HISTORY OF SUFFOLK

VOLUME I

Medieval Suffolk

An Economic and Social History

1200–1500

T0311318

HISTORY OF SUFFOLK

ISSN 1754-1506

This series is designed to offer a scholarly but accessible multi-volume history of Suffolk, from the earliest times until the present day, written by leading experts in the field. Drawing upon both primary and secondary sources, it will utilise the remarkably rich resources of the county to present Suffolk's history within a wider regional, national and international context.

Medieval Suffolk

An Economic and Social History

1200–1500

Mark Bailey

THE BOYDELL PRESS

First published 2007
The Boydell Press, Woodbridge

ISBN 978 184383 315 4

Transferred to digital printing

The Boydell Press is an imprint of Boydell & Brewer Ltd
PO Box 9, Woodbridge, Suffolk IP12 3DF, UK
and of Boydell & Brewer Inc.
668 Mt. Hope Avenue, Rochester NY 14620, USA
website: www.boydellandbrewer.com

A CIP catalogue record for this title is available
from the British Library

This book is printed on acid-free paper

Designed and typeset in Adobe Caslon Pro by
David Roberts, Pershore, Worcestershire

Contents

List of Plates

The plates appear between pp. 178 and 179.

List of Maps

List of Tables

Foreword

THIS important book will be the first in a series of monographs which together will constitute a scholarly but accessible multi-volume history of Suffolk from the earliest times until the present day. Written by leading experts in the field, the series has been designed to fill a striking gap in the area of regional studies. It will draw upon primary as well as secondary material, and by utilising the county's rich resources to the full, will present Suffolk's history within a wider regional, national and international context.

Notwithstanding its outstanding resources in terms of archaeology, landscape, material culture and archival evidence, and the prominent part that it has played in shaping the history of south-eastern England, Suffolk remains curiously neglected. There is, for example, no *Victoria County History* or comparable broad chronological survey for use by local historians and others who wish to extend their knowledge beyond the tourist guide or parish history. Moreover, although a number of valuable theses, articles and monographs have appeared on aspects of Suffolk's past, no sustained attempt has yet been made to bring much of this specialist research out of the university library to the attention of a wider public.

The series is supported by the School of History and the Centre of East Anglian Studies at the University of East Anglia, and is funded by a bequest made to the School by Miss Ann Ashard Webb, BA, BSc, MA, who died in 1996 at the age of ninety-four. Her aim was to produce a county history that would combine high standards of scholarship with readability, and thus enjoy an appeal both within and beyond the academic community. Miss Webb devoted her career to education, and so was well aware of the need for clarity and accessibility. Having spent many years as a teacher, not least at Haverhill Middle School in Suffolk, she took up a post as senior lecturer at Goldsmiths' College, University of London, where she trained others to teach. As early as 1978 she began discussing with the University of East Anglia the possibility of making an endowment that would facilitate the production of a history of Suffolk. Her aim was the creation of a series which would follow the tradition of W. G. Hoskins' classic, *The Making of the English Landscape*, and Norman Scarfe's *The Suffolk Landscape*, works which she regarded as models of their kind. By the time of her death, the bequest had grown considerably, although she remained convinced that the money should be devoted to a project that would bring the history of Suffolk to a wider public.

In addition to the main volumes in the series, it is also intended to produce a select number of more specialised monographs and collections of essays, of which the following have already appeared with support from the bequest:

Judith Middleton-Stewart, *Inward Purity and Outward Splendour: Death and Remembrance in the Deanery of Dunwich, Suffolk, 1370–1547* (2001)

Christopher Harper-Bill, Carole Rawcliffe and R. G. Wilson, eds., *East Anglia's History: Studies in Honour of Norman Scarfe* (2002)

Christopher Harper-Bill, ed., *Medieval East Anglia* (2005)

NORWICH, 2007

Acknowledgements

MOST of the research for this book was undertaken in the 1990s, for which I gratefully acknowledge the support of the Masters and Fellows of Gonville and Caius College, and of Corpus Christi College, Cambridge, and the University's Institute of Continuing Education. Serving as an academic historian in Cambridge for 13 years was an immense privilege. Various versions of chapters of this book were presented to seminars at the Universities of Cambridge, Leeds and Manchester, and I am grateful for the feedback and comments received. The University of Cambridge's Unit for Landscape Modelling welcomed me warmly and kindly granted permission to publish the aerial photographs.

I owe much to a number of historians active in Suffolk for their kindness and support. Rosemary Hoppitt and John Ridgard provided some primary references and allowed me to cite from their unpublished material; Audrey McLaughlin placed at my disposal her transcriptions of original sources from fifteenth-century Walsham; Ray Lock offered his early versions of the fourteenth-century Walsham court rolls; John Walker talked me through the technicalities of late-medieval house construction; Peter Northeast was a willing and knowledgeable source of information on a wide range of local medieval subjects; Oliver Rackham has provided information and discussed a variety of topics on the landscape; Tom Williamson gave permission to reproduce two of his maps, and his passionate views have shaped my thoughts on the Suffolk landscape; while Timothy Easton offered advice on possible photographs to include in this book.

Steve Rigby and Richard Smith have been generous with their ideas, encouragement and expertise; James Davis has allowed me to cite from his unpublished work, and kindly commented upon an early draft of the general chapter on 'Towns'; David Stone has provided references from Hinderclay and instruction upon medieval agrarian techniques, in addition to fine company and conviviality; and Bruce Campbell read three early chapters, generously gave permission to reproduce a number of maps, and has shaped various lines of argument in this book in a way that he will readily recognise. Finally, John Hatcher has commented incisively whenever his former PhD student reappeared with yet more rough drafts to read, and he has also provided friendship, advice and hospitality well beyond the call of academic duty.

Steve Cherry at the University of East Anglia has been a marvellously relaxed contact for the *History of Suffolk* series, guiding this volume through some choppy waters to completion with a deceptive ease; Carole Rawcliffe was also tough-minded and supportive; while Christopher Harper-Bill first broached the subject and for many years has been very patient with an inarticulate but eager young economic historian. At the Boydell Press Caroline Palmer and David Roberts were very efficient, helpful and supportive. David Dymond has readily discussed many of my emerging ideas over many years, and commented on a number of chapters. Nick Amor has read much of the book in draft form, despite a busy professional and full domestic life, offering criticisms and further examples with humbling speed and generosity. In the early 1980s Duncan Bythell furnished me with the confidence to break free from the shackles of the stereotypical sportsman to develop my passion for history, and his shrewd scrutiny of every page of this book has rescued it from arcane digressions and stylistic peccadilloes. In a lively professional life, where medieval Suffolk is irrelevant, Julie Noy-Bailey has provided practical support and laboured onerously while 'that damned book' has consumed her husband. Our children, Katie and Harry; my parents, Ron and Maureen; and the enthusiasm of many local historians, have provided its inspiration.

Note on Currency & Units of Measurement

The coinage used in medieval England was pounds (£), shillings (s.) and pennies (d.). There were 12 pennies to a shilling and 20 shillings to a pound. One shilling is equivalent to 5p, although price inflation since the medieval centuries renders direct comparisons meaningless. For example, a labourer might earn 2d. per day in the fourteenth century, or perhaps nearly £2 per annum, whereas an aristocrat was fabulously wealthy with an income of £3,000 per annum. The most common unit of area was the acre (0.4 hectare), comprising 4 roods: the rood itself comprised 40 perches.

Abbreviations

AgHR	*Agricultural History Review*
AHEW	*The Agrarian History of England and Wales*, 8 vols. (Cambridge, 1967–2000)
Bacon	Bacon Collection, Joseph Regenstein Library, University of Chicago
Bacon, *Annals*	*The Annals of Ipswich by Nathaniell Bacon AD 1654*, ed. W. H. Richardson (Ipswich, 1884)
BL	British Library
CIM	*Calendar of Inquisitions Miscellaneous*, 7 vols. (HMSO, 1904–69)
CCR	*Calendar of Close Rolls*, 67 vols. (HMSO, 1902–63)
CPR	*Calendar of Patent Rolls*, 60 vols. (HMSO, 1901–74)
CUL	Cambridge University Library
EcHR	*Economic History Review*
EDC	Ely Dean and Chapter
HistA	*An Historical Atlas of Suffolk*, ed. D. P. Dymond and E. Martin, 2nd edn (Ipswich, 1989)
1283 Lay Subsidy	*A Suffolk Hundred in 1283*, ed. E. Powell (Cambridge, 1910)
1327 Lay Subsidy	*Suffolk in 1327: being a Subsidy Return*, ed. S. H. A. Hervey, Suffolk Green Books 9 (Woodbridge, 1906)
1334 Lay Subsidy	*The Lay Subsidy of 1334*, ed. R. E. Glasscock, Records of Social and Economic History n.s. 2 (London, 1975)
1524 Lay Subsidy	*Suffolk in 1524: Being the Return for a Subsidy Granted in 1523*, ed. S. H. A. Hervey, Suffolk Green Books 10 (Woodbridge, 1910)
NRO	Norfolk Record Office
NRS	Norfolk Record Society
PR	*Pinchbeck Register of the Abbey of Bury St Edmunds and Related Documents*, 2 vols., ed. F. Hervey (Brighton, 1925)
PRO	Public Record Office
PSIA	*Proceedings of the Suffolk Institute of Archaeology and History*
RH	*Rotuli Hundredorum temp. Hen. III et Edw. I*, 2 vols., ed. W. Illingworth and J. Caley (London, 1812–18)
SCS	Suffolk Charter Series
SR	*Suffolk Review*
SROB	Suffolk Record Office, Bury St Edmunds
SROI	Suffolk Record Office, Ipswich
SRS	Suffolk Records Society
TRHS	*Transactions of the Royal Historical Society*
UH	*The Cambridge Urban History of Britain*, vol. 1: 600–1540, ed. D. M. Palliser (Cambridge, 2000)
VCH	*Victoria County History of Suffolk*, ed. W. Page, 2 vols. (London, 1907)

– CHAPTER I –

Introduction

To the casual observer or the incurious visitor the county of Suffolk might appear to be a pleasant, but undistinguished, backwater. Its landscape is not dramatic, and may be easily dismissed as flat and monotonous, while leading towns such as Ipswich, Lowestoft and Felixstowe have relatively few monuments of great historical interest. Yet the real Suffolk is a county of subtle contrasts and wide variety, and the discerning eye can identify a rich heritage of medieval religious and vernacular architecture. Many features of the modern rural and urban landscapes of Suffolk are centuries old, and were influenced significantly by developments in the Middle Ages. Modern Suffolk still reflects much of its medieval past.

In Suffolk, as elsewhere, the influence of physical geology and soil type is considerable in shaping the development of different regions and local land-scapes.[1] The county's gently undulating countryside seldom rises higher than 200 feet (approx. 65 m) above sea-level, although one-third of west Suffolk lies above 300 feet (approx. 105 m), rising to a high point of 420 feet (140 m) near Chedburgh. Its soils are dominated by clay, which stretches in a wide crescent from Haverhill to Beccles, and also by glacial deposits of various sands, gravels and loams, which create a subtle but important diversity in both landscape and land use (map 1). This diversity was even more apparent and influential in the Middle Ages than it is today. For example, the peat fens in the north-west, and the alluvial soils around the coast, were uncultivable before widespread reclamations in the seventeenth century, and in the Middle Ages comprised extensive freshwater fens and saltwater marshlands. Similarly, the acidic sands lying to the north-west of Bury St Edmunds, and to the north-east of Ipswich, were marginal for arable farming, and harboured vast tracts of colourful and hauntingly beautiful heathland. Even the dominant clay soils are subject to variations and differences in composition – from acidic clays interspersed with glacial sands south of Ipswich, to chalky clays in the south-west, to heavy intractable clays in the north-west – which provided subtly different challenges for medieval farmers. These variations in soil types are the primary explanation for the local differences in farming patterns within Suffolk, which

[1] A general background to the early history and geology of Suffolk is provided in P. Warner, *The Origins of Suffolk* (Manchester, 1996).

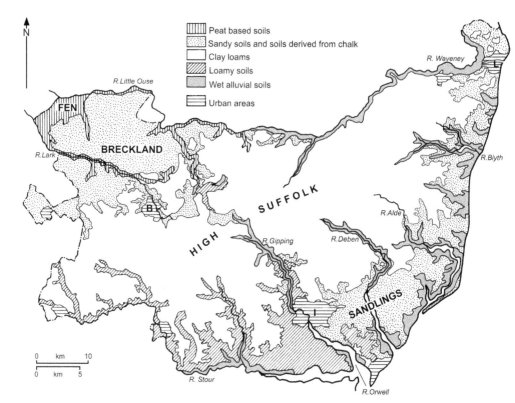

MAP 1 Soil types, rivers and regions

created distinctive regions, such as the Fenland, the Breckland, the Sandlings and 'High' Suffolk.

Communications – the movement of people and goods – across Suffolk are relatively easy. The major river valleys are mainly wide and shallow, and penetrate deep into central areas of the county; consequently the Stour valley, the Gipping and the Lark valleys, and the Waveney and Little Ouse valleys shape the three main east–west routeways across the south, middle and north of the county respectively. The main north–south routes follow either tributaries of these major rivers (such as the A134 road between Sudbury and Bury St Edmunds) or forge across the easily traversed sandy soils in the west and east. The road from Ipswich to Lowestoft (latterly the A12) skirts the western fringe of the Sandlings, while that from Thetford to Newmarket (the A11) drives straight across the open heaths of the Breckland. The accessibility of the coast and tidal rivers has also facilitated seaborne travel and trade, particularly with London and the Low Countries, a factor which significantly influenced the economy and society of medieval Suffolk.

By the time of the Norman Conquest in the eleventh century the county

of Suffolk was already an identifiable administrative entity, based on the original southern territory of the kingdom of East Anglia. Its affairs were run on
behalf of the king by an annually appointed sheriff, who was responsible for
supervising any royal estates within the county, and for many other aspects
of royal administration and jurisdiction, such as taxation, defence and justice.
By the thirteenth century the work of the sheriff was supplemented – and
to some extent superseded – by the dispatch of royal justices into the shires
to hear and decide legal cases, through the mechanism of either occasional
'assizes' or individual commissions of 'oyer and terminer'. By the fourteenth
century Justices of the Peace also sat four times a year in each county and
offered more immediate justice dispensed by men with a closer understanding of the locality. The rule of law – as constructed and implemented by the
king – was well established in medieval England, but there was no police force
or standing army to enforce it. Effective law enforcement depended partly
upon royal officials discharging their work efficiently and fairly, but mainly
upon local landlords implementing the king's will. Upholding this law was an
obligation upon landlords, and their ability to discharge it derived from their
social status and local standing, as well as from the size and effectiveness of
their supporters or 'retinues', some of whom were armed. It follows that on
occasions such armed muscle could also be diverted to serve the private interests of the lord, rather than the king, and such occasions were more common
when royal authority was weak. Hence in practice the operation of medieval
law was influenced not only by the facts of the matter, but by whom you knew,
and what you could get away with.

For administrative convenience all English counties were further subdivided into 'hundreds', of which twenty-five existed in Suffolk by the end of
the eleventh century (map 2). Suffolk hundreds came in a variety of sizes, from
the 87,000 acres covered by the 'double' hundred of Blything to the 17,000
acres occupied by Colneis. In fact, these hundreds pre-date the county itself
as administrative units, reflecting their early importance in the governance of
England. Each vill (broadly equivalent to the parish) sent representatives to
regular meetings of the hundred, who in turn sent representatives to the sheriff,
and to other royal officials and courts. By these means the vill and the hundred
oiled the mechanisms of royal administration, by ensuring the punishment of
petty criminal acts and the reporting of major ones to higher courts, by organizing jurors and witnesses to attend hearings in higher courts, by carrying out
the instructions of royal officials, and by supporting the assessment and payment of fiscal and military dues on the ground. Yet the Crown had, unusually,
granted the privileges and obligations of a number of hundreds in Suffolk into
the hands of two great monastic landlords, effectively creating privatized legal
franchises. Eight hundreds in west Suffolk (the large hundred of Blackbourne

N

Liberty of St Edmund

Liberty of St Etheldreda

Mutford
and
Lothingland

Wangford

Lackford

Blackbourne

Blything

Hartismere   Hoxne

Thingoe B

Thedwastre

Stow

Thredling

Loes

Plomesgate

Risbridge

Bosmere

Claydon

Carlford Wilford

Babergh   Cosford

Samford

Colneis

0 miles 5

0   km   10

MAP 2 Adminstrative organization: hundreds and liberties

was regarded as a double hundred) had been granted in the middle of the eleventh century to the abbey of Bury St Edmunds and were known as the Liberty of St Edmund, a territory which formed the basis for the later administrative unit of West Suffolk (map 2). The Liberty of St Edmund was effectively run as a separate county, in which the abbey exercised and profited from many of the legal privileges vested in the hundred and usually associated with the Crown. Hence it appointed and ran the office of coroner, held a great court at Bury equivalent to a county court, administered hundred and leet courts, and dealt with all petty criminal and legal cases within the liberty. Similarly, in the mid-tenth century the Crown had granted to the prior and convent of Ely five and a half hundreds in east Suffolk. These were also run as a privatized legal franchise known as the Liberty of St Etheldreda: the monastery even maintained its own gaol at Melton, the administrative centre of the liberty.[2]

---

[2] *VCH*, ii, pp. 157–9; Warner, *Origins of Suffolk*, chap. 6; J. Campbell, 'Hundreds and Leets: A Survey with Suggestions', in Harper-Bill, *Medieval East Anglia* (2005), pp. 153–67. For additional background to the Liberty of St Edmund, see H. Cam, *Liberties and Communities in Medieval England* (Cambridge, 1942), pp. 188–92.

For this reason, it could be argued that medieval Suffolk possessed three 'county towns': Bury St Edmunds, Melton and Ipswich. It also meant that the size of the territory supervised by the sheriff from Ipswich was relatively small, and consequently the office was eventually combined with that of Norfolk to create a single sheriff of Norfolk and Suffolk. The administrative influence of Norwich and Norfolk over the south folk of the old kingdom of East Anglia also extended to religious matters, for the whole of Suffolk was contained with the diocese of Norwich. However, the political and religious history of medieval Suffolk is not the subject of this book, although these issues will eventually be considered in a companion to this volume in the *History of Suffolk* series.

This book focuses on the economic and social history of Suffolk between *c.* 1200 and *c.* 1500. The sources for such a study are good compared to those surviving from many parts of medieval Europe. The strength and sophistication of English royal government from an early date is reflected in a wealth of extant fiscal, legal and public documents which throw considerable light on the localities: taxation and arcane legal disputes may have been a bane to medieval communities, but their documentation is a boon to the historian. The management of landed estates generated a substantial archive of written records, the most numerous and useful of which are manorial accounts, surveys and court rolls. Accounts reveal details of farming practices and economic activity on the larger farms of landlords ('demesnes'); surveys detail landholding by their tenants, often providing useful topographical information; and seigneurial regulation of the lives of tenants is recorded in manor court rolls, which provide the historian with important – but partial – insights into the world of ordinary people. Survivals from these categories of manorial documents are patchy before 1300, and are most numerous from the period 1320–1450. The greater landlords maintained household and estate documents, only a small proportion of which have survived, but kept few personal documents such as letters and diaries. The number of surviving wills increases after *c.* 1400, offering valuable information about the wealth and belongings of ordinary people. Borough authorities enjoyed a degree of autonomy to run their own affairs, recording their rules, decisions, their income and expenditure. In addition, physical remains such as artefacts and buildings provide further evidence of daily life.[3]

Collectively, these sources constitute a large and impressive body of evidence with which to reconstruct and to understand late medieval Suffolk. Yet there is much we can never know about the medieval economy and society, because

---

3 For general introductions to the main sources for local studies of medieval England, see C. Dyer, 'Documentary Evidence', in *The Countryside of Medieval England*, ed. G. Astill and A. Grant (Oxford, 1988); M. Bailey, ed., *The English Manor, c. 1200 to c. 1500* (Manchester, 2002).

of the selectivity, subject matter and bias of the sources. For example, we have no census material with which to calculate accurately the county's population, let alone changes over time, and no dairies, household accounts or letters have survived from the lower orders of medieval society, so we have hardly any way of knowing directly about their daily lives or how they felt about the world around them. Furthermore, the chronological, social and geographical distribution of the surviving sources is uneven. The greater concentration of local records after *c.* 1320 permits a more detailed assessment of late medieval than thirteenth-century Suffolk; a few manors are very well documented, but most have left no archive; east Suffolk is less well documented than west; and survivals from the estates of aristocratic landlords are more numerous than those from lesser landlords and freemen. Any history of medieval Suffolk risks placing a disproportionate reliance upon the archives of the great landlords – such as the abbey of Bury St Edmunds – who were powerful and prominent, but who were also atypical.

The main shortcoming of a county-based study is that it runs the risk of being either too detailed to be manageable or too thinly stretched to be credible. For example, an in-depth account of a small sample of rural manors and urban centres in Suffolk would yield much quantifiable and comparable data, and would enable the narrative to engage intimately with a number of specific academic debates, but it would then become exposed to the criticism of being arcane and unrepresentative of the county as a whole. Such criticism is avoided by adopting a wider-ranging approach, drawing more liberally upon the evidence generated by a large number of manors and towns, although such individual studies would perforce lack the depth of fewer, but narrower and more detailed, investigations. This risk is unavoidable, but is justified by the quest to identify broad characteristics and general themes of the economy and society of medieval Suffolk: further historical research will confirm, refute or refine them. Consequently, this survey draws upon the published research on the medieval history of the county, in addition to a substantial quantity of original research into the primary sources of around two dozen well-documented manors spread across the county.[4]

Economic and social history is timeless in the sense that, for any period, it focuses upon long-term processes: the interactions of thousands of people as they earned their livelihood, the exploitation and utilization of natural resources, the shaping of the landscape, the relative distribution of wealth and

---

4 The main manors used in the study are: Akenham, Aldham, Barton Magna, Brandon, Cratfield, Dunningworth, Easton Bavents, Fornham All Saints, Fornham St Martin, Huntingfield, Lakenheath, Laxfield, Leiston, Loudham, Lidgate, Mildenhall, Melton, Staverton, Tattingstone, Ufford, Walsham and Walton. However, primary sources from scores of other manors have also been used.

power between social groups, the dependence upon custom and law, the limits of technology and the unremitting struggle for survival. The concentration upon processes over long periods of time poses two peculiar challenges to the economic and social historian. First, it is difficult to identify with any certainty or precision the key turning points in significant historical changes, or precise dates for them; and, second, this type of history tends to lack prominent or influential individuals, even though history is about people. In contrast, political history is often more immediately accessible and colourful, featuring the actions and motives of key individuals – perhaps heroic or villainous – and precise dates for the most significant events. Yet the historian has a duty to understand the lives of the mass of the populace as well as those at the top of the political hierarchy, and to chart the evolution of the economic and social institutions which underpin modern society.

Good historical enquiry involves a dialogue between the general and the particular, in which the elucidation of grand themes and the sketching of the bigger picture informs – and is informed by – an understanding of developments in the locality. The difficulty lies in ensuring that this dialogue does not become too one-sided, so that either the sweeping historical generalization is unrepresentative of many local events, or the parochial study lacks a wider context. Unfortunately, in the 1960s and 1970s the economic and social historiography of medieval England was characterized by an uneven dialogue between the general and the particular, and historians were prone to offer bold generalizations on the basis of a small number of isolated local or regional case studies. In contrast, during the 1980s and 1990s a dramatic rise in the volume of historical research generated many studies focusing narrowly over both time and place. The sheer weight and volume of local studies in the recent past has been impressive, but a great mass of parochial detail and example can obscure that which is significant and typical, and is often difficult to assimilate in a manageable form. As Tom Williamson recently bemoaned in his survey of research on the medieval landscape, the problem for the historian in the early twenty first century is not a shortage or paucity of data, but its effective integration into a coherent whole. His lament echoes David Morgan's wry observation that, 'having with much profit gone into provincial society, we may in due course, laden with our historical booty, consider getting out'.[5]

One of the aims of this book is to marshal the expanding volume of local research during the past twenty years or so into a coherent and comprehensible survey of Suffolk's medieval economy and society, and to identify the

---

5 T. Williamson, *Shaping Medieval Landscapes: Settlement, Society, Environment* (Macclesfield, 2003), p. 27; Morgan quoted in R. E. Horrox, 'Local and National Politics in Fifteenth-Century England', *Journal of Medieval History* 18 (1992), p. 402.

major patterns of change. Wherever appropriate, those observations will be placed within the context of wider academic debates, contrasted with developments elsewhere in medieval England, and embellished with the author's original research. In fact, the prospect of succeeding in this ambitious task is enhanced by the high quality and wider academic horizons of many recent local studies, a development due in part to a marked increase in the number and popularity of 'Local History' courses and qualifications offered by university departments of continuing education. The historical research undertaken by non-professional and local historians has shed much of its amateur and parochial image by demonstrating a keener awareness of academic debates and issues, of relevant statistical methods, and of the need to work to the exacting standards of modern scholarship. It has also become more innovative and interdisciplinary in its methodology, as evidenced by the interweaving of elements of economic history, archaeology and historical geography in the development of field walking and landscape history. Hence this book is self-consciously conceived and written as part of an ongoing dialogue between the general and the particular.[6]

Although placing Suffolk within a wider historical context should broaden the appeal of this study, there is much in its medieval history that should prove absorbing to those with little interest in the county *per se*. First, its sheer diversity is intrinsically interesting, and provides many instructive economic and agrarian contrasts within relatively short distances. In this sense, a study of this varied county further aids our understanding of the complexity and variety in the English economy and society. Second, its social structure was highly distinctive, dominated by a large proportion of freemen and landlords of low status who exhibited a robust independence of mind and will, in contrast to the traditional image of a society made up of unfree peasants and powerful landlords. Finally, its economy lay in the vanguard of economic development in the later Middle Ages. One could claim that by *c*. 1500 this was the most industrialized and urbanized county in England: indeed, at this date one might reasonably regard Suffolk as the most likely candidate to become the first industrialized region of Britain. A study of one of western Europe's prominent false starts along the road to industrial capitalism is itself a worthwhile enterprise.

The approach to this study is essentially thematic, rather than chronological, and it begins properly with a discussion of the people of medieval Suffolk, the basic structure of society and the distribution of wealth (chapters 2 and 3). It then considers agriculture, and the close interrelationship between landscape and land use, because farming was the main source of livelihood for

---

[6] E. Royle, 'Need Local History be Parochial History?', *University of Cambridge, Institute of Education, Occasional Paper* 4 (2001), pp. 1–8.

the majority of the populace (chapters 4 and 5). Towns, trade and industrial activities were less important, although they increased in scale and influence during the Middle Ages (chapters 6 and 7). Wherever possible, these broad processes are illustrated by the actions and experiences of real people. Yet there is one fundamental discontinuity in the period 1200–1500 caused by a crisis of unparalleled severity, one of those rare moments in economic and social history which can be legitimately regarded as a key turning point on a precise date: the Black Death of 1349. This crisis also provides the central turning point in the organization of this book, and the final chapters consider how society, agriculture, towns and trade fared in its wake.

CHAPTER 2

Landlords and their Estates, 1200–1349

S UFFOLK society in the Middle Ages was neither simple nor unchanging, yet throughout the period it was dominated by a small group of land-lords who held a disproportionate amount of land. Few of these lords were regular soldiers (although male members of their family, such as younger sons, may have pursued a military career), and most were ecclesiastics, administrators and/or engaged in agriculture. Their standing in society was determined largely by their wealth, which in turn owed much to the size of their landed estate, although it was also influenced to some degree by the tenure on which that land was held, the standing of their family and the status of their social contacts. This explains why even the relatively small proportion of well-to-do people who earned most of their living away from the land, such as career soldiers, merchants or lawyers, sought to convert their financial success into the acquisition of land. Degrees of wealth also determined degrees of political power, which was exercised as Members of Parliament, in the retinue of a greater lord, or in the service of the Crown. A wealthy earl or bishop could be a major player in national politics and government, while a wealthy knight could wield significant political power within a single county as the holder of a local government office – such as sheriff, escheator, tax collector or Justice of the Peace – or as a prominent estate official of a major landlord.[1]

Wide differences in wealth and power were evident among the ranks of landlords. The uppermost ranks comprised the aristocracy (earls, barons and, from the late fourteenth century, the new rank of duke), together with closely analogous ecclesiastical landlords such as bishops and the wealthier abbots. The links between lay and ecclesiastical landlords were often close, because their lifestyles displayed similarities and the religious orders drew many recruits from aristocratic families. Aristocrats often held extensive lands scattered across sizeable areas of England, enjoyed a range of jurisdictional rights and privileges, maintained a number of residences, and enjoyed an income

---

[1] For a general introduction, see C. Dyer, *Standards of Living in the later Middle Ages* (Cambridge, 1989), chap. 2; C. Carpenter, 'England: The Nobility and Gentry', in Rigby, *Companion* (2003); P. J. Goldberg, *Medieval England: A Social History, 1250–1550* (London, 2004). For two general histories of the period, see M. Rubin, *The Hollow Crown: A History of Britain in the Later Middle Ages* (London, 2005) and R. E. Horrox and W. M. Ormrod, eds., *A Social History of England, 1200–1500* (Cambridge, 2006).

in excess of about £500 per annum. The lower ranks of landlords comprised knights, whose annual incomes extended to a few hundred pounds, and minor local landlords, with tens of pounds. Their landed estates were smaller and concentrated within a narrower geographical area, and administered from a single residence. The protection, augmentation and inheritance of estates were major preoccupations for lay lords, because the status and livelihood of their immediate family depended upon it, and prudential marriage to the children of other lords offered clear opportunities in this regard. Marriages were therefore business arrangements, sometimes concluded by parents during the childhood of their progeny, and consequently a high proportion of lords were married: for example, according to the 1381 Poll Tax returns 86 per cent of identified landlords in Thingoe hundred were married.[2]

All lords acted as the head of a household, which extended beyond the immediate family to include followers and employees. Servants of various kinds comprised the bulk of the household, employed in menial tasks in the kitchen, buttery, pantry, or stables; in cleaning and maintaining the buildings; or in personally attending the lord. The exact size and structure of each household varied according to the status of the lord. The household of a leading magnate was itinerant, travelling around the country on personal or royal business with small group of retainers, while his 'inner' household – leaded by his wife – was more sedentary. The major items of expenditure in every seigneurial household were food, fuel, clothing and buildings, with food comprising around half of all expenditure. In addition to providing food and shelter for its members, the household also existed to administer the lord's estate, protect him and his interests, dispense justice, nurture relations with tenants, and to affirm his status by displays of patronage and hospitality.[3]

THE GENTRY

In late-medieval England the lower ranks of lords are dubbed 'the gentry', comprising knights, esquires, armigers and lesser landlords. Knights were the wealthiest subgroup of the gentry, nominally with land valued in excess of £100, although the award of knighthood was an honour which also implied identifiable patterns of behaviour based on contemporary notions of chivalry and, in some cases, military experience and prowess. During the course of the thirteenth century the number of knights in England declined by over one-half, due to a complex mixture of social and military changes. We may

---

[2] B. A. Hanawalt, *The Ties that Bound: Peasant Families in Medieval England* (Oxford, 1986), p. 96; V. B. Redstone, 'Social Condition of England During the Wars of the Roses', *TRHS* 16 (1902), p. 170.

[3] Dyer, *Standards of Living*, chap. 3.

estimate that in *c.* 1200 fewer than 100 knights were resident in Suffolk, and perhaps just over thirty in *c.* 1300. Sir William de Pakenham met the knightly definition of the late thirteenth century admirably, receiving an annual income of between £25 and £40 from each of four manors in Norton, Ixworth Thorpe, Thurston and Bardwell, and about £10 each from his manors and land in Great Ashfield, Pakenham and elsewhere. With an annual income approaching £200 in the 1280s, he could afford to spend £140 over subsequent years acquiring land in Ixworth Thorpe to provide a decent estate for his younger son, Thomas. Sir William was politically well connected, serving as a senior administrator on the estates of both the abbey of Bury St Edmunds and the bishop of Norwich; as a royal official on various legal commissions in East Anglia; and as one of just two tax collectors in Suffolk for the Lay Subsidy of 1283. His household may have contained around thirty people, although no evidence has survived to confirm this. However, in 1381 the household of Robert de Ashfield of Stowlangtoft, an esquire occupying the social stratum just below William de Pakenham, contained sixteen servants, including a shepherd and full-time brewer.[4]

Sir William de Pakenham was essentially a wealthy farmer and administrator, not a soldier. In contrast, from the 1250s Sir Richard de Holbrook was an active member of the entourage of Roger Bigod III, the bellicose earl of Norfolk. He was therefore closely involved in the national political and military manoeuvring of the early 1260s, although – following the lead of his lord – he chose to avoid action at the battles of Lewes (1264) and Evesham (1265). Similarly, Sir Philip de Buckland served both Roger III and Roger IV Bigod loyally for forty years before his death in 1294, initially as an armed knight but latterly as steward of Roger IV's extensive estates in county Carlow, Ireland. The trusty and elderly de Buckland spent the last few months of his life as a guest in the tranquil setting of earl Roger's Hollesley manor, despite holding five manors of his own in east Suffolk.[5]

Knights such as Richard de Holbrook and William de Pakenham were wealthy by the standards of the majority of the English gentry. Bruce Campbell argues that in *c.* 1300 English lay landlords of 'genteel' status received a mean annual income of £12, but it is likely that many Suffolk lords earned less than this. Suffolk society was dominated by minor lay landlords, men of

4 P. R. Coss, 'An Age of Deference', in Horrox and Ormrod, *Social History* (2006), pp. 36–8; S. D. Church, ed., *The Pakenham Cartulary for the Manor of Ixworth Thorpe, Suffolk, c. 1250 to c. 1320*, SCS 17 (Woodbridge, 2001), pp. 1–3, 5, 11; *1283 Lay Subsidy*, p. xiii; P. R. Coss, *Lordship, Knighthood and Locality: A Study in English Society, 1180–1280* (Cambridge, 1991), pp. 149, 254; E. Powell, *The Rising in East Anglia in 1381* (Cambridge, 1896), p. 109.

5 M. Morris, *The Bigod Earls of Norfolk in the Thirteenth Century* (Woodbridge, 2005), pp. 69–94, 142–3.

local – often merely parochial – significance, who held a small manor and were therefore not conspicuously wealthier than the leading villagers. For example, Nicholas de Walsham, lord of High Hall manor in Walsham, paid 4s. in tax in the Lay Subsidy of 1327, the same sum as peasants such as Walter Osborne and William Hawys. Their modest wealth and political standing means that we know infuriatingly little about them, and we can only glimpse their existence: they hardly feature in the records of central government, and any manorial documents or land titles they generated are unlikely to have been retained for long in a secure archive. In *c.* 1300 the typical landlord in Suffolk held one – at most two – small manors in close proximity, was resident upon one of them, and therefore received an annual income between £7 and £15. There were several hundred such lords in Suffolk, who stood well below the rank and status of knight, and did not even warrant the title of esquire or armiger. Their households were small, hardly differing from those of successful peasants: in 1381 the household of Thomas Ickworth, a minor landlord in the eponymous village, contained merely four servants. By the fifteenth century this residential local elite would become known as 'gentlemen', but in the thirteenth century they did not conform to any clear contemporary social ranking and therefore they could not be readily labelled: they were neither fighting men nor royal administrators, but mere agriculturalists who exercised little political power. The proportion of such low-ranking lords was probably higher in Suffolk than many parts of the country.[6]

Those situated at the upper end of this loose social group of minor landlords were still financially comfortable. For example, in the late thirteenth century William de Thelnetham held one manor in Troston and some lands in Barnham, generating income of around £15 per annum, and he carried enough local influence to serve as a juror in 1285 for Blackbourne hundred at an assize held by the king's itinerant justices. Ralph de Bardwell was also a juror that year, but as the lord of two modest manors in Bardwell and Hunston, each yielding perhaps £10 per annum, he was wealthier than William. Both Ralph and William enhanced their social status and local standing by serving in the extended household of Sir William de Pakenham, witnessing his legal transactions, providing counsel and supporting his political actions. Their close affiliation with such a powerful local figure also protected their own positions and estates against other members of the gentry who might attempt to undermine their political standing or acquire their land: this was a highly competitive and, at times, volatile stratum of medieval society. Bardwell and

---

[6] B. M. S. Campbell, 'The Agrarian Problem in the Early Fourteenth Century', *Past and Present* 188 (2005), table 1; B. M. S. Campbell, 'The Land', in Horrox and Ormrod, *Social History* (2006), table 7.1 and pp. 204–5; *HistA*, pp. 80–1; *1327 Lay Subsidy*, p. 183; Powell, *Rising in East Anglia*, p. 78.

Thelnetham were wealthy by the standards of the men at the middle and lower end of this group, such as Walter le Pouer of Knettishall or Roger de Cotton of Cotton, whose landed holdings were scarcely bigger than those of the most prominent peasants. Such men may have forged allegiances with more powerful local figures, or bolstered their political influence by serving in the local administration of the Crown at its lowest level, as jurors at hundred courts, or as hundredal bailiffs, constables or sub-keepers of the peace.[7]

A few of these lesser lords served as active soldiers in the inner circles of nobles. John Algar was an esquire holding a manor in Brockley and some land in Loddon (Norfolk), but he was also a personal friend of Roger Bigod III, and accompanied the earl to Lyon in 1245. Algar would have received free board and lodging from the earl when in active service, and also a cash retainer of between £10 and £20 each year, which probably doubled his annual income. Yet most low-status lords had few military interests, and their main source of income came from cultivating their demesne (i.e. that part of the manor which the lord could exploit for his own benefit, often no bigger than 30 to 60 acres on the typical Suffolk manor). Hence the lord of the average Suffolk manor was likely to be actively and personally involved in the exploitation of the demesne, which was worked principally by a hired rather than customary labour force. The remainder of their revenue came mainly from the rents paid by their land tenants (see chapter 3), which tended to be relatively modest, and similarly the proportion generated by perquisites, such the manorial court, was often insignificant: for example, court income from the manor of Eriswell in 1235 was rated at only 13s. 4d. per annum out of a total manorial valuation of £25, and in one year the court of Loudham yielded a mere 6s. 2d. Lesser lords lacked the power and privileges to generate much income from seigneurial rights over their tenantry, so their manorial court was more likely to be an assertion of status than a successful money-spinning exercise: after all, they had only a small number of tenants, most of whom were free and therefore relatively independent. Nicholas de Walsham, lord of Walsham High Hall manor, attended each session of his manor court, was actively involved in the running of his only manor, and would have known his twenty or so tenants personally.[8]

7 C. Carpenter, *Locality and Polity: A Study of Warwickshire Landed Society, 1401–1499* (Cambridge, 1992), pp. 42–4; C. Dyer, *Making a Living in the Middle Ages: The People of Britain, 850–1520* (London, 2002), pp. 147–52; Campbell, 'Agrarian Problem', table 3; Church, *Pakenham*, pp. 14–15, 33; *PR*, ii, pp. 229–30 (Knettishall).

8 Morris, *Bigod Earls*, pp. 65–7, 147; Campbell, 'Agrarian Problem', p. 39; J. T. Munday, *Eriswell Notebook*, SROB (acc. 1938); SROI HD1538/295/3 (Loudham). For examples of lay manors with little or no villein land, see *PR*, ii, pp. 70–1. R. Lock, ed., *The Court Rolls of Walsham-le-Willows*, vol. 1: *1303–1350*, SRS 41 (Woodbridge, 1998), pp. 6–7, 13; and SROB HA504/3/1 (Walsham).

Rectors and the smaller monastic landlords occupied the same social stratum as the lesser lay landlords. The average rectorial income was around £10 per annum, and therefore directly comparable to the income of the average manorial lord. The size of the glebe (the rector's own holding) varied from parish to parish, although David Dymond estimates that most contained around 40 acres, and in the 1280s the average size of eleven glebes in Blackbourne hundred was 29 acres. A holding of this size was broadly comparable to the demesne land held by the average lay lord, and it was comfortably big enough to feed the rector's own household: consequently it is likely that rectors were regular suppliers of surplus agricultural produce to the market. The smallest monastic houses possessed similar amounts of land, but the consumption needs of their own households were greater than those of rectors and lesser lords. In the 1320s St Bartholomew's priory in Sudbury held an endowment of around 130 acres and received an annual income of about £10, most of which would have been absorbed in supplying the basic needs of the canons and their servants, and in 1291 Letheringham priory received a modest income of £13.[9]

Lesser lay lords were acutely conscious of status, and coveted symbols of lordship that could distinguish them from prominent local freemen and associate them with the greater lords. For example, Edmund de Pakenham retained for his own use the gaming and fishing rights of the manor of Ixworth Thorpe when it was granted to his younger brother as part of their father's inheritance settlement, and other lesser lords created parks on their manors in the thirteenth century. The economic value of minor parks and gaming rights was slight, so their primary purpose was to emphasize the superior social status of their owners. Nicholas son of Reyner, lord of the manor of Witnesham in the 1280s, took such symbols seriously, as he ostentatiously rode around the parish on a splendid horse with a hawk on his arm, attended by a small entourage of valets.[10]

A moat, proudly embracing the seigneurial dwelling, was another important

[9] Campbell, 'Agrarian Problem', table 1; D. P. Dymond, 'The Parson's Glebe: Stable, Expanding or Shrinking?', in Harper-Bill *et al., East Anglia's History* (2002), p. 90; *PR*, ii, pp. 198–241 (Blackbourne). The glebes at Felsham, Gislingham and Mildenhall contained 13, 50 and 60 acres respectively, while the Melford glebe was enormous, comprising 220 acres of arable, 16 acres of meadow, 11 acres of pasture and 4 acres of wood, *PR*, ii, pp. 46 (Gislingham), 67 (Melford), 243 (Mildenhall). Thetford priory routinely bought produce from rectors, see, for example, D. P. Dymond, ed., *The Register of Thetford Priory*, part 1: *1482–1517*, NRS 59 (Oxford, 1994) and part 2: *1518–1540*, NRS 60 (Oxford, 1995): part 2, pp. 778, 784; R. Mortimer, ed., *Charters of St Bartholomew's Priory, Sudbury*, SCS 15 (Woodbridge, 1996), pp. 7–8; *VCH*, ii, p. 108.

[10] Coss, *Lordship, Knighthood*, pp. 157–8; Church, *Pakenham*, pp. 5–6; *1283 Lay Subsidy*, pp. xvi–xvii.

status symbol among the lesser landlords who lived on the claylands of Suffolk. Moats became highly fashionable in the late twelfth and thirteenth centuries, when scores were constructed on the heavier soils: many were three- or four-sided, and covered anything between one-quarter acre to 4 acres, and those larger than an acre are generally assumed to have been manorial sites. Within these moats, lords built houses which copied the style, although not the scale, of the aristocratic households, including wide aisled halls with two bays and perhaps some ancillary rooms. Most of these were constructed of timber, because stone proved too expensive for their relatively modest incomes, although higher-status gentry lords built grander residences. Little Wenham hall is a very early example of a brick manor house, dated to the late thirteenth century; the use of brick – rather than timber – and the incorporation of crenellated walls has convinced some historians that its architecture was principally defensive in purpose. Yet Edward Martin's fascinating reinterpretation of the building shows that in reality the hall possessed little defensive capability, so that the use of brick and battlements must represent innovative and fashionable architecture emphasizing wealth and status, probably with Flemish influences.[11]

THE NOBILITY

At various times in the fourteenth century four prominent aristocrats had major residences in Suffolk (the earls of Norfolk, Suffolk and Clare, and the abbey of Bury St Edmunds). The last of these was comfortably the county's most powerful and dominant landlord. The abbey's vast estate comprised numerous large manors strung across East Anglia in general and Suffolk in particular, and its judicial privileges exercised through the Liberty of St Edmund were extensive and highly valuable. The abbey's total income at the end of the thirteenth century exceeded £3,000 per annum, which made it one of the wealthiest (and largest) monasteries in England, and its lucrative estate was subdivided to support its various officers. Hence the cellarer, responsible for feeding the monastic household, held a number of large manors close to the abbey in west Suffolk (notably Bradfield, Barton Mills, Cockfield, Elveden, Fornham St Martin, Groton, Herringswell, Horringer, Ingham, Mildenhall, Nowton, Risby, Rougham, Semer, Timworth and Whepstead) and administered them separately from manors held by other abbey officers (such as the abbot, sacrist and chamberlain) as a loosely integrated estate to provide vast quantities of cash, grain, malt, wool, meat, dairy produce, game and timber for the monks' needs. Such produce was consumed by the large number of people

---

[11] *HistA*, pp. 60–1, 174–5; E. Martin, 'Little Wenham Hall', *PSIA* 39 (1998), pp. 151–64; E. Sandon, *Suffolk Houses: A Study of Domestic Architecture* (Woodbridge, 1977).

who constituted the various sub-households that existed within the abbey, each belonging to the major officers (known as obedientaries). In the early thirteenth century the abbey comprised over eighty monks and perhaps three times as many household members: the cellarer (responsible for the board and lodging of the monks) alone retained forty-eight servants, the sacrist (responsible for the upkeep of the church) had twenty-four, and the infirmarium, almoner and guestmaster retained a further twenty-six.[12]

No other landlord possessed land or influence within Suffolk to rival the abbey of Bury St Edmunds, although the prior and convent of Ely wielded similar judicial powers over the Liberty of St Etheldreda in east Suffolk, and held the manors of Melton, Sudbourne, Winston, Stoke-by-Ipswich, Kingston (south of Woodbridge) and Lakenheath. The bishopric of Ely also held eight large manors concentrated across the south of the county: Barking, Bramford, Brandon, Glemsford, Hartest, Hitcham, Rattlesden and Wetheringsett. The most important lay estate belonged to the earls, later dukes, of Norfolk, comprising eleven large and strategically important manors along the rivers of east Suffolk, including Walton, Staverton (covering land between Eyke and Butley), Dunningworth (near Snape), Bungay, Hollesley, Kelsale and the baronial seat at Framlingham. The earls of Suffolk held a handful of manors in the east and north-east of the county (including Ufford, Wingfield and Sutton) and the de Veres, earls of Oxford, ran Aldham and Lavenham from their seat at Castle Hedingham in north Essex. The estate of the earls of Clare was distributed widely across England and Wales, but its holdings in Suffolk were concentrated upon three large manors located close to the residential seat at Clare (Erbury, in Clare itself, Desning and Hundon), and included other manors in Lakenheath, Woodhall, Ilketshall and Southwold. None of these estates was sufficiently large and evenly distributed to enable a single aristocratic lay landlord to dominate medieval Suffolk in the way that some dominated counties such as Devon and Warwickshire, although a single magnate could wield considerable power over parts of the county for short periods.[13]

Aristocrats expended much of their income in supporting a large household

---

[12] The assessment of Bury abbey's income in 1291 in the *Victoria County History* is inaccurate and contradictory: for example, compare *VCH*, ii, p. 69, with *Taxatio Ecclesiastica Angliae et Walliae* (London, 1807), pp. 129–53; V. B. Redstone, ed., *Memorials of Old Suffolk* (London, 1908), pp. 99, 102.

[13] E. Miller, *The Abbey and Bishopric of Ely* (Cambridge, 1951), map 2; M. Bailey, 'An Introduction to Suffolk Domesday', in *Little Domesday Book: Suffolk* (London, 2000), pp. 10–12; *PSIA* 39 (1996), p. 109; G. A. Holmes, *The Estates of the Higher Nobility* (Cambridge, 1957), pp. 30, 144; Carpenter, 'Nobility and Gentry', p. 274. The influence of William de la Pole, earl of Suffolk, over central and north-east Suffolk between the mid-1430s and 1450 is cited in Coss, 'Age of Deference', pp. 54–5.

in a grand style: the contrast with the small households of the majority of Suffolk's minor lords was striking, as, indeed, it was meant to be. Elizabeth de Burgh inherited the extensive estates of the earls of Clare, which in 1330 generated around £3,500 a year (to which her eight Suffolk manors and boroughs contributed around £450), making her one of England's wealthiest aristocrats. Most of this annual income was spent in sustaining her household in a manner appropriate to her standing and status, and on maintaining her various properties, including the main residence at Clare (plate 2). Household expenditure comprised everything from food, clothes, salaries, travel expenses, horses, entertainment and maintaining buildings. Hospitality was a key feature of medieval lordship, and the greater lords routinely fed kin, guests, visitors and estate officials. Dame Alice de Bryene's household in Acton consumed over 20,000 lb of meat in one year, including nearly 1,600 poultry, and at Christmas her hospitality included a meal for over 200 tenants and followers. In the 1330s Katherine de Norwich's manors in north-east Suffolk supplied her two residences in Mettingham and Norwich with large quantities of meat, grain and vegetables, whilst ale, herrings, eels and oysters were purchased frequently. Wine, game and meatier fish such as cod and haddock were also consumed on special occasions, although Elizabeth de Burgh had a particular taste for wine from the Rhineland, salmon and swans. De Burgh spent nearly half her annual income on food. Similar patterns of expenditure were apparent in monastic households. In 1337 Stoke-by-Clare priory received a total income of about £200, of which almost half was absorbed by expenditure on various pensions, salaries and alms, and a further £81 on supporting the monastic household of the prior, seventeen monks and numerous servants and retainers.[14]

The consumption of huge quantities of food partly reflects the high volume of visitors to aristocratic households, but it also reveals that their membership extended well beyond the handful of valets and servants found in many gentry households. The size of the household reflected the status of the lord, and included knights, other armed escorts, and household and estate administrators, whose numbers could fluctuate in size and composition according to circumstances. Hence when in 1294 the household of Roger Bigod IV, earl of Norfolk, was preparing for war, it had expanded to more than seventy people, mainly fighting men, including two standard bearers, fifteen knights and twenty-three men-at-arms, whilst in the 1330s Elizabeth de Burgh's sedentary household at Clare castle contained a greater proportion of falconers,

[14] Holmes, *Higher Nobility*, pp. 144, 149; M. C. Morgan, *The English Lands of the Abbey of Bec* (Oxford, 1946), pp. 121–2; Dyer, *Standards of Living*, pp. 53, 59, 63; C. M. Woolgar, ed., *Household Accounts from Medieval England*, part 1 (Oxford, 1992), pp. 177–227; F. A. Underhill, *For Her Good Estate: The Life of Elizabeth de Burgh* (London, 1999), pp. 69–74.

tailors, chaplains and goldsmiths. De Burgh consciously cultivated goodwill by drawing a social circle around her household, which included minor local lords and government officials, although such affinity also enhanced her security, prestige and influence. Some of these people were simply provided with periodic gifts and hospitality, but around thirty knights and squires wore her livery and received an annual stipend, all of whom could be called upon to serve on a council of advisors helping to direct her affairs, to escort her on her travels and to decide upon legal and political courses of action. Her chief household officer was a local knight, Sir Andrew de Bures, who directed and managed this extended household. The practice of paying annual retainers to lesser lords for their loyalty and service, an arrangement known as 'bastard feudalism', developed during the fourteenth century and added to the costs of the household: an esquire might receive around £10 per annum, and a knight closer to £30. The web of 'affinity' created by bastard feudalism and its attendant allegiances was tightly drawn across the upper echelons of Suffolk society, if the example of a royal commission of 1338 is typical: the commissioners were unable to assemble a disinterested jury to hear the evidence in a particular case, because most of the knights whom they summoned were affiliated to, or in the service of, one of the four commissioners.[15] Service was a pervasive concept in medieval England, creating powerful bonds of allegiance and loyalty, especially among the nobility and gentry. It was reinforced by a strong culture of deference, as illustrated by the language deployed in contemporary letters and correspondence. A deferential society is a hierarchical society, where people knew their place.[16]

ESTATE MANAGEMENT

All landlords needed to exploit their lands carefully if they were to maintain a lifestyle befitting their status and to dispense appropriate patronage to followers. At the core of the estate were demesne manors, which the lord could either exploit directly to provide cash, food and other produce or lease (or 'farm') to another person for an annual rent to generate a steady income. A lord might also hold other parcels and slivers of land as a tenant of other manors, which usually were leased for a cash rent to local farmers: it was not economical for lords to cultivate small, miscellaneous parcels of land directly. In addition, powerful nobles and aristocrats obtained further income from a range

[15] Holmes, *Higher Nobility*, pp. 77–8, 82–3; J. Ridgard, ed., *Medieval Framlingham: Select Documents, 1270 to 1524*, SRS 27 (Woodbridge, 1985), p. 48; Underhill, *For Her Good Estate*, pp. 73–81, 119–34; Morris, *Bigod Earls*, pp. 145–53.

[16] Coss, 'Age of Deference', pp. 45–6, citing correspondence to Dame Alice de Bryene of Bures.

of jurisdictional rights. The large and complex estates of aristocratic landlords were managed by an increasingly professional team of administrators, led by one or more estate stewards with responsibility for particular groups of lands: stewards were drawn from the ranks of the gentry, while those charged with running individual manors – bailiffs and reeves – were often local tenants. In contrast, the small and localized estates of the minor landlords – comprising little more than a manor or two, and few jurisdictional privileges – were usually managed directly by the lord and his family, with perhaps a manager to support his work.[17]

Most demesne manors on the estates of higher-status landlords had been leased during the twelfth century, but during the thirteenth century many were brought into direct exploitation. This meant that landlords managed the rents, services, perquisites and resources of the manor themselves (either personally or delegated to their own officials), rather than devolving the whole business to a lessee for an annual rent. This change in managerial policy reflects a concern to raise levels of income during an inflationary period, a more active and professional approach to estate management, and the increased opportunities for commercial profit from demesne exploitation. By these means, many landlords increased the revenues from their estates over the course of the thirteenth century, to reach a peak at the beginning of the fourteenth. The contribution of direct demesne cultivation to seigneurial incomes was greatest on the manors and estates of the lesser landlords. Bruce Campbell calculates that in *c.* 1300 nearly half of all income on gentry estates was generated from the demesne land. For example, in 1360 Sir John Jernegan's manor of Somerleyton produced a mere £3 11s. 6d. from rents, compared with £33 from sales of grain and dairy produce; similarly, Kersey priory depended upon the rectory of Lindsey, and its demesne land around Kersey, for the bulk of its £33 income each year; and St Bartholomew's priory, Sudbury, had few tenants and exploited most of its 130-acre endowment as a home farm. In contrast, only around 20 per cent of the income of aristocratic landlords came from the produce of their demesnes, with the majority sourced from rents of various sorts: only a small percentage was generated by perquisites such as markets, court income and jurisdictional rights.[18]

Our knowledge of how individual manors were exploited draws heavily upon the details contained within manorial accounts, which enable historians to establish with precision their financial yield, and the extent to which demesnes were geared towards production for the market or for the lord's

---

[17] For a general introduction, see Dyer, *Making a Living*, pp. 119–37.

[18] C. Dyer, *An Age of Transition? Economy and Society in England in the Later Middle Ages* (Oxford, 2005), p. 98; Campbell, 'Agrarian Problem', table 3; *VCH*, ii, p. 107; Mortimer, *St Bartholomew's Sudbury*, p. 8.

own consumption. In *c.* 1300 the largest manors in Suffolk each yielded nearly £100 per annum, although a few generated comfortably more, mainly through a combination of rental income, sales of demesne produce, and the monetary value of supplies sent to the seigneurial household. For example, the monks of Ely used their manor at Lakenheath mainly as a home farm to supply produce worth at least £60 each year for consumption at the monastery, ranging from swans and rabbits to enough malted barley to brew 20,000 gallons of ale, yet in the 1320s and 1330s they also squeezed significant sums of cash to help finance the construction of the octagon tower at Ely cathedral. The single most valuable manor in Suffolk was undoubtedly Mildenhall, comprising an enormous arable demesne of 1,200 acres, which in 1323 sent more than £130 in cash to the coffers of the cellarer of Bury St Edmunds abbey, in addition to large quantities of grain, livestock and other produce of equivalent value. Of course, not all of the manors of the aristocratic landlords were large and valuable: both the earl of Clare's manor in Lakenheath, and the prior and convent of Ely's manor of Kingston, comprised arable demesnes of about 35 acres and yielded around £10 per annum in the early fourteenth century.[19]

During the course of the thirteenth century landlords became increasingly sophisticated in the way that they mixed production strategies on the various manors across their estates, and also exploited the growing opportunities for commercial profit. By *c.* 1300 around one-third of all grain produced on English demesnes was reserved as seed corn for the next year's crop; approximately 38 per cent was sold, with the proportion of sales rising to around one-half on the estates of the greater landlords; and the remainder was consumed either by the lord's household or as part of the running expenses of the manor. These general figures demonstrate that demesne output in England was significantly orientated towards market production. In some places, the decision to sell corn was a deliberate commercial strategy, while in others the policy was more incidental: lords simply sold any corn that was left over after their own consumption needs had been satisfied.[20]

To what extent are these characteristics evident in Suffolk? Many manors sold a large proportion of the wheat and barley they produced, which is indicative of commercialized cash cropping. For example, most Breckland manors sold the majority of their barley, encouraged by proximity to Bury St Edmunds and the navigable stretches of the Little Ouse and Lark rivers.

[19] M. Bailey, 'The Prior and Convent of Ely and their Management of the Manor of Lakenheath', in *Ecclesiastical Studies in Honour of Dorothy M. Owen*, ed. M. Franklin and C. Harper-Bill (Woodbridge, 1995), pp. 3, 7; Bodleian Suffolk Rolls 21 and *PR*, ii, p. 243 (Mildenhall); CUL EDC 7/14/c/1–10 (Kingston).

[20] B. M. S. Campbell, *English Seigneurial Agriculture, 1250–1450* (Cambridge, 2000), table 5.01, p. 203. These figures, like all those presented here, are net of tithe payments to the church.

Barley production at South Elmham was highly commercialized, with 60 per cent of output sold to unspecified buyers in the 1340s, while between 1314 and 1348 the Hinderclay demesne sold 68 per cent of all its wheat (a further 22 per cent was used as seed corn) and 58 per cent of its barley (25 per cent seed). Between 1276 and 1300 54 per cent of the wheat (30 per cent seed) and 58 per cent of the barley (35 per cent seed) produced at Blakenham was sold (it lay 5 miles from Ipswich), and the income from these sales constituted almost half of the manor's annual revenue. Yet most of its rye and oats was consumed as fodder for livestock, which confirms that deliberate choices were being made about those crops produced for sale and those for consumption. In general, the wheat and barley produced on demesnes in Suffolk were usually sold; rye features as a cash crop only on a few demesnes around Ipswich; and oats was usually consumed.[21]

The sophistication of commercial decision-making on demesnes could be impressive. The exact balance of crops sown each year at Hinderclay was adjusted in response to subtle shifts in the relative prices of the two cash crops, wheat and barley. Such commercial sensitivity is remarkable, given that Hinderclay was land-locked and far distant from large urban markets: most of its grain was sold nearby for local consumption. The example of Hinderclay reinforces the point that farms did not have to be located on a prime site close to major markets or a navigable waterway, nor did they have to operate a highly intensive arable regime, to be responsive to market opportunities. In 1328–9 Gipping Newton, stuck in the middle of the county, sold 52 per cent of its wheat (21 per cent seed), 68 per cent of its mongerall (a wheat/oats mix) and 51 per cent of its oats (24 per cent seed), mainly in the vicinity of nearby Stowmarket, although it also used a middleman to try and sell some corn 'in Norfolk and elsewhere'. Canny managers deliberately stockpiled and withheld sales of grain until prices were higher during the summer months before the next harvest. For example, in the late autumn of 1321 nearly 7 quarters of wheat were sold by the Hinderclay manor for around 8s. a quarter, yet 16 quarters in the summer of 1322, just prior to the next harvest, fetched around 16s. per quarter; the manor of Layham sold no wheat in the months following the harvest of 1331, but then made all of its sales in the spring and summer of 1332; and Gipping Newton held back most of its wheat for sale in the

[21] M. Bailey, *A Marginal Economy? East Anglian Breckland in the Later Middle Ages* (Cambridge, 1989), tables 4.11, 4.12, 4.13; *AHEW*, ii, p. 302 (South Elmham); D. Stone, 'Medieval Farm Management and Technological Mentalities: Hinderclay before the Black Death', *EcHR* 54 (2001), p. 617; M. C. Chibnall, ed., *Select Documents of the English Lands of the Abbey of Bec*, Camden Society 3rd series 73 (London, 1951), pp. 94, 174–85; M. C. Chibnall, ed., *Compotus Rolls of the English Lands of the Abbey of Bec, 1272–1289*, Camden Society, 4th Series 34 (London, 1987), pp. 81, 106–7, 134–5 (Blakenham).

spring and summer months. There is nothing here to surprise a modern farmer, except perhaps the discovery that such commercial tactics were deployed in the Middle Ages.[22]

Pastoral farming was more commercialized than grain production on the vast majority of demesnes. Wool was sold for commercial profit on almost every Suffolk manor where sheep were reared. Many demesnes slaughtered only their oldest sheep for meat in order to maximize the wool-bearing capacity of their flocks, and wool was a reliable and lucrative source of cash each year. The largest flocks generated wool sales of over £30 each year, and even a modest demesne flock of 100 sheep might produce wool worth £3. Fleeces were usually sold in a single batch to merchants operating from East Anglia's leading towns: it is instructive that in the 1280s wool features prominently among the taxable goods of Ipswich residents. Similarly, most dairy herds were reared solely for commercial profit. A few demesnes (such as Blakenham and Lawshall) exploited their herds directly, using manorial workers to milk the cows and to produce butter and cheese for sale, but the majority of herds were simply leased to local people for an annual 'lactage' fee for each cow, who then produced and sold the butter and cheese themselves. In the 1330s large herds of over thirty cows generated fees well in excess of £10 per annum on manors such as Kelsale, South Elmham and Worlingworth. Demesne herd sizes could be very sensitive to variations in lactage rates, and those at both Dunningworth and Melton were expanded in the 1290s as these rates rose and then contracted in the 1300s as they fell.[23]

Stock rearing was locally significant and became more important during the fourteenth century. The fattening of cattle for slaughter was a particular feature of tenant, rather than demesne, farms, but some landlords reared bullocks commercially. A few landlords holding large manors on light soils reared rabbits for domestic consumption before the Black Death, but thereafter shifted to commercial strategies and exploited their warrens to sell fur and meat in London. A few others looked to fatten sizeable herds of pigs for market. The Exning demesne concentrated strongly upon pig rearing, and in the 1320s and 1330s the size of the pig herd at Hinderclay was very sensitive to variations in prevailing market prices: it was expanded to around seventy pigs as prices rose in the late 1320s and early 1330s, when around a third of the herd was fattened and sold each year. Yet, when their price fell severely after

---

[22] Stone, 'Hinderclay', pp. 619–23; SROI HD1538/236/16 (Gipping); Bacon Ms 451 (Hinderclay); SROB E3/1/1 (Layham).

[23] Bailey, 'Lakenheath', p. 5; *1283 Lay Subsidy*, p. xxv; Campbell, *English Seigneurial Agriculture*, p. 163; Chibnall, *Compotus Rolls*, pp. 65, 118 (Blakenham); SROB E7/17/9 (Lawshall); *AHEW*, ii, pp. 301–2; SROI HD1538/279/2 (Kelsale); PRO SC6/995/21–24 (Dunningworth); CUL EDC 7/16/11/2–5 (Melton).

1339, the manor rapidly sold off the herd and abandoned pig rearing entirely. The production of fuel, particularly turves, bracken and wood, was also highly commercialized on many demesnes: for example, thousands of faggots from the large woods at Chevington found their way to the Bury market every year.[24]

For all the evidence for the commercialization of agricultural production on Suffolk demesnes around 1300, there is still much that is paradoxical and unknowable about the commercial mentality of landlords. The decision-making on some demesnes confounded market forces. For example, the manor of Easton Bavents possessed all the prerequisites for a successful commercial enterprise – easily worked land, a coastal location with its own port and market, and ready access to large urban markets (Dunwich and Yarmouth) – but in the fourteenth century most of its arable and pastoral produce was consumed by the household of the resident lord and hardly any was sold. Although in the 1370s the manor of Tattingstone was very commercialized, selling nearly half its rye and barley and fattening many bullocks and lambs for market, by the late 1390s its production had become very uncommercialized. Much of its produce was now consumed by the lord's household, which reinforces the rather obvious point that production strategies could change dramatically on a single manor over a short period for non-commercial reasons.[25]

The example of Easton Bavents highlights the danger of making judgements about the production strategies on a single manor in isolation from those on other manors on the same estate, because landlords usually adopted an estate-wide policy when deciding how to deploy the resources of each individual manor: in this case, Thomas de Bavent may well have orientated production on all of his other manors towards the market, but unfortunately their accounts have not survived. Similarly, the example of Tattingstone highlights the danger of profiling the strategies on a single manor using a small sample of accounts over a short period, rather than using a larger sample over a longer period: a change of lord, of residency arrangements, or in the composition of an estate could all result in a significant change in the production strategy on any one manor. Both of these examples emphasize that all lords usually relied upon their own estates to supply most of the basic food and provisions for their household, and therefore some production on some of their manors was inevitably geared to subsistence. In determining where on their estates to deploy subsistence or commercial strategies, or a mixture of both, some lords appear to have been more influenced by custom and convenience than

---

[24] C. Richmond, *John Hopton: A Fifteenth-Century Suffolk Gentleman* (Cambridge, 1981), p. 37; Campbell, *English Seigneurial Agriculture*, p. 168 (Exning); Stone, 'Hinderclay', pp. 629–32; SROB E3/15.3/2.20(b) (Chevington).

[25] SROI v5/19/1.1 – 1.6 (Easton); SROI H8/1/817–825 (Tattingstone).

by a hard-edged assessment of the competitive commercial advantage of each manor. Consequently, the outstanding commercial potential of some manors passed unexploited. The demesne land on the vast manor of Lakenheath was deployed largely as a home farm by the prior and convent of Ely, despite its accessibility to a navigable river system and its capacity for producing large quantities of highly marketable malting barley, for the simple reason that it was conveniently located near Ely. Production on the earl of Norfolk's manors of Kelsale and Staverton was geared primarily to the needs of the lord's house-hold (at nearby Framlingham castle), despite their favourable locations near the coast and navigable stretches of the rivers Alde and Deben. However, the earl did exploit the excellent coastal location of his Walton manor, generat-ing the remarkable sum of nearly £90 (or 38 per cent of manorial revenue) in 1282–3 from grain sales alone.[26]

Clearly, landlords did not always attempt to exploit all of their manors in the most economically rational and profitable fashion, because they were strongly influenced by the desire to supply their own household(s). Monastic landlords were especially focused upon the subsistence needs of their house-holds, because they had a fixed and sizeable community of monks, nuns or canons to feed, heat and clothe, and consequently their manors were usually the most weakly commercialized in England. So although medieval landlords had an eye for commerce and profit, such opportunities tended to be exploited once their own households had been provisioned: an attitude which indicates that they were not yet 'capitalist' in their outlook.[27]

Most of the examples presented so far, and most of the research on medi-eval commerce, draw upon the evidence of aristocratic manors, because their surviving records are most informative and voluminous. We still know too little about production strategies on the manors of lesser lay landlords, the very category of lords who dominated Suffolk society. In particular, we know hardly anything about the demesne output of the most humble landlords. His-torians have sometimes assumed that, if anything, the lesser landlords were more commercialized and innovative producers than aristocrats, for the obvi-ous reasons that they were more directly and closely involved with husbandry, and needed to make less land and capital go further. Some scraps of evidence from Suffolk support this contention. An inventory of the goods of Walter de Merton at Freckenham in the 1280s reveals that barley was seven times more important than the next crop (wheat), a far higher proportion than was evi-dent on proximate demesnes held by ecclesiastical landlords; the gentry-held manor of Icklingham Berners was strongly geared towards barley production,

---

[26] Bailey, 'Lakenheath', pp. 4–7; SROI HD1538/279/1–2 (Kelsale); PRO SC6/1007/11 (Walton); PRO SC6/1005/10–12 (Staverton).

[27] Campbell, *English Seigneurial Agriculture*, p. 208.

of which over 70 per cent – a very high proportion – was routinely sold on the open market each year; and the demesne at Akenham was highly commercialized, selling most of its barley, wheat and peas in nearby Ipswich, and leasing for profit its sizeable dairy herd of twenty-five cows. Yet the lesser landlords still had to meet the demands of their households, as the example of Easton Bavents graphically reveals, and Shardelowe's manor in Santon Downham sold merely 11 per cent of its rye and one-third of its barley in the 1340s and 1350s. In a similar fashion, Sir William Elmham used the manor of Walsham to supply his guest house at nearby Westhorpe with provisions as required, but sold any wheat and barley to market if no such need arose: hence much of its wheat and barley were consumed at Westhorpe in 1402–3 and much of it was sold in 1406–7. There is no clear evidence before 1350 that gentry manors were *significantly* more commercialized than those of other landlords.[28]

The most humble lay landlords probably adopted strategies similar to those of the wealthy peasantry, responding flexibly to market conditions to maximize their net income while tailoring their household expenditure and consumption according to need. A part-year account for Walsham High Hall, the only manor held by Nicholas de Walsham, generated just over £6 cash in 1327–8, mainly through sales of wheat – sown largely as a cash crop (60 per cent sold, 24 per cent seed) – and surplus barley (39 per cent sold, 22 per cent seed): all other grain was used for domestic purposes. The majority of grain sales were made after Christmas, when prices were higher, and the proportion sown with legumes (17 per cent) was unusually high for this part of Suffolk. Although the manor raised poultry for the market, all its other animals were draught livestock and therefore Nicholas had to purchase whatever other meat he consumed. The area of pasture and meadow on this demesne was small and leased to local tenants, which might have encouraged a mutually beneficial relationship in which Nicholas supported his tenants by buying his meat from them. The practice of withholding grain sales until the spring and summer months, when prices were rising in advance of the next harvest, was probably commonplace on the small demesne farms of the lesser lay landlords, and any grain sales made earlier in the year often attract a careful explanation for the sale in manorial accounts: they were usually driven by a pressing need to generate cash for a specific purpose, such as the sale of small batches of grain to pay workers for winnowing corn and for undertaking small chores on manorial buildings, or to buy seed corn. The manors of lowly landlords appear to have been carefully managed, with direct involvement from the lord himself: such people were under heavy financial pressure in the late thirteenth century,

---

[28] Holmes, *Higher Nobility*, p. 89; *AHEW*, ii, p. 301 (Freckenham); NRO Mss 13190–13200 (Icklingham); SROI HD1469/7, 8 (Akenham); SROB 651/35/2–6 (Downham); SROB HA504/3/5a, 5b (Walsham).

and perforce they had to manage their lands and households with utmost care.[29]

MANORIAL STRUCTURE

Having considered the ways in which different lords managed their various manors, we should consider regional variations in the distribution of manors of different sizes and composition. Reconstructing and understanding regional differences in manorial structure across medieval England is important for two reasons. First, it provides useful insights into the nature and structure of local society. A community split between numerous small manors held by a variety of low-status landlords was likely to be ordered and governed very differently from another community dominated by a large single manor held by a powerful aristocrat. Second, a good correlation exists between the character of manorial structures and the level of regional economic development.

The manorial structure of medieval England is traditionally portrayed as dominated by 'classic' manors, each conterminous with the village and parish of the same name and possessing a large arable demesne and predominantly unfree tenures and tenants. Such manors were usually subject to the exercise of strong lordship by the aristocrats who held them. Areas where such manorial forms predominated are deemed to possess a 'strong' manorial structure. In contrast, areas where small manors proliferated, held by low-status landlords and characterized by free tenures, are deemed to possess a 'weak' manorial structure. Here most vills and parishes were split between numerous manors, and seigneurial demands upon the majority of manorial tenants were not onerous. Regions of weak manorialism often exhibit more symptoms of social and economic individualism, and higher levels of economic development, than those which were strongly manorialized.[30]

On these criteria Suffolk possessed a weak manorial structure, a characteristic which had been evident in the Domesday Survey of 1086 when many Suffolk manors were much smaller than the national average. In 1086 the average English manor was rated at around 600 acres, but only 11 per cent of Suffolk manors rated higher than this, and 45 per cent were less than 120 acres. Manors containing 30 acres or less were no rarity in Suffolk, prompting Maitland to conclude that 'there are many holdings called manors which are

---

[29] SROB HA504/3/1b (Walsham); SROI HD1538/236/16 (Gipping); SROI HA68/484/318 (Horham), especially 1328–9 and 1369–70; Carpenter, 'Nobility and Gentry', pp. 269–70.

[30] S. H. Rigby, *English Society in the Later Middle Ages: Class, Status and Gender* (London, 1995), pp. 40–5; for a general introduction to the manor, see Bailey, *English Manor*, pp. 1–12.

so small that we, with our reminiscences of the law of later days, can hardly bring ourselves to call them manors'. The precise definition of a 'manor' in the late eleventh century is uncertain, although Maitland concluded that it was a legal term used to describe a hall against which the geld (i.e. taxation) was charged. In every other respect the precise difference between the smallest manors and the holdings of the larger freemen is impossible to distinguish, such that 'freemen' held tiny manors in Tuddenham and Wenham. Five manorial units are explicitly identified in Chediston, the largest of which was rated at 100 acres, and lay alongside a further five holdings of around 13 acres each, shared among joint-holders of freemen. Chediston is typical of the Domesday entries for many places in east Suffolk, where numerous lords of relatively low social status, and a 'middle class' of freemen who were relatively independent of seigneurial control and who were hardly distinguishable from the lesser lords, dominated landholding.[31]

These general characteristics became even more pronounced over the next two centuries, as larger manors fragmented into smaller ones and as the holdings of freemen became increasingly complex and fluid, a process that culminated around 1300. Historians have sought to reconstruct the outcome of this process by utilizing the *Nomina Villarum* of 1316, which lists the 'head lords' contained within each vill, to recreate local variations in manorial structure. Unfortunately, these returns for Suffolk seriously under-numerate the actual number of lords (and, by extension, the number of manors) in each vill. For example, the *Nomina Villarum* records only one 'head lord' in each of Brockley and Stowlangtoft, yet the chance survival of a copy of part of the Hundred Rolls for that part of Suffolk made in the 1280s reveals at least seven manors in Brockley and three in Stowlangtoft. The tendency for many vills in *c.* 1300 to be split between a number of manors is abundantly clear from other sources: for example, at least six manors are identifiable in Whatfield, seven in Cretingham, and eight each in Debenham and Westleton. Map 3 attempts to reconstruct variations in the number of manors per vill across early fourteenth-century Suffolk by utilizing W. A. Copinger's early though no means exhaustive research into its manorial history, rather than relying upon the *Nomina Villarum*. It illustrates clearly that most Suffolk vills contained more than one manor; many vills were subdivided between at least three manors; and the degree of subdivision and fragmentation was highest in the north-east.[32]

---

[31] Bailey, 'Suffolk Domesday', p. 14; *Little Domesday Book*, ff. 293a, 332b, 444b; F. W. Maitland, *Domesday and Beyond*, 3rd edn (Cambridge, 1987), pp. 107–11, 117–18, 120–5.

[32] The manorial structure of eastern Norfolk was significantly 'weaker' than that of Suffolk on the basis of the information contained within the 1316 returns. B. M. S. Campbell, 'The Complexity of Manorial Structure in Medieval Norfolk: A Case Study', *Norfolk Archaeology* 39 (1986); V. B. Redstone, '*Nomina Villarum*,

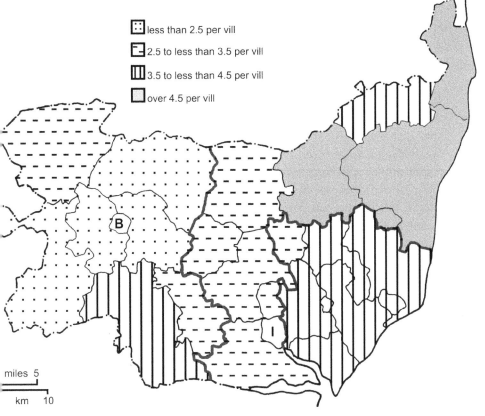

less than 2.5 per vill

2.5 to less than 3.5 per vill

3.5 to less than 4.5 per vill

over 4.5 per vill

miles 5

km 10

MAP 3 Density of manors per vill (by hundred)

The manorial subdivision of many vills in *c.* 1300 was the culmination of an accelerating process of fragmentation between the eighth and thirteenth centuries, and emphasizes that manors were not static or immutable entities, but changed size, shape and composition over time. Manors were held freely, which meant that all or some of their land could be bought and sold with few restrictions (although new laws in the 1290s imposed further restrictions), and they could also become split between heirs as part of an inheritance settlement. Both of these processes caused large manors to be broken up

Suffolk, 1316', *PSIA* 11 (1902), pp. 197–8; *PR*, ii, pp. 158–62, 204–5 (Brockley and Stowlangtoft); Bailey, 'Suffolk Domesday', p. 14; W. A. Copinger, *The Manors of Suffolk*, 7 vols. (Manchester, 1905–11), iii, pp. 238–45 (Cretingham); *PSIA* 12 (1906), pp. 218–22 (Debenham); P. Warner, *Greens, Commons and Clayland Colonisation: The Origins and Development of Greenside Settlement in East Suffolk*, University of Leicester Department of English Local History, Occasional Papers series 4 no. 2 (1987), p. 40. Yet Copinger himself overlooked many lesser manors in Suffolk: see D. Allen, 'The Descent of the Manor of Ampners in Thrandeston', *PSIA* 40 (2002), p. 145.

into smaller ones. The descriptions of landholdings in the Domesday Book of 1086 provide a snapshot of the cumulative effect of the manorial fragmentation that had occurred during the late Anglo-Saxon period, but the process continued, and probably accelerated, over the following two centuries. Sustained economic and demographic expansion during the twelfth and thirteenth centuries increased the pressure to subdivide and split manors into smaller units, which explains the proliferation of manors held by fractions 'of a knight's fee'. Hence in 1242 Robert Darnel held a manor in Poslingfield as 'one-third of a knight's fee', reflecting the fragmentation of an original, larger, manor into at least three smaller manors. The number of manors in Westleton increased from two in 1086 to eight in *c.* 1300, and from two to at least four in Wickhambrook. Similarly, by the 1280s some land from the main manor in Brockley (held by John Algar, who was introduced earlier in this chapter) had been carved off to create two small manors, and another manor – originally around the same size as Algar's – had become split into four other manorial units. It is also evident that the 'manor', which in the late eleventh century could be legally defined as a unit against which the geld was charged, had lost this precise technical meaning by the thirteenth century as forms of taxation changed.[33]

The effects of this fission 'from above' were complicated by the tendency for some manors to change their form as a consequence of engrossing activity 'from below'. Manors could be created, or the size and composition of an existing manor could be altered, by the acquisition of additional land parcels from other lords and free tenants. For example, Berards manor in Whatfield was constructed from land originally acquired from at least two other manorial holdings, while the manor of Ixworth Thorpe was forged from three large holdings obtained from two different sources, the Blund family and Gilbert de Thorpe, and its composition was further altered between the 1250s and 1320s by the acquisition of scores of small parcels of land purchased from local freemen. In Ashfield Parva a small manor held by the prior of Ixworth was constructed from land obtained from both the abbot of Bury St Edmunds and Thomas Nowell. The evidence contained in map 3 indicates that the cumulative effects of the processes of fragmentation and reorganization were most pronounced in east Suffolk, where once large manors had been broken down into smaller units, and acquisitive freemen in secondary settlements

---

33 Bailey, 'Suffolk Domesday', p. 14; J. C. Ward, 'The Honour of Clare in Suffolk in the Early Middle Ages', *PSIA* 30 (1964), pp. 94–111, provides a good discussion of subinfeudation and its effect upon the relationship between the nobility and their lesser lords. Warner, *Greens, Commons*, p. 40; R. Hoppitt, 'A Study of the Development of Parks in Suffolk from the Eleventh to the Seventeenth Centuries' (PhD thesis, University of East Anglia, 1992), p. 197; *PR*, ii, pp. 158–60; Maitland, *Domesday and Beyond*, p. 128.

bought up land and reorganized their holdings into small but identifiable manors.[34]

In *c.* 1300 most Suffolk manors possessed a high proportion of free tenants, a low proportion of villeins, small demesnes, and were held by lesser lay lords. (The status of peasants and their land tenures are explained in chapter 3.) In fact, Suffolk stands out among English counties for its very high proportion of small lay manors where free tenures dominated, and for the relative unimportance of unfree (or customary) rents and services. Free rents were two to three times more valuable than customary rents on the lay manors in Suffolk sampled by Campbell, and were many times more valuable in south-east Suffolk around Ipswich and along the Stour valley: the latter represents one of the highest such ratings in medieval England (map 5). These general characteristics can be readily illustrated. In the 1280s the average size of the arable demesne on thirty-seven lay manors in Blackbourne hundred was only 120 acres, and the average area of villein land was a mere 30 acres: over one-half of these manors contained no villein land at all. Free tenants held nearly 500 acres of land, and unfree tenants a mere 13 acres, from the manor of Stowlangtoft. The manor held by John Algar in Brockley comprised a sizeable 320-acre demesne, seven free tenants, and included 64 acres held by an undisclosed number of villeins. No villeins were recorded on any of the other six manors in Brockley, where the arable demesnes were significantly smaller than Algar's: Nicholas Gedding held the smallest, with a 20-acre demesne and seven freemen. In Pakenham, William de Pakenham's manor was a similar size to that of John Algar, but its structure was very different. The demesne was much smaller, at 56 acres of arable and 4 acres of meadow, and his free tenants held over 300 acres of arable: only 42 acres were held in villeinage. In Hunston, John de Hunston's manor comprised an arable demesne of 64 acres, eight free tenants and 12 acres held by villeins, and that of William Godbarlik had no villeins, a 60-acre arable demesne and seven free tenants holding three messuages and 27 acres.[35]

In a few places these small arable demesnes were supplemented by endowments of other landed resources, particularly in the Breckland, where arable farming was relatively insignificant. Hence Robert Lengynour's 49-acre arable demesne in Knettishall was complemented by 16 acres of heathland, and Walter le Pouer's paltry 15-acre arable demesne was enhanced by 5 acres of heath:

34 Bailey, 'Suffolk Domesday', pp. 14–15; Church, *Pakenham*, p. 3; *PR*, ii, pp. 199–200; Warner, *Greens, Commons*, p. 40.

35 Campbell, 'Agrarian Problem', maps 1 and 2; E. A. Kosminsky, *Studies in the Agrarian History of England in the Thirteenth Century* (Oxford, 1956), pp. 130–1; *PR*, ii, pp. 198–241 (Blackbourne), 204–9 (Stowlangtoft), 158–62 (Brockley), 201–2 (Hunston); Church, *Pakenham*, p. 2.

similarly, his villeins held 18 acres of land and 4 acres of heath. The example of Walter le Pouer reiterates the point that some manors are so small that they hardly warrant the title. In the 1280s Roger, son of William, de Cotton held 24 acres in Cotton from the abbey of St Edmund, together with 4 acres 'which his cottars hold from him', and Robert de Pirar held the 'capital hall' of Oakley as half a knight's fee with 23 acres of arable, 6 acres of meadow and 2 acres of pasture. Manors such as these, which do not fit the conventional definition of a manor, were numerous in Suffolk, but few of them have made any impression upon the surviving documentary record. Hence, if almost one-half of all lay manors in England between 1300 and 1349 generated less than £10 per annum, we might reckon that the average Suffolk manor generated only around £5–7 each year.[36]

The fluidity of manorial forms and the existence of numerous manors in each vill were only two aspects of the complexity of Suffolk's manorial structure, which was exacerbated further by the tendency for the land of a single manor to be scattered in the fields of more than one vill or parish. This characteristic was widespread, and it was not confined to any particular type of manor or landlord. For example, 36 acres of demesne arable, 30 acres of heath and 42 acres in villeinage belonging to Peter de Thelnetham's manor of Great Livermere actually lay in Troston; some land belonging to the manor of Melton lay in Ufford and across the river Deben in Bromeswell; Thrandeston Ampners extended into Stoke Ash, Yaxley, Thornham Parva and Mellis, and its court was held in Yaxley; and some lands belonging to Tattingstone manor lay in Belstead, Brantham and Copdock. The open fields of Culford contained land belonging to the manors of Ingham, Lackford, West Stow and Wordwell; elements of the manor of Culford itself extended into Wordwell and Fornham St Genevieve; and the fields of Westleton contained land belonging to fifteen different manors, although Westleton itself contained only eight manors. Similarly, the arable demesne of the manor of Fornham All Saints, belonging to the abbot of Bury St Edmunds, was distributed in separate parcels located across the parishes of Fornham All Saints, Fornham St Genevieve and Fornham St Martin, with the furthest-flung block of land abutting Timworth heath.[37]

This survey of variations in the internal structure of the small manors that dominated Suffolk should not obscure that fact that some classic manors – with large demesnes (in excess of 250 acres), a high proportion of unfree

---

[36] *PR*, ii, pp. 47 (Oakley), 48 (Cotton), 229–30 (Knettishall).

[37] *PR*, ii, p. 225 (Troston); CUL EDC 7/14/c/30 (Melton); Allen, 'Manor of Ampners', p. 147; SROI HB8/1/822 (Tattingstone); BL Add. Ms 42055, ff. 28, 30, 34, 37, 43, 45 (Culford); Warner, *Greens, Commons*, p. 40; BL Add. Ms 34689, ff. 26–9 (Fornham).

tenures, and held by a high-status landlord – did exist: perhaps 5 per cent, and certainly no more than 10 per cent, of all Suffolk manors in *c.* 1300 fitted this description. Large demesnes required a large servile workforce to cultivate them, and hence were usually accompanied by a sizeable allocation of villein land and by strong seigneurial control over the villein tenants. Inevitably, such sizeable manors dominated the vill in which they lay, and are particularly associated with the estates of the great ecclesiastical landlords, such as Bury St Edmunds abbey, and those of powerful lay lords, such as the earls of Norfolk, who possessed the will, power and status to resist the fragmentation of their manors into smaller units. For example, in the 1280s the size of the arable demesne on seven manors held by the abbey of Bury St Edmunds in Blackbourne hundred averaged 320 acres (three times greater than the average size of the demesne on thirty-seven lay manors in the hundred), while the area held in villeinage averaged 280 acres (nine times the area on lay manors). Classic manors could be found all over the county, but they were most prevalent in west Suffolk. A single manor, held by the bishop of Ely, dominated Brandon, and contained an arable demesne of 564 acres and a similar area of villein holdings: free tenants were relatively unimportant. Only two manors existed in Lakenheath, one held by the earl of Clare, containing around 100 acres of arable, and the other by the prior and convent of Ely, containing a 600-acre arable demesne and a similar area on customary tenures. A number of manors existed in Melford, which was nonetheless dominated by one huge manor with an 800-acre demesne, together with 600 acres of villein land, held by the abbot of Bury St Edmunds.[38]

In general, Suffolk in *c.* 1300 was lightly manorialized compared with many areas of England, but parts of east Suffolk were particularly so, and strongly independent of wealthy and dominant lordship. The area stretching from the Stour to the Waveney, lying between the lighter sands to the east and the heavier upland clays to the west, contained vills which were divided into greater numbers of small, low-value, manorial units, mainly held by lay landlords and dominated by free tenures: villein tenures and villeins were largely non-existent. The fertile soils and relatively dense population in this area facilitated the development of small, multiple, manors. In contrast, the poor, sandy, soils and low population density of the Breckland are associated with a different manorial structure, in which most vills contained just one or two large, high-value, manors, mainly held by great ecclesiastical landlords and dominated by villein tenures. North-west Suffolk was heavily manorialized (map 3).

The characteristics of many Suffolk manors in *c.* 1300 challenge the

---

[38] M. Bailey, 'Villeinage in England: A Regional Case Study, 1200 to 1350' (forthcoming); *PR*, ii, pp. 68–71 (Melford), 198–241 (Blackbourne); Bailey, 'Lakenheath', pp. 1–20.

conventional legal definition of the manor. Legal historians state confidently that a manor exists only if it can be proven to have all of the following characteristics: demesne land, more than two tenants, and a court baron. Yet Frederic Maitland realized long ago that some medieval manors simply do not fit this clean, modern, definition: after testing the medieval evidence against these defining characteristics, he concluded that 'one after another, all the familiar propositions seem to fail us … we must expressly reject some suggestions that the later history of our law may make to us'. Maitland's observations and reservations are reinforced time and again by the evidence from medieval Suffolk. As we have seen, Robert de Pirar held the 'capital hall' of Oakley with no tenants attached to it, and there is nothing to distinguish William de Cotton's 24-acre holding in Cotton from those of many local freemen: nor was it worth William – nor many other Suffolk lords in his position – holding a manorial court for the handful of cottars or other tenants who loosely held land from him. Manorial forms in Suffolk in *c.* 1300 were more varied and fluid than in many areas of medieval England and, indeed, than later manorial forms, and many simply do not fit the modern legal definition of a manor. The English manor acquired a tighter technical and legal definition during the course of the sixteenth and seventeenth centuries, which has strongly influenced modern notions of 'the manor'. The definition of a manor under modern law would have perplexed many residents of medieval Suffolk, where the manor was a genus with many more species.[39]

CONCLUSION

The structure of landed society in thirteenth-century Suffolk was unusual in two ways: first, the most powerful aristocrats were ecclesiastics not laymen, two of whom enjoyed greatly extended judicial powers over sizeable areas of the county. The landed estates of the abbey of Bury St Edmunds dominated west Suffolk, and its additional judicial rights associated with the Liberty of St Edmund enabled the abbey to protect its interests effectively and to control the local political landscape with an iron grip. Likewise, the landed holdings and judicial liberties of the prior and convent of Ely in parts of east Suffolk provided similar power and control. The estate of the earls (later dukes) of Norfolk was the major aristocratic presence outside these liberties, with eleven manors loosely scattered around his baronial seat at Framlingham. Second, lordship in general was characterized by a high proportion of minor landlords whose estates hardly extended beyond a single vill. The majority of lords in Suffolk were nothing more than moderately wealthy local farmers, although a few might seek favour and advancement in the retinues of lay aristocrats.

39 Maitland, *Domesday and Beyond*, pp. 119–20, 128.

Most remained politically anonymous, and very few were required to perform any military service, which explains why they are largely invisible and
unknowable to the historian.

The complex political implications of this unusual seigneurial structure will
doubtless be explored further in a companion medieval volume in this *History
of Suffolk* series. Lords operating exclusively within the Liberty of St Edmund
or St Etheldreda could not afford to antagonize their monastic overlords if
they wished to prosper in their territories, and Sir William de Pakenham
grasped and manipulated this political reality shrewdly. As William's estates
were located in west Suffolk, he served the abbey of St Edmund loyally and
well, but also took the wise precaution of aligning himself with the bishop
of Norwich, who was the only other competing ecclesiastical authority in
the area. With such powerful local patrons, William had little need to seek
support or enhance his status through affiliation with members of the lay
nobility. Because large areas of Suffolk were controlled by two powerful and
relatively apolitical monastic landlords, its political life was relatively subdued
in comparison to other counties where competing factions of lay lords vied
for supremacy, except in extreme circumstances. The tight control exercised by
Bury and Ely abbeys in Suffolk helps to explain the relish and vehemence with
which local people reacted in rare moments of national revolt.

The economic implications of this social structure are clear. Suffolk was
a county of weak manorialism, where the average vill was split between a
number of manors, the typical manor was small, and the average landlord
exercised limited powers (either *de facto* or *de jure*) over his tenantry. Many of
the lesser lords experienced mounting financial pressures during this period,
forcing them to exploit what lands they possessed with care, efficiency and,
perhaps, innovation. Together, these forces encouraged greater economic freedom, independence and enterprise, attributes which were further encouraged
by the range of commercial opportunities available in Suffolk (chapter 7). The
widespread shift to the direct exploitation of demesnes during the course of
the thirteenth century was also associated with the spread of commercialized
agricultural production, although few lords ignored the consumption needs
of their own households entirely. The relative importance of the demesne as
a source of revenue was greatest on the small manors which proliferated in
Suffolk, and so it follows that many lesser landlords were personally commit-
ted to maximizing the income from this, their single most valuable resource.
The willingness of landlords to pursue profit-making opportunities, and their
pragmatism in adapting manorial institutions for commercial benefit (chapter 6), reflects an economically progressive seigneurial mindset and attitude,
which was some distance removed from the stereotype of the feudal lord.

CHAPTER 3

Peasants and their Lifestyles, 1200–1349

ANY discussion of the lower orders of Suffolk society in the thirteenth century could usefully begin by dispelling some common misapprehensions. Medieval England is traditionally viewed as a peasant society, where a 'peasant' is assumed to be a dependent landholder, subject to exacting lordship, whose family worked its holding as subsistence farmers: land was not bought or sold, but merely passed on to relatives. Yet this traditional view is unhelpful, for two reasons. First, hardly any agriculturalists in thirteenth-century Suffolk fit this definition of a peasant. The majority sold much of the produce of their holdings to market; their geographical mobility was relatively high; they were not tied to a particular family holding; and they bought and sold land readily, usually on a commercial basis. Second, many people were not primarily farmers, but smallholders who earned most of their livelihood through wage labouring, domestic service or petty trade and craftwork. (The opportunities available to them are explored in chapter 7.) A sizeable, but unknowable, minority were landless, often renting rather than owning low-grade housing. The diversity of rural society is reflected in the wide range of labels used to describe people. In the thirteenth century these were based predominantly upon their legal status, such as freemen, mollmen, villeins and serfs. Thereafter, the labels were increasingly based upon their economic status, such as yeomen, husbandmen, artisans, labourers and servants. When referring to themselves collectively, these people would have used the term 'the commons', not 'the peasantry'.[1]

Hence when medieval historians use the word 'peasant', they tend to deploy it as a handy, catch-all, label for 'a farmer below the status of a lord' and to use it interchangeably with 'tenant': this book is no exception.[2] The majority of

---

[1] For a general introduction to the lower orders of English rural society, see Dyer, *Standards of Living*, chap. 5; Hanawalt, *Ties that Bound*; Dyer, *Making a Living*, chap. 5; P. R. Schofield, *Peasant and Community in Medieval England, 1200–1500* (Basingstoke, 2003); Goldberg, *Medieval England*, pp. 88–9. For the medieval East Anglian peasantry, see Lock, *Walsham*, i, p. 14; R. M. Smith, *Land, Kinship and Life Cycle* (Cambridge, 1984), pp. 87–195; J. Whittle, *The Development of Agrarian Capitalism: Land and Labour in Norfolk, 1440–1580* (Oxford, 2000), pp. 54–62.

[2] Medievalists tend to avoid using the term 'farmer' or 'farm', which carried a subtly different meaning. A farm was a lease of land, and so a farmer was, strictly speaking, a person leasing land. Most peasants and tenants before 1350 held their land

rural dwellers had a landed holding of some description, although the average size was just a few acres, and only a minority possessed sufficient land to feed all of their family and generate surplus produce (i.e. more than about 10 acres). Few peasant households in the thirteenth century would have generated an income in excess of a couple of pounds each year, and the living standards of the majority were low. An unskilled labourer might earn 1½d. for a day's work, but was unlikely to find work every day. Peasant diet was narrow, founded on pottage, bread, sprats, oysters, fruit, coarse cheese and thin ale: meat eating was not common among this social group. Personal possessions were few and basic, and clothing was threadbare. Barbara Hanawalt also reckons that 'by our standards these peasants would have been offensively malodorous, although it is all too easy to be over-refined in this matter'. Life expectancy at birth was low (roughly estimated at around twenty years), reflecting high levels of infant mortality, but those who survived adolescence could expect to live until their early 50s. An analysis of the skeletons of adults from a medieval cemetery in Haverhill reveals that osteoarthritis and dental disease were widespread.[3]

Marriage was a central cultural institution in medieval England, the major pre-condition of household and family formation, and only those who had acquired some land to support a household would contemplate it. Consequently, child bearing outside wedlock was rare, marriage was not entered into lightly or easily, and women were usually in their early 20s when first married: however, ordinary people exercised greater choice in their marriage partners than their social superiors. This pattern of behaviour was founded on the highly practical principle that only those with the landed resources to support a family should be rearing children, a belief which explains the readiness of manorial courts to regulate illegitimacy: in the overcrowded settlements of thirteenth-century Suffolk this was a practical problem as much as a moral issue. Little hard evidence exists to indicate the proportion of people who married, although the 1381 Poll Tax returns for Thingoe hundred reveal that 94 per cent of agriculturalists were married, 86 per cent of labourers, 77 per cent of artisans and 54 per cent of servants: many servants lived in the home of their employer on an annual contract, and therefore they were usually young and unmarried.[4]

Households tended to be smaller in thirteenth-century Suffolk than in most areas of England, when its family structure exhibited many of the characteristics usually associated with that of the early modern period. The

on free and villein tenures, not leasehold, and therefore to label them as 'farmers' in this context creates ambiguity.

3 Hanawalt, *Ties that Bound*, pp. 60–1; *PSIA* 41 (2005), p. 39.

4 Dyer, *Making a Living*, pp. 155–86; Schofield, *Peasant and Community*, pp. 25–35, 83–93; Hanawalt, *Ties that Bound*, p. 96.

households of wealthier peasants contained about five people, and perhaps a live-in servant, and they often sought to acquire land on the open market to provide their sons with an independent livelihood: they also tended to have elderly relatives and other relations established nearby. Poorer families had about two children per household, no servants, and few kin in the locality, reflecting a higher degree of geographical mobility. In contrast, most households in the west Midlands contained nearer six persons, with close relatives or married sons living with the head of house. Provision for the elderly or the sick everywhere was often arranged through formal maintenance contracts, in which relatives or friends were contracted to provide food and accommodation in return for land. The household was the chief unit of work, most of which was dictated by the rhythms of the agricultural year. Children worked from an early age, helping the women to tend livestock, to process pastoral produce, such as eggs, cheese, butter and milk, and perhaps to bake bread and brew ale. Few were formally educated in the county's five grammar schools, although rather more would have received informal elementary instruction in reading and writing at the parish church or in the household. Many children left the family home in their early teens to become servants in other households or to seek paid employment elsewhere.[5]

Well-to-do peasants lived in sturdy timber houses constructed by specialists, usually featuring an aisled hall with some screening of internal space to create a degree of privacy. A late thirteenth-century house at Purton green in Stansfield comprised an aisled hall of two bays measuring 10 × 5 metres, featuring a dominating central hall, and wooden shutters rather than glass windows (plate 3): at this time the subdivision of houses into smaller rooms and the presence of a first floor were mainly features of urban, not rural, housing. On the clay soils the houses of higher-status freemen were often located within a small moated enclosure, which mirrored the fashion though not the scale of manor houses. Only a minority of peasants could afford stylish moated residences, so that the majority lived in modest accommodation. Some rented small houses, or just a room, while most owner-occupiers lived on subdivided plots in flimsy, small and inexpensive buildings which had to be rebuilt every few years: in 1329 the reusable construction materials of a cottage in Walsham were valued at a mere 18d.[6]

---

5 Smith, *Land, Kinship*, pp. 23–38; Z. Razi, 'The Myth of the Immutable English Family', *Past and Present* 140 (1993), pp. 6–20; Hanawalt, *Ties that Bound*, pp. 91–5, 145; see J. Blatchly, *A Famous Antient Seed Plot of Learning: A History of Ipswich School* (Ipswich, 2003), pp. 2–3, for the early grammar schools at Dunwich, Beccles, Bury St Edmunds, Ipswich and Mildenhall.

6 Hanawalt, *Ties that Bound*, pp. 37–42; J. Walker, 'Purton Green, Stansfield: Some Later Observations on the Early Aisled Hall', *PSIA* 38 (1994), pp. 126–37; Lock, *Walsham*, i, p. 132.

Before *c.* 1350 the lives of the lower orders of society were both arduous and precarious. A holding of 10 acres is usually assumed to have been sufficient to feed a household of five people (although some historians argue that 15 acres were necessary), but in *c.* 1300 at least three-quarters of all Suffolk holdings were smaller than 10 acres, and most were under 5 acres. Consequently peasants had to eke out all they could of their meagre arable land, gardens and orchards, because ingenuity and industry could mean the difference between survival and starvation. Unfortunately no farm or household accounts survive from this section of society, although historians generally assume that, if anything, the peasantry were generally more efficient, commercialized and innovative farmers than the great aristocratic landlords, because they were more directly and closely involved with husbandry, and needed to make less land and capital go further. After all, the commercial acumen exhibited on the sacrist of Bury's manor of Hinderclay was provided by a succession of 'amateur' reeves, drawn from his local villeins. Similarly, tenants *had* to sell some of their produce to raise cash for rent, court fines, taxation and to buy essential goods that they could not produce for themselves. Snippets of evidence from manorial court rolls indicate that peasants exploited their holdings with a high degree of intensity, lavishing their labour on the soil in order to maximize output per acre. They also tended to be strongly orientated towards commercial production, judging by the extent to which their production was concentrated on the principal cash crops of wheat and barley. Cash crops feature regularly in debt and damage litigation recorded in manorial court rolls when the grain was specified. For example, barley dominates court entries in the Breckland, and in the 1340s it comprised 91 per cent of all debt cases involving grain in the Staverton court; and wheat dominated debt and detention cases at Walsham. Detailed cases occasionally state the destination of grain sales, so that in 1304 Thomas Curteys of Fornham St Martin sold a large batch of barley (valued at 50s.) to a merchant of Bury St Edmunds, and malted barley from Barton Mills also found its way to Bury.[7]

Pastoral production on tenant holdings was strongly orientated to the market. Chris Dyer's estimate that around two-thirds of the wool exported from medieval England in *c.* 1300 was sourced from peasant flocks also seems about right for Suffolk. In 1341 the county's contribution to the national wool tax was above the national average, despite the absence or unimportance of

7 Campbell, 'Agrarian Problem, pp. 11, 14; H. Kitsikopoulos, 'Standards of Living and Capital Formation in Pre-Plague England: A Peasant Budget Model', *EcHR* 53 (2000), pp. 237–61; SROI HD1538/357/2, mm. 1–16 (Staverton); Lock, *Walsham*, i; Bailey, *Marginal Economy*, p. 140; SROB E3/15.9/1.1, m. 17 (Fornham), and see E3/15.9/1.2, m. 8, for examples of barley dominating debt presentments; SROB E18/151/1, especially courts held in 1370 (Barton).

sheep on many demesnes, which implies that tenant sheep were the main local source of wool. For example, in the 1340s peasants owned a total of 2,340 sheep in Lakenheath, and wool frequently appeared as the subject of debt litigation elsewhere in the Breckland. Peasants dominated dairy farming and stock rearing, the produce of which routinely entered regional markets. They also specialized in the commercial production of the smaller and more troublesome goods, such as poultry, eggs, fruit, vegetables, honey and wax, which were grown in gardens tended by family labour. Such produce hardly features in the accounts of the larger demesnes, but it was regularly available in urban markets: for example, the statutes of Ipswich refer to the sale of items such as onions, garlic and brooms. The size of individual gardens and orchards could extend up to an acre, which warns against underestimating their capacity to supply good quantities of petty produce for both consumption and sale. Unfortunately, contemporary documents rarely mention either gardens or their produce, but chance references can be highly revealing. For example, a quarter-acre garden in East Bergholt was rented for 18d., well above the normal value of arable land. In Lackford gardens and orchards were also rented separately: in 1399 John Hethe leased half a rood of garden for ½d., Robert Nokkard leased an 'enclosed garden' for 1d., while Nicholas Champayn held another enclosed garden for 2s.: in 1397 John Page paid the substantial rent of 3s. 4d. per annum for an *ortum* called Ladysyerd. Some families had 'canobars' attached to their houses, small enclosures dedicated to the cultivation of hemp, whose output comfortably exceeded their domestic needs. Tithe evidence from 1341 indicates that flax and hemp comprised 6 per cent of agricultural production in East Anglia, sourced almost entirely from peasant holdings: these crops were widely available in local urban markets and used in rope making and linen manufacture.[8]

The willingness of peasants to exploit commercial opportunities is also implicit in the extent to which they leased the non-arable components of demesnes. On manor after manor, peasants paid substantial sums of money to lease the lord's dairy herds, large areas of pasture and meadow, fisheries, heathland and even rabbit warrens. The herd of twenty-two cows leased for one year by John and Margaret Plumb for over £7 from the manor of Loudham

---

[8] Dyer, *Making a Living*, pp. 164–7; Campbell, *English Seigneurial Agriculture*, p. 163; J. L. Phillips, 'Collaboration and Litigation in Two Suffolk Manor Courts, 1289–1364' (PhD thesis, Cambridge University, 2005), pp. 110–11; Bailey, *Marginal Economy*, pp. 149, 173–4, 246, 250; Bacon, *Annals*, p. 55; for 'canobars', see SROI HD1538/357/5, mm. 33, 46, 50, 58, 70, 86 (Eyke); C. Dyer, 'Gardens and Garden Produce', in *Food in Medieval England: Diet and Nutrition*, ed. C. M. Woolgar, D. Serjeantson, and T. Waldron (Oxford, 2006), p. 33; SROB E3/15.12/2.3 and 3.2 (Lackford); Bacon Mss 294/16, 17, and 295/9 (Brandon); BL Add. Roll 40715 (Dunwich market).

probably yielded over 2,000 lb of butter and cheese, and was obviously a substantial commercial enterprise; the unnamed woman who in 1331 paid nearly 7s. per acre for the bracken and broom growing on the heath at Easton Bavents was purchasing fuel or making brooms that far exceeded the needs of her own household; and the willingness of John Knight (either as a sole agent or with a variety of associates) to pay up to £4 every year between 1361 and 1390 for exclusive fishing rights along 3 miles of the Little Ouse at Brandon only hints at the scale of his trade as a wholesaler of fresh fish. The geographical range of the commercial contacts of residents in the Breckland, who enjoyed access to the navigable Ouse river system, was impressively wide: those of Lakenheath and Brandon had established links throughout the Fenland, west Suffolk, west Norfolk and east Cambridgeshire.[9]

Between 1200 and 1349 peasants were usually distinguished in written records in terms of their social and legal status, but on the ground it was economic criteria – such as their wealth and the size of their landholdings – which shaped the key differences between them. We shall consider both forms of differentiation in turn.

SOCIAL DIFFERENTIATION: FREEMEN AND FREE TENURE

Free peasants inherited their status through the male line, and, as their name implies, they were relatively free from the tight control of lordship. Similarly, free tenure was hereditary and secure, and its title could be defended in the royal courts. Freemen were the largest category of landholders in medieval Suffolk, constituting around 45 per cent of its recorded tenant population in the Domesday Book of 1086, compared to the national average of 14 per cent. As map 4 illustrates, they were mainly concentrated along the Gipping valley, between Ipswich and Bury St Edmunds, and on the claylands of east and north Suffolk, where over 50 per cent of the recorded population was free: only in a small area of north-west Suffolk did the proportion of freemen fall below 10 per cent. As George Unwin commented long ago, 'the typical holder of land in [medieval] Suffolk was the freeman of small estate', and he typically held his land on free tenure. Map 5 indicates that the relative value of free rents – and by extension the proliferation of free tenures – was greater in Suffolk (and especially the south-east of the county) than many parts of England. By *c.* 1300 free tenures comprised at least 80 per cent of tenanted land in Suffolk and freemen comprised about the same proportion of all tenants (compared with approximately 50 per cent nationally). Unfortunately, reconstructing the

9 SROI HD1538/295/10 (Loudham); PRO SC6/1304/29 and Bacon MS 653 (Brandon); Bailey, *Marginal Economy*, pp. 146–8.

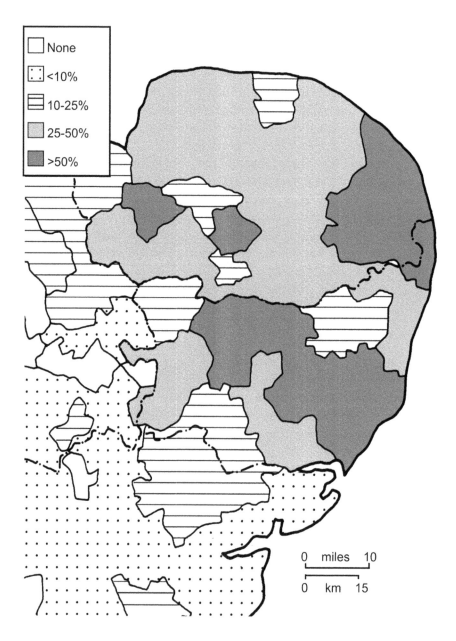

MAP 4 Proportion of freemen in 1086 in East Anglia (after Williamson)

lives of this dominant social group is very difficult, because their landholdings and activities are poorly recorded in extant documentation. A few enjoyed wealth, if not status, equivalent to that of the lesser lords, but, as we shall see, the majority were smallholders: personal freedom did not necessarily equate with wealth or prosperity.[10]

The growing proportion of free tenants between the late eleventh and early fourteenth centuries was paralleled by an increase in the number of free holdings. This growth is partly explained by the conversion of pasture grounds into arable tenures, particularly on the clay uplands of east Suffolk, and by the conversion of some demesne land to free tenure. Yet it was also a consequence of the mounting pressure to absorb a rising population through the subdivision of existing holdings, which in turn meant that by *c.* 1300 the size of many free holdings was very small by national standards. For example, the number of freemen at Hawstead increased, but average holding size fell, between 1086 and 1300; between 1221 and 1251 the number of separate free holdings doubled on seven Suffolk manors of the bishop of Ely; and in *c.* 1300 around 75 per cent of free tenants held less than 10 acres of land on the estates of the abbey of Bury St Edmunds. Good economic sense dictated that land parcels were not subdivided to absurdity, and so some land was held and exploited jointly by 'co-parcennars' (co-landholders). Free holdings were more prone to fragment under the pressure of rising population than either demesne or even villein holdings, because free land could be bought and sold at will during the lifetime of a tenant, and upon death was often subject to partible inheritance and therefore liable to be split among the heirs. Furthermore, the rents per acre charged on free land by the thirteenth century were invariably some way below the real market value of land and could therefore sustain a high level of subdivision. Although the land market in free tenures leaves little direct record in extant sources, all of this evidence indicates strongly that it was extraordinarily active, characterized by a high volume of transactions featuring very small parcels of land. Indeed, Phillipp Schofield argues convincingly that it was probably active as early as the eleventh century and may well have established the precedent for the subsequent development of the market in customary land.[11]

---

[10] Bailey, 'Suffolk Domesday', p. 13; Williamson, *Shaping Medieval Landscapes*, pp. 47, 49–52; Campbell, 'Agrarian Problem', p. 36; Copinger, *Manors of Suffolk*, iii, pp. 235–6; Warner, *Greens, Commons*, pp. 25–8; Warner, *Origins of Suffolk*, pp. 195–203; *VCH*, i, p. 635; Bailey, 'Villeinage in England'.

[11] *VCH*, i, pp. 645–6; *AHEW*, ii, pp. 603–7; B. Dodwell, 'Holdings and Inheritance in Medieval East Anglia', *EcHR* 20 (1967), pp. 59–64; Dyer, *Standards of Living*, p. 119; P. R. Schofield, 'The Market in Free Land on the Estates of Bury St Edmunds, *c.* 1086–*c.* 1300', in *Le Marché de la terre au Moyen Âge*, ed. L. Feller and C. Wickham, Collection de L'École Francaise de Rome 350 (2005), pp. 273–90.

The fall in mean holding size and mounting population pressure in many places encouraged some freemen to seek a living elsewhere. During the twelfth and thirteenth centuries freemen were key figures in the reclamation of the remaining reserves of wood-pasture and woodland, and the colonization of greens and commons, on the clay lands of central and north-east Suffolk. For example, they were responsible for the creation of isolated farms and the development of hamlets around greens on the clay uplands of Blything hundred, and they dominated settlement around Sawyer's tye in Bures. At Worlingworth the houses of many freemen were dispersed around the southern end of the vill, hinting at their role in colonizing its upland margins. The wealthier freemen on the clay lands occupied a social stratum just below the lesser lay landlords and tended to follow the example of their seigneurs by surrounding their messuages with moats. Moated sites covering less than 1 acre probably belonged to these upper ranks of freemen, and the numbers could be impressively high: at least twelve such sites are scattered around the parish of Felsham. As Oliver Rackham reminds us, 'they belonged to middle class people who left few records'.[12]

The fragmentation of free holdings, through both sale and inheritance, is a common theme in the economic history of twelfth- and thirteenth-century England, but less attention has been paid to the growing tenurial complexity among freeholders that occurred as a by-product of this process. The high velocity and volume of exchanges of free land in thirteenth-century East Anglia meant that any simple tenurial linkages between a lord of the manor and his freemen were quickly replaced by linkages of greater complexity, because freemen constructed their holdings from various parcels of land purchased or inherited from a variety of other freemen or manorial lords. For example, in the 1280s Reginald Peche held the main manor in Stowlangtoft, William de Norwich held a small manor from Reginald, and Walter Langtot held another from William. William's manor included six free tenants, one of whom, Elias son of Odo, also held 3 acres and a further 25 acres as a free tenant of Reginald Peche's main manor. Likewise, Walter Langtot had augmented the small quantity of land on his manor through the acquisition of a further 32 acres from another freeman of Reginald's main manor. Therefore Langtot was simultaneously a manorial lord and the tenant of a more humble freeman. The difference in social status between lesser lords and the upper ranks of the free tenantry was slight, and is obscure to the historian: however, one suspects that the

[12] Warner, *Greens, Commons*, pp. 26–8; *PSIA* 39 (1998), pp. 400–1; S. E. West and A. McLaughlin, *Towards a Landscape History of Walsham le Willows, Suffolk*, East Anglian Archaeology 85 (Ipswich, 1998), p. 108; *HistA*, pp. 60–1, 86–7, 174–5; O. Rackham, *The History of the Countryside* (London, 1986), pp. 360–4.

difference would have been apparent to, say, Elias son of Odo and Walter Langtot.[13]

By the end of the thirteenth century even contemporaries found some aspects of the tenurial structure of freeholdings confusingly complex. The Crown had acquired a considerable amount of land in the extreme north-east of the county after the battle of Hastings, which in 1086 was already split into many small manors dominated by independent freemen. These landholdings became further subdivided over the next two centuries, so that in the 1270s royal commissioners compiling the Hundred Rolls were unable to record them with any claim to precision. Instead they identified by name the chief tenant of each major landholding, whether a manorial lord or freeman, but then simply noted in entry after entry that 'other [unnamed tenants] hold the residue of the land from him'. For example, we are told that 'Gilbert de Colkyrke used to hold a free holding from the king in Lound for 8s. per annum, of which Oliver Wight holds one messuage 48 acres 3 roods for this rent, and others hold the residue from the said Oliver': we simply do not know how much land was held by how many tenants, and suspect that the Crown did not know either. Even Bury St Edmunds abbey, a notoriously bureaucratic landlord, had released its grip from some free lands: a survey of Great Barton lists a number of 'alienated' lands, where the rents and services were unknown.[14]

The complex tenurial structure of free holdings in places such as Stowlangtoft and Lothingland hundred was typical of conditions in eastern and northern Suffolk where the incidence of freemen of low status was greatest. An individual freeman might simultaneously be a tenant of a number of different lords of varying status for some of his land and the subtenant of lesser freemen for other land. Under these circumstances the relationship between the freeman and the majority of his lords and superior tenants must have shifted more towards one that was strictly contractual rather than personal. In the late eleventh century the tenurial link created a social allegiance and personal bond between a freeman and his lord, often involving military service, but by the late thirteenth century the complexity and multiplicity of free tenures had significantly eroded the importance of both the personal tie and military service. Freemen now entered the land market principally to acquire land to construct a viable landholding, not to cement a particular position within a simple social hierarchy, because there is little sense that the social ties between a freeman and his superior landholders still carried much importance in the late thirteenth century. Although the resulting tenurial complexity is difficult

[13] *PR*, ii, pp. 204–5; see also D. C. Douglas, *The Social Structure of Medieval East Anglia* (Oxford, 1927), pp. 136–42.

[14] *RH*, ii, p. 163; BL Harley Ms 3977, f. 88.

for the historian to unravel, it should not obscure the topographical and economic logic that undoubtedly lay behind some of these multiple acquisitions: the freeman who held five small parcels of land from five different lords in the same vill was probably constructing a farm concentrated in a particular area. Other freemen acquired land in a number of different vills, sometimes in order to sublet the land at higher rents. For example, individual freemen from Bury St Edmunds, Coney Weston, Roudham and Somersham held land in Fornham St Martin, and freemen in Fornham itself held land in other local vills.[15]

So far, 'freemen' have been described as if they formed an homogenous group, and 'free holdings' as if they were held by a standard tenure, but the reality was inevitably more complex. Documents refer to different categories of free peasants, such as 'freemen', 'sokemen' and 'mollmen', and Douglas reckons that the line between these categories was irregular and fluctuating. Similarly, precise forms of tenure varied. Some held their land in return for performing an office for their lord (a form of 'sargeantry'), while most held their land on socage tenure, although different forms of socage tenure existed (such as *de antiquo* and *de cartem*). Distinctions in status and tenure were fine and subtle, which encourages us to think in terms of broad ranks of peasants in Suffolk rather than clearly defined groups and categories. Ironically, the superior social status of freemen contrasted with the deteriorating economic status of many of them during the thirteenth century, because the subdivision of many free holdings by *c.* 1300 severely constrained the income of their households. Some freemen sought to supplement their meagre holdings by acquiring villein land and were prepared to render the onerous and, for them, demeaning rents and services attached to such tenures. In 1328 William Jacob, 'freeman', held a cottage on villein tenure in Yoxford, and John Horsman and Alice ate Therne co-held 4 acres of villein land. Occasionally the acquisition of villein land by freemen was driven by entrepreneurial, rather than subsistence, motives. In the 1310s and 1320s Thomas Piscar, a freeman of Lakenheath, held villein land which he routinely sublet to other tenants, for which he would certainly have extracted a worthwhile rent.[16]

Personal legal status in the Middle Ages was hereditary through the male line and, in general terms, freemen were 'freer' from manorial obligations than sokemen, mollmen and, especially, villeins. The precise nature of 'free' obligations varied from manor to manor, although they were lightest on manors held by the lesser landlords, and cash rents constituted a large proportion

---

[15] SROB E3/15.9/1.2, mm. 7, 8, 15, and 449/2/257, 258, 259, 264.

[16] Douglas, *Social Structure*, pp. 70, 79, 109–10; Dodwell, 'Holdings and Inheritance', p. 55; Bailey, 'Suffolk Domesday', p. 15; A. H. Denney, ed., *The Sibton Abbey Estates: Select Documents, 1325–1509*, SRS 2 (Ipswich, 1960), pp. 70–1; CUL EDC 7/15/11/1/4 (Lakenheath).

of the overall rent package. Indeed, most free tenures in Suffolk owed little more than an annual cash rent, some liability for occasional levies and duties, and the payment of a 'relief' on entering the holding. For example, in 1325 a number of free tenants of Berneys manor in Rendham paid both a cash rent and a payment for 'wardage' (a form of military service), while others owed cash only: the tenement of John Hoxne rendered 10d., plus ½d. in lieu of wardage, while the tenant of 1 acre 'of the tenement Scot' owed just 2d. Most free tenants at Hadleigh rendered just a cash rent, while those at Walsham paid a cash rent plus a few labour services on the lord's demesne during the harvest. Occasionally some component of rent was paid in kind, such as the pair of gloves rendered in 1299 by John son of William of Bardwell to the lord of Ixworth. Freemen were not required to attend their lord's manorial court on a regular basis and the requirement for them to attend at all was recorded less frequently during the course of the thirteenth century. Those at Walsham were expected to attend one manor court each year and the first court of a new lord of the manor. This reflects a general tendency during this period for lords to regulate freemen less closely, and land transfers between freemen are recorded infrequently if at all in manorial court rolls.[17]

The cash element of free rents was fixed and non-negotiable, and the rising demand for land meant that by the thirteenth century many of these rents stood at levels well below the market value of land. Campbell estimates that by the early fourteenth century rents of free land were at least 50 per cent below their real value, and the evidence from Suffolk strongly supports this observation. For example, before the Black Death leasehold rents for arable land varied from around 6d. to 20d. per acre in Suffolk, but average freehold rents in the same era rarely exceeded a couple of pennies: those at Culford, for example, averaged a mere 0.6d., and those at Stowlangtoft 1.8d. per acre. The rate per acre paid by individual tenants varied, even on the same manor. Hence among free tenants at Stowlangtoft in the 1280s, Henry Britwym held 14 acres for a paltry 13d. per annum, while Peter le Swour owed 4d. for 1 acre, and Ralph Britwym rendered 27d. for 3 acres. Differences in the rates of free rents must have reflected the different dates when the rent level was first fixed: the lowest rates probably relate to the most ancient free holdings, and the higher rates reflect new tenancies created in the twelfth and thirteenth centuries from newly colonized land, or demesne land that had been converted to free tenure, during a period of rising land values. The only way that landlords might obtain something like the market value of the land was through the 'relief' payable when a new tenant entered the holding. However, even here the

---

[17] Douglas, *Social Structure*, pp. 109–10, 136–42; Denney, *Sibton Abbey*, p. 61; *PSIA* 11 (1903), pp. 154–5; Lock, *Walsham*, i, p. 13; PRO c133/89 (Ixworth), thanks to Nick Amor.

landlord's scope for action was often constrained by manorial custom, which determined the amount that a lord could charge for relief: for example, entry fines on free holdings at Walsham were levied at the very modest rate of a year's rent, so that one tenant is recorded as paying a mere 1d. on entering 1 acre of free land.[18]

Free holdings were liable for a few occasional levies. Most were associated with ancient military services, such as the wardage owed by those free tenants at Rendham, or involved a contribution to the administrative expenses of the sheriff. Again, these were more likely to be attached to the older free holdings. Some free holdings were required to render 'aid' (*auxilium*) to their lord, an irregular levy usually confined to events determined by custom. For example, in 1328 free tenants of Cornard Parva contributed aid totalling 12s. 6d. when their lord, John Peacock, was required to contribute towards the marriage expenses of the eldest son of his superior lord, and those at Walsham aided the expenses incurred by their lord at the knighting of his first son. In addition to these basic renders, some freeholdings, notably those on aristocratic manors, were required to render a few bodily services to their lord, such as light labour services, or the odd render in kind. For example, some freemen on the manors of the abbot of Bury St Edmunds in the 1250s were required to do a few reaping and weeding 'boonworks' (i.e. a boon to the lord), and to pay some rent in kind (a few eggs, capons or a small quantity of oats). Similarly, in 1222 a freeman holding 30 acres of land on the bishop of Ely's manor at Hartest had to provide annually a cash rent of 2s. 8d., two works a year with food provided by the lord; four men to perform one boonwork with food, two men for one boonwork without ale, and had to attend the county and hundred courts. The requirement to attend the hundred courts was increasingly a function of tenure rather than personal obligation.[19]

A peculiarity of the social structure of medieval East Anglia is the existence of 'mollmen' and 'molland', a category of personal standing and tenure which occupied an intermediate status between free and unfree. The existence of mollmen underlines the subtle gradations of personal and tenurial status in

[18] J. Kanzaka, 'Villein Rents in Thirteenth-Century England: An Analysis of the Hundred Rolls of 1279–80', *EcHR* 55 (2002), pp. 593–618; P. R. Schofield, 'Seigneurial Exactions in Eastern England, *c.* 1050 to 1300', in *Pour une anthropologie du prelevement seigneurial dans les campagnes medievales*, ed. M. Bourin and P. Sopena (Paris, 2004), pp. 393–4; Campbell, 'Agrarian Problem', pp. 24–8; Bailey, *Marginal Economy*, p. 228; SROB E3/1/1 (Layham); SROB E3/15.6/2.1b (Fornham); *1283 Lay Subsidy*, p. 33 (Culford); *PR*, ii, pp. 204 9 (Stowlangtoft); Lock, *Walsham*, i, p. 89; Lock, *The Court Rolls of Walsham-le-Willows*, vol. 2: *1350–1396*, SRS 45 (Woodbridge, 2002), p. 13.

[19] The Cornard document is in private hands, kindly shown to me by Andrew Phillips; Lock, *Walsham*, i, p. 110; *VCH*, i, p. 645; Douglas, *Social Structure*, p. 208.

this region, where the distinction between free and unfree was more blurred and uncertain than in other areas of medieval England. Similarly, the range of rents owed by mollmen varied from estate to estate, although they usually owed seasonal labour services but no week works. Douglas suggests that moll-men may have originated as unfree tenants who bought out ('commuted') their week works at some stage in the eleventh or twelfth centuries.[20] Mollmen and molland could be found throughout Suffolk, and often owed a rent package based on cash rents and a few labour services. For example, in 1247 mollmen at Blakenham rendered cash, a light range of services, and, crucially, were liable for merchet, a common determinant of unfree status. Thus Simon Treddewell held 1 acre of molland for 6d., and owed one harvest work with food, and one without; scotage and lotage; one hen at Christmas and six eggs at Easter; and could not marry his daughter without the lord's licence. Mollmen are most evident and best documented on the estates of the greater landlords, especially those of Bury St Edmunds abbey. In 1302 twenty free tenants, three mollmen and sixteen customary tenants are recorded on the abbot's manor of Fornham All Saints, and fourteen mollmen are documented at Rickinghall. They tended to hold their land partibly, and were often required to render a few labour services. On other manors, such as Staverton and Thorpe Morieux, the exist-ence of molland is implied in references to 'free land liable to heriot'.[21]

SOCIAL DIFFERENTIATION: VILLEINS AND UNFREE TENURE

Just as any history of lordship in medieval Suffolk risks focusing dispropor-tionately upon the lives and estates of the greater landlords, so a history of the peasantry risks placing undue attention upon the unfree (also known as 'villein' or 'customary') tenants. Villein holdings were liable for a wider and more onerous range of obligations than free holdings, and consequently the activi-ties and lives of villeins are recorded in impressive detail in surviving manorial documents: little wonder that villeins and villeinage have dominated the social history of medieval England. Most villein holdings were occupied by peo-ple who were personally unfree (serfs, *nativi de sanguine*), a status inherited through the male line. Serfs were *personally* obligated to their lord, irrespective of whether they held villein land or not, and were unable to migrate from their home manor without their lord's permission, to acquire free land, or to

---

[20] Douglas, *Social Structure*, pp. 82–9; P. Vinogradoff, *Villeinage in England* (Oxford, 1892), pp. 183–6.

[21] Chibnall, *Select Documents*, p. 92; Schofield, 'Seigneurial Exactions', p. 396; *VCH*, i, 642; BL Harley Ms 230, f. 148 (Fornham); SROI HD1538/357/1 (Staverton); SROB 1700/1/1 (Thorpe Morieux).

prosecute cases in the courts of either other lords or the king. Villeins comprised at least half of the tenant population across much of midland England, compared with a maximum of 20 per cent in Suffolk. However, the relative absence of villeins and serfs does not mean that villeinage was unimportant, because in some places they comprised a much higher proportion of the local population. This was particularly true in west Suffolk, where the estates of Bury St Edmunds abbey were concentrated, although they were not unknown in east Suffolk. Hence in the early fourteenth century around 45 per cent of the tenant population of Fornham All Saints were villeins, and 90 per cent of that of Sibton abbey's manor of Sibton, 43 per cent of Peasenhall and 25 per cent of Yoxford; similarly, the proportion of serfs ranged between one- and two-fifths of tenants on the manors of Bredfield, Dunningworth, Earl Soham and Iken.[22]

The relatively low proportion of villeins in thirteenth-century Suffolk is matched by a low proportion of land held by villein tenure. As map 5 reveals, the value of customary rents were at least equal to, or greater than, free rents across large areas of midland and southern England, but they were much less important in Suffolk. In parts of south-east Suffolk free rents were more than four times more valuable than unfree, one of the highest ratings in England. It is likely that villein tenures comprised a maximum of 20 per cent of all tenanted land in the county, and numerous small manors contained no villein land at all. Once again, however, customary land was usually important where it did exist, particularly on the great ecclesiastical estates, so that villein tenures comprised around two-thirds of all tenant land on a manor such as Lakenheath. Customary holdings tended to be organized and maintained in standard sizes to facilitate the administration of the rents and services attached to them throughout England, although the terms by which they were known varied from manor to manor. The 'virgate' was a common term in midland England, but was rarely found in East Anglia, where 'tenementum' was the preferred name. Tenementa were commonly organized into 10-, 20- and 30-acre holdings, although 8-, 16-, 24- and 30-acre holdings were the norm on the extensive estates of Bury St Edmunds abbey.[23]

[22] This section draws heavily upon Bailey, 'Villeinage in England', to which the reader is referred for more examples, and more detailed development of the arguments. The estimate of the proportion of serfs nationally is from Campbell, 'Agrarian Problem', p. 36, and the local examples are taken from C. Dyer, 'The Rising of 1381 in Suffolk: Its Origins and Participants', *PSIA* 36 (1988), p. 275; SROI HD1538/207/3 (Dunningworth); SROI HA91/1, m. 88 (Bredfield); Denney, *Sibton Abbey*, p. 16.

[23] Dodwell, 'Holdings and Inheritance', pp. 56–7; Douglas, *Social Structure*, pp. 24, 45–7, 57, 97;

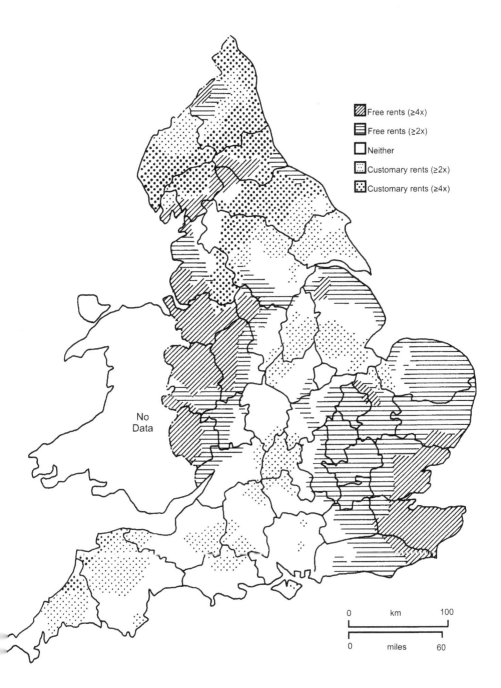

Free rents (≥4x)

Free rents (≥2x)

Neither

Customary rents (≥2x)

Customary rents (≥4x)

No Data

0   km   100

0   miles   60

MAP 5 Proportion of free and customary rents in England in *c.* 1300
(after Campbell)

Land on villein tenure was burdened with a heavier rent charge than freeholdings. The exact weight and composition of this charge varied from manor to manor, but most villein holdings rendered a mixture of cash and food rents, and labour services on the lord's demesne, and were additionally liable for a range of incidental payments and dues. The cash rent was fixed, non-negotiable and relatively low. Seasonal renders of hens and eggs were common, and tenants on ecclesiastical estates were often required to pay part of their rent in grain, eels and herring. Labour services fell into one of four main categories: week works, seasonal works, boonworks and carrying services. Week works were the most demanding and onerous type of labour service, in which tenants might perform a wide range of agricultural tasks at the discretion of the lord's officers, from dung-spreading, fencing and ditching to reaping and threshing. Seasonal works related to specific tasks at key moments in the agrarian year, such as a set amount of ploughing, harrowing, haymaking or shearing, while boonworks often related to work at the harvest and often carried an obligation for the lord to provide food and drink to the workers. Carrying services were particularly important to the greater landlords, whose estate administration and commercial interests often required the transportation of goods and agrarian produce over long distances. Other incidents and levies on villein holdings and serfs could be onerous, and included entry fines (a fee to take a holding), merchet (a duty on marriage), heriot (death duty on a tenant), chevage (paid by a migrant), mill suit, childwite (duty on illegitimate births), tallage (a tax at will) and foldage (the requirement to keep their sheep in the lord's fold). On many manors the larger villein landholders were also required on strict rotation to hold a manorial office for one year (usually the reeve and the messor, or harvest reeve), but a few manors also required additional officers, such as keepers of the park, the woods or the heath, to be appointed annually from their villein tenants.

The exact weighting of these obligations varied from holding to holding, manor to manor, and region to region. Furthermore, the extent to which landlords imposed all of their dues and rents upon their villeins also reveals much variation, because the theory of villeinage, as conveyed by contemporary legal treatises and royal courts, contrasted markedly with the more liberal reality of villeinage as implemented by manorial courts. Lords did not, in practice, possess the ability to act wilfully or arbitrarily in their own manor courts, where many procedures, judgements and fines were regulated by local custom, which in turn shaped the way in which lordly power was wielded.[24] For example, the head rents charged on villein holdings – whether paid in cash and or grain – were theoretically changeable at the will of the lord, but in practice they were

---

[24] J. Hatcher, 'English Serfdom and Villeinage: Towards a Reassessment', *Past and Present* 90 (1981), pp. 7–10; Rigby, *English Society*, p. 35; Razi, 'Myth', p. 38.

fixed by custom. The rent levels on villein holdings in Suffolk were low by national standards. Campbell has estimated that in 1300 these rents averaged around 7d. per acre in England, compared with closer to 5d. in Suffolk, which is significantly lower than the open market rate for land (which in Suffolk varied between 12d. to 22d. per acre).[25]

Labour services in general – and week works in particular – constituted an unusually high proportion of the villein rent package in Suffolk. Labour services formed between 10 and 20 per cent of the total value of rent on villein holdings on lay manors over much of England, but between 20 and 30 per cent across much of East Anglia, and over 30 per cent in west and north Suffolk. A heavy burden of labour services suited both lords and tenants in this densely populated region: it enabled tenants to convert a relatively cheap and plentiful resource (their family labour) into rent, while landlords could extract some economic value from their customary landholdings without overburdening their tenants. Finally, the burdens of villeinage were greatest on the tightly administered manors of the great landlords. Labour services were most oner-ous in such manors, especially on the major ecclesiastical estates in north and west Suffolk, but they were lighter on manors held by lower-status landlords, especially in east and south Suffolk. For example, the main villein landholders on the bishop of Ely's manor of Hartest owed at least four days of week works each week of the year, yet a standard 8-acre villein holding on the gentry manor of Cockfield Hall in Yoxford owed merely a weekly ploughing work between November and June, one labour service a week during October, and another single week work between mid-May and 1 August.[26]

How rigorously did landlords implement and enforce the dues associated with villeinage in Suffolk? Some aspects of villeinage were enforced firmly and consistently. The collection of annual rents owed in cash and kind was generally thorough and efficient, and the holders of the main villein landhold-ings were held to their obligation to serve on rotation in a major manorial office for one year. Court rolls routinely record the 'election' of leading villeins to the main manorial offices of hayward (or 'messor') and reeve. The messor supervised the harvest and communal rights over the fields, while the reeve acted as farm manager on the lord's own demesne. Refusals to serve resulted

---

[25] Campbell, 'Agrarian Problem', pp. 28–9; Denney, *Sibton Abbey*, pp. 69–74, although this calculation includes cottages, messuages, and some woodland and meadow, so that the actual rents charged for villein arable here were even lower; CUL EDC 7/15/1/14; Bailey, *Marginal Economy*, p. 228. Barley rents at Risby in 1330 were rated at merely 1.8 bushels per acre, SROB E3/15.13/2.8.

[26] E. Miller and J. Hatcher, *Medieval England: Rural Society and Economic Change, 1086–1348* (London, 1978), p. 123; Douglas, *Social Structure*, pp. 80–1; Campbell, 'Agrarian Problem', map 4; Bailey, *English Manor*, pp. 46–58 (Hartest); SROI HA30/314/8 (Yoxford).

in the seizure of land, although a villein could buy exemption from office, albeit for a hefty sum (30s. on both the earl of Norfolk's estate and abbey of Bury St Edmunds estate, but only 2s. at Drinkstone), and landlords routinely ordered seizure of the land of those who refused.[27]

Labour services not only lay heavily on villein holdings in Suffolk, but they were also routinely deployed by landlords to supplement the labour force on their demesnes. Even the onerous week works were widely enforced, in contrast to the practice on many estates in England where week works were extensively commuted for cash. Indeed, Bruce Campbell has estimated that commutation was so commonplace that only around one-half of all labour services were used in early fourteenth-century England. Yet, on a sample of twelve Suffolk manors between 1280 and 1348, week works were utilized on every manor, and, on eleven of the twelve, well over one-half of all week works were physically performed by tenants. Merchet was also routinely enforced. In some parts of England, merchet was payable only for the marriage of the daughter, and in others it was levied only upon the progeny of landholders and not those of landless serfs: most Suffolk manors charged only daughters, but a sizeable minority applied it to sons as well, and eligibility was occasionally extended to serfs who did not hold land. Childwite (due from any unfree woman who bore a child outside wedlock) was not owed by all villeins, but it was implemented consistently wherever it was liable, especially among the poorer female sections of society. The fee charged for childwite in fourteenth-century Suffolk was often 2s. 8d. (the same sum was widespread in Norfolk), which is significant for two reasons. First, it was higher than the charge levied for this offence in many parts of the country, and, second, the imposition of a standardized fee on manors held by different lords is indicative of a regional custom. The Suffolk evidence strongly supports Bennett's argument that manorial courts used this levy discriminately to control birth rates among servile women at the margins of society during a period of severe demographic pressure.[28]

The effective implementation of these aspects of villeinage contrasts markedly with the lax approach adopted to other aspects. Most obviously, by *c.* 1300 many of the standardized villein holdings had become highly fragmented between a number of tenants, and landlords had failed to preserve them as integral holdings. This was a feature of all types of manors in Suffolk, including the estates of the greatest landlords such as the abbot of Bury St Edmunds.

[27] Whittle, *Agrarian Capitalism*, p. 69; see Lock, *Walsham*, i, pp. 261–2, 266; SROB E7/10/1.1 (Drinkstone).

[28] Bailey, 'Villeinage in England', table 2; Campbell, 'Agrarian Problem', p. 37; J. M. Bennett, 'Writing Fornication: Medieval Leyrwite and its Historians', *TRHS* 13 (2003), pp. 131–62.

For example, by 1348 none of the standard villein tenementa had survived as an integral unit on his manor of Culford, where the tenementum of John son of Robert, containing 27 acres 1 rood, was split between eleven tenants, and the original messuage had been divided into three parcels upon which five cottages were now built.[29] The failure, or unwillingness, of even the greatest and most powerful landlords in Suffolk to prevent the break-up of villein tenementa mirrors the failure of other major landlords, such as Norwich cathedral priory, to prevent similar fragmentation in Norfolk, but it contrasts with the success of other landlords in midland England, who maintained their villein holdings more or less intact. Why did Suffolk landlords fail where others succeeded? One explanation is the local custom regarding inheritance. Villein land was traditionally inherited impartibly (i.e. by a single heir), which clearly helped to maintain them as integral holdings, but villein holdings on a number of Suffolk manors were inherited partibly (i.e. split between a number of heirs). Another reason is that population pressure in Suffolk was high, and the opportunities for bringing more land under the plough were limited, which made further subdivision the most effective way of absorbing more people on the land. Finally, although villein land could not be bought and sold without the lord's permission, landlords recognized that they could profit from the sale and redistribution of villein land as long as their manor courts regulated each transaction and charged a fee for the privilege. Consequently, by the late thirteenth century the villein land market was exceptionally lively in Suffolk, where it was characterized by a high turnover of small parcels of land (at Rickinghall between 1259 and 1293 75 per cent of all land transfers were less than 1 acre), most of which involved exchanges between unrelated parties. This high volume of activity in the villein land market generated tidy sums of money for manorial lords: between 1260 and 1289 219 sessions of the Redgrave court handled a remarkable total of 969 *inter vivos* transactions, 87 per cent of which were between unrelated parties, generating a total income of £55. The existence of an extraordinarily active market in unfree land is another example of the lax enforcement of villeinage in Suffolk.[30]

Entry fines were payable to the lord by the incoming tenant when villein land

---

[29] Subdivision in Suffolk is documented in Lock, *Walsham*, i, p. 14; R. M. Smith, 'Kin and Neighbours in a Thirteenth-Century Suffolk Community', *Journal of Family History* 4 (1979), p. 246; *VCH*, i, pp. 655–6; Dodwell, 'Holdings and Inheritance', p. 60; BL Add. Ms 42055, ff. 8–22 (Culford).

[30] CUL EDC 7/15/11/1–2 (Lakenheath); Lock, *Walsham*, i, p. 15; R. M. Smith, 'English Peasant Life-Cycles and Socio-Economic Networks' (PhD thesis, Cambridge University, 1974), p. 60; R. M. Smith, 'A Periodic Market and its Impact upon a Manorial Community. Botesdale, Suffolk, and the Manor of Redgrave', in Razi and Smith, *Medieval Society* (1996), p. 466.

changed hands and therefore, in theory, presented lords with an opportunity to recoup the market value of the land through a one-off charge. Yet, in practice, the size of these fines was remarkably low and usually determined by custom. Dyer reckons that entry fines were often set at three times the annual rental charge of the holding, which – though higher than those on free land – is hardly punitive. The level of entry fines for inheritances in East Anglia were usually even lower than those charged in the Midlands, indicating a more permissive approach to land transfers.[31] A heriot – or the 'best beast' – was also payable after the death of a tenant from the estate of the deceased, in return for which the villein's land and property could be transferred according to the custom of the manor and, increasingly in the fifteenth century, according to their own will and testament. The heriot was therefore another potent symbol of villeinage and was liable from many villein holdings across Suffolk. However, it was not a universal feature, and was notably absent from many of the manors of the earls of Norfolk, such as Dunningworth and Staverton.[32] Even on those manors where heriot was liable from villein holdings, it was not always enforced. First, a heriot was not usually charged if the land of the deceased had passed to an heir who had already paid an entry fine for admission: this custom was widespread in Suffolk and Norfolk, but was unusual in many parts of England. Second, tenants could evade heriot by surrendering their land on their deathbed to another tenant in front of witnesses. This tactic was widely deployed in late fourteenth- and fifteenth-century England to counter the unwillingness of lords to sanction the wills of customary tenants, but it was already well established in early fourteenth-century Suffolk.[33] Third, tenants who died without owning any livestock routinely rendered a cash payment instead, but the sum was usually modest and on a number of manors held by different landlords was fixed at 2s. 8d., which was well below the value of a horse, ox or cow. Through a combination of such practices,

---

[31] Miller and Hatcher, *Medieval England: Rural Society*, pp. 45–9; Dyer, *Making a Living*, p. 141; J. Whittle, 'Individualism and the Family–Land Bond: A Reassessment of Land Transfer Patterns among the English Peasantry, c. 1270–1580', *Past and Present* 160 (1998), pp. 51–9; Whittle, *Agrarian Capitalism*, p. 67; L. Poos, Z. Razi and R. M. Smith, 'The Population History of Medieval English Court Rolls: A Debate on the Use of Manor Court Rolls', in Razi and Smith, *Medieval Society* (1996), pp. 346–8.

[32] Vinogradoff, *Villeinage*, p. 162; SROB HA504/1/3, m. 9 (Walsham); SROI HD1538/207/2 (Dunningworth); SROI HD1538/357/1 (Staverton); SROI HD1469/1 (Akenham).

[33] Vinogradoff, *Villeinage*, pp. 160–1; Whittle, *Agrarian Capitalism*, p. 67; L. Bonfield and L. Poos, 'The Development of Deathbed Transfers in Medieval English Manor Courts', in Razi and Smith, *Medieval Society* (1996), p. 137; Lock, *Walsham*, i, p. 120.

not one heriot was rendered on the manor of Drinkstone between 1316 and 1326.[34]

The right of landlords to insist that villeins ground their corn at the seigneurial watermill or (after the twelfth century) windmill for a fixed toll, called millsuit, was well established in manorial law. Langdon has shown that the mean value of demesne mills, the importance of mill revenues and the size of the toll taken as millsuit were all relatively low in East Anglia, and many manors in Suffolk did not have demesne mills at all: this was not unusual on small lay manors, but even some of the large manors did not have demesne mills.[35] Clearly, Suffolk landlords did not have a monopoly of mills, and they operated in one of the most competitive markets for milling in the country, where tenant and domestic mills proliferated, a fact reflected in the modest incomes generated by manorial mills in Suffolk in the early fourteenth century (around £5 per annum). This local competition weakened their ability to enforce millsuit consistently and effectively, and it also forced them to charge tolls that were competitive. Langdon has argued that villeins used demesne mills because they offered competitive rates, not necessarily because they were forced to; this fits the Suffolk evidence well. Millsuit violations appear infrequently in many court rolls, and long periods in which no violations are recorded were usually punctuated by short enforcement waves. These periods of occasional enforcement of millsuit can usually be explained by particular circumstances, such a drive to counter a fall in mill revenue in the 1290s at Worlingworth. Most landlords in medieval Suffolk were very lax in their enforcement of millsuit, a pragmatic response to market forces that had largely moved beyond their control.[36]

Villeins and serfs were theoretically required to obtain the lord's permission to live off the manor for more than a year, although, in practice, they simply rendered a fee (known as chevage) to the manorial court to do so, which confirmed the peasant's continued subjugation to the lord. Chevage was paid mainly by landless serfs seeking better prospects elsewhere, although

---

34 The fixed fine of 2s. 8d. is recorded in a number of places: for example, SROB E18/151/1, courts held in March 1279 and September 1307 (Great Barton); CUL EDC 7/15/11/ box 2/25, m. 29 (Lakenheath); Bailey, *English Manor*, p. 52 (Hartest); SROB E7/10/1.1 (Drinkstone).

35 J. Langdon, 'Lordship and Peasant Consumerism in the Milling Industry of Thirteenth- and Early Fourteenth-Century England', *Past and Present* 145 (1994), pp. 5, 22–5, 31; J. Langdon, *Mills in the Medieval Economy: England, 1300–1540* (Oxford, 2004), pp. 259–73, 279–83.

36 Langdon, 'Lordship and Peasant Consumerism', pp. 22–5; Langdon, *Mills*, pp. 283–7; SROB E7/10/1.1 (Drinkstone); Lock, *Walsham*, i, pp. 48, 151, 243, 265; see also Dunningworth, SROI HD1538/207/1–2; J. M. Ridgard, 'The Local History of Worlingworth to 1400 AD' (PhD thesis, University of Leicester, 1984), p. 51.

the court's interest in females ceased upon their marriage. Yet before the Black Death very few manors enforced the payment of chevage consistently if at all. The amercements levied were usually small, from 1d. to 12d. per annum, and rarely reached the high levels (3s. 4d. to 6s. 8d.) charged in parts of midland England. This cannot indicate a lack of geographical mobility by local villeins and serfs, for everything we know about the growth of towns and the expansion of the economy in this period indicates that migration was commonplace, and there was considerable geographical mobility among the lower orders of Suffolk society. Instead, it must reflect seigneurial indifference to the migration of serfs from their manors, and a willingness to forego their customary dues in this respect. However, this indifference evaporated rapidly after the Black Death.[37]

Potentially one of the most onerous burdens on medieval villeins was tallage, the right to 'tax' villeins 'whenever the lord wishes', and in this stark form it represents the most arbitrary and punitive liability associated with villeinage. Yet tallage as an annual charge in Suffolk is only recorded on the earl of Norfolk's estates, where it generated several pounds each year; on all other Suffolk manors it was either not imposed or assumed a different, less onerous form, known as a 'recognition' fine. Recognition was a one-off payment levied on villein tenants and serfs whenever a new lord acceded to his estate, but the sums charged tended to run into shillings rather than pounds. Tallage, in whatever form, was neither a regular nor onerous burden across most of Suffolk. From all of these examples, it is clear that a sizeable gap existed between the theory and practice of villeinage in Suffolk.[38]

ECONOMIC DIFFERENTIATION

For all the differences between freeman and villein, and free and customary tenures, legal status was not the main determinant of a family's wealth and income: both wealthy villeins and destitute freemen could be found throughout Suffolk. Economic well-being was primarily dependent upon the size of a family's landholding, but the small size of many Suffolk farms in *c.* 1300 meant that the majority of the populace was poor. The rise in the population of Suffolk during the thirteenth century to its peak in the 1340s coincided with a fall in average farm size: for example, between 1222 and 1251 the median holding size fell below 5 acres at Glemsford and Wetheringsett. By *c.* 1300 average farm size was extremely low across the county. In 1285 71 per cent of unfree tenants and 73 per cent of free tenants on the estates of Bury St Edmunds abbey held under 10 acres of land and in 1301 the median holding size was

---

37 Bailey, 'The Decline of Villeinage in Suffolk' (forthcoming).

38 Bailey, 'Villeinage in England'; SROI HD1538/394/1, court held December 1369.

below 5 acres on the manors of Eye priory. In 1289 92 per cent of customary tenants at Redgrave held less than 10 acres, 44 per cent held less than 2 acres, and, similarly, 45 per cent of freeholders held under 2 acres: only 11 per cent of all peasant holdings were larger than 10 acres. At Hinderclay the average holding size was 7 acres, only one peasant held more than 30 acres, and 30 per cent of tenants held less than 1 acre. Overall, at least 75 per cent of peasant holdings comprised less than 10 acres of arable land, compared with only 60 per cent of freeholdings and 40 per cent of villein holdings across many Midland counties.[39]

The small minority who worked more than 10 acres were well placed to exploit the generally high prices of agricultural produce between 1200 and 1349, and to lead a comfortable existence. For example, Peter de Thorpe, who held at least 30 acres in Pakenham, and Robert ultra Aquam of Bardwell were prominent and relatively wealthy freemen who were among the leading taxpayers in their communities in the 1283 Lay Subsidy. Similarly, Richard Brakeberewe of Ixworth improved his lot in the last two decades of the thirteenth century, from a modestly successful farmer taxed on assets worth £3 in 1283 to one of the vill's wealthiest residents in 1299, when he worked at least 27 acres. The wealthier freemen were well connected to lordly society, and both Peter de Thorpe and Robert ultra Aquam were active in the social circle of Sir William de Pakenham and in the local administration of justice. Men such as these contributed to local public administration through their attendance at the leet and hundred courts, and as officials of those courts, and such service provided them with both status and a place within the wider political community.[40]

Although the social and legal status of freemen was higher than that of villeins, they were not necessarily wealthier. In some places the active market in villein land enabled enterprising villeins to construct larger holdings, while in others villein tenementa did not fragment as badly as freeholdings. In 1283 Thomas Prympil, a villein, was second only to the abbot of Bury St Edmunds among wealthy taxpayers in Elmswell. Most of the wealthiest residents of Walsham in the subsidies of 1283 and 1327 were villeins. Ironically, one Walsham villein, William Lene, who was unquestionably wealthy enough to pay tax, escaped mention in the 1327 Lay Subsidy, presumably due to evasion or omission. When he died in a fire two years later, William held over 40 acres of

39 *AHEW*, ii, pp. 603–7; J. Hatcher and M. Bailey, *Modelling the Middle Ages: The History and Theory of England's Economic Development* (Oxford, 2001), p. 45; Smith, 'Families and their Land in Redgrave Suffolk, 1260–1320', in Smith, *Land, Kinship and Life Cycle* (1984), pp. 135-95, p. 143; Smith, 'Periodic Market', pp. 466–7; Lock, *Walsham*, i, p. 14; Razi, 'Myth', pp. 14–17; Dyer, *Standards of Living*, p. 119.

40 Church, *Pakenham*, pp. 14–15; Coss, *Lordship, Knighthood*, pp. 155–6; I owe the Brakeberewe example to Nick Amor, drawing upon PRO c133/89.

land, a flock of over 100 sheep, a dairy herd of eight cows and three calves, 16 quarters of grain in his granary, and he also dabbled as a butcher. He possessed a varied range of basic personal and household possessions, but few luxury goods.[41]

The wealthier peasants were influential figures within their community. They employed hired labour on their holdings, lent money to poorer peasants on a commercial basis, acted as pledges (guarantors) for the debts or good behaviour of neighbours, featured prominently as jurors in manorial courts, served as leading manorial officers, helped in the assessment and collection of royal taxes, and discharged the other civil responsibilities of the vill. In all of these ways the leading peasants contributed to the daily life of their community and nurtured the relationships essential to the good order of local society. Yet they could also be competitive, seizing opportunities for individual advancement and profit. Wealthier peasants were prominent among those who used private suits in local courts to seek redress against each other, usually for economic gain. For example, in the 1290s and 1300s Nicholas le Wodeward repeatedly sued Robert son of Adam in the manor court of Hinderclay. Nicholas was heavily indebted to Robert, and did this as a device to protect his deteriorating financial position. He also suspected Robert of having an affair with his wife; this tryst was open knowledge in Hinderclay, and Nicholas deliberately played upon the gossip as a tactic to ease pressure on his financial plight. He was reasonably successful, too, winning a series of minor settlements against Robert through the manor court, although the locals clearly reckoned that Robert was simply collecting his interest from the Wodeward family through sexual favours.[42]

The competitiveness of the leading peasants is also evident in their regular forays into the local land market, using the profits of their commercial farming to acquire more land, often preying upon the desperate plight of smallholders who were struggling to survive. In the 1283 Lay Subsidy William son of Adam of Hinderclay was assessed on moveable goods rated at over £5, mainly in cereals and livestock, and over the next fifteen years he invested considerable sums of cash in property: between 1294 and 1299 he bought land on eight occasions from five different individuals, by which time his holding comprised around 50 acres. William Lene of Walsham entered the land market regularly to purchase small pieces of land from poorer tenants who were selling to obtain desperately needed cash to pay for food or to meet their debts. Adam Pistor of Redgrave possessed 19 acres of land and a varied property portfolio,

---

[41] *1283 Lay Subsidy*, p. xxi; Lock, *Walsham*, i, pp. 14, 18–19, 135; *1327 Lay Subsidy*, p. 183.

[42] P. R. Schofield, 'Peasants and the Manorial Court: Gossip and Litigation in a Suffolk Village at the Close of the Thirteenth Century', *Past and Present* 159 (1998), pp. 14–15, 18–24, 41–2.

containing two messuages, two cottages, two stalls and a shop in Botesdale market, which he presumably sublet to others: by his death in 1320 he had acquired a further 20 acres in Redgrave and 4 acres in Rickinghall. All these men are representative of the small but wealthy minority of peasants who were able to produce surpluses for the market, and who were aggressive and successful in their acquisition of land.[43]

Middling peasants – those holding between 3 and 10 acres of land – experienced mixed fortunes. They may have employed labourers to work their holdings, or to help with their petty trading activities, on an occasional basis, but they were more likely to seek co-operation with their peers by sharing equipment and draught animals in order to exploit their land effectively. Some peasants in this group were just wealthy enough to attract the attention of royal tax collectors. Gilbert le Shepherd was ranked twenty-seventh out of forty taxpayers in Hinderclay in 1283, with moveable goods valued at 28s. 9d., which placed him in the top quartile of Suffolk peasants by wealth. When he died in 1308 Gilbert held a house and 4½ acres, but even during his life he had not been an active accumulator of land, acquiring, for example, just two parcels of land in the 1290s. In fact, his wealth was founded on stock rearing, because in 1308 his holding included seven pigs, fourteen piglets, three cows, two oxen and seven sheep. This example illustrates powerfully the pitfalls of judging economic well-being solely on the size of a family's arable holding, because the mixed nature of Suffolk farming meant that livestock, poultry and garden crops (such as hemp and flax) could significantly boost farm income. Peasants such as Gilbert must have worked their gardens hard and lavished labour on their arable holdings to maximize output. Yet, for all their endeavours, many of these middling peasants were downwardly mobile after *c.* 1280 in Redgrave and Rickinghall, because a succession of harvest failures and royal taxes forced them into a spiral of debt and land sale. During the course of the 1290s Henry Crane of Hinderclay sold small parcels of land to wealthier peasants and lost a succession of debt pleas in the manor court as he failed to keep up with repayments to other villagers for money he had borrowed. Some middling peasants tried to ride out difficulties by subleasing part of their land for a fixed period in order to raise cash, but such tactics were often no more than a palliative.[44]

Below these middling peasants, the vast majority of rural dwellers were

43 Smith, 'Families and their Land', p. 176; P. R. Schofield, 'Dearth, Debt and the Local Land Market in a Late Thirteenth-Century Village Community', *AgHR* 45 (1997), pp. 10–14.

44 Smith, 'Kin and Neighbours', p. 249; Smith, 'Families and their Land', p. 193; Schofield, 'Dearth, Debt', pp. 14, 15, 17; P. R. Schofield, 'The Social Economy of the English Village in the Early Fourteenth Century' (forthcoming).

land-deficient and struggling to make ends meet. Robert Saresson, William Hermer and Robert de Castre – all residents of Yoxford in the late 1320s – were typical of many Suffolk freemen, holding no more than a cottage and a couple of roods of land each and deemed too poor to be taxed in the Lay Subsidy of 1327 (only the wealthiest 15 to 30 per cent of peasants were taxed in these Lay Subsidies). We know nothing else about them, and can only assume that they reared a few poultry, kept a cow and turned a penny through sales of garden produce and petty trading activities. They lived in flimsy hovels on cramped and subdivided plots, so that their lives were grimly consumed by their own interests within a petty enterprise culture: their 'superiour' free status brought neither material wealth nor comfort. They certainly possessed a sense of their personal independence from the demands of lordship, but the harsh reality of their daily existence meant that they were unlikely to have shared Peter de Thorpe and Robert Ultra Aquam's sense of responsibility to, and active service in, a wider political community. Their main responsibility was far more prosaic: to survive.[45]

In economic terms poor freemen and their families were hardly distinguishable from poor villein familes. John Kynde supplemented the produce of his meagre 1½-acre arable holding in Redgrave with regular odd jobs for the wealthier Oky family: the regularity of this employment, and Simon Oky's willingness to act as a personal pledge for John in the Redgrave court, indicates an element of patronage and perhaps an indirect form of charity from one wealthy villein to another less fortunate. Smallholders and landless residents here were increasingly dependent upon commercial brewing and baking to survive, buying small quantities of grain and processing and selling it as best they could: 88 per cent of brewing fines in late thirteenth-century Redgrave were paid by people who were either landless or held under 5 acres of land, and a number of full-time brewers who held stalls in Botesdale market had no arable land. May le Gannoker was another landless brewer, who in 1324 was deemed too poor to pay a paltry fine for breaking the assize of ale, and depended upon Robert Titton of Fornham St Martin for a roof over her head. Records of the material goods and possessions of such people simply do not exist, but they must have been few and almost worthless.[46]

The land deficiency of the majority of Suffolk families increased their dependency upon wage labouring, retailing, fishing and craft manufacturing. The scale of such opportunities was higher in places close to thriving markets or those blessed with a wide range of natural resources, such as the Fenland. However, by the early fourteenth century greatly swollen rural and urban

---

45   Denney, *Sibton Abbey*, pp. 70–1; *1327 Lay Subsidy*, p. 73.

46   Smith, 'English Peasant Life-Cycles', pp. 116, 152–3, 174, 378; Smith, 'Periodic Market', pp. 466–7; Smith, *Land, Kinship*, pp. 27–8; SROB E3/15.9/2.2 (Fornham).

populations created greater competition for work and widespread underemployment, so that trade and commerce do not appear to have significantly enhanced the income or wealth of smallholders and the landless. Richard Smith argues that the combination of fragmented holdings and a dependence on the market did not improve the standards of living among the lower orders of Redgrave society, despite the presence of a local market (Botesdale), but merely served 'to create a large body of near landless individuals who were given an opportunity to exist at levels marginally above the barest of subsistence requirements'. Any beneficiaries of commercialization 'may have been too small in number to offset the deteriorating or deteriorated ratio of population to land … we can have little confidence that their advances stimulated beneficial commercialisation throughout the local economy as a whole'.[47]

Furthermore, the challenges facing ordinary people increased in severity between *c.* 1280 and *c.* 1340, when the difficulties created by the high demographic pressure were exacerbated by a variety of other factors: a significant rise in the burden of taxation imposed by the Crown, soaring grain prices, static wage rates and a succession of harvest failures. The precariousness of the lives of the majority was brutally exposed in those years when taxation was levied or the harvest was poor, when many smallholders could barely cope. A strong correlation is evident between years of taxation, poor harvests, high grain prices and a hair-trigger sensitivity in the land market, especially during the 1290s and 1310s. A succession of external shocks provoked a disproportionate response in the land markets of both Redgrave and Hinderclay, because increasingly desperate families were forced to sell land to buy food for survival, even though this strategy pushed them into a downward cycle of deprivation. Their options were reduced by a tendency for the supply of credit within the community to contract at the very time that demand for it among the poorer sections of local society was greatest, as lenders feared that debts could not be honoured. Hence Henry Thatcher of Hinderclay was forced to sell successive pieces of land, culminating in the sale of his only cow, before his death in 1320. Schofield concludes that 'the social economy at Hinderclay failed in the worst years of this decade'. Furthermore, the availability of work off the farm in craft manufacture and petty retailing tended to dwindle in these years of crisis, at precisely the time it was most needed.[48]

The examples of Hinderclay and Redgrave are probably representative (to a greater or lesser degree) of many parts of late thirteenth- and early fourteenth-century Suffolk. The exceptionally high proportion of smallholders

---

[47] Smith, 'Periodic Market', pp. 460, 468, 480–1.

[48] M. Bailey, 'Peasant Welfare in England, 1290–1348', *EcHR* 51 (1998), pp. 223–51; Smith, 'Kin and Neighbours', pp. 219–56; Schofield, 'Dearth, Debt', pp. 11, 13, 17; Schofield, 'Social Economy'.

and landless reflects the commercial advances of the previous century or so, and the wide availability of by-employments, but these developments did not result in an improved standard of living for the majority of people. The small size of many holdings, the growing dependence upon non-farm income that was poorly paid, and fluctuations in both grain yields and the availability of employment, all combined to increase their vulnerability to economic disruption and to expose them to greater instability when the population peaked in the first half of the fourteenth century. The disproportionate response of the land market to poor harvests and to taxation demands, especially in the half century or so after the 1280s, is a clear sign of the immiseration of the majority of the populace and the economy's heightened sensitivity and vulnerability to external shocks. In the three generations before 1350 the majority of Suffolk residents were impoverished and debt-ridden.

CONCLUSION

Centuries of sustained population growth culminated at the beginning of the fourteenth century, which created severe pressure to fragment holdings and increased both the number and proportion of freemen. These forces were especially pronounced in Suffolk, where by *c.* 1300 the proportion of free tenures rose to around 80 per cent, one of the highest in England: at about 20 per cent, the proportion of villeins and serfs was among the lowest. Irrespective of tenurial status, around 75 per cent of peasant holdings comprised less than 10 acres, and perhaps one-half of the population were landless labourers, servants and townsfolk. Among English counties, only the social structures of Norfolk and Kent appear to have been freer and more fragmented. Yet such freedoms came at a price, because the tail of poor and landless was long, and their susceptibility to poor harvests and economic crises was high. Standards of living for the majority were low.

By *c.* 1300 neither freedom nor villeinage was particularly onerous in Suffolk. The range of personal obligations a freeman owed his lord was usually narrow, and the lion's share of rent on free tenures was rendered in cash. A few elements of villeinage – such as labour services and merchet – were enforced rigorously, but even the requirement to perform weekly labour services on the demesne was not necessarily a significant economic burden upon tenants, because it represented a relatively efficient method of extracting rent from villein holdings. Labour was one of the thirteenth-century villein's most abundant and underutilized resources, with a relatively limited opportunity cost: the tenants' interests were often better served by sending a son to perform labour services than paying the rent in precious cash or in kind. The reality of villeinage in this predominantly free region was far removed from the onerous burdens of its legal theory, or the experience of villeins in midland England, although this does not mean that Suffolk villeins resented their status any less. The influence of lords on local society, and the proportion of peasant outgoings rendered to lords as rent, appears to have been lower here than in many areas of England.

D. C. Douglas once commented admiringly upon the 'remarkable distinctiveness of social organisation in East Anglia', based upon the region's high proportion of freemen, the fragmentation of holdings and the lack of coincidence between manor and vill. The social constraints imposed by traditional family structures, lordship and local custom had been severely eroded by the multiplicity of lordships (which meant that many tenants held land from more than one lord), high levels of commercial activity, a fluid and active labour market, and the high degree of geographical mobility (chapter 7). The tight bonds, which are traditionally assumed to have shackled feudal society, had been loosened in Suffolk, where peasants possessed greater freedom of time and action. The low levels of seigneurial exactions, and the consistently lax manner in which villeinage was implemented on the ground, indicate that regional practice had heavily infiltrated manorial custom, as evidenced by the consistency with which millsuit and chevage were ignored, and by the deployment of a standard fine for childwyte across a variety of different manors. Suffolk society at all levels was outward looking by contemporary standards, keenly aware of events and issues beyond the immediate locality.

Did this distinctiveness produce a distinctive mentality or sense of regional identity among East Anglians? Such a question is difficult to answer, because the characteristics that shape a common mentality – the habits, attitudes, social interactions and sense of belonging of thousands of ordinary people – are difficult to recover and were not usually captured in the written record. Yet the existence of regional customs, such as those which influenced local manorial courts, is suggestive of a sense of regional identity. Another strong regional focus was the cult of St Edmund, which remained popular throughout the period 'not only with simple superstitious people but with the most practised potentates', as evidenced by the alacrity with which the townsfolk of Bury reacted to save his shrine during a damaging fire at the abbey. The folklore associated with St Edmund, and his status as the patron saint of East Anglia, constituted a powerful force in binding regional identity. Similarly, the area's distinctive and widespread economic and social characteristics must have acted as a unifying force, and Roger Virgoe detects that medieval East Anglians did possess a sense of a historical community. The preponderance of freemen and the weakness of lordship generated a culture of independence and autonomy, as illustrated by the central role played by freemen from an early date in organizing community responsibilities. It also nurtured anti-authoritarian and nonconformist behaviour, and stirred resentment among villeins towards their servile status. Furthermore, the pervasive influence of commerce encouraged self-help, opportunism and the pursuit of profit. Norfolk folk in the fourteenth century were stereotyped as crafty, cunning and avaricious, as caricatured in Chaucer's hard-bargaining and shrewd reeve. The influence of high levels of personal freedom and commerce, combined with proximity to London and trade with the Low Countries, enhanced the receptiveness of local people to new ideas and their willingness to embrace radical solutions. It seems eminently plausible to suppose that the north and south folk of medieval East Anglia shared a discernible and distinctive mentality.[49]

---

[49] On regional mentalities, see G. Platts, *Land and People in Medieval Lincolnshire* (Lincoln, 1985), pp. 284–95; Douglas, *Social Structure*, pp. 202–3, 205, 218; N. Scarfe, 'The Body of St Edmund', *PSIA* 31 (1967), p. 304; Campbell, 'Hundreds and Leets', pp. 166–7; C. Barron, C. Rawcliffe and J. T. Rosenthal, eds., *East Anglian Society and the Political Community of Late Medieval England: Selected Papers of Roger Virgoe* (Norwich, 1997), p. 89; B. M. S. Campbell, 'The Livestock of Chaucer's Reeve: Fact or Fiction?', in *The Salt of Common Life*, ed. E. B. DeWindt (Kalamazoo, 1995), pp. 304–5.

– CHAPTER 4 –

The Agrarian Economy, 1200–1349

POPULATION AND SETTLEMENT

The Domesday Survey of 1086 records nearly 20,000 landholders in Suffolk, suggesting a total population of around 100,000. The population certainly expanded over the next two centuries, although its exact magnitude is unknowable, because estimating medieval population levels is notoriously difficult on the scant evidence available. Dymond and Northeast reckon that it doubled between 1086 and *c.* 1300, although even higher rates of growth are evident in some places. For example, between 1086 and 1251 the landholding population of eight Suffolk manors belonging to the bishop of Ely increased by a factor of 2.5. The Lay Subsidy of 1327 lists 11,720 taxpayers in Suffolk, which crudely converts to a minimum population of about 180,000. Yet on the eve of the Black Death (1349) many Suffolk villages contained more residents than at any time before the mid-nineteenth century. Lidgate housed more people in the early fourteenth century than in 1801, and the population of Walsham (1,250) was not surpassed until 1851. Overall, the evidence encourages a more optimistic estimate of Suffolk's medieval population, which may have peaked in the 1340s at around 225,000 inhabitants.[1]

Although the actual population level of medieval Suffolk will always remain uncertain, we can gain a good sense of its relative density and distribution from the Domesday survey of 1086 and later tax assessments. In 1086 the population density of much of eastern England lay between five and ten landholders per square mile, compared with an average of thirteen in Suffolk (map 6), and the density of landholders in parts of central Suffolk, and around Ipswich, was among the highest in eleventh-century England. Lay subsidies from the early fourteenth century reveal that England possessed an average of 5.6 taxpayers per square mile, compared with nearly eight in Suffolk (map 7). At both dates, and especially 1086, Suffolk contained some of the most densely populated areas of England. The impression of a heavily populated region is reinforced by evidence from other early fourteenth-century sources: for example, the population density of rural Redgrave in

[1] E. Campbell, 'Domesday Suffolk', in Darby, *Domesday Geography* (1952), p. 169; D. Dymond and P. Northeast, *A History of Suffolk* (Chichester, 1995), pp. 42–3; *AHEW*, ii, pp. 140, 542; *1327 Lay Subsidy*, p. ii; R. Lock, 'The Black Death in Walsham-le-Willows', *PSIA* 37 (1992), p. 328.

c. 1300 was seven times greater than that of urbanized Halesowen in the west Midlands.[2]

Within Suffolk, in 1086 the distribution of population was least concentrated in the far west of the county, particularly the Fenland and Breckland, where there were barely four landholders per square mile, and most concentrated in the central belt stretching from the river valleys of the Deben and Gipping in the east to Bury St Edmunds in the west, where the density reached twenty (map 6). The distribution of taxpayers in the early fourteenth century conformed to a similar pattern, when the population was still heavily concentrated in the river valleys between Bury St Edmunds and Ipswich. However, the density of population on the chalk uplands to the west of Bury and in much of north-east Suffolk had increased relative to other parts of the county since 1086, and especially in comparison to the sandy soils east of Ipswich (map 7). The strong growth of population in the Waveney valley reflects similar developments across the county border in Norfolk, while that on the clay uplands of north-east Suffolk is consistent with the expansion of settlement and the sharp reduction of woodland in this area during the twelfth and thirteenth centuries (map 8).[3]

The growth in population between *c.* 1100 and *c.* 1300 represented the final phase in a long period of demographic expansion, which had begun around the eighth century and ceased abruptly with the arrival of the Black Death in 1349. More people meant more houses, and consequently demographic growth was accompanied by an extension of settlement. Earlier settlement in Suffolk had been concentrated in the river valleys and its expansion thereafter resulted in both the denser occupation of existing sites and the colonization of new ones on the plateaux above the valleys. By *c.* 1100 Suffolk was already a densely settled and populous region, thus reducing the scope for further reclamations. Hence most new settlement between 1100 and *c.* 1349 took the form of either isolated farmsteads or small hamlets in marginal sites, usually around the edges of greens near parish boundaries, rather than the colonization of vast tracts of virgin territory. These communal greens occupied patches of soil that were difficult to cultivate, and during the late Anglo-Saxon period they had been deliberately protected, or perhaps set aside, by lords or groups of freemen to provide pasture and other resources for local communities. Some greens covered several hundred acres on the heavy clay uplands of north-east Suffolk, where they often occupied waterlogged depressions in the wide clay plateaux on the interfluves. In contrast, the clay uplands of south Suffolk were

---

[2] H. C. Darby, *Domesday England* (Cambridge, 1977), p. 90; Razi, 'Myth', pp. 17–18; Campbell, 'Agrarian Problem', p. 66; Phillips, 'Collaboration and Litigation', p. 109.

[3] Williamson, *Shaping Medieval Landscapes*, p. 32; *HistA*, p. 64.

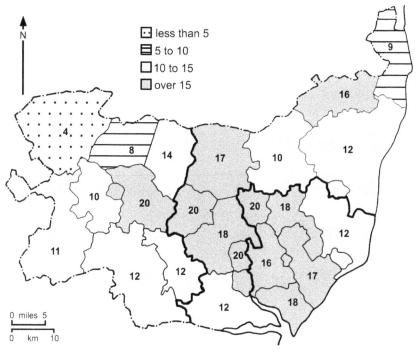

MAP 6 Number of landholders per square mile in 1086 (by hundred)

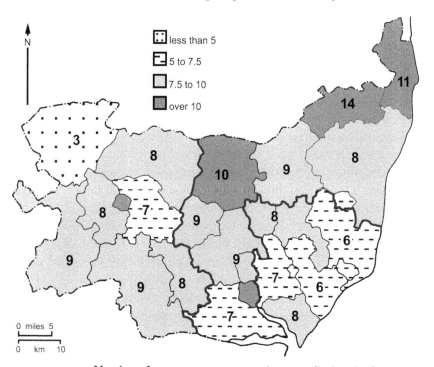

MAP 7 Number of taxpayers per square mile in 1327 (by hundred)

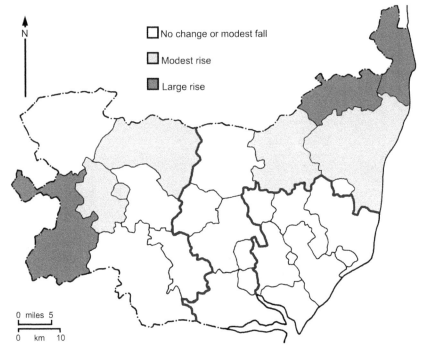

N

☐ No change or modest fall

☐ Modest rise

■ Large rise

0 miles 5

0   km   10

MAP 8 Changes in relative population density between 1086 and 1327 (by hundred)

narrower and more dissected, and consequently greens here – known locally as 'tyes' – tended to be smaller.[4]

By *c.* 1100 some settlement had already developed around these greens in marginal locations, but thereafter the rate of colonization accelerated.[5] In the twelfth and thirteenth centuries new settlement is evident at Rush green, straddling the parish boundaries of Bardwell and Stanton; at Cocks green in the north-west corner of Otley; around the edge of Whittingham green in Fressingfield; and around greens on the edges of the parishes of Capel St Andrew, Woolpit, Hopton, Ickworth and Ixworth Thorpe. The number of house sites around Cranmer green in Walsham doubled during the course of the thirteenth century, and new ones were still being established in the early fourteenth century. In some places the development of secondary sites was extensive enough to transform the local settlement pattern. For example, the early focus of settlement in Hoxne was concentrated around the church in the north of the parish, but during the twelfth and thirteenth centuries it extended to the edges of five greens scattered to the south, thus shifting the distribution of settlement decisively and creating a dispersed pattern of

4 Williamson, *Shaping Medieval Landscapes*, pp. 161–2; *HistA*, pp. 62–3.

5 T. Williamson, *The Origins of Norfolk* (Manchester, 1993), pp. 168–70; Warner, *Greens, Commons*, pp. 13–27; Williamson, *Shaping Medieval Landscapes*, pp. 98–9.

small hamlets. Greenside development during the thirteenth and early four-teenth centuries was extensive in the South Elmhams: for example, Greshaw green cut across the parish boundaries of South Elmham St Cross and St James, and was extensively settled in the thirteenth century (see plate 4). In some places, the pattern of secondary settlement included the creation of isolated, often moated, farmsteads: six have been identified in Mendham and thirteen in Metfield, all of which appear to date from this period. In exceptional cases the scale of colonization was sufficiently great to justify the creation of a new parish, so that Linstead Parva was carved out of Chedis-ton and Linstead to embrace new settlement around Blacksmith and Collopy greens.[6]

The movement of settlement from primary sites in river valleys to dispersed secondary sites around the edges of upland greens was most pronounced on the wide clay interfluves of north-east Suffolk, where the greens were espe-cially large and ubiquitous, and where in *c.* 1100 the reserves of wood-pasture were still relatively high. The exception to this trend was in the Breckland, where the absence of water on the heaths above the river valleys presented an insuperable barrier to further settlement.[7] By *c.* 1300 the settlement pattern of Suffolk had acquired many of its distinguishing modern characteristics: loose-knit centres of primary settlement along river valleys, with scatterings of isolated farmsteads and greenside hamlets on the interfluves and around upland parish boundaries. Nucleated villages – where settlement is almost exclusively concentrated within tight-knit and planned villages with a sin-gle focus – were rare. The colonization of secondary sites represents the local response to rising demographic pressure and a growing scarcity of resources, just as nucleation represents a different response to the same pressures in many other parts of the country. Suffolk's communal greens carried grazing rights for local residents, which enhanced their importance in a period when an extension in the area under cultivation reduced grazing grounds for live-stock. Such rights were especially important in north-east and parts of south Suffolk, where the absence of communal grazing rights over the fallow arable exacerbated shortages of pasture.

[6] *PSIA* 37 (1992), pp. 378–9 (Capel); *PSIA* 37 (1989), p. 69 (Otley); *PSIA* 37 (1992), p. 377 (Fressingfield); *PSIA* 35 (1986), p. 49 (Woolpit); *PSIA* 38 (1993), p. 90 (Hop-ton); *PSIA* 39 (2000), pp. 21–2 (Ickworth); *PSIA* 38 (1994), 205–7 (Ixworth); West and McLaughlin, *Walsham le Willows*, pp. 12, 108 (Walsham); Hoppitt, 'Parks', pp. 239–41 (Hoxne); *PSIA* 36 (1986), pp. 147–9 (South Elmham, St James and St Cross); *PSIA* 36 (1987), pp. 234–5 (All Saints); *PSIA* 36 (1988), pp. 315–16 (St Michael and St Peter); *PSIA* 36 (1985), p. 48 (Mendham); *PSIA* 35 (1984), p. 324 (Metfield); Warner, *Greens, Commons*, p. 17.

[7] *HistA*, p. 62; Williamson, *Shaping Medieval Landscapes*, pp. 54–60, 91–106, 108–19, 130.

The proliferation of nucleated villages in central parts of England is associated with strong lordship and/or powerful village communities, who possessed the authority to reorganize settlement in such an ordered and co-ordinated fashion. The existence of a more fluid and dispersed pattern in Suffolk
implies that neither lords nor village communities were strong enough to
impose such an ordered settlement plan upon the landscape, and it is significant that the areas of weakest lordship – the clay lands in the central,
northern and eastern parts of Suffolk – coincide with the highest incidence
of isolated farmsteads and greenside hamlets. The proportion of freemen was
also high, and Peter Warner has explicitly linked the development of secondary settlement on the clays of east Suffolk to the piecemeal colonizing activities of hundreds of low-status freemen operating within a system of loose
manorial control. Individual freemen and kinship groups responded to the
economic and demographic pressures of the twelfth and thirteenth centuries by gradually colonizing the upland clay landscape, relatively free from
the restrictions of lordship: he cites Stoven as a classic example of secondary
and dispersed settlement developed by low-status freemen. The tightest and
most formal settlement pattern in Suffolk occurred in the Breckland, where
lordship happened to be strong (map 3). However, we should not read too
much into this particular coincidence, because many of the Breckland settlements were formed by the fusion of separate loci into loosely nucleated vills,
rather than through a formal reorganization of settlement into nucleated
villages.[8]

By the early fourteenth century, after almost six centuries of sustained
expansion in settlement, the Suffolk countryside was full of people, and the
pressure of providing sufficient housing for a very dense population was everywhere apparent. Greenside hamlets and isolated farmsteads had been established all over the heaviest clays and in the far-flung corners of many parishes.
Primary settlement sites in river valleys were brimful after the sustained infilling of empty sites and the subdivision of existing house plots. By 1305 very
small pieces of demesne land at Hadleigh had been granted out to tenants as
'new rents', almost certainly for new housing, and small cottages had sprung
up on other slivers of land around the manor. By 1323 Roger de Cowlinge
was paying 1d. new rent annually 'for a certain house on the common at
Mildenhall' and small parcels of arable land had been 'built upon' in other
parts of west Suffolk. The extent of subdivision and infilling is reflected at
Culford in 1348 by the many residents who held fractions of 'messuages' with
cottages squeezed upon them, and in 1328 Matilda Clerk held a cottage 'with

---

[8] Warner, *Greens, Commons*, pp. 25–8; Williamson, *Shaping Medieval Landscapes*,
     p. 88.

houses built upon it' in Yoxford. Suffolk's fields and villages were fair crowded with folk.[9]

AGRICULTURE

Arable farming

More people required more food. Grain provided the readiest source of carbo-hydrate, and its production could be increased by either ploughing up more land for cultivation or raising the output of existing arable: both methods were used in twelfth- and thirteenth-century Suffolk. However, the scope for extending the area under cultivation was limited, because around one-third of the land surface of Suffolk was already cultivated in 1086, a high figure by contemporary standards. Yet this figure hides some significant local varia-tions: in 1086 over 40 per cent of the district north of Ipswich was under the plough, compared with only about 20 per cent of the Breckland. Hence after *c.* 1100 the conversion of woodland, pasture and heath to arable land was small scale and piecemeal in many places, and consequently documentary evidence of the process is often hard to find on any scale. For example, at the end of the twelfth century small parcels of pasture were 'assarted' (ploughed up for arable) in the Waveney valley; 2½-acres of woodland were converted to arable in Weybread; a few acres of heathland were assarted here and there in Blyford, Mells and Theberton; and in the early fourteenth century odd parcels of marsh along the margins of the river Deben were granted to local tenants for enclo-sure and reclamation, probably for pasture rather than arable.[10]

The greatest potential for increasing the area under cultivation existed among the woods and pastures of north-east Suffolk and in the Breckland. Reserves of wood-pasture still remained in *c.* 1100 on the clay plateaux of Blything and Wangford hundreds, where the subsequent colonizing activities of independent freemen passed largely unrecorded. Reclamations for arable were probably greater here after 1100 than in any other area of Suffolk, as reflected in the marked increase in the relative density of population between 1086 and 1327 (map 8), and the decline in its reserves of woodland. Similarly, between 1086 and *c.* 1300 the area under cultivation may well have doubled in

---

9　*PR*, ii, pp. 236–7; *PSIA* 11 (1903), pp. 169–71 (Hadleigh); Bodleian Suffolk Rolls 21 (Mildenhall); BL Add. Ms 42055, ff. 8–22 (Culford); Denney, *Sibton Abbey*, p. 71 (Yoxford).

10　M. Hesse, 'Domesday Land Values', *Landscape History* 22 (2000), pp. 24–5, and Bailey, *Marginal Economy*, p. 97; *AHEW*, ii, pp. 160–1; C. Harper-Bill, ed., *The Cartulary of Blythburgh Priory*, vol. 1, SCS 11 (Woodbridge, 1980), p. 81 (Blyford) and vol. 2, SCS 12 (Woodbridge, 1981), p. 185 (Mells), p. 235 (Theberton); W. G. Arnott, *Suffolk Estuary: The Story of the River Deben* (Ipswich, 1950), p. 38.

and around the Breckland. For example, in the late twelfth century Warden abbey carved a new farm, called Livermere grange, on the boundary of Brandon parish next to Wangford heath, mainly for sheep rearing but including an arable demesne of 60 acres, and arable land at Coney Weston was extended by various assarts named 'whetebreche', 'barleybreche', 'westbreche', 'breche' and 'brakelond'. A 103-acre 'breche', or intake, is recorded at Culford, again close to heathland on the parish boundary with Wordwell, and was apparently a joint enterprise between the two manors in the vill, Easthall receiving 50 acres in one block and the abbot of Bury St Edmunds holding the remainder in three blocks of 40, 8 and 4½ acres. However, the soil quality of these large intakes was poor, because they were valued significantly lower than other arable land on the same manor.[11]

By the early fourteenth century the area of land devoted to arable cultivation had reached its peak. Rough comparisons between Domesday Book and late thirteenth-century surveys suggest that the area under cultivation south of Bury St Edmunds had increased by 10 per cent, although locally the proportion could be much higher: by the 1280s a remarkable 74 per cent of the land surface of Ickworth parish was ploughed for grain farming, which probably represents a 25 per cent increase on the eleventh century. Grain prices and land values may have doubled during the thirteenth century and prices also rose relative to the cost of labour: grain production was highly profitable, and the growth of towns and markets increased the opportunities for commerce (chapters 6 and 7). It is likely that by *c.* 1300 at least one-half of Suffolk's land surface was under the plough, a much higher proportion than in the twentieth century, making arable farming the dominant sector of Suffolk's agriculture, and, indeed, economy.[12]

The value of Suffolk's arable land was generally higher than in many parts of England, and similar to that recorded in most parts of Essex and western Norfolk, although it fell some way short of the levels reached in north and east Norfolk. At the high point of the medieval economy, between 1300 and 1349, the mean value of demesne arable land in England was 4.6d. per acre, while much of that in Suffolk was rated closer to 6d. The highest valuations in the county, around 8d. per acre, were mainly found in a belt stretching from south-west Suffolk to the east and north-east. The lowest valuations (3d. per acre) were recorded in the poor soil regions of the Breckland and the Sandlings, although even these values compare favourably with those of more fertile soils elsewhere in England. The above-average valuation of

---

[11] Warner, *Greens, Commons*, pp. 18–28; *HistA*, pp. 64–5; *SR* 4 (1973), pp. 20–4 (Brandon); Bodleian Ms Gough Suffolk 3 (Coney Weston); BL Add. Ms 42055, f. 45 (Culford).

[12] M. Hesse, 'The Early Parish and Estate of Ickworth', *PSIA* 39 (2000), pp. 17–18.

most of the arable land in Suffolk indicates that the productivity of its arable farming was higher than in much of England. This in turn reflects higher levels of demographic pressure, commercial opportunity and local grain prices.[13]

The main field crops were wheat, rye, maslin (an equal mix of rye and wheat), barley, peas, oats and drage (an equal mix of barley and oats), supplemented on peasant holdings by flax and hemp. Wheat was the preferred bread grain, barley the preferred malting grain, and oats the main fodder crop. Seeding rates and yields were very modest by modern standards. Winter-sown crops (wheat and rye) were usually sown at the rate of 2–3 bushels per acre, and spring-sown crops closer to 4 bushels an acre, although rates in the Breckland were even lower. Mean yields per acre on Suffolk demesnes in *c.* 1300 were similar to the average for south-east England, at around 6 or 7 bushels per acre for wheat and oats, and around 10 bushels per acre for barley and rye, but were some way below those achieved on the most commercialized and productive demesnes in eastern Norfolk: for example, yields per acre at Hinderclay were around half those at Martham. The proportion of arable land cultivated in any one year varied according to local conditions, and was lowest in the infertile Breckland at around 40 per cent, but demesnes across most of Suffolk sowed around 75 per cent of their arable each year in the early fourteenth century. Again, this was a relatively high proportion by contemporary standards, but below the level of the most advanced regions of medieval England, where fallows had been eliminated almost completely. Demesne arable cultivation in Suffolk was moderately intensive.[14]

Between 1250 and 1350 arable farming on Suffolk demesnes fell into one of four main categories (map 9). One group of demesnes returned good yields per acre, sowed a high proportion of legumes, and had significantly reduced the area left as fallow each year, and therefore had attributes in common with the highly productive and technologically advanced demesnes of eastern Norfolk. However, this group was small and its members were concentrated in north-east Suffolk. These are known as *Category 1* demesnes, following Bruce Camp-

---

[13] Demesne valuations of arable land offer the best evidence for comparing land values across England, although they relate to a calculation of financial yield taken from manorial extents and are not a direct indication of the open market value for land: they tend to be lower than the contemporary *leasehold* values of demesne and tenant arable, which often rate between 10d. and 20d. per acre in Suffolk. The values are assessed in Campbell, *English Seigneurial Agriculture*, pp. 348–56. Within Suffolk the Hadleigh demesne rated at 8d. per acre in 1301, *PSIA* 11 (1903), p. 153, and the Great Barton glebe at 18d. per acre, Dymond, 'Parson's Glebe', p. 76. Some leasehold valuations can be found in Bailey, *Marginal Economy*, p. 98.

[14] Campbell, *English Seigneurial Agriculture*, pp. 213–23, 253–70, 309–10; table 7.06; Stone, 'Hinderclay', p. 616; Bailey, *Marginal Economy*, pp. 99–108.

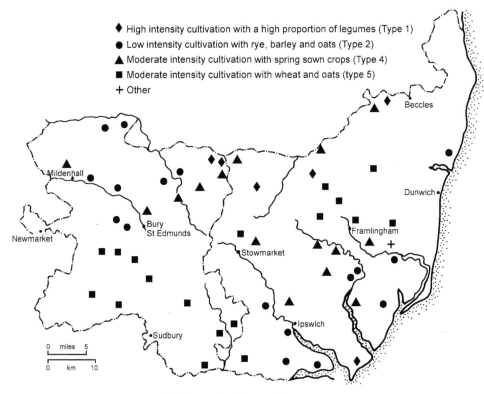

- ◆ High intensity cultivation with a high proportion of legumes (Type 1)
- ● Low intensity cultivation with rye, barley and oats (Type 2)
- ▲ Moderate intensity cultivation with spring sown crops (Type 4)
- ■ Moderate intensity cultivation with wheat and oats (type 5)
- ＋ Other

MAP 9   Arable production on demesnes, 1250–1349

bell's national classification of demesne types.[15] Most demesnes fell into two
other groups, both of which were widespread on the loamy and clay soils. The
first group comprised those which concentrated on a mixture of spring-sown
crops (mainly barley, peas and oats), cultivated with moderate intensity (*Category 4* demesnes in Campbell's scheme): the second group was dominated by
the production of wheat and oats, often sown on a three-course rotation, and
these demesnes (*Category 5*) were usually located on the heavier clays.[16] A final
group of demesnes was confined to the lightest soils of the Breckland and the

[15] There are eight national demesne classifications in Campbell's scheme, detailed
in Campbell, *English Seigneurial Agriculture*, pp. 262–76, 449. The Suffolk
information comes from the same source, supplemented by my own research into
manorial accounts. Examples of Category 1 demesnes in this period are Denham,
Gislingham, Hinderclay, Walton, Mettingham and Thelnetham.

[16] Category 4 demesnes include Bungay, Clopton, Cretingham, Earl Stonham,
Fornham, Glemham, Henley, Ixworth, Kettleburgh, Mildenhall, Redgrave,
Rickinghall, Syleham, Walsham and Woodhall. Category 5 demesnes include
Aldham, Boulge, Chevington, Clare, Cratfield, Earl Soham, Framlingham,
Gipping Newton, Hargrave, Holton, Horham, Hundon, Kelsale, Lawshall,
Layham, Monks Eleigh, Nayland and Whepstead.

Sandlings, and were characterized by the production of rye, barley and oats (hardly any wheat or peas were sown), modest yields, extensive fallows and therefore a relatively low intensity of cultivation (*Category 2*).[17]

As no accounts have survived from tenant holdings, our knowledge of their cropping preferences is poor in comparison. Detailed local tax assessments are the scarcest but most informative source, because they provide information about the grain surpluses of the wealthier peasants. The assessment for the Lay Subsidy of 1283 for Blackbourne Hundred is the best such example to survive from Suffolk, and reveals that the choice of crops on tenant holdings, perhaps unsurprisingly, resembled those on local demesnes. Hence barley was the preferred crop on both demesnes and peasant holdings, and hardly any-one in the Breckland grew wheat or legumes. If anything, the Blackbourne returns suggest that tenants concentrated on the known cash crop of barley to a greater degree than lords (48 per cent of all grain on tenant holdings but only 38 per cent on demesnes). The stronger preference for cash crops on peasant holdings is also revealed by other sources of evidence. The tithe payments made by parishioners to the rectories of Lakenheath and Milden-hall reveal that, of peasant crops at Lakenheath between 1336 and 1461, barley constituted a remarkable 79 per cent, and rye 15 per cent (compared with 53 per cent and 25 per cent on the Lakenheath demesne in the 1390s), and 69 per cent barley and 29 per cent wheat/maslin at Mildenhall over a similar period (compared with 53 per cent and 26 per cent on the Mildenhall demesne in the 1420s). Similarly, tithe receipts in Wickham Market and Loudham were dominated by barley (53 and 73 per cent respectively) and wheat (27 and 12 per cent). Court rolls sometimes note the crops sown on tenant land on the rare occasions when it had been seized by the lord. For example, John Archer of Brandon had 42 acres sown with crops in the summer of 1418, of which 62 per cent were barley, 24 per cent rye and 14 per cent oats, compared with 64, 22 and 14 per cent on the Brandon demesne (1390s), and the sown area of the hold-ing of Robert Harry in Fornham All Saints comprised 83 per cent barley and 11 per cent peas (46 per cent barley and 4 per cent peas on the demesne). Of thirteen recorded holdings (not all arable land) abandoned at Iken after the plague epidemic of 1349, seven had barley growing upon them and no other crops were mentioned, and barley is the only crop mentioned on land aban-doned at Easton Bavents in that year. Most of these examples are taken from the lighter soil regions of Suffolk, and wheat dominated on the heavier soils. The sown area of William Carter's abandoned holding in Aldham comprised

---

[17] Examples of Category 2 demesnes include Barton Mills, Blakenham, Brandon, Downham, Dunningworth, Easton Bavents, Fakenham, Harkstead, Icklingham, Lakenheath, Loudham, Melton, Risby, Sapiston, Staverton, Stoke-by-Ipswich, Tattingstone and Westley.

52 per cent wheat and 48 per cent bullemong (an equal mix of oats and peas), and the grain among John Hankerhacches' chattels comprised 70 per cent wheat and 30 per cent drage (compared with 50 per cent wheat and 43 per cent oats on the demesne). Bequests of crops recorded in wills are dominated by wheat, barley and malted barley.[18]

Evidence for the intensity of cultivation on tenant holdings is exceptionally rare, although it is widely assumed that necessity forced peasants to squeeze more out of them by increasing the proportion of land sown each year. The most effective methods of reducing the area left fallow each year were to increase labour inputs, to deploy plenty of manure, and to extend the area sown with legumes, because in the absence of chemical fertilizers additional work on ploughing, weeding, hoeing and dung-spreading helped to prevent soils from leaching nutrients during grain cultivation, and legumes fixed nutrients back into the soil. We have no evidence with which to assess the deployment of labour on these holdings, but in *c.* 1300 the combination of smallholdings and relatively high population densities in Suffolk would have encouraged high labour inputs, and, by extension, an intensive arable regime. Bruce Campbell has calculated that the labour–land ratio on tenant holdings in eastern Norfolk was six times greater than on demesnes during this period, and David Stone has suggested that more intensive use of labour and manure meant that they were also around 40 per cent more productive. This general supposition is supported by the few snippets of indirect evidence from Suffolk. For example, a holding called Smithslond was abandoned in the summer of 1332 at Brandon, with only 21 per cent of its 7 acres laid to fallow, and in 1310 William Rok of Lakenheath leased 6 roods from another peasant, of which one-third was sown with barley, one-third with peas, and one-third fallow: the proportion left fallow around this time on the demesnes of Brandon and Lakenheath was nearer 50 per cent, and peas were hardly sown. Leguminous crops comprised less than 10 per cent of all demesne-sown crops nationally, yet a quarter of the sown area of thirteen peasant holdings abandoned at Bredfield in 1349 was sown with peas; 2½ acres of villein land illegally sublet at Walsham were sown entirely with peas; peas comprised the second most important crop

[18] Bailey, *Marginal Economy*, pp. 139, 238, 240; SROI HD1538/424/1 (Wickham); SROI HD1538/295/11, 13 (Loudham); Bacon Ms 294/11 (Brandon); SROB E3/15.7/1.9(a), court held 1 January 1384 (Fornham); CUL Vanneck Ms, boxes 1 and 2, courts held June 1345 and October 1341 (Aldham); SROI HD32/293/387, m. 25 (Iken); SROI v5/19/1.3 (Easton Bavents); P. Northeast, ed., *Wills of the Archdeaconry of Sudbury, 1439–1474*, vol. 1, SRS 44 (Woodbridge, 2001), pp. 67, 73, 86, 100, 104, 128, 154, 190, 224, 343, 349, 368, 431, 435, 442, 451, 495. When John Symond of Eyke died intestate in the winter of 1339, he left 7 quarters of barley, 4 quarters of rye and no other crops, and barley constituted 54 per cent of the crops abandoned by a serf in Walton, SROI HD1538/357/1, m. 12 (Eyke) and HA119/50/3/18, m. 50 (Walton).

on the seized holding of another serf in Walton; and the Aldham example cited above indicates a preference for bullemong rather than oats.[19] Another useful indicator of the high productivity of some peasant landholdings is the manner in which some lords chose to cultivate them alongside the demesne when they fell into the lord's hands after the death of the tenant who did not possess an obvious heir: the usual practice would have been to grant the holding to another tenant. Significantly, such lands were sometimes sown intensively with the most demanding rotations and crops, such as on Wysman's and Trusshare's *tenementa* in Hinderclay. Similarly, in the 1340s two small villein holdings were sown as part of the arable demesne at Fornham All Saints, and a similar practice is recorded at Kelsale and Thelnetham. All these examples imply that high inputs of labour enabled many peasants to raise the output of their holdings and to cultivate them with a greater degree of intensity than on neighbouring demesnes.[20]

Pastoral farming

In the century before the Black Death the intensity of pastoral farming in Suffolk was higher than of arable. Historians judge the intensity of pastoral regimes by the composition of farm livestock and by the local value of grassland, especially meadowland. The first characteristic of intensive pastoral farming is that draught animals (those used to pull ploughs and carts) comprised a relatively low proportion of all farm stock, because a lower proportion of draught animals enabled more supplies of grass and hay to be diverted to support larger numbers of non-working animals, which in turn permitted the greater development of other sectors of pastoral farming, such as dairying. The second characteristic is that horses are more important than oxen as draught animals. Horses could work longer and faster than oxen, thus enabling the size of the ploughteam to be reduced, but they also incurred higher depreciation costs than oxen, because they could not be fattened and sold for meat at the end of their working life in the same manner: they also incurred higher running costs, because they required larger quantities of fodder crops than oxen, which had to be grown for the purpose. Hence, a greater emphasis on horses rather than oxen as the main source of traction carried implications

[19] B. M. S. Campbell, 'Agricultural Progress in Medieval England: Some Evidence from Eastern Norfolk', *EcHR* 36 (1983), p. 39; D. Stone, *Decision-Making in Medieval Agriculture* (Oxford, 2005), pp. 262–72; Stone, 'Hinderclay', pp. 634–5; Bacon Ms 289/9 (Brandon); CUL EDC 7/15/II/1/2, court held September 1310 (Lakenheath); Bailey, *Marginal Economy*, pp. 139, 214; SROI HA91/1, m. 61 (Bredfield); Lock, *Walsham*, i, p. 100; Dymond and Northeast, *History of Suffolk*, p. 44; SROI HA119/50/3/18, m. 50 (Walton).

[20] Bacon Mss 451, 459 (Hinderclay, thanks to David Stone); SROB E3/15.7/2.2(b) (Fornham); SROI HD1538/279/2 (Kelsale); SROI HD1538/380 (Thelnetham).

both for arable farming, which had to shift its production towards fodder crops to accommodate their needs, and for the efficiency of the local economic system, which had to yield greater rewards to cover and justify the higher costs of rearing horses.[21] The third characteristic is that cattle, rather than pigs and sheep, dominated stocks of non-draught animals, and cows in particular. Dairying was an expensive form of pastoral farming, because it required additional capital investment in stables, byres and cowhouses, and was highly labour intensive, but it provided a good return, especially in areas where labour was abundant and cheap, offering milk (around 100 gallons per cow annually), butter and cheese, and ultimately meat and leather at the end of a cow's productive life. The fourth, and final, characteristic of intensive pastoral farming is the high returns obtained from dairy farming, measured through the annual lactage rate (the amount charged by the demesne for the rent of one of its cows, including pasture, in which the lessee received the milk and usually any calves born during the year), and by the high value of grassland, reflecting the premium placed on hay as a source of fodder.

Many farms in Suffolk exhibit all four of these characteristics strongly, to a degree which placed them at the very forefront of intensive pastoral farming in medieval England. First, as table 1 shows, the proportion of draught animals was very low by the standards of English demesnes, and even lower among peasants, which encouraged a concentration upon dairy cattle rather than sheep or pigs, although sheep did feature more prominently on demesnes on the lighter soils, such as the Breckland and Sandlings. The concentration upon cattle, mainly cows, was especially pronounced on tenant holdings.[22] Second, draught animals not only comprised a relatively small proportion of farm livestock in Suffolk, but there were also fewer oxen. Oxen comprised around 75 per cent of all draught animals on English demesnes, but only 55 per cent on Suffolk demesnes, where instead the small and versatile 'stott' (a small horse) was popular. Oxen were less popular among peasants, comprising around 45 per cent of all their draught animals nationally, but in Suffolk they hardly feature at all: around 75 per cent of their draught animals were horses, the highest recorded proportion in England. In 1283 78 per cent of draught animals in Blackbourne Hundred were horses: in Coney Weston they comprised 83 per cent, and not one ox was rendered as a heriot at Walsham in the Black Death of 1349. The importance of horses was especially pronounced on the light soils of west Suffolk, where horse rearing was an important activity. For example, horses accounted for 44 per cent of all damage and trespass presentments

---

[21] Campbell, 'Chaucer's Reeve', pp. 279–89; Campbell, *English Seigneurial Agriculture*, pp. 106–20.

[22] Most Suffolk demesnes fit 'Type 2' pastoral system in Campbell's classification, Campbell, *English Seigneurial Agriculture*, p. 449.

TABLE I   The profile of pastoral husbandry on Suffolk farms, 1250–1350

Farm type	Percentage of livestock units			
	Draught animals	*Cattle*	*Pigs*	*Sheep*
English demesnes	47%	29%	3%	22%
Suffolk demesnes	33%	44%	13%	17%
Suffolk tenant holdings	22%	55%	3%	20%

Sources: Demesne data taken from Campbell, 'Chaucer's Reeve', pp. 280–1; tenant data taken from *1283 Lay Subsidy*, pp. xxx–xxxi. Livestock units calculated following Campbell, *English Seigneurial Agriculture*, pp. 102–4.

involving livestock recorded in the court rolls of Lackford (1361–1459) and 46 per cent in Brandon (1377–99). This part of the county provided a pool of replacement horses for farms elsewhere in East Anglia.[23]

The low proportion of draught animals in general, and oxen in particular, in Suffolk created greater opportunities for cattle rearing across the county (map 10). Large demesne herds of between thirty and 130 cows are recorded in parts of east Suffolk, milk output per cow was high, and cheese routinely features in tithes and other gifts and rents to religious houses: it is instructive that 59 per cent of all animals rendered as heriot during the Black Death of 1349 in Walsham were cows.[24] Dairy production was usually managed by women, five of whom ran the dairy of Sibton abbey and generated an impressive annual profit of around £45 per annum. A good indicator of the intensity of dairying is the level of the annual lactage rate paid to demesnes for the lease of their cows. Little systematic work has been undertaken on demesne lactage rates, despite their significance, although Farmer reckoned that between 5s. and 6s. per cow was typical in southern England, and Campbell has shown that 4s. to 6s. per cow was common in Norfolk (with a range of 3s. 4d. to 6s. 8d.).[25] Lactage rates in Suffolk are spread across a similar range (table 2), with the lowest values recorded on the light soils, yet nearly two thirds of all valuations from this sample of twenty-eight demesnes were 6s. or greater. On the heavier soils of east Suffolk, and in the Stour and Waveney valleys, lactage rates consistently reached between 6s. and 7s. per cow, which rank among the highest recorded

[23] J. Langdon, *Horses, Oxen and Technological Innovation* (Cambridge, 1986), pp. 88, 204–5; *1283 Lay Subsidy*, pp. xxx–xxxi; BL Harley Ms 230, ff. 62–3 (Coney Weston); Lock, 'Black Death', pp. 329–36; Campbell, *English Seigneurial Agriculture*, pp. 127–8; SROB E3/15.12/1.2 – 1.5 (Lackford); Bacon Ms 292 (Brandon).

[24] See below, pp. 219–26; Denney, *Sibton Abbey*, p. 38; *PSIA* 14 (1912), pp. 319, 333; Lock, 'Black Death', pp. 329–36.

[25] Denney, *Sibton Abbey*, p. 38; Campbell, 'Chaucer's Reeve', pp. 283, 291–4, 301; Campbell, *English Seigneurial Agriculture*, pp. 143–6; *AHEW*, iii, p. 464.

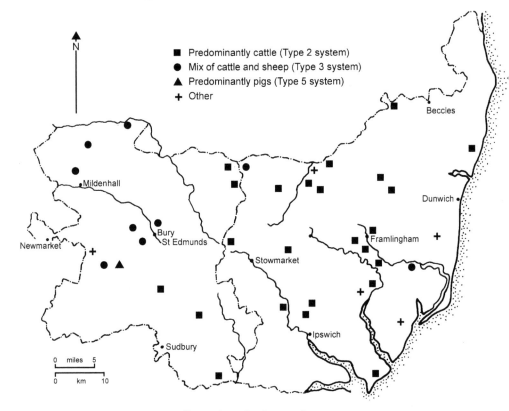

MAP 10 Pastoral production on demesnes, 1250–1349

in medieval England. The local people who paid such high rentals worked within an intensive regime of dairy farming.

The valuations of meadowland reinforce the evidence for intensive pastoral farming. Meadow values on demesnes in eastern England were usually rated at around 2s. to 3s. per acre, yet those in Suffolk were at the upper end of this range and rose as high as 5s. to 6s. in a few places, more than four times the value of arable. Meadow values were uniformly high across the county, higher than those recorded in neighbouring Essex and Norfolk. The lowest valuations seldom fell below 2s. per acre (and were usually found in the Breckland), the majority were around 4s., and the highest valuations were mainly found in eastern Suffolk, especially on the heavier clays and along the lower reaches of the Stour valley: these are the highest mean values for meadowland recorded in medieval England. Similarly some of the highest values of demesne grassland relative to arable were recorded along the Stour, Gipping and Deben valleys and in north-east Suffolk. These valuations reflect the handsome financial returns that could be obtained from specialized and intensive forms of pastoral husbandry, rather than any superior 'natural' endowment of grassland.

TABLE 2   Annual lactage rates for demesne cows

Manor	Lactage Rate*		Year
Dunningworth	4s.	0d.	1296–7
Tattingstone	4s.	0d.	1378–9
Fornham St Martin	4s.	0d.	1301–2
Lakenheath	4s.	6d.	1347–8
Risby	5s.	0d.	1329–30
Great Fakenham	5s.	0d.	1329–30
Framlingham	5s.	0d.	1324–5
Kelsale	5s.	0d.	1356–7
Fornham All Saints	5s.	3d.	1360–1
Brandon	5s.	4d.	1341–2
Melton	5s.	6d.	1331–2
Boulge	6s.	0d.	1356–7
Harkstead	6s.	0d.	1341–2
Walsham	6s.	0d.	1400–1
Hinderclay	6s.	0d.	1320s
Ufford	6s.	0d.	1401–2
Easton Bavents	6s.	8d.	1330–1
Akenham	6s.	8d.	1392–3
Chevington	6s.	8d.	1335–6
Cretingham	6s.	8d.	1371–2
Hargrave	6s.	8d.	1338–9
Horham	6s.	10d.	1328–9
Loudham	7s.	0d.	1371–2
Holton	7s.	0d.	1376–7
Layham	7s.	0d.	1331–2
Winston	7s.	0d.	1327–8
Worlingworth	7s.	0d.	1320s
Glemham	7s.	6d.	1328–9

* Annual rate for the lease of one cow, including all or half of any calves born in the year and pasture grounds.

Sources: PRO sc6/999/22 (Dunningworth); SROI hB8/1/819 (Tattingstone); SROB E3/15.9/2.12 (Fornham St Martin); CUL EDC 7/15/1/4 (Lakenheath); SROB E3/15.13/2.8 (Risby); BL Add. Roll 9100 (Fakenham); Ridgard, *Framlingham*, p. 55; SROI HD1538/279/2 (Kelsale); SROB E3/15.6/2.28 (Fornham); SROB E3/15.13/20b (Chevington); PRO sc6/1304/23 (Brandon); SROB HA504/3/5a (Walsham); Stone, 'Hinderclay', p. 630; CUL EDC 7/16/11/4 (Melton); SROI HD1538/139/1 (Boulge); SROI s1/10/6.6 (Harkstead); SROI HD1538/400/1 (Ufford); SROI v5/19/1.1 (Easton); SROI HD1469/7 (Akenham); SROI HA10/50/18/4.4 (8) (Cretingham); SROB E3/15.10/2.2 (Hargrave); SROI HA68/484/319 (Horham); SROI HD1538/295/3 (Loudham); SROI HA246/A4/7 (Holton); SROB E3/1/1 (Layham); CUL EDC 7/17/1/3 m. 2 (Winston); Ridgard, 'Worlingworth', p. 51; SROI HD1538/238/1 (Glemham).

The demand for grassland in Suffolk is reflected in the readiness of local tenants to compete for very small strips of grass and the high monetary value of both pasture, which often rated at least twice the value of arable, and meadow, which rated even higher. Peasants in early fourteenth-century Hinderclay leased the smallest slivers of verges and herbage from the demesne, those in Layham even rented 'the herbage between the hedges', and uncultivated arable was leased as pasture at 6d. per acre in Gipping Newton in 1346.[26]

In *c.* 1300 the proportion of draught animals on most Suffolk farms was low, and the proportion of cattle high, by national standards, and consequently the county contained a very high incidence of 'intensive' pastoral demesnes (map 11). The coincidence of exceptionally high lactage rates and high valuations of meadowland in many areas of east Suffolk, and in the Stour and Waveney valleys, is indicative of the most intensive dairy farming regime in medieval England. The development of such an advanced pastoral system is remarkable given the limited amounts of grassland in Suffolk, for East Anglia was one of the least grassy areas in the country. Its development must reflect the strength of commercial opportunities for dairy farmers, who were responding to concentrated demand in East Anglia and south-east England.

Suffolk agriculture in 1300 was largely mixed. Its pastoral farming was highly intensive and commercialized, while arable farming was probably intensive on tenant holdings and moderately so on demesnes. This generalization disguises some broad differences across the county. Most farms in southern, central and northern Suffolk were dominated by either the production of wheat and oats, or by a combination of spring-sown crops with barley prominent, where around 70 to 80 per cent of the arable was sown each year. This was combined with an intensive pastoral regime where dairying and stock fattening predominated, and meadow valuations and lactage rates were high. Layham in the 1330s provides a good illustration of a demesne operating within this system: it was sown with 49 per cent wheat and 42 per cent oats (the wheat mainly for sale and the oats for fodder), and maintained a middling flock of about 120 sheep and a decent dairy herd of about twenty cows. In contrast, a few demesnes in north-east Suffolk combined high intensity arable and pastoral farming, to a degree which was exceptional in England. Finally, only farms situated on the lightest soils of the western and eastern extremes of the county – notably the Breckland and the Sandlings – display a significantly different character, where both arable and pastoral pursuits were more extensive.

[26] Campbell, 'Chaucer's Reeve', pp. 285–7, 301; Campbell, *English Seigneurial Agriculture*, pp. 146–7; and for local examples of meadow values in demesne extents, see PRO c135/87/27 (Cavenham); CUL EDR G3/27, ff. 166, 172, 177, 183; BL Harley Ms 230, f. 147; BL Add. Ms 34689, f. 6 (Fornham); *VCH*, i, p. 642. These valuations are from manorial extents, and leasehold values were much higher; Stone, 'Hinderclay', p. 618; SROB E3/1/1 (Layham); SROI HD1538/236/17 (Gipping).

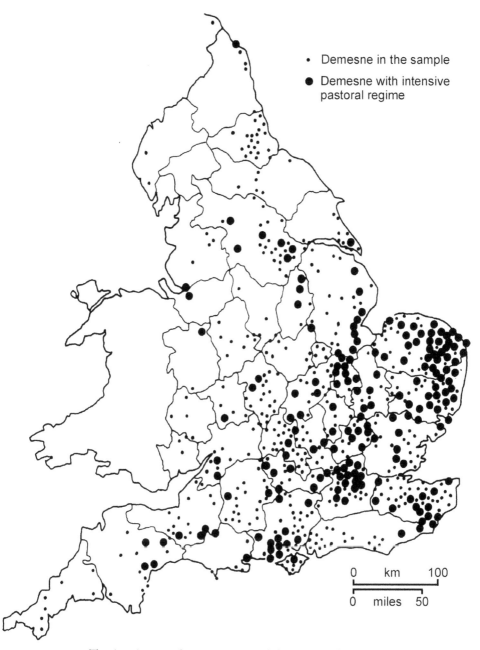

MAP 11 The distribution of intensive pastoral demesnes in England, 1250–1349
(after Campbell)

Here rye, barley and oats dominated arable farming, but as little as one-half of the arable was sown each year, and yields were relatively low. Pastoral farming was dominated by sheep and horse rearing, especially where extensive areas of marshland supplemented vast heathland pastures, such as the parishes on the Breck-Fen edge. These sheep produced lightweight fleeces, seldom exceeding 2 lb each, which were considered inferior to the wool of Lincolnshire and the east Midlands. Valuations of arable land, meadow and lactage rates here were about average by national standards, but below those recorded elsewhere in Suffolk. These features are well illustrated at Lakenheath, a huge parish containing 1,500 acres of sandy arable land and 9,500 acres of heath and marsh, where the large demesne sowed rye, barley and oats in equal measures on less than half of the available arable each year, and kept a huge flock of 2,500 sheep with some cattle.[27]

AGRARIAN FORTUNES

The period between *c.* 1200 and *c.* 1349 represents the high point of the medieval economy, when the number of people, the area under cultivation, the level of grain prices, the extent of settlement, land values and the profitability of grain production all peaked. It also coincides with the expansion of trade and towns, and the growing commercialization of the economy (chapters 6 and 7). These features are interconnected, in the sense that the increase in the intensity and output of agricultural production, and the improvement in economic efficiency engendered by trade, enabled the Suffolk economy to absorb the sizeable growth in its population since 1086. This represents a significant achievement, and reflects the fact that the medieval economy was more sophisticated, diversified and commercialized than historians once imagined. In 1334 the taxable wealth of Suffolk was assessed at £14 per square mile (compared with £24 in Norfolk and £11 in Essex), which ranked sixteenth out of forty-one English counties. The assessable wealth of communities along the Stour, Gipping and Waveney valleys was among the highest in England, and contrasted starkly with the low valuations recorded in areas of poor soil and sparse population, such as the Breckland, Fenland and Sandlings (map 12).[28]

The relative absence of demesne accounts before *c.* 1300 inhibits any detailed assessment of temporal changes in agricultural fortunes during the course of the thirteenth century, but the inexorable rise in grain prices and the quickening of commercial activity in the second half of the century indicate

---

[27] Campbell, *English Seigneurial Agriculture*, pp. 252–72; SROB E3/1/1 (Layham); Bailey, *Marginal Economy*, pp. 126–7; Bailey, 'Lakenheath', pp. 2–6.

[28] R. E. Glasscock, 'England in 1334', in Darby, *New Historical Geography* (1973), pp. 138–40.

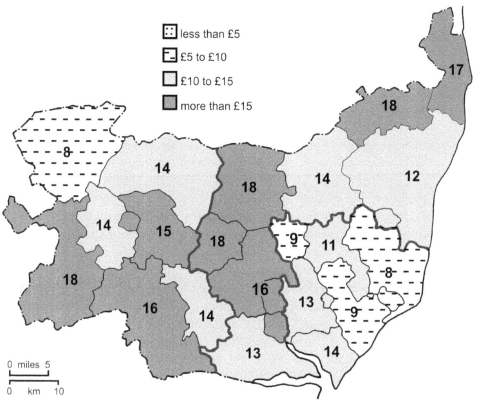

less than £5

£5 to £10

£10 to £15

more than £15

MAP 12 Taxable wealth per square mile in 1334 (by hundred).

that the general trend was upwards to a peak in the first half of the four-teenth century. Yet it was also the period in which a number of stress lines became exposed, as the economy struggled to cope with the weight of popu-lation in the face of successive harvest failures and high taxation. One of the most dramatic external variables acting upon Suffolk's economy around 1300 was the weather. This period has been identified as one of sudden climatic change, characterized by dramatic swings in annual weather patterns and a high incidence of violent storms and marine surges in the North Sea, whose local impact could be catastrophic. Hundreds, perhaps thousands, of acres of salt marsh were permanently inundated around Suffolk's coast during the first half of the fourteenth century, and turf pits around Lowestoft were flooded to create the southern end of what we now know as the Broads. The fate of Dunwich – once Suffolk's premier port – was finally sealed in this short period, when six parishes, over 600 buildings, and its harbour mouth were washed away in a series of violent marine inundations between 1275 and 1345 (plate 16). The rate of deposition of sand and shingle along Orford Ness increased markedly, relegating the borough of Orford to the status of an up-river port as the extending finger of the spit deflected the mouth of the river Alde further southwards.[29]

The variability of the weather was responsible for a series of exceptionally poor harvests in the 1310s and 1320s, followed by a bountiful series in the 1330s. The 1310s witnessed some of the most appalling famines in the history of north-west Europe, when perhaps 10 per cent of the population died of starvation-related illnesses. The impact of the harvest failures of 1315–22 in Suffolk has received little scholarly attention, partly because of the patchiness of local sources, although the limited evidence that exists encourages us to downplay their long-term significance. Certainly, the harvest failures of 1315, 1316, 1321 and 1322 resulted in a dramatic rise in local grain prices in response to scarcity, and, for example, between 1314 and 1316 the prices of wheat, barley and rye sold in Eye market rose by over 50 per cent, and the price of oats by 80 per cent. Many poor families were forced to steal to survive, and rises in rates of petty larceny are evident in many places. At Lakenheath in 1316 reports of petty crimes by vagrants and nocturnal malefactors, of the illegal sale of fish in the market, of illegal fishing in the fens, and of the clandestine cropping of the corn of others all increased. Theft of foodstuffs increased at Worlingworth in the years of crisis, and in 1321 Catherine Kembald stole handfuls of the lord's oats from the fields of Walsham. The most vulnerable members of society were badly exposed, and in 1317 Matilda de Neue died in Hinderclay with hardly any food among her possessions. Other families relied on charitable handouts (in 1321–2 the manor of Hinderclay distributed wheat worth 60s. as alms to local people), while others had no option but to liquidate assets such as land or livestock to cope with the crisis: between 1316 and 1319 William Lene of Walsham acquired thirty-three pieces of land from poor families forced to sell up their assets. In 1317–18 animal murrain decimated livestock on many farms, followed by drought in 1321–2, which particularly affected farmers on the lightest soils.[30]

This succession of catastrophes between 1315 and 1322 has been dubbed the 'Agrarian Crisis'. It was sufficiently sustained and serious in large areas of midland and northern England to trigger a decisive downturn in economic fortunes, the point at which the expansion of previous centuries finally and definitively ceased. Yet its impact was less severe in Suffolk: for all the evident

---

[29] M. Bailey, '*Per Impetum Maris*: Natural Disaster and Economic Decline in Eastern England, 1275–1350', in *Before the Black Death: Essays in the Crisis of the Early Fourteenth Century*, ed. B. M. S. Campbell (Manchester, 1991), pp. 191–9.

[30] I. Kershaw, 'The Great Famine and Agrarian Crisis in England, 1315–22', *Past and Present* 59 (1973), pp. 1–50; Ridgard, 'Worlingworth', pp. 103–5 (Eye and Worlingworth); Lock, *Walsham*, i, pp. 14–15, 92; Schofield, 'Social Economy'; Bacon Ms 451 (Hinderclay, reference supplied by David Stone); CUL EDC 7/15/11/1/6, m. 14 (Lakenheath); Bailey, *Marginal Economy*, pp. 201–2.

distress of the famine years, places such as Lakenheath, Redgrave, Walsham and Worlingworth do not reveal abnormal death rates among tenants, and the court rolls of Drinkstone and Fornham St Martin reveal little out of the ordinary between 1315 and 1317, with the exception of a barn flattened by a tempest in 1315.[31] At Hinderclay the number of heriots rendered to the lord doubled in 1316 and 1322, albeit from a small base, and a concentration of deaths in the September court of 1316 is highly suggestive of an outbreak of some gastro-enteric disease in the wake of famine. The Agrarian Crisis did not mark the turning point in the fortunes of the Suffolk economy. Certainly, the 1320s and 1330s were a period of relatively low grain prices and a sluggish agrarian economy. After a peak in the 1290s, both the area under cultivation and the value of arable land dipped in the 1320s and 1330s on many Suffolk demesnes, and livestock herds and sheep flocks contracted in the wake of successive outbreaks of animal disease. Yet by the 1340s most economic indictors point to a complete recovery. Demesne-sown acreages and arable values had returned to the levels of the 1290s, the peasant land market remained strong, livestock herds were rebuilt, and the numbers of petty traders operating in many market towns peaked in the 1340s. The *Inquisitiones Nonarum* reveal clear evidence for a contraction in the area under cultivation between 1290 and 1341 in many parts of England (including parts of Cambridgeshire and Hertfordshire), but, apart from a small area west of Bury St Edmunds, no such contraction in Suffolk. In terms of aggregate output, the 1340s mark the highpoint of the medieval Suffolk economy.[32]

The Suffolk economy rode the Agrarian Crisis more successfully than many parts of central and northern England. The explanation for this might lie in its resilient and flexible nature, which was able to absorb such exogenous 'shocks' without suffering long-term damage. Perhaps the high price of land, or the diversity of the local resource base, provided sufficient reserves of capital and food for most families to cope with the crisis. Alternatively, Suffolk folk may simply have been lucky, in that East Anglia escaped the worst weather conditions in 1315 and 1316, and again in the early 1320s. Whatever the reason, Suffolk – like neighbouring Norfolk – had weathered a series of violent economic storms between the 1290s and the 1340s. Nothing, however, could prepare either the Suffolk economy or its society for the greatest human catastrophe in recorded history: the Black Death of 1349 (chapter 8).

[31] Lock, *Walsham*, i, pp. 30–92; Phillips, 'Collaboration and Litigation', p. 147; Ridgard, 'Worlingworth', p. 105; SROB E7/10/1.1 (Drinkstone); SROB E3/15.9/1.2, mm. 17–25 (Fornham); Schofield, 'Social Economy'.

[32] Campbell, *English Seigneurial Agriculture*, pp. 235, 368; Bailey, *Marginal Economy*, pp. 208–15, 246–7, 261–2, table 4.2; Ridgard, 'Worlingworth', pp. 186, 215; Holmes, *Higher Nobility*, p. 93; R. H. Britnell, *Growth and Decline in Colchester, 1300–1525* (Cambridge, 1986), pp. 21–2.

– CHAPTER 5 –

The Suffolk Landscape, 1200–1349

WHAT did the landscape of Suffolk look like in the century and a half before the Black Death of 1349, and would it have been recognizable to the modern eye? Unfortunately, finding clear answers to such straightforward and interesting questions is problematic, because medieval sources do not describe explicitly how the landscape looked. However, they do provide partial information about how much of the land was managed. This enables us to recreate elements of the landscape, which was itself shaped by the particular ways in which local communities organized their arable fields, exploited other natural resources, such as woodland and marshes, and laid out their farms: this was especially true in an era when the economy was dominated by agriculture, and in a period of extensive colonization and intensive management of the land. Of course, the medieval landscape also owed some of its character to the imprints left by many earlier generations of settlers and agriculturalists, because thirteenth-century people were adapting some property boundaries and settlement patterns dating back hundreds of years. Indeed, historians have increasingly emphasized the importance of continuity in explaining the character and evolution of the British landscape, and consequently there are ample grounds for arguing that tracts of the medieval Suffolk landscape would have been readily recognizable to the modern eye.

The settlement pattern of medieval Suffolk was described in chapter 4. The earliest settlements tended to congregate in river valleys, but they were not planned nucleated villages like those in central England. By the thirteenth century valley settlements usually took the form of loosely integrated, polyfocal sites, while those on the plateaux above the river valleys, and those congregated around parish boundaries, comprised a mixture of greenside hamlets and isolated farmsteads. Towns were small by modern standards, containing hundreds rather than thousands of people, and so the extent of urban sprawl was limited: however, towns developed a distinctive topography during this period, when many marketplaces and street plans were laid out in ways that are readily identifiable today (chapter 6).

An important component in determining the appearance of the medieval landscape was the organization, layout and operation of arable fields, because grain was the most important source of food in medieval England, and around one-half of the land surface of Suffolk was ploughed for grain cultivation in *c.* 1300. Although field systems have justifiably generated an extensive body of academic research, less attention has been paid to the types of irregular fields that dominated Suffolk. Furthermore, the appearance and utilization of non-arable resources has also attracted limited scholarly attention, even though vast tracts of the medieval countryside were not ploughed up for arable cultivation. Yet these other forms of land use merit close consideration, particularly in a county such as Suffolk, which possessed a diverse resource base and a strong pastoral economy. Indeed, meadowland was highly valued, marshland was locally significant in coastal areas and the Fenland, heathland dominated the light soils of the Sandlings and Breckland, and patches of woodland characterized central areas (see map 1 for the location of these regions). Calculating with precision the relative extent of these forms of land use is impossible, but we might roughly estimate that in *c.* 1300 meadowland comprised around 1 per cent of Suffolk's land surface, woodland about 5 per cent, heathland about 10 per cent, other pasture grounds about 25 per cent (including commons, greens, verges), marshland about 5 per cent, and arable land just over 50 per cent.

Arable and pasture throughout much of medieval England were widely subject to common rights, which provided local people with specific rights of access at various times of the year. Hence local people might have certain common rights over a stretch of marshland – such as a right of way and the ability to pasture their cattle there during the summer months – even though it belonged to another individual. However, in Suffolk the extent of common rights was often relatively restricted, and in many cases the land was 'several', meaning that no common rights existed over it and so all usage was exclusive to the holder of the land. Significant areas of heath and marshland were subject to limited or no common rights, while large areas of Suffolk's woodland and meadowland were several. Freedom from the constraints of common rights might enable the landholder to exploit the land more intensively, a process further encouraged during the thirteenth century by the rise in both agricultural profits and demographic pressure. By *c.* 1300 both arable and pasture in Suffolk were intensively managed and carefully nurtured to yield an eclectic range of valuable products, and the value of different forms of non-arable land was usually higher than arable. At this date an acre of heathland could fetch 6s. per acre at leasehold, an acre of cropped woodland up to 8s., and the 13s. 4d. per acre achieved at Melton in the 1300s rates among the highest leasehold valuations of meadowland yet discovered in medieval England: all of these valuations were higher than the value of arable land, which usually fetched between 12d. and 20d. per acre at leasehold.[1]

---

[1] For high heathland valuations, see SROI v5/19/1.1 and PRO sc6/1000/1. For meadowland in general, see Williamson, *Shaping Medieval Landscapes*, pp. 163–73; CUL EDC 7/16/11/4 (Melton).

MARSH AND FENLAND

Three basic types of marshland are distinguished in medieval documents: tidal marsh, freshwater marsh (fenland) and turbary. Tidal or salt marshes, comprising deposits of marine clay and silt which flooded at each high tide, were far more commonplace around the coast and estuaries of thirteenth-century Suffolk than today, partly due to the cumulative effect of marshland reclamations in subsequent centuries, but also due to changing sea-levels: sea-level at Great Yarmouth is estimated to have been about 4 metres lower in the mid-thirteenth century than at present. Hence the place now known as Easton [Bavents] Broad comprised the landward edge of an extensive tidal salt marsh in the Middle Ages, which was open to the North Sea through a series of meandering creeks. However, after *c.* 1275 increased storm activity and, perhaps, a sudden rise in the sea-level resulted in marine inundation at vulnerable spots and the subsequent destruction of salt marsh: 80 acres were submerged at Aldeburgh between 1290 and 1341.[2] Tidal marshes were colonized by a narrow range of species of short grasses, which provided extensive grazing for sheep in particular: sheep were more agile over the uneven ground than cattle, and better able to graze on the low grass. Communal access to these marshes was often limited, and lords leased their grazing rights to local farmers, which generated annual revenue of more than £4 at Easton Bavents in the 1330s, and in 1304–5 the herbage from 2 acres of salt marsh near Woodbridge fetched 17s. Marsh was sometimes included in the landholdings of lesser tenants: in the 1270s Adam de Blundeston's holding contained 6 acres of arable land and 7 acres of salt marsh.[3]

Tidal marshes also presented opportunities for salt making, although the number of salt pans around Suffolk's coast had declined during the late eleventh century and few signs of the industry are detectable in the later Middle Ages. The tidal creeks and fleets that intersected these marshes presented other opportunities for profit. Numerous baskets, nets, kiddles and weirs (built of wattle and wood, and shaped like the letter V) were fixed inside the mouths of the rivers Alde, Deben and Orwell on mudflats exposed at low tide to trap fish swept along by tidal flows. The largest estuarine weirs were highly valued, judging from the substantial entry fines paid when their ownership changed hands, and the illegal construction of weirs was closely monitored: the jurors of Lothingland hundred reported disapprovingly to royal commissioners in 1279

---

[2] Rackham, *Countryside*, pp. 376, 381; Bailey, 'Suffolk Domesday' pp. 18–19 (Easton); Bailey, '*Per Impetum Maris*', pp. 192–3; *Inquisitiones Nonarum* (London, 1807), p. 92 (Aldeburgh).

[3] SROI v5/19/1.2 (Easton); CUL EDC 7/16/11/3 (Woodbridge); *RH*, ii, p. 185 (Blundeston).

that Roger de Colville had wrongly raised a weir in the Wicfleet in Carleton. Oyster beds abounded along these rivers. Finally, and most obviously, these marshy creeks provided a safe anchorage for small boats: around a dozen boats were routinely beached in Easton marsh each winter, for which a small charge was levied, and the lord also raised a few more pennies by permitting fishermen to dry their nets.[4]

Freshwater marshes are described as either marsh (*mariscus*, which was either silt or peat fen) or turbary (*turbarium*), the distinction being that peat turves could be dug from the latter. They existed in close proximity, for the canons of Blythburgh priory noted the existence of both among their landholdings in Henham. The most extensive areas of freshwater peat fen were located in the extreme north-west and north-east of Suffolk, the former comprising the south-east edge of the vast medieval Fenland. These fens contained outcrops of rough grassy pasture, although large areas were waterlogged in winter. They were navigable in shallow-draft boats, and in some places 'lodes' had been cut to improve navigation. An inland port at Lakenheath was linked to the Little Ouse by a navigable lode, and almost two-thirds of this vast parish comprised peat fen. Communal rights existed over some areas of marsh, yielding a wide range of resources for local communities. The manor of Lakenheath appointed a 'marsh reeve' each year to supervise this process, charged with protecting wildfowl and fish, and ensuring 'the use of customary nets and traps, and no others'.[5]

Peat itself (*turba*) was dug from small patches of wetland throughout Suffolk, including places that were some distance from the Fenland. In the 1280s the manor of Coney Weston included a small turbary of 2 acres; a small lay manor in Hopton included 10 acres of turbary among the resources of the demesne; and the villeins of Hinton were required to dig turves as part of their labour services. The careful record and exploitation of even small turbaries reflects the importance of peat, which was probably the single most important source of fuel in East Anglia in the twelfth and thirteenth centuries. Likewise, expanses of marsh could be found along river valleys some distance from either the Fenland or the coast, and were evidently valued. In 1251 the Bramford demesne included 32 acres of freshwater marsh valued at 14d. per acre; in 1305 a free tenant of Hadleigh paid 6d. rent each year for half an acre of marsh

4 Bailey, 'Suffolk Domesday', pp. 29, 41, 49–50; Bacon, *Annals*, p. 125; W. G. Arnott, *Orwell Estuary: The Story of Ipswich River* (Ipswich, 1973), p. 90; W. G. Arnott, *Alde Estuary: The Story of a Suffolk River* (Ipswich, 1952), pp. 49, 54; M. Bailey, 'Coastal Fishing off South East Suffolk in the Century after the Black Death', *PSIA* 37 (1992), p. 110; *RH*, ii, p. 192 (Carleton); SROI v5/19/1.1 – 1.10 (Easton).

5 Harper-Bill, *Blythburgh*, ii, pp. 166–7 (Henham); Bailey, 'Lakenheath', pp. 2–3; CUL EDC 7/15/11/1/4, m. 3 (Lakenheath).

in Layham fen; and the tenants of the abbey of St Edmund in Pakenham enjoyed rights over 400 acres of 'common pasture and of marsh and turbary in the vill'.[6]

The largest turbaries supported major peat workings, especially in the wetlands of north-east Suffolk and south-east Norfolk, where in the thirteenth century perhaps over 12 million turves were extracted each year. The large pits created by this work were flooded by successive marine surges after the end of the thirteenth century, which severely disrupted the industry and formed the Broads. Fritton had a thriving peat-digging industry, the sales from which generated over three-quarters of the manor's income in 1317–18. This regular activity created a huge hole, 2 miles long, 200 yards wide and five yards deep, which filled with water in the fourteenth and fifteenth centuries to form Fritton lake. Manor courts carefully controlled the cutting of peat, reflecting its importance as a resource, regulating when it was cut (usually the spring), who could cut it (usually residents with common rights), how much they could take, and where they might dispose of it. Residents of Eriswell were each allowed to cut 4,000 turves a year for domestic use, while in Brandon thousands of peat turves were sold to outsiders for a nominal fee. In the early fourteenth century around 100,000 turves were prepared annually at Lakenheath and sent to the monastery at Ely. Sods of turf covered with vegetation (known as 'flakkes') were also cut to construct field banks and to line house roofs. The income from such activities could be lucrative. Peat marshes along the upper reaches of the Butley river between Eyke and Chillesford – which were not especially extensive – yielded between £11 and £16 each year at the end of the thirteenth century.[7]

Freshwater marshes offered a plentiful supply of fish. Settlements along the Fenland edge contained many residents described as 'fishermen', who leased or owned their own boats and worked designated fisheries. The rights of the Lakenheath demesne over freshwater fisheries were habitually leased, and could fetch over £15 per annum, which equalled the cash yield of rents from land holdings on the manor. These fisheries were equipped with stipulated numbers of weirs and kiddles, and carried boating rights over them. Lakenheath market was well known for its freshwater fish, where hungry traders could buy hot eel

6 *PR*, ii, pp. 142, 212, 215 (Coney Weston, Hopton, Pakenham); Rackham, *Countryside*, p. 359; Harper-Bill, *Blythburgh*, ii, pp. 157–8 (Hinton); CUL EDC G3/27, f. 194 (Bramford); *PSIA* 11 (1903), p. 157 (Layham).

7 N. Scarfe, *The Suffolk Landscape* (London, 1972), p. 182; Rackham, *Countryside*, p. 358 (Fritton); Bailey, *Marginal Economy*, pp. 163–4; Bailey, 'Lakenheath', p. 7; PRO SC6/1005/7, 8, 10, 12 (Butley); A. Winchester, *The Harvest of the Hills: Rural Life in Northern England and the Scottish Borders, 1400–1700* (Edinburgh, 2000), pp. 126–8.

pasties, a local delicacy perhaps. Eels were sufficiently common in Lakenheath to be used as a currency for rent, and to be sold in large quantities: for example, in 1333 Thomas Doune was accused of failing to deliver to another merchant 8,000 eels worth £7. Marshes also provided a rich supply of wildfowl, although it was the preserve of lords. The monks of Ely received an ample supply of ducks and swans from the fens of Lakenheath, where cranes and bitterns were also commonplace, and the lord of Iken battled against the use of illegal snares to trap his ducks. A swannery was developed as a commercial venture at Easton Bavents in the fifteenth century, and heron farms were developed on manors in the Waveney valley: that at Mettingham produced around forty herons a year, some for commercial profit. The rearing of geese was a legitimate enterprise for local residents with access to marsh, where large numbers were raised on a commercial basis.[8]

Freshwater marshes provided a suitable habitat for a wider range of grasses and plants than salt marshes, some of which had other uses. Reeds (*arundo*) were cut annually from shallow water, and made good thatch: they were well regarded, judging by the regularity with which bundles were sent from Mildenhall fen to other manors on the Bury abbey estates, and by the ease with which the manor of Dunningworth disposed of thirty-two cartloads of reed. Sedge (*lesch*) was an even better thatch, although it could only be found in large quantities in the Fenland, and its sharp edges made it notoriously painful to work. The Lakenheath demesne raised nearly £6 in 1348 from the sale of 7,000 bundles of sedge, and by the early sixteenth century its residents regularly supplied large quantities to the Cambridge market. Any sedge cut in certain common areas of Mildenhall fen could be taken by boat to Ely for sale, yet residents and outsiders routinely cut and distributed sedge from other areas. In October 1429 a total of twenty-one people were amerced 61s. 6d. for illegally removing an astonishing 147,000 bundles of sedge from Mildenhall fen, and many of these illicit bundles were shipped down the river Lark to unknown destinations.[9]

---

[8] Bailey, 'Lakenheath', pp. 4, 6; CUL EDC 7/15/11/1/4, m. 3, lease of fisheries to Richard de Venella in June 1311; CUL EDC 7/15/1/10; 7/15/11/1/5, court held 30 May 1314; 7/15/11/1/9, m. 21; CUL EDC 7/15/11/1/4, m. 3; 7/15/1/10 (all Lakenheath); Richmond, *John Hopton*, pp. 88–90 (Easton); SROB HA507/1/33 (Mettingham); SROI HD32/292/390, m. 66 (Iken).

[9] Bailey, *Marginal Economy*, p. 164; PRO SC6/999/25 (Dunningworth); Rackham, *Countryside*, p. 382; J. S. Lee, 'Feeding the Colleges: Cambridge's Food and Fuel Supplies, 1450–1560', *EcHR* 56 (2003), pp. 253–4; CUL EDC 7/15/1/14 (Lakenheath); SROB E18/451/3, courts held July 1401 and July 1404, and E18/451/4, October 1429 (Mildenhall).

HEATHLAND

The landscape of medieval Suffolk's eastern and western extremities was dominated by heathland, which covered thousands of acres in the Breckland and the Sandlings. Heaths are associated with light, sandy and acidic soils, and characterized by heather, ling, furze and bracken. Heathland is not a 'natural' landscape feature, and will quickly revert to woodland if left alone, because its existence depends upon regular human intervention and management. As heathland was widespread in these parts of medieval Suffolk, it follows that local communities nurtured it as a valuable resource. It also follows that the destruction of this striking, evocative and starkly beautiful medieval landscape during the nineteenth and twentieth centuries was a consequence of the declining usefulness of heathland during a period of rapid and extensive agricultural change. In the post-medieval centuries it became regarded as 'wasteland', desolate and agriculturally useless, and the inevitable target for improvement by progressive farmers.[10]

Heathland provided a valuable use for soils that were uncultivable under medieval agrarian technology. It offered low-grade permanent pasture mainly for sheep and rabbits, both of which grazed close to the ground and therefore perpetuated the conditions under which many heathland plants flourished. It is not coincidental that the largest sheep flocks were located on the Sandlings and Breckland, particularly where heath lay in close proximity to marshland. Medieval rabbits flourished only on sandy heathlands and were rare and fragile beasts, unlike their ubiquitous and robust modern descendants. They had been introduced to East Anglia by the early thirteenth century, and within 200 years greatly enlarged commercial rabbit warrens were intensively managed for huge profits. Heathland plants could be put to other uses. When permitted to grow to maturity, gorse (*whynnes, genecta*) was extremely useful as a clean hot-burning fuel, and a good fencing material in dry hedges. Heather or ling was fast-growing and could be used as either thatch or fuel. Bracken (*fugerium*) was also an excellent fuel, capable of fuelling furnaces for brickmaking, and it could also be used as litter for livestock, thatch and even food. Broom (*myrica*) was cut for use as either a fuel or to make broomsticks. The sandy soils on which heaths thrived, and the underlying chalk, were also dug and quarried for use in building projects.[11]

10 J. Sheail and M. Bailey, 'The History of the Rabbit in Breckland', in *Thetford Forest Park: The Ecology of a Pine Forest*, ed. P. Ratcliffe and J. Claridge, Forestry Commission Technical Paper 13 (Edinburgh, 1996), pp. 16–20; P. Armstrong, *The Changing Landscape* (Lavenham, 1975), figs. 34, 35.

11 M. Bailey, 'The Rabbit and the Medieval East Anglian Economy', *AgHR* 36 (1988), pp. 1–20; Rackham, *Countryside*, pp. 282–96; Winchester, *Harvest of the Hills*,

Some communal rights existed over most heaths. The tenants of Hardwick paid 22d. each year for access to a specified amount of bracken on the heath, and tenants in Westley had rights to graze fixed numbers of animals at stipulated times on their common heath. Yet 'a certain several heath containing 27 acres of pasture' also existed in Westley, whose sole use was restricted to the landholder. Several (or private) heaths were valued resources, judging by the care with which they were recorded and the disputes they occasionally attracted. Eustace de Berningham held 20 acres of heathland (*bruera*) on his demesne at Barningham, and Roger de Akethorpe's holding near Lowestoft in the 1270s comprised a mere 20 acres of arable land but 60 acres of heath: in the 1280s the jurors of Blackbourne hundred accused St Salvator's Hospital (in Bury St Edmunds) of holding 120 acres of heath at West Stow in severalty 'when it ought to be common to the vill'. Some tenant holdings also contained heath, such as the 20 acres held by twenty unnamed sokemen in Troston and the 3 *acreware* of heathland held by Thomas de Nauton near Snape. In 1336 an Iken resident held 1 acre of heath on villein tenure, and a several heath belonged to the borough of Ipswich.[12]

Whether several or common, heathland had to be managed carefully if its resources were to be sustainable. Manorial courts routinely punished those who overstocked the heaths with livestock or used them when they had no common rights. The manorial court at Leiston was quick to amerce local residents for cutting heathland plants in the wrong season, commoners at Brandon were not permitted to mow bracken before 25 March each year, the court at Great Barton temporarily banned furze cutting in 1478, when stocks were low, and the Lackford court moved persistently to counter the use of mattocks to dig out the roots of bracken and furze. The careful management of heaths by medieval communities is evident in the election annually of a 'keeper of the heath' from among the unfree landholders at Staverton, a post that was still active in the fifteenth century. His responsibility was to ensure that pasturing and the removal of fuel by commoners were properly observed.[13]

Grazing by sheep and rabbits prevented certain plants from growing to maturity, and so designated areas of heath were routinely withdrawn from

pp. 133–8. For an example of the illegal cutting of broom at Walton, see SROI HA119/50/3/18, m. 69.

12 *PSIA* I (1895), pp. 183–4 (Hardwick); SROB 449/6/18, ff. 1–4 (Westley); SROI HD1538/207/2, court held November 1333 (Snape); *PR*, ii, pp. 214, 224, 241 (West Stow, Barningham, Troston); *RH*, ii, p. 184 (Lowestoft); Bacon, *Annals*, p. 128 (Ipswich).

13 CUL Vanneck Ms, box 9, court held January 1449 (Leiston); Bacon Ms 294/4 (Brandon); SROB E18/151/3, court held October 1489 (Mildenhall); Bailey, *Marginal Economy*, p. 55; PRO SC6/1005/10; SROI HD1538/357/5, m. 4 (Staverton).

grazing to ensure that the furze, bracken and heather could flourish. Furze and bracken were often cultivated in carefully managed cycles of four to five years, and then cut and sold for profit. In the mid-thirteenth century furze grow-ing on 7 acres of heath at Elmswell was cut on a seven-year cycle (i.e. 1 acre every year), a harvest valued at 18d. per annum. The direct income from these activities could be lucrative on larger expanses of heathland, and in 1291–2 the manor of Dunningworth received £4 8s. from the sale of 'heathland', plus a further 36s. 3d. for 'dried furze': in 1293–4 the sale of 'heath' generated over £7 at Staverton, and in 1305–6 heather alone raised over £2. Small parcels on the 'north' and 'south' heaths of Easton Bavents were sold each year, often to local women, who presumably cut, dried, prepared and then sold various heathland plants for sale as fuel: interestingly, women also appear among those amerced at Walton for cutting furze illegally. Their labour must have been worth while, because the prices paid for leasing heathland were sometimes remarkably high: for example, 15s. for 2½ acres of heath in Easton in 1330–1, and in 1286–7 'heathland' fetched 3s. per acre at Staverton – significantly higher than the prevailing value of arable land on the manor. The local availability of large quantities of high-quality hot-burning fuel stimulated some industrial activity based on kilns, such as the pottery manufacture carried out on Hollesley heath in the 1280s.[14]

WOODS AND PARKS

Suffolk was not a well-wooded county at the time of Domesday Book (woods occupying no more than 10 per cent of its land surface), and some areas – most notably the Breckland, Fenland and Sandlings – had hardly any recorded woodland in 1086. Woodland tended to be concentrated on the heavier clays, and was most prominent in north-east Suffolk. Hence, when an eleventh-century benefactor offered the abbey of Bury St Edmunds a choice of three diverse Suffolk estates, the abbey chose Fressingfield because it 'abounded in woods'. The nature of the Domesday entries in northern Suffolk also indi-cates the existence of small areas of 'wood-pasture', open woodland where local communities had rights to graze animals and collect firewood, so that a sizeable area of the parish of Sotherton was devoted to wood-pasture in the late eleventh century. However, demographic and economic expansion in the twelfth and thirteenth centuries created pressure to convert wood-pasture to arable, and perhaps around one-half of Suffolk's woodland was grubbed

14 BL Harley Ms 230, f. 148 (Elmswell); PRO sc6/999/19 (Dunningworth); PRO sc6/1005/7, 11 (Staverton); Rackham, *Countryside*, p. 295; SROI v5/19/1.1 (Easton); SROI HA119/50/3/17, m. 24, and HA119/50/3/19, m. 105 (Walton); Scarfe, *Suffolk Landscape*, p. 182 (Hollesley).

out and ploughed for cultivation between 1086 and 1349. Rising pressure on resources also resulted in more intensive management of the remaining wood-pasture and woodland, which was increasingly parcelled off, enclosed by banking or fencing, exempt from communal rights, and intensively managed.[15]

Woodland consisted of many different types of trees, although oak was the dominant species in most woods, and hornbeam was widespread in north-east Suffolk. Staverton wood contained mainly oaks, but also elm, poplar, maple and elder. Woods dominated by other species were not unknown: for example, in the early thirteenth century John de Cove granted Blythburgh priory a holly wood in Covehithe, and a mix of oak and ash was common around Lax-field and Huntingfield.[16] The least wooded areas of Suffolk tended to contain fewer, but larger, woods, while the most wooded areas tended to contain more woods of smaller size. In western Suffolk, where woodland was relatively scarce, large woods are frequently recorded: a 160-acre wood in Elmswell, a 246-acre wood in Hitcham, and a 100-acre wood, and a separate 'grove' of 12 acres, in Hartest. In contrast, Jurdyez grange, located around Sibton and Peasenhall, included 143 acres of woodland split into ten separate woods: significantly, the largest – the 33-acre Falshamhall wood – was described locally as a 'great wood'. Sibton abbey held a 3-acre wood in Rendham, the 'great wood' of Westleton contained a mere 16 acres, and the six demesne woods of Hunt-ingfield were mainly between 3 and 8 acres in size, with one of 100 acres. As these examples imply, most woods were part of the demesnes of high-status landlords, although some tenants also held slivers of woodland as part of their landholdings. In the 1280s William de Monastery was the tenant of 8 acres of wood in Ricklinghall, of which he held 1 acre himself and John de Croue held 7 acres. In the 1280s eight separate woods, varying in size from 2 to 10 acres, held by small lay manors or free tenants are recorded in Whelnetham Parva.[17]

By *c.* 1300 woodland was scarce and valuable in Suffolk, and therefore carefully managed to provide mature timber, coppice and faggots, and some fodder for animals. Timber was matured for twenty five to 100 years before being cut for beams and planks. Often these mature trees were felled to

---

[15] I have learned much from discussing and visiting the woodland of Suffolk with Oliver Rackham, whose scholarship strongly influences the following discussion. Williamson, *Shaping Medieval Landscapes*, p. 162; *HistA*, pp. 64–5; Warner, *Greens, Commons*, pp. 20–4.

[16] Hoppitt, 'Parks', p. 190; Harper-Bill, *Blythburgh*, ii, p. 190 (North Hales); CUL Vanneck Ms, box 6 (Huntingfield), and box 7, court held April 1462 (Laxfield).

[17] BL Harley Ms 230, f. 148 (Elmswell); CUL EDR G3/27, ff. 162, 172 (Hitcham, Hartest); Denney, *Sibton Abbey*, pp. 45–6, 62 (Peasenhall, Rendham, Sibton, Westleton); Richmond, *John Hopton*, p. 57; CUL Vanneck Ms, box 6 (Huntingfield); *PR*, ii, pp. 152–5, 214 (Whelnetham, Rickinghall).

order for construction projects some distance from the wood: in the 1440s oaks from Wetheringsett wood were chosen, felled and then dispatched to Ely for this purpose. In 1391 estate officials assessed the value of standing trees at an extraordinary £6 13s. 4d. per acre in the demesne woods at Lidgate and Badmondsfield, which equates to an overall capital value of £3,275 for the two woods: a fortune by any medieval standard. A single oak from Hundon park could fetch 18s. in the 1370s, and oaks from Lidgate were sold for around 13s. 4d. each in the 1420s, which indicates trees of considerable size and maturity. Other types of wood were felled in shorter cycles of five to twenty years, yielding smaller beams, poles or rods, and firewood. In 1250 Elmswell wood contained 160 acres, 'of which it is possible to sell 10 acres per annum', implying that timber was matured for felling on a cycle of sixteen years; Badmondsfield manor had 50 acres of underwood in le Esthey, of which 5 acres were cut each year, realizing around 4s. per acre; the underwood in Hepworth wood was cut on a three-year cycle yielding 3s. 4d. per acre. Nuts were also collected each year. Woodcutters worked felled wood to order. Poles from Lidgate park were prepared *in situ* for use in tenter frames, and small sharp 'spets' – used to suspend herring and sprats in smokehouses – were made in large quantities in Laxfield wood. Bundles of faggots were made in many woods, and those at Hinderclay sold at 3s. per hundred in the 1320s: other woodland products, such as loppings and bark, were sold, and underwood (*subboscum*) fetched 3s. 4d. per acre. Clearly, the income from such activity could be substantial, and the sale of timber and faggots comprised comfortably the major source of revenue on the small manor of Westhall. Even manors in relatively unwooded areas, such as Hinderclay, could receive around £11 per annum in the early fourteenth century from the sale of various woodland products.[18]

After the Norman Conquest some land was enclosed to create private parks, status symbols that provided deer and recreation for their owner. Many of the earliest and biggest parks belonged to the greater landlords, and were situated close to their residential seats: the earls of Clare established one at Hundon; the abbot of Bury St Edmunds created parks at Assington and Elmsett; and by *c.* 1300 Roger Bigod IV, earl of Norfolk, possessed nine in Suffolk. Yet park ownership had also descended the social scale during the course of the thirteenth century, as lesser landlords sought to establish them as an assertion

18 *HistA*, pp. 64–5; Hoppitt, 'Parks', p. 164 (Wetheringsett); PRO DL 43/14/3, ff. 20, 24 (Lidgate, Badsmondfield); PRO sc6/999/26 (Hundon); SROB E3/11/1.2, court held April 1414 and E3/11/1.4 (Lidgate); BL Harley Ms 230, f. 148 (Elmswell); *PSIA* 1 (1895), pp. 39–40 (Hepworth); in 1311 officials of the prior of Ixworth collected nuts in Badwell Ash wood, BL Add. Roll 9131 (reference from Nick Amor); CUL Vanneck Ms, box 7, court held April 1479 (Laxfield); Bacon Ms 451 (Hinderclay); Richmond, *John Hopton*, pp. 75–6 (Westhall).

of their status at a time when their incomes were buoyant: for example, two minor landlords developed parks in Badingham. Parks contained different types of land use, segregated into discrete subdivisions by hedges, ditches, banks and gates, but were usually dominated by woodland and wood-pasture, interspersed with open 'launds'. In 1200 around fourteen parks had been established in Suffolk, but over a hundred by 1350. Most parks were located on clay soils (they were relatively rare in the Breckland and Sandlings) and often situated on higher ground around parish boundaries, where reserves of pasture and waste were greatest at the time of their creation. Rishangles park was created during the twelfth century by enclosing existing woodland and common pasture around the edge of the parish. The greatest parks covered hundreds of acres (e.g. Framlingham and Hundon at 600 acres), and most contained between 200 and 300 acres: yet Glemsford park contained 92 acres, and Barking 9 acres.[19]

The main objective of park management was to raise deer for hunting or culling (and then dispatch to the lord's table), which involved tending the herd and the maintenance of the boundary fence, hedging and ditching, the park gates and perhaps a park lodge. This was an expensive business, and the costs of upkeep of even moderate parks could be high, perhaps around £5–10 per annum. Consequently, parks were managed to provide other sources of income, especially after the mid-fourteenth century, when spiralling costs, and perhaps rising mortality among fallow deer as the climate cooled, caused interest in hunting and game to dwindle. Staverton park was reported to be without deer in 1382, although this may have owed something to the Peasants' Revolt the previous year, and Hundon park experimented with a stud farm of nearly thirty horses to generate income. In most places woodland became the most lucrative and dependable source of cash from parks. The main responsibilities of the park-keeper at Wetheringsett (who in the 1440s received a handsome salary of £4 11s. 3d. per annum) were to supervise the felling of mature oaks, the coppicing of hornbeam, and the generation of a small income from the sale of pannage and undergrowth. By the end of the fifteenth century the management of woodland represented the major use of parks, although the largest still offered some prospect of genteel pleasure: in the early sixteenth century the duke of Suffolk and Mary 'the French queen' hunted foxes in Staverton park and then enjoyed a meal and undisclosed 'fun and games' beneath the oaks.[20]

19 *HistA*, 66–7; Hoppitt, 'Parks', pp. 9, 34–5, 64–72, 81, 82, 111, 118, 221–4, 231, 277–8; CUL EDR G3/27, ff. 156, 177 (Glemsford, Barking).

20 Hoppitt, 'Parks', pp. 132–46, 164–7, 181–4.

FIELD SYSTEMS

The layout and pattern of arable fields had a significant influence upon the Suffolk landscape. The majority of this cultivated land lay in irregular open fields, rather than in large 'Midland'-style fields, although a sizeable minority was arranged in manifold smaller fields enclosed by hedges and ditches. Each irregular field contained many parcels of land belonging to different farmers, and was 'open' in the sense that no permanent barriers – such as ditches, hedges or fences – stood between each parcel. These individual parcels were known as 'pecia' (comparable to the Midland 'selion'), and their boundaries were marked by stone markers, wooden posts (known as metes or bounds) or narrow access paths. The most common size of pecia was half an acre (2 roods), and consequently many vills contained hundreds of pecia within their open fields. In a few parts of Suffolk groups of contiguous pecia were aggregated into identifiable, and often compact, units called 'quarentena', equivalent to the Midland 'furlong'. The size of individual quarentena varied: Thanklesfurlong in Wangford contained 114 acres, and Downdale 86 acres 1 rood.[21] In many places the open fields of one settlement ran into those of another, delimited only by a grassy bank.

At this point, however, similarities with the Midland system cease. Midland furlongs were aggregated into two or three great, and relatively permanent, fields, but this arrangement was exceptional in medieval Suffolk, where fields were sufficiently unimportant as an agrarian unit that residents did not bother to enumerate them routinely. In Suffolk the term 'field' is used indiscriminately to describe both great fields created by groups of quarentena and a single quarentena. At least eleven 'fields' are mentioned in medieval Brandon, although a later survey of the town in 1566 records twelve, including the 'amalgamation' of the earlier named North and East fields into 'Townlandfield'. In sixteenth-century Mildenhall, a large and complex settlement, around forty 'fields' are recorded.[22] Another significant difference with the Midland system is the prevalence of larger blocks of (usually demesne) land and of hedged enclosures and crofts interspersed among the open fields. In some places these enclosures were neither numerous nor large (containing perhaps an acre or two), yet in others they comprised many acres and dominated the local landscape. Some of the larger enclosures even had distinct subdivisions within them or contained land held by more than one tenant: a demesne enclosure

---

[21] Bailey, *Marginal Economy*, p. 41.

[22] Bailey, *Marginal Economy*, p. 41; G. A. Thornton, *A History of Clare, Suffolk* (Cambridge, 1928), pp. 19–20; CUL EDR G3/27, f. 189; SROI VII/2/1.1 (Brandon); M. R. Postgate, 'The Field Systems of East Anglia', in *Studies of Field Systems in the British Isles*, ed. A. R. H. Baker and R. A. Butlin (Cambridge, 1973), pp. 292–3.

in Hinderclay called Westcroft, containing at least 30 acres, had five notional subdivisions or 'wents'.[23] The layout of fields in medieval Suffolk was thus highly complex and varied, and, at times, challenges the conventional distinction between 'open' and 'enclosed' land.

The fluidity and limited importance of the 'field' in Suffolk reflects significant differences in the way its open fields were organized and exploited compared with the Midlands. The existence of three regular fields in the Midland system reflected the imposition of a three-course rotation of cropping (winter-sown crop, spring-sown crop, then fallow) upon each of them in turn, whereas the irregularity of Suffolk's open fields reflects the fact that they were not subject to communal regulations anything like as formal or wide ranging. Some communal rights existed over most of the open fields of medieval Suffolk, because the continued use of strip farming and open fields only made real sense if local farmers possessed some kind of common rights over the land of others, but they were mainly restricted to a narrow range of pasturing rights over the fallow arable: very little cropping was organized communally.

The most basic, and widespread, communal regulation in Suffolk was the right to pasture animals on the stubble of the open fields for a few weeks after the harvest, when animal feed was scarce, a period known locally as the 'shack'. This right of shack started once the sheaves of corn had been removed from the fields following the harvest (notionally 1 August), when the stubble still provided some 'bite' for livestock, but ceased sometime in September according to local custom, when the quality of grazing had diminished and farmers needed to prepare the land for the next crop. In some parts of Suffolk, communal grazing rights over the fallow arable ceased after shack; in others, these rights continued until February or March and then ceased until the beginning of the next period of shack. The six months between February and the harvest, when no communal rights existed over the fallow arable, were often called the 'several' or 'closed' time. Communally imposed cropping rotations, in which farmers were required to sow specified areas of their land with winter crops and other areas with spring crops, did not apply. Instead individuals were largely free to crop their land as they saw fit. In late September and October they would plough, weed and manure some of their land for sowing with 'winter' crops (mainly wheat and rye): any animals on a neighbouring strip of fallow arable would be tethered or penned by their owners to prevent trampling on the sown strips. Other lands were grazed, ploughed and manured until the spring months and then sown with crops such as barley, peas and oats, and thus were effectively half-year fallows. Arable land left fallow during the whole of the year was manured, weeded, marled and ploughed ready for

---

[23] Stone, 'Hinderclay', p. 619; Postgate, 'Field Systems of East Anglia', p. 287; H. L. Gray, *English Field Systems* (Cambridge, Mass., 1915), p. 310.

sowing in the following agrarian year (*terra warecta*). Occasionally arable land was left uncultivated for more than one agrarian cycle to allow the recuperation of the soil and the regeneration of rough pasture, known as ley land (*terra frisca*).[24]

The management of Suffolk's field systems by the local community was also different from the Midland system. The formal regulations of the Midlands were enforced by common herdsmen and the heavy use of village bye-laws, but neither is much in evidence in medieval Suffolk for the obvious reason that a less rule-bound field system needed less formal management. In Suffolk the manorial court of the main landlord in each vill (the 'chief lord') assumed responsibility for enforcing agricultural regulations, usually through cases brought by either the presentment jury or manorial officials (usually the messor). They prosecuted individuals who overstocked common pastures and fallows; those who pastured animals on the fields, but did not possess rights of common within the vill; and those whose wandering animals had trampled the lord's corn. Bye-laws were rare in the thirteenth and fourteenth centuries, but became more numerous and significant in the fifteenth century, when they usually focused upon controlling animals and access to the stubble after harvest. The growing use of the bye-law to regulate fields reflects a more general increase in its usage by local communities.

For all these generalizations about field systems in medieval Suffolk, subtle variations in their layout and operation are evident across the county. Three main subcategories of field systems are discernible: irregular commonfield systems with partially regulated cropping, irregular commonfield systems with non-regulated cropping, and non-common subdivided fields.

Irregular commonfield systems with partially regulated cropping

The most formal field system in Suffolk existed on the poorest and lightest soils at the western and eastern fringes of the county, particularly in the Breckland and on the chalk clays of the south-west. The layout of fields here bears most resemblance to those of the Midlands: land parcels were small; a tenant's holdings tended to be scattered fairly evenly around the fields; arable enclosures were largely absent; and fields tended to be enumerated more formally. The small size of individual land parcels reflects the effects of fragmentation and the relative scarcity of arable in these areas. For example, the mean size of demesne pecia on the two main manors in Barnham was 1¼ acres and 1 acre, and 1½ acres at Wangford. In 1348 277 acres of customary land at Culford lay

---

[24] B. M. S. Campbell, 'Commonfield Origins: The Regional Dimension', in *The Origins of Open-Field Agriculture*, ed. T. Rowley (London, 1981), pp. 113–14; Bailey, *Marginal Economy*, pp. 56–85; open and closed seasons were also known in north-west England, Winchester, *Harvest of the Hills*, pp. 54–6.

in 554 pecia, an average of 2 roods, while in 1357 the demesne lay in 47 pecia averaging 5 acres 2 roods: 94 per cent of the demesne arable lay in open fields. The Culford demesne was evenly distributed around the fields of the vill, and most of the original villein tenementa exhibited a similar tendency. Although the tenementa of Henry Clark and Geoffrey Aylwy were mainly concentrated in the north and west of Culford's fields, the majority of other holdings were spread more-or-less equitably around the open fields: the tenementum of Henry Acke was widely distributed and the 14-acre holding of Henry le Huxter was spread in small strips (of mainly 2 roods) from Lemmerswong in the north-east of Culford to Wickethornhill in the south-west. Some aggregation of quarentena into a few larger fields is apparent, although fields operating on a classic two- or three-field system are unknown. Brandon had around twelve fields, Exning seven, Herringswell five, and Newmarket one field.[25]

Communal regulations over the arable in this system were relatively formal by East Anglian standards. All tenants were allowed to graze their animals on the grain stubble with few restrictions during the shack. They were also permitted daytime access to any fallow arable until 2 February.[26] Night-time access to the fallow arable after the shack was more carefully regulated. All sheep were organized into private or collective folds and each fold was tightly penned on a small area of fallow within a defined area of the open fields. The folded sheep were gradually moved across the fallows during the course of the year to ensure that their valuable manure (known as 'tathe') was targeted effectively on the thin soils. Thus tenants in Lidgate who failed to put their sheep in the lord's fold, either for short periods (e.g. 'between Michaelmas and All Saints') or for the whole year, were promptly amerced in the manor court. After 2 February, when of course the area sown with crops gradually increased, all access to the fallows was restricted solely to herds and flocks organized by the owner of a foldcourse. This was also known as the 'several time', and, for example, the Lidgate court demanded to know on what grounds a tenant claimed to have access to 'several pasture [over the fallow] at Northfeld between and February and 1st August'.[27]

A foldcourse was the right to graze animals, principally sheep, across a

---

[25] BL Add. Ms 42055, ff. 25–46 (Culford demesne) and ff. 8–22 (villein holdings); SROB HA513/30/2, final folios (Barnham); Bailey, *Marginal Economy*, p. 45; CUL EDR G3/27, f. 189; SROI VII/2/1.1 (Brandon); PRO DL 43/14/3, f. 24 (Lidgate); *AHEW*, ii, p. 278; P. May, *Newmarket: Medieval and Tudor* (published privately), p. 10.

[26] SROB E18/451/6 and see also E18/451/3, court held 6 September 1404 (Mildenhall); E3/11/1.4, m. 2 (Lidgate); E3/15.12/1.13, courts held November 1390 and October 1409 (Lackford); E7/24/5.1 (Herringswell).

[27] E. Kerridge, *The Common Fields of England* (Manchester, 1992), p. 27; SROB E3/11/1.1 and 1.3, court held September 1416 (Lidgate).

specified area of both arable and pasture. The sheep would graze on the pasture during the day, and then be penned on a small area of fallow arable at night. Hence a designated area of the open fields and heath constituted one fold-course, other areas constituted another, and so on. The number of foldcourses in each vill varied, from perhaps two or three to a dozen or so, which indicates that their ownership was restricted to just a few, privileged, individuals. The biggest and most important foldcourses in every vill belonged to the manorial lord, who often maintained flocks containing hundreds of sheep. Lords who possessed foldcourses, but chose not to run a demesne flock, could fill them instead with peasant sheep and charge for the privilege. The organization of the foldcourse system was the responsibility of the capital lord of the vill, who used his manorial officials to organize cropping and folding on the ground, and his manor court to amerce dissidents.[28]

Villeins were normally compelled to place their sheep in the lord's fold (usually without charge), either in the demesne fold or, where their sheer number made this arrangement impractical, in a separate village fold: the number of peasant sheep at Barnham in 1283, and those at Lakenheath in the 1340s, exceeded 2,300. In vills such as these a separate communal flock, called a 'common' or 'collect' fold, ran as one foldcourse, although the responsibility for its organization and shepherding was firmly vested in the lord. In some vills all cattle – with the exception of oxen and milking cows – were also organized in a communal herd. A few peasants, including some villeins, had the right to hold their own foldcourse, but these were smaller and inferior to the demesne folds: indeed, any tenant of the manor of Easthall in Culford who held his own fold was still required to place his sheep in the main fold of the capital lord, the abbot of Bury St Edmunds, for two nights out of three. The presence of a number of folds, belonging to either different manorial lords or peasants, within the fields of a single vill created a complex system. The complexity, however, brought operational flexibility, and the lords responsible for supervising field arrangements in a given vill were prepared to adjust foldcourse arrangements temporarily, as the balance shifted between the numbers of sheep and the extent of permanent pasture and fallow in the vill.[29]

The foldcourse was therefore a complex and relatively formal system of organizing and regulating the use of the fallow arable, and its primary purpose was to ensure that the light soils, whose nutrients were very prone to leach

[28] Bailey, *Marginal Economy*, pp. 65–74.

[29] *1283 Lay Subsidy*, pp. xxx–xxxi; Bailey, *Marginal Economy*, p. 250; 'a common fold of customary sheep' was run at Great Barton, BL Harley Ms. 3977, f. 86; BL Add. Ms 42055, f. 8 (Culford); for a communal cattle herd, see BL Harley Ms. 3977, f. 82; NRO Ms 13200 (Icklingham).

during arable cultivation, received as much replenishing manure as possible. This objective was best achieved by organizing sheep into large collective flocks and then folding them each night on compact blocks of fallow arable, which in turn required some communal co-ordination of sowing patterns by all those whose arable land lay within the area of that particular foldcourse. Consequently, quarentena were grouped together and organized into 'shifts', onto which a communal cropping and fallowing pattern was imposed for perhaps two or three years, to ensure that compact areas of fallow were available to the foldcourse. The demesne land at Stansfield was allocated evenly among three 'seasons' or shifts: 31 per cent in the 'first season', 37 per cent in the 'second season' and 32 per cent in the third.[30] A shift was a short-term arrangement, a grouping of lands for cropping purposes with no permanence beyond its cycle, whereas Midland fields – and the cropping/fallowing patterns imposed upon them – were more regular and permanent. The flexibility of this system enabled sheep folds to be concentrated upon the better soils lying in the river valleys, which consequently could sustain more demanding rotations than the poorer arable on the higher land. Hence the better land was cultivated regularly, and known as 'infield', while the poorer arable was cropped for, say, two or three years and then left as a ley to recuperate for a number of years ('outfield'). This system of 'infield–outfield' was widely employed on the poorest soils of medieval East Anglia. The unploughed outfield soon reverted to scrub pasture.[31]

This type of irregular system is strongly associated with areas of poor soil and extensive low-grade pasture, either heathland or downland, which formed an integral and vital element of the pasturing arrangements. A good deal of this pasture was subject to common rights designed to accommodate livestock according to the needs of the foldcourses. Some areas of heathland were deemed 'intercommon', and therefore shared between more than one vill, while other areas were 'several' and could only be pastured as part of a designated foldcourse. Sheep were better suited to such rough pastures than other livestock, because they could graze lower and were good walkers, and consequently they dominated pastoral farming: flocks of thousands of sheep were kept in many Breckland vills in the thirteenth century.[32] The inherent infertility of the soil dictated that the intensity of farming was low by East Anglian standards, and that rye, barley and oats comprised the main crops. Up to half of the arable on demesnes was left unsown each year in the 1340s, and both yields per acre and yields per seed were poor to indifferent. About 60 per cent

[30] SROB E7/10/10.

[31] Bailey, *Marginal Economy*, pp. 57–63.

[32] Bailey, *Marginal Economy*, pp. 54–6; Campbell, *English Seigneurial Agriculture*, pp. 252–73, 449.

of the crops sown each year were spring sown, thus creating more half-year fallows which extended the amount of time available each year to manure and prepare the soil. Manure, supplied either by carts or direct from animals, was essential if these soils – whose nutrients were prone to leaching – were to be kept in regular cultivation, and the foldcourse system was effective at targeting the manure of sheep where it was most needed. In the 1320s an impressive 56 per cent of the demesne-sown area at Lakenheath was manured each year, a quarter of the enormous Mildenhall demesne was 'manured by men of the vill' in 1324, and 80 per cent of the fallow (*warecta*) at Eastern Bavents was manured in 1376–7. The high value placed upon manure in this system is clearly illustrated by the demand of the Lakenheath court that Robert Bolt answer 'for loss of dung to the lord' when he failed to put his sheep in the foldcourse and by the value of the compost of the lord's fold in Coney Weston, which was rated at 12d. per acre. Similarly, the homage of Fornham St Martin was amerced a hefty 20s. in 1344, when the 'lord's fold did not fertilize in the places where by custom it ought'.[33]

Irregular commonfield systems with non-regulated cropping

In *c.* 1300 this category of irregular open field system dominated the loams and clays of southern, central and eastern Suffolk. It is likely that in *c.* 1300 around three-quarters of the land area in many of these parishes was occupied by irregular open fields, and the area of permanent pasture was, by extension, relatively small.[34] The general layout of these open fields differed from those operating the 'foldcourse' system in four significant ways.

First, individual pecia tended to be larger, especially those belonging to the manorial demesne. For example, in 1289 the average parcel of tenant land in Redgrave was almost 2 acres (1,440 acres in 725 parcels), while in 1250 477 acres of the manor's demesne arable lay in 16 pecia at an average size of 30 acres: similarly, 15- to 17-acre blocks of demesne were common at Wetheringsett.

Second, the open fields were frequently interspersed with arable land enclosed by hedges and ditches, whose presence can be detected by field names containing the suffix '-croft'. Crofts comprised 12 per cent of the demesne arable at Fornham All Saints in 1302, 11 per cent at Redgrave in 1250, 15 per cent at Barking in 1251, 11 per cent at Wetheringsett and 12 per cent at Hitcham. Nor were enclosures confined to demesne land. A tenant at Cornard Parva held '2 acres lying in a croft called le Birches' in 1322, some tenant land

33 Bailey, *Marginal Economy*, tables 4.3, 4.10, and pp. 89–93; Bodleian Suffolk Rolls 21 (Mildenhall); SROI v5/19/1.6 (Easton); CUL EDC 7/15/11/1/6, m. 9 (Lakenheath); BL Harley Ms 230, f. 156 (Coney Weston); SROB E3/15.9/1.2, m. 13 (Fornham).

34 Hesse, 'Ickworth', pp. 17–18; Church, *Pakenham*, p. 7.

in thirteenth-century Ixworth Thorpe lay in places called 'Leyerescroft ... le Toftys ... Wodecroft ... Scymplingcroft and Coliscroft', the fields of Stowmarket were a mixture of crofts and irregular open fields, and a 20-acre 'close with ditches and hedges' lay in Rushfeld in Gislingham.[35]

Third, both demesne and tenant holdings tended to be clustered within certain parts of the open fields, rather than widely dispersed throughout them. This characteristic is evident among tenant holdings in Redgrave, and the arable belonging to Paynes tenementum in Walsham comprised a number of small strips in the open fields at the east end of the parish clustered around Paynes' messuage. The demesne at Fornham All Saints was clustered into four distinct groups: on the road to Westley, the road to Bury St Edmunds, the southern portion of the parish of Fornham St Genevieve, and the eastern portion of the parish of Fornham St Martin. Fourth, the relative absence of large areas of permanent pasture meant that numerous small greens and tyes feature more prominently in the landscape, many of which provided grazing rights to the residents colonizing their edges during the twelfth and thirteenth centuries.[36]

The existence of larger blocks of land in single ownership, the concentration of holdings in particular areas of the open fields, and the presence of enclosures reflects the limited importance of communal arrangements in this system. Fold rights were less commonplace and confined to the lighter loams (in places such as Blakenham, Hepworth, Hinton, Ixworth Thorpe, Norton, Pakenham, Redgrave, Rougham and Walsham): they were unknown on the heavier clays. However, these folds did not extend over large areas of arable and pasture land, but were mainly restricted to the fallow land of the owner. The lord enjoyed the right to fold his own sheep and those of his villeins on his own demesne, with perhaps small areas of contiguous peasant land. A few peasants enjoyed similar rights over their own land, while others sometimes obtained from their lord the right to erect a *temporary* fold on their own fallows. For example, six folds were granted in Great Barton in October 1323, mainly for sixty to eighty sheep in each fold. one operated until 2 February 1324, and the other five ran until the end of that farming year. Part of the explanation for fewer and less formal folding rights is that sheep tended to be

---

35 BL Add. Ms 34689, f. 6 (Fornham); BL Harley Ms 239, f. 184 (Redgrave); *AHEW*, ii, pp. 277–8; CUL EDR G3/27, ff. 162, 171, 177, 183 (Barking, Wetheringsett and Hitcham); Cornard Parva court rolls in private hands; Church, *Pakenham*, pp. 46, 75, 77, 88; N. Amor, 'Late Medieval Enclosure: A Study of Thorney near Stowmarket, Suffolk', *PSIA* 41 (2006), pp. 178–83; SROI HD1538/237/9 (Gislingham).

36 Smith, 'English Peasant Life-Cycles', pp. 181–2; A. McLaughlin, personal communication; reconstruction from BL Add. Ms 34689, ff. 26–9 (Fornham); *HistA*, p. 63.

less important in these districts, and the soils were less likely to leach.[37] The absence of formal foldcourses in this irregular system, and the restriction of fold rights to the land of the owner, reduced the need for regulated communal cropping patterns. Anyone with a liberty of fold simply drove the sheep from daytime pasture to the fallow arable each evening and penned them tightly on the land for the night with wattle fences. Light, portable wattle fences enabled farmers to create temporary 'enclosures' to protect crops on adjoining strips from wandering sheep, and were essential to the success of this system. Evidence from manors such as Fornham, Hinderclay and Redgrave indicates that each large block of demesne land was cropped and fallowed as an independent unit, and not integrated into some larger communal cropping scheme.[38]

Communal rights over the fallow arable were heavily restricted, although their precise nature is difficult to ascertain, because they are seldom described explicitly in court rolls. The right to pasture animals on the harvest shack was widespread, and in many places this right extended to any arable land lying fallow between the end of shack and 2 February, a period known as 'the open time'. For example, in 1251 it was recorded that the demesne land of Hartest was 'several to the lord' after 2 February each year, implying that the period beforehand was 'common'. In Ixworth, and perhaps a few other places, communal access to fallows extended from the shack to 25 March.[39] After this period, access to any fallow at any time of the day or night was exclusive to the holder of the land. Any crops sown during the 'open' time (i.e. the 'winter' crops of wheat, rye and maslin) were protected from wandering animals during the day by the close supervision of herds and by penning the animals during the night to small areas of the fallow with wattle hurdles (or 'clats'). Hurdles were readily available, because the manor of Mildenhall routinely bought them from local suppliers, and Downham manor also looked to Mildenhall market for its needs. After 2 February each farmer could cultivate or fallow his land as he pleased, and no communal rights pertained until the shack began

---

37 Chibnall, *Select Documents*, p. 94; Bailey 'Suffolk Domesday', p. 24; *AHEW*, ii, pp. 283–4; *PSIA* 1 (1895), p. 25; M. Bailey, 'Sand into Gold: The Evolution of the Foldcourse System in West Suffolk, 1200–1600', *AgHR* 38 (1990), pp. 43–55; Church, *Pakenham*, p. 79, the Ixworth Thorpe fold is explicitly limited to the tenant's own land, operating each night; SROB E18/451/1 (Mildenhall).

38 Gray, *English Field Systems*, pp. 342–3; Campbell, *English Seigneurial Agriculture*, pp. 263–5; Stone, 'Hinderclay', pp. 619–23. The interpretation offered by H. E. Hallam in *AHEW*, ii, pp. 272–81 should be used with extreme caution.

39 D. P. Dymond, 'The Suffolk Landscape', in *East Anglian Studies*, ed. L. Munby (Cambridge, 1968), p. 30; N. Amor, 'Riding out Recession: Ixworth and Woolpit in the Late Middle Ages', *PSIA* 40 (2002), p. 132 (Ixworth); CUL EDR G3/27, f. 162 (Hartest); see also Thornton, *History of Clare*, pp. 19–20; Bacon Ms 912, court held March 1481 (Ixworth, thanks to Nick Amor); for common fields in Hadleigh, see *PSIA* 11 (1903), p. 153.

in August. The lack of communal access to the fallow arable heightened the importance of wide roadside verges, greens and 'tyes' as a source of permanent, all-year pasture for livestock, where animals were either closely supervised or tethered. In 1251 Barking tye comprised 50 acres 'in which the whole vill ought to common for pasture with beasts with the lord bishop [of Ely]'.[40]

The advantage of this system is that it provided individual farmers with the flexibility to sow their individual land parcels as they pleased: they could sow spring or winter crops, and could vary the area left fallow, with few restrictions. The disadvantage is that the supervision costs were high, because the intermingling of livestock and crops – segregated only by flimsy fences or the watchfulness of herdsmen – increased the risks of trampling and damage. Yet the advantages outweighed the disadvantages before the Black Death, when grain was scarce and labour costs were low. Hence the combinations of crops sown in this system were varied, and the pattern of cropping on individual parcels was often highly idiosyncratic and demanding. Some demesnes concentrated upon the production of wheat and oats, while others concentrated upon spring-sown crops, mainly barley with some oats and legumes. Around 75 per cent of the demesne arable was usually cultivated each year in these areas, a higher proportion than in the Midland system. Consequently, farmers placed greater emphasis on preparing the soil through the use of legumes and marling: for example, 5 per cent of the Elmswell demesne was marled in 1250, and at Akenham around 15 per cent of the demesne-sown crops were occupied by legumes.[41] The flexibility afforded to farmers by the absence of communal cropping regulations is well illustrated by the demesnes of Redgrave and Rickinghall, where a different and independent cropping pattern was applied to each individual pecia in each year of the 1340s. A standard three-course rotation of wheat, oats, then fallow was applied to a number of individual parcels of demesne land, but, on a group of others, rye and barley were sown alternately year after year without any relieving fallows. Finally, a third group of pecia was subject to intensive sowing of wheat, barley and legumes, with a fallow inserted perhaps every half dozen years or so. These strategies are impressive for their variety, flexibility and complexity, but did not obtain high yields, and consequently have been described by Bruce Campbell as a 'relentless rotational regime of dubious agronomic wisdom'. However, David Stone perceives some wisdom in equally complex and irregular cropping strategies on the Hinderclay demesne, where a logical and consistent underlying pattern

[40] BL Add. Roll 53126 (Mildenhall); SROB 651/35/2 (Downham); SROB E3/15.9/1.1, mm. 19–20, and 1.2, court held December 1302 (Fornham); CUL EDR G3/27, f. 177 (Barking); for verges see West and McLaughlin, *Walsham le Willows*, p. 108.

[41] Campbell, *English Seigneurial Agriculture*, pp. 252–73, 449; BL Harley Ms 230, f. 186 (Elmswell); SROI 1469/7–8 (Akenham); Stone, 'Hinderclay', pp. 619, 623–6.

is discernible. Soil preparation was meticulous on land where the main cash crops of wheat and barley were due to be sown next, either by targeting it with manure or conditioning it with a prior crop of legumes. He also argues that the unusual combination of a high sown area and modest yields was a deliberate policy, aimed at improving cash profits rather than maximizing output. Similarly, in the 1340s over 80 per cent of the demesne arable at Fornham All Saints and Risby was cropped each year, a remarkably high proportion on relatively poor soils. It was achieved by irregular cropping rotations and a shift towards spring-sown crops, but at the cost of indifferent yields. This was probably a matter of rational choice, for it resulted in higher gross returns per acre.[42]

Non-common subdivided fields

Enclosed fields of both arable and pasture dominated the landscape of the heavy clay uplands in the hundreds of Hoxne, Wangford and the western portion of Blything, and also some areas of heavy soil south of the river Gipping. For example, in 1325 59 per cent of the demesne arable land of Sibton abbey's North Grange (located in the northern part of the parish), 43 per cent of its arable in Peasenhall, and 54 per cent in Cookley was enclosed, and Rumburgh priory's arable in Rumburgh lay entirely in seven closes. 'Geneysclose' in Gislingham contained 82 acres, and probably comprised the entire demesne of the small manor of Gislingham Geneys. In 1306 75 per cent of the arable demesne of Flixton-by-Bungay was enclosed, and in 1250 33 per cent of that at Worlingworth lay in crofts. Some enclosures contained pasture rather than arable land – the manor and church at Westhall were entirely surrounded by enclosed pastures and woods – but most contained arable land: for example, in 1325 86 per cent of all Sibton abbey's demesne land in Cookley, Linstead, Peasenhall, Rendham and Sibton was arable.[43] These figures indicate that, even in this enclosed landscape, some patches of arable were arranged in irregular open fields, especially in the river valleys.

Another distinguishing feature is that individual holdings tended to be very compact and geographically concentrated, whether open or enclosed. The glebe land in Westhall, for example, was mainly concentrated around the church at the east end of the parish. Demesne land often lay in very large blocks and closes. The demesne at Worlingworth was located exclusively around the manor house and church in large and contiguous parcels, and that

[42] Campbell, *English Seigneurial Agriculture*, pp. 263–5; Stone, 'Hinderclay', pp. 619, 623; Bailey, *Marginal Economy*, tables 4.3 – 4.5; Stone, *Decision-Making*, pp. 260–1.

[43] Denney, *Sibton Abbey*, pp. 14–15, 148; Scarfe, *Suffolk Landscape*, p. 180; BL Harley Ms 230, f. 185 (Worlingworth); SROI HD1538/237/9 (Gislingham); *PSIA* 37 (1992), pp. 309–10; Richmond, *John Hopton*, p. 213; *PSIA* 14 (1912), pp. 320–1 (Rumburgh).

at Glemsford was located in just four enormous fields and one enclosure. The four demesne crofts at Worlingworth averaged over 19 acres each; the seven demesne closes in Rumburgh averaged 25 acres each; many individual enclosures at Huntingfield ranged from 16 to 35 acres; closes of 15 acres and 32 acres are recorded in Mettingham; and in Sibton Osmundcroft contained 51 acres and Newoxecroft 46 acres. Similarly, parcels of demesne land lying in the open fields tended to lay in larger blocks and were less likely to be intermingled with other small strips of open field: part of the Cookley demesne comprised 'one pecia of land called Couleswefeld lying next to the way next to Deysescroft containing 41 acres', and a single pecia in the open fields of Heveningham Thorpe contained 30 acres 2 roods. However, smaller parcels of 1 or 2 acres could still be found in the open fields: for example, one pecia of land contained 2 acres 'in the field called Snakemerefeld' in Chediston, and Sibton abbey held 'one pecia at the head of del Culeswefeld lying next to Deysescroft containing one acre' in Cookley.[44]

Tenant holdings also tended to comprise a mixture of enclosures and strips in the open fields, although individual parcels of land were inevitably smaller than on the demesne. A survey of some tenant land in Yoxford in 1358 reveals numerous small crofts and pightles (a local name for small enclosures) of undisclosed sizes, interspersed with 32 acres lying in 21 pecia in irregular open fields. Peasants in Huntingfield and Linstead Magna held a mixture of closes, such as the 12-acre Jamesclose and 18-acre Newhattclose, together with a few small parcels in the open fields. Tenant land also tended to be concentrated in certain areas of the fields and on the clay uplands usually lay around the farms. In Worlingworth arable was distributed either in contiguous blocks around the owner's messuage or in small strips among irregular open fields around the boundaries of the vill, and Martin argues that tenant land in Hitcham lay clustered around the tenant's messuage in enclosures rather than in open fields.[45]

No common rights – not even shack – existed over the vast majority of closes, although they pertained over the small patches of irregular open fields. Some open-field parcels in Sibton and Peasenhall are explicitly described as 'common land' [*terre communis*], but the exact nature of those common rights is not defined: it was most likely restricted to shack. Livestock certainly grazed legitimately upon some of the fallow arable in fourteenth-century

44 *PSIA* 37 (1992), pp. 37, 303, 309 (Westhall); Ridgard, *Framlingham*, p. 87; CUL EDR G3/27 f. 156 (Glemsford); BL Harley Ms 230, f. 185 (Elmswell); CUL Vanneck Ms, box 6 (Huntingfield); Denney, *Sibton Abbey*, pp. 48, 52–4, 59; *PSIA* 14 (1912), pp. 320–1 (Rumburgh); SROB HA507/1/33 (Mettingham).

45 SROI HA30/314/8 (Yoxford); CUL Vanneck Ms, box 6, account 1420–1, and box 5, court held December 1465 (Huntingfield and Linstead); *HistA*, pp. 86–7; E. Martin, 'Suffolk', *Medieval Settlement Research Group* 15 (2000), pp. 5–7.

Huntingfield, and tenants could stock both fallows and greens in Linstead with a set number of sheep determined by the amount of land they held. In contrast, common rights over the irregular open fields of Glemsford were minimal, because in 1251 the demesne arable was stated explicitly to be several to the lord throughout the year.[46] Patches of irregular open fields, subject to some common rights, interspersed among vast tracts of enclosures which were not, constitutes a very complex but interesting field system. This mixed landscape was also characterized by deep ditches, large greens and pockets of enclosed woodland. Extensive greens dominated the clay interfluves of northeast Suffolk and provided permanent pasture for livestock, although stocking levels were carefully regulated and each tenant's 'stint' was linked to the size of his landholding. Many greens, such as Sotherton moor, were located on slight depressions in the higher clay plateaux, rendering them wet and uncultivable to medieval farmers. However, they were a vital source of pasture for smallholders in a system where communal rights to access the fallow arable or other pastures and meadows were minimal or non-existent.[47]

Demesne cropping patterns were usually intensive within this system. Wheat (as a cash crop), oats and legumes (both for fodder) dominated; many demesnes cultivated more than 75 per cent of their arable each year; and individual enclosures and parcels in the open fields were cropped as independent units. The relatively high proportion of land sown each year was achieved on some demesnes by the extensive sowing of legumes instead of oats, which comprised an impressive 25 per cent of the sown area of demesne land in Gislingham belonging to the Knights Templar at the time of their suppression in 1313.[48] The fodder was mainly fed to cattle, especially dairy herds, and sheep hardly featured. The concentration upon dairying, the limited use of fallows, the greater use of legumes, and the exceptionally high valuations of meadowland in these areas all indicate a mixed farming regime operating at one of the highest levels of intensity in medieval England.

CONCLUSION

The Suffolk landscape in *c.* 1300 contained a number of elements that would be recognizable to the modern traveller. The dispersed rural settlement pattern, peppered with single farmsteads and hamlets strewn around isolated greens;

---

[46] Denney, *Sibton Abbey*, pp. 53, 59; CUL Vanneck Ms, box 5, court held January 1412 (Linstead); CUL EDR G3/27, f. 156 (Glemsford).

[47] Dymond, 'Suffolk Landscape', p. 33; *HistA*, p. 62; Williamson, *Shaping Medieval Landscapes*, pp. 67–8; Warner, *Greens, Commons*, p. 6, and chap. 2.

[48] Ridgard, 'Worlingworth', p. 215; Campbell, *English Seigneurial Agriculture*, pp. 253, 449; PRO sc6/1006/30 (Gislingham); SROB HA507/1/33 (Mettingham).

narrow sinuous lanes, deeply embanked, hedged or ditched; pockets of wood-land, such as those at Bradfield St George and Staverton, broadly the same size and shape then as now; and the familiar location and basic elements of urban topography. Many of these elements of the landscape have changed little in seven centuries. The major changes have been the eradication of the former open fields; the draining of the fenland and salt marshes; the destruc-tion of heathland, and its replacement with coniferous forests; and the inexo-rable advance of urban sprawl.

In *c.* 1300 around one-half of the land surface of Suffolk was ploughed for arable, a very high proportion by the standards of any age, of which no more than three-quarters lay in irregular open fields and no less than one-quarter in hedged or fenced enclosures. The irregular field systems of Suffolk were varied and complex in their layout and operation, and few communal rights pertained over them, but they were well adapted to local farming needs. The integration of arable and sheep farming in the Breckland through the device of the foldcourse is an extraordinary example of the adaptability and fitness for purpose of an irregular field system. They also provided local farmers with considerable choice and flexibility in the types of crops they could grow and the intensity with which they could sow them, especially when demand for grain and commercial opportunities rose in the thirteenth century, although this flexibility could only be achieved through high labour inputs and at the cost of some damage to corn by wandering livestock.

Verges and greens offered a vital source of common pasture to ordinary people, but in general communal rights over land were relatively restricted. Even where commoners enjoyed rights to graze or take fuel from heath or marsh, their activities were usually subject to time restrictions and closely monitored by heath wardens and marsh reeves. The supervisory care taken to ensure that such resources were prudently managed and exploited made good economic sense in this period when land was scarce relative to labour, especially in a county where pastoral farming was more intensive than arable. The value of meadow, decent pasture, woodland and even some heathland in Suffolk was often higher than arable land, representing some of the high-est such valuations known in medieval England in the century before the Black Death. There was no such thing as wasteland at this time, because even non-arable resources were exploited with care and intensity.

CHAPTER 6

Towns and the Urban Environment

BOROUGHS, MARKETS AND FAIRS, 1200–1349

At the end of the eleventh century Suffolk contained three of England's most important towns and four other boroughs. In 1066 Ipswich had been comfortably the county's largest town, but was strongly associated with resistance to William I's conquest, and by 1086 – the date of the Domesday Survey – had suffered severe depopulation and destruction. In stark contrast, Bury St Edmunds and Dunwich flourished under Norman patronage and expanded rapidly between 1066 and 1086, by which date they both rated among England's top ten towns. The Normans actively developed Dunwich as a commercial centre and port to rival Ipswich, and its impressive growth continued during the twelfth century, so that by 1200 it was the only place in Suffolk to be ranked among England's ten wealthiest towns. However, none of Suffolk's towns was large by modern standards, and even Dunwich's population in 1086 probably did not exceed 3,000. Domesday Book also records the existence of burgesses at Beccles, Clare, Eye and Sudbury; markets at Blythburgh, Haverhill, Hoxne, Kelsale and Thorney (Stowmarket); and a fair at Aspall. Others must have escaped mention, and there is no doubt that the urban and commercial structure of late eleventh-century Suffolk was already well developed by the standards of the time.[1]

Demographic and economic expansion over the next two centuries resulted in a two- to threefold growth in the population of many of these early boroughs and towns, peaking in the early fourteenth century. The expanding economy also encouraged the foundation of new boroughs, markets and fairs, which reduced the costs and risks of trade by bringing traders together in an environment that offered some legal protection. It has been estimated that between *c.* 1100 and *c.* 1349 the Crown granted charters for over 2,000 weekly markets and 400 boroughs in England. After 1100 hardly any new boroughs were created in Suffolk, although the scale of market and fair foundation was prodigious. Fifteen markets had been established in Suffolk before 1200, and

---

[1] For a general introduction to town life, see E. Miller and J. Hatcher, *Medieval England: Towns, Crafts and Commerce, 1086–1348* (London, 1995), chap. 5. For the specific examples mentioned here, see *UH*, i, pp. 752, 754; M. Bailey, ed., *The Bailiffs' Minute Book of Dunwich, 1404–1430*, SRS 34 (Woodbridge, 1992), p. 1; *VCH*, ii, pp. 201, 203; N. Scarfe, *Suffolk in the Middle Ages* (Woodbridge, 1986), pp. 130–3; *HistA*, p. 159; Bailey, 'Suffolk Domesday', pp. 25–7.

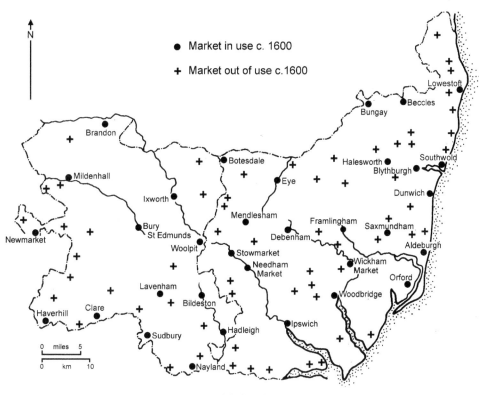

MAP 13 Medieval markets

by 1349 a total of eighty-nine markets are formally recorded, although the actual total was nearer 100. Similarly, seven fairs are recorded before 1200, and 106 by 1349. The main phase of new foundations occurred in the second and third quarters of the thirteenth century, when a total of 49 markets and 51 fairs were formally established. Most were located in small or medium-sized rural settlements, and held on either a specified day each week (markets) or date (fairs). Weekly markets became the main medium for the trade in basic provisions and foodstuffs, and only the markets at Dunwich, Ipswich and Bury St Edmunds attracted sufficient trade to justify holding a market daily.[2]

Some of these new grants merely 'legalized' existing arrangements in places where informal marketing had occurred for years, while others proved little more than speculative and short-lived ventures. Mildenhall was known as a trading centre from the late eleventh century, but its first formal market was granted in 1220 (held each Tuesday), while the thirteenth-century markets at Felsham and Wisset may never have been held for more than a brief period.

[2] J. Davis, 'The Representation, Regulation and Behaviour of Petty Traders in Late Medieval England' (PhD thesis, Cambridge University, 2001); *HistA*, pp. 76–9.

However, many of Suffolk's markets and fairs were genuinely new and successful enterprises which reflected both the commercial and demographic developments of the age, and a seigneurial determination to control, regulate and
profit from the growing volume of trade through formal outlets. The relative
absence of borough plantations in twelfth- and thirteenth-century Suffolk is
partly explained by the high volume of market foundation: by 1348 Suffolk
possessed nearly 10 weekly market sites per 100 square miles, comfortably
the highest recorded density in England and well above the national average
of 3.7.[3]

The growth of new markets, fairs and boroughs was paralleled by legal developments which facilitated the regulation of trade and commercial activity by
the Crown, and provided a context for defining more closely the legal concept
of a market and the precise legal rights of a borough. These developments
established the dual principle that royal permission was required to create a
market, borough or fair, and that all markets and boroughs were subject to
some form of lordship. A market grant was essentially a franchise to organize, control and profit from trade on a stipulated day and place, usually weekly,
and bestowed upon the holder the right to profit from the proceeds of trade,
by charging tolls on transacted goods and collecting rent for stalls and shops
occupied for the duration of the market, and the obligation to ensure that all
trading activity there was conducted according to certain rules.[4]

Although the rules governing trade were based upon an emerging body
of law, the method and rigour of implementation varied according to local
custom. All trade in the market had to take place openly, so that it could be
supervised by nominated officials, and within stipulated times: many markets
opened at dawn and closed during the afternoon, and few operated on holy
days. Traders who attempted to buy goods before the market formally opened
(forestallers), or who bought legitimately but then resold them later in the day
when prices were higher (regraters), acted contrary to market rules and were
punished accordingly. All markets were expected to enforce the various royal
assizes, which standardized weights and measures, and many also regulated
the sale of bread and ale by ensuring their quality and linking their price to
the prevailing price of grain. The holder of a market had to enforce these
rules consistently if the market was to attract potential traders, and the obvious mechanism was through a special court: consequently the existence of a
market grant implies the right to hold a market court.

3 *HistA*, p. 77; Dymond and Northeast, *History of Suffolk*, p. 46; Smith, 'Periodic
   Market', p. 453, tables 13.1, 13.2.

4 R. H. Britnell, *The Commercialisation of English Society, 1000–1500* (Cambridge,
   1993), pp. 10–19, 81–5; Miller and Hatcher, *Medieval England: Towns, Crafts and
   Commerce*, pp. 155–66.

The general principles governing the creation, control and administration of markets also applied to fairs: indeed, manorial lords often acquired a market and fair charter simultaneously. A fair was associated with a particular religious festival, and was therefore an annual not weekly occurrence, running for a specified and consecutive number of days around it (normally three in total). The holy day chosen for some fairs was dedicated to a saint with local significance, and therefore became a celebratory and social occasion as well as a trading opportunity. Booths and stalls were erected on either the marketplace or a local field, and officials were appointed to ensure that tolls were collected and trading activity conformed to standard rules and procedures. Larger fairs, such as Newmarket, held special courts to settle disputes and to handle cases, while others, such as Wentford (Clare), simply used the mechanism of the manor court. Some places held more than one fair each year, and three were held annually at Stoke-by-Nayland and Sudbury.[5]

The type of business conducted at fairs tended to differ from that in weekly markets. Markets mainly handled the small volume, high turnover, trade in basic foodstuffs and goods, whereas traders at fairs often dealt in bulk purchases or more specialist trades, such as livestock, cloth and luxuries. This is reflected in their timing. The majority of Suffolk fairs were held in either June or September, and most of the others in either May, July or August, thus coinciding with the period when the trade in young livestock or bulk grain purchases was most buoyant. Although the majority of fairs were modest enterprises, some concentrated on a particular trade. Halesworth fair was known for its trade in northern bullocks, and by the late fifteenth century Woolpit had established a high reputation for its trade in horses, attracting merchants from across East Anglia and cattle drovers from the north of England. Clearly, the most successful and specialized fairs attracted traders from farther afield than did weekly markets.[6]

Most of these new fairs were relatively humble and rural, and consequently little documentary evidence has survived to chart their fortunes. In contrast, by the late twelfth century the annual fair at Bury St Edmunds was established as one of the greatest in England, attracting clothiers from the leading English textile towns and from Flanders: the latter were so prominent and influential that the borough authorities passed edicts to prevent them from monopolizing the trade in leather and velvet goods. Henry III sent his royal tailor to Bury fair to obtain cloth from Ghent and Ypres, and as late as 1320 a London merchant regarded Bury fair as sufficiently important to have

5 Britnell, *Commercialisation*, pp. 14–16, 88–91; Miller and Hatcher, *Medieval England: Towns, Crafts and Commerce*, pp. 268–74; SROB 1476/1/22; Thornton, *History of Clare*, pp. 177–8; *HistA*, pp. 78–9.

6 Davis, 'Petty Traders', p. 14; *HistA*, p. 78; Amor, 'Riding out Recession', p. 135.

spices and dyestuffs forwarded to him from Lynn to supplement the stock he had brought with him from the capital. The fair was probably held on Angel Hill, and properties fronting the fairground were sublet to visiting traders for its duration. In common with many of England's great international fairs, it declined after the late thirteenth century.[7]

A landlord had to pay 5 marks into the royal coffers before the Crown would grant a market or fair charter, and even then the grant was conditional. If existing franchise holders complained that the location or the day of the week of the new market or fair was likely to injure their own, the Crown would direct the county sheriff to investigate and, if the complaints were upheld, to rescind the grant: as a rule of thumb, just under 7 miles was regarded as an acceptable distance between markets. Founders sometimes chose the day of week for their proposed market to complement existing ones, which might create a local circuit of markets for traders to visit on consecutive days. Richard Smith provides the example of Kersey, Lavenham, Bildeston, Brent Eleigh and Felsham markets, which were geographically proximate and held on different weekdays, and he argues that such circuits are symptomatic of a periodic marketing system orientated principally towards traders rather than consumers. One suspects that some markets had an unofficial or experimental existence before a lord formally acquired a charter, and in some cases – such as Haverhill, East Bergholt and Lidgate – there is no evidence that one was formally acquired at all. Most successful markets were located on the manors of higher-status landlords.[8]

Over 400 new boroughs were founded in England after 1086, mainly during the twelfth and thirteenth centuries. The foundation of a borough bestowed personal privileges upon its leading inhabitants (the burgesses), who were therefore able to pursue trade free from the burdens and obligations of manorial and agricultural life. A borough was therefore a particular type of town, one with specific legal and institutional privileges granted by the Crown. However, the great surge of English borough creation during this period largely by-passed Suffolk, in direct contrast to the tidal wave of new markets and fairs that engulfed the county, for only Bungay, Exning, Orford and Lidgate were added to the seven boroughs recorded in 1086. Orford was already a fledgling port in the late eleventh century, and acquired the status of a royal borough in the 1160s as part of Henry II's hasty redevelopment of

---

7 M. D. Lobel, *The Borough of Bury St Edmunds: A Study in the Government and Administration of a Medieval Town* (Oxford, 1935), pp. 65–6; R. S. Gottfried, *Bury St Edmunds and the Urban Crisis, 1290–1539* (Princeton, 1982), p. 90; Miller and Hatcher, *Medieval England: Towns, Crafts and Commerce*, pp. 118, 166, 170, 172; *VCH*, i, p. 637.

8 Davis, 'Petty Traders', p. 24; Smith, 'Periodic Market', pp. 460–1; Dymond and Northeast, *History of Suffolk*, p. 46.

the site as a port and military stronghold. Land from the existing manor was allocated to the new borough, and a large rectangular marketplace and distinctive grid street pattern were laid out upon it. Regular-sized burgage plots were created, some of which are still recognizable from the air (plate 9), and by 1307 there were seventy-two such plots, each paying 6d. rent. The land belonging to the borough contained very little arable, reinforcing the sense of an urban – rather than agricultural – community. Orford experienced considerable early success, paying more tax upon its imports and exports in 1203–4 than any other Suffolk port, although it subsequently lost ground to Ipswich. Its success enhanced the attractiveness of prime sites around the marketplace, because by the 1270s houses and shops had already begun to encroach.[9]

Orford is a classic example of a medieval borough plantation and, although the original motive for its creation was military, the site was already attracting some trade before the 1160s. It thereafter became quickly established as a successful town independent of its military function. In contrast, Lidgate was much smaller in scale and lower in status, scarcely warranting the status of a borough. A castle had been built here during the civil war of King Stephen's reign, and the subsequent presence of a garrison and, occasionally, an aristocratic household must have stimulated some local trade. At some point in the thirteenth century part of the castle's abandoned outer bailey was converted into a marketplace, and burgess plots were created along its side – part of a speculative attempt by the lord to implant a successful town (plate 5). A handful of burgesses and burgess plots are still recorded there in the fifteenth century, when it was nothing more than a rural settlement with a weekly market. Lidgate occupied a position at the bottom of the burghal hierarchy, and never possessed any of the economic and social characteristics of a town.[10]

The relative absence of boroughs in medieval Suffolk is something of a paradox, because we might reasonably expect its commercialized, densely populated and wealthy economy to be founded upon a well-developed urban structure comprising a good number of large and successful boroughs. After all, Devon contained seventy-one medieval boroughs, most of them founded after 1100. However, we must not confuse the relative absence of *boroughs* in Suffolk with an absence of *towns*. Historians rightly define a medieval town in

9 PRO sc6/1003/3; *RH*, ii, p. 199; T. H. Lloyd, *The English Wool Trade in the Middle Ages* (Cambridge, 1977), p. 12.

10 For Orford, see Bailey, 'Suffolk Domesday', p. 20. Lidgate castle was probably abandoned in the 1260s, and was certainly overgrown and derelict by the fifteenth century, see *CPR, 1258–66*, p. 621; PRO DL43/4/3, f. 24. Other references to its burgesses are recorded in SROB E3/11/1.3, courts held December 1415, September 1416, July 1420, April 1421; E3/11/1.4, courts held October 1425 and May 1460; E3/11/1.5, court held March 1474.

MAP 14 Towns, 1200–1500

terms of its economic and social, as well as its legal, characteristics: it possessed occupational variety, at least twenty different crafts and trades, perhaps a population in excess of 300 people, a distinct and tight topography, a degree of social stratification among its inhabitants, an ability to govern itself to some extent, and distinctive cultural activity. In *c.* 1300 nearly thirty settlements in Suffolk met these criteria (and by *c.* 1500 well over thirty places – see map 14). Suffolk was a county of small market towns rather than boroughs, and only Hertfordshire and Kent contained a higher density of such places in medieval England.[11]

Successful boroughs, markets and fairs generated considerable amounts of revenue for either the burgesses or the landlord. Tolls charged on transactions in the market, the rents paid by properties, shops, stalls, houses and buildings, and the proceeds of the various courts (manorial, market and/or borough)

---

[11] C. Dyer, 'How Urbanised was Medieval England?', in *Peasants and Townsmen in Medieval Europe*, ed. J-M. Duvosquel and E. Thoen (Ghent, 1995), p. 173; *UH*, i, pp. 4–5, 507–9, reckons that Suffolk contained 29,000 acres per town, compared with the median of 46,000; C. Dyer, 'Small Places with Large Consequences: The Importance of Small Towns in England, 1000–1540', *Bulletin of the Institute of Historical Research* 187 (2002), pp. 8–12.

constituted the most common sources of income. Although the individual toll charged on each transaction in the market was usually relatively small (½d.), and certain people and goods were exempt, a thriving market could generate significant sums of money from the sheer volume of transactions. Ipswich market was the greatest in the county, sufficiently large to be subdivided into constituent parts: in 1344 the corn market was leased for £22, the meat market for £9 6s. 8d., the fish market for £7 6s. 8d. and the remaining 'small' markets for £4 6s. 8d. Only the markets at Bury St Edmunds and, for a while, Dunwich generated comparable sums of money, and the £10 produced by the tolls and stalls of Clare market in 1262, and the £15 at Bungay at the end of the thirteenth century, appear modest in comparison. However, this represents a healthy return, especially when added to the £5 generated by the borough properties of Clare and the perquisites of its court. Similarly, in 1308 the royal borough of Orford raised around £30 per annum, comprising rents from land, houses and buildings (approx. £9), tolls and stallage from the market and port (approx. £7), the lease of corn and fulling mills (approx. £11), and revenues from the borough and market courts (approx. £3). Boroughs that were also ports increased their revenue by charging boats for using their docking facilities, and in 1344 the tolls from the common quay at Ipswich exceeded £17. In addition to these sources of income, the largest boroughs such as Ipswich and Dunwich also raised revenue from supplementary sources. For example, by charging an annual levy on all fishing boats operating from the port, and imposing *ad hoc* levies (i.e. rates) on the townsfolk, the total borough income of Dunwich comfortably exceeded £100 per annum in the early thirteenth century, easily comparable to the income from the largest manors in the county.[12]

Market revenues in small towns usually generated between £5 and £10 per annum, equivalent to the income generated by an average Suffolk manor, although these often declined after *c.* 1350. In the 1280s market tolls generated around £5 per annum at Newmarket, £4 at Woodbridge market in the 1340s, 40s. at Framlingham in the 1270s, 3s. 4d. at Lidgate in the 1390s, and 18d. at Laxfield in the 1380s. Additional income was generated through rents from the properties crowding around a thriving marketplace. Botesdale market generated around £5 in tolls each year in the late thirteenth century, and an additional £4 in fines and rents: the total income of £9 compares very favourably to the £1 that the same land would have generated from

[12] Bacon, *Annals*, p. 71; Thornton, *History of Clare*, pp. 21–2; Scarfe, *Suffolk Landscape*, p. 164; PRO sc6/1003/3 (Orford); Bailey, *Dunwich*, p. 5; R. Parker, *Men of Dunwich: The Story of a Vanished Town* (New York, 1979), p. 42, reveals that in the 1190s the borough paid an annual fee-farm of £108, which implies that its income was sufficient to cover such a large sum.

agricultural use.[13] Fair income was generated mainly from tolls on trading transactions and the rent paid by traders for temporary booths and stalls. At the upper end of the scale, St Leonard's fair had been established at Dunwich in 1075 and may have generated up to £20 per annum at the peak of its prosperity, although it had ceased to be held by the mid-fourteenth century. More typically, Wentford (Clare) fair was worth £1 in 1307, the Michaelmas fair at Mildenhall returned between 20s. and 30s. in the early fifteenth century, in the 1410s the October fair at Newmarket raised about £3 per annum, and at the end of the fifteenth century Laxfield fair generated around 2s.[14]

Not all markets or fairs proved successful. The acquisition of a franchise was no guarantee of success, and some failed soon after their initial foundation: others limped on for a number of years before finally disappearing in the radically different economic conditions of the later Middle Ages. The failure of some rural markets and fairs soon after their foundation is a reflection of the nature of commercial activity in medieval Suffolk, which, no less than in the rest of England, was neither consistent nor persistent enough to sustain all of the new trading franchises that had been established in the thirteenth century. Competition was fierce even among the major markets. During the 1270s officials of the earl of Norfolk's manors at Walton and Dovercourt prevented ships entering the Orwell/Stour estuary from reaching Ipswich, and instead forced them to sell their merchandise at Harwich, which provoked bitter responses from the burgesses of Ipswich. This particular earl of Norfolk, Roger Bigod IV, readily resorted to strong-arm tactics to obtain some advantage for his own market franchises, for he was also accused of blockading the port of Dunwich by land and sea for six days, and imprisoning some of its burgesses at his manor (and market) of Kelsale. Ironically, the burgesses of Dunwich were not averse to using similar tactics themselves in their prolonged dispute with successive lords of neighbouring Blythburgh and Walberswick over trading rights in the Byth estuary, which smouldered for two centuries and vividly illustrates the ferocity and persistence of commercial competition in medieval Suffolk.[15]

---

[13] *UH*, i, p. 524; May, *Newmarket*, p. 7; the Ipswich burgesses were entitled to half the income from the Woodbridge market, a concession to buy off their opposition to its establishment, Bacon, *Annals*, p. 71; Ridgard, *Framlingham*, pp. 19–20; PRO DL43/4/3, f. 23 (Lidgate); CUL Vanneck Ms, box 6 (Laxfield); Smith, 'Periodic Market', pp. 464–5.

[14] *UH*, i, p. 524; Parker, *Men of Dunwich*, p. 174; Thornton, *History of Clare*, p. 22; BL Add. Rolls 53121–53134 (Mildenhall); M. Bailey, 'Trade and Towns in Medieval England: New Insights from Familiar Sources', *The Local Historian* 29 (1999), p. 207; May, *Newmarket*, p. 25; CUL Vanneck Ms, box 6 (Laxfield).

[15] *RH*, ii, pp. 197, 200; Bailey, *Dunwich*, pp. 11–15.

However, some of the contemporary complaints about unfair competition between markets smack of greed and special pleading. In 1201 the newly founded market of Lakenheath was attacked by armed thugs sponsored by the abbey of St Edmund on the spurious grounds that this foundation would be injurious to the great market at Bury. Certainly, the existence of a market and riverine port at Lakenheath constituted a threat of sorts, yet the same abbey had run an informal market for many years on its manor of Mildenhall – a mere 6 miles from Lakenheath – which had hardly proved detrimental to the development of Bury St Edmunds. Similarly, the complaints by burgesses of Dunwich that the market at humble Sizewell damaged their own standing and trade (like the complaints by the borough of Orford concerning the market at distant Saxmundham) are more disingenuous than substantive.[16]

URBAN TOPOGRAPHY, SIZE AND FUNCTION IN *c.* 1300

All medieval towns, including the largest boroughs, retained some rural features, a characteristic which reinforces the point that – for all the commercial advances of the age – the economy remained essentially agrarian. The agrarian roots of small towns like Halesworth and Ixworth were readily apparent, but even in Ipswich in 1282 the main source of wealth lay in grain and livestock. Bury St Edmunds had arable fields large enough to support over 2,400 of the abbey's sheep, and also contained some cultivated land within its town boundary: 3 roods of arable land were cultivated in Friars Lane, and the parish of St Nicholas in Dunwich also contained a fair amount of arable. Likewise, the topography of the largest boroughs was similar in style, although not in scale, to that of small towns. Most show signs of planned alterations to their physical layout to accommodate their expanding role as trading centres. Streets, houses and buildings were often realigned or relocated to create an appropriate space for the marketplace and to ensure that the density of house plots in prime locations was high. The market squares at Framlingham and Lavenham, both small towns, bear a strong resemblance to the planned market squares at boroughs like Clare and Orford. The triangular marketplace at Lakenheath was probably created in the early thirteenth century, soon after its lord acquired a market grant for the manor, and was located at the heart of the settlement, which must have involved some reorganization of existing house plots and property boundaries at the time of its construction. In contrast, the marketplaces at Mildenhall

---

[16] *Curia Regis Rolls*, vol. 16, p. 414, and vol. 17, pp. 1137–8; D. Greenway and J. Sayers, eds., *Jocelyn of Brakelond's Chronicle of the Abbey of Bury St Edmunds* (Oxford, 1989), pp. 117–18; *RH*, ii, p. 199.

(plate 7) and Saxmundham appear to have been laid out over fields or common pasture as 'urban' extensions to the original rural settlements.[17]

A marketplace was organized to group together particular trades for the convenience of consumers. For example, a tollhouse was situated on the north side of the market at Bury St Edmunds, next to rows of stalls held by tanners and skinners. Drapers, spicers and mercers were concentrated at the east end, and ironmongers at the west: in the middle were rows of stalls devoted to foodstuffs. Newmarket was just one-tenth the size of Bury, yet its fourteenth-century marketplace was laid out in a similar fashion, with around 100 stalls arranged by rows of commodities: le Draperie, le Bocherye, le Merserie, le Spyserye, le Lyndraperie, le Barkersrowe and le Cordewenerrowe, together with other rows for ironmongers, ropers and cheesemongers. A 'butcher's house' stood at the centre of Woodbridge marketplace, where the corner stalls attracted higher rents due to their prominent position. Other markets included 'selds', which were smaller stalls or simply chests stuffed with goods.[18]

In a few places, usually on important route ways, a new market settlement was carefully and deliberately laid out on a virgin site. In the early thirteenth century uniform and narrow house plots were created on either side of a major roadway at both Needham Market (market granted in 1226) and Newmarket (*c*. 1200). Both sites lay in marginal locations within their respective manors, some distance from the main settlement (Barking and Exning), at places where informal trading had probably sprung up along the roadside without seigneurial permission. However, in both cases the landlord (the bishop of Ely at Barking and the Argenteins at Exning) recognized the potential for profiting from this unauthorized trade, and first legalized and controlled it by the acquisition of market charters, and then stimulated commerce further by developing a purpose-built market settlement that was attractive to traders. The start-up costs of what was effectively a town plantation must have been substantial, but were handsomely repaid in these two cases. In 1251 a survey of Barking dryly records forty-five 'new fees in the market of Needham', which were actually houses and workshops that had been laid out along the main road and marketplace. The number of forges and smiths among the tenants is striking, underlining the importance of passing road traffic to Needham Market's burgeoning economy. Similarly, over seventy long and narrow house plots were laid out on either side of the road at Newmarket, and by the fourteenth

---

[17] *PSIA* 12 (1906), pp. 137–57 (Ipswich); *PSIA* 13 (1909), pp. 207, 215 (Bury St Edmunds); Bailey, *Dunwich*, pp. 19–20; Dymond and Northeast, *History of Suffolk*, p. 46; see also *HistA*, pp. 162–3.

[18] *PSIA* 13 (1909), pp. 198–9 (Bury St Edmunds); SROB 376/3; May, *Newmarket*, p. 45; Davis, 'Petty Traders', p. 218 (Newmarket); SROI HD1538/435/3 (Woodbridge). Market crosses were common, although few have survived; see *PSIA* 23 (1939), p. 20.

century the weekly market was sufficiently busy to justify the construction of a purpose-built marketplace adjacent to the main road. By the later Middle Ages both Needham Market and Newmarket had eclipsed their parental settlements in size, wealth and reputation.[19]

The risks of a market franchise failing, especially if it was located close to established markets, were sufficiently large to discourage the prudent landlord from investing too much start-up capital in the venture (in laying out a fine marketplace, realigning property boundaries and constructing an imposing shambles or tollbooth) until its success seemed likely. Thomas de Bavent acquired a market charter for his manor of Easton Bavents at the relatively late date of June 1330; the manorial account for 1330–1 reveals little more than the expenditure of a few shillings on constructing a small tollbooth and a few shops and stalls, and certainly no evidence of any reorganization of the settlement to accommodate a marketplace. Thomas was evidently realistic about its chances of success against local competition such as Northales (Covehithe) and Southwold. His caution was well founded, for the market failed to survive the Middle Ages.[20]

The plantation of new market towns, and the speculative addition of commercial centres to older rural settlements, were paralleled in the established boroughs by denser infilling of existing spaces and the development of suburbs. Buildings encroached upon both the disused outer defences of Eye castle and the large marketplace at Orford, and in the late thirteenth century housing was built across parts of Eastgate field in Bury St Edmunds. The medieval marketplace at Sudbury was itself an eastward extension of the Anglo-Saxon borough, and another medieval suburb developed to the south-west. The high density of buildings in prime urban locations set towns apart from rural settlements. Tenements, some two storeys high, were packed around the Cornhill in Ipswich, and on the approaches to Stoke bridge and the quay. Ribbon development even sprung up along the main roads on the edge of a market settlement like Debenham. Yet small market towns usually lay within a single parish, whereas Ipswich contained fourteen medieval parishes: indeed, its growth in the thirteenth century is evident in the construction of two new churches within the original borough and the creation of the three suburban parishes of St Matthew, St Helens and St Clements.[21]

[19] CUL EDR G3/27, f. 178; Dymond and Northeast, *History of Suffolk*, p. 45.

[20] S. Letters, ed., *Gazetteer of Markets and Fairs in England and Wales to 1516*, part 2, List and Index Society, Special Series 33 (2003), p. 327; SROI v5/19/1.2.

[21] *RH*, ii, p. 199; *PSIA* 13 (1909), pp. 220–1; *HistA*, pp. 158–9, 163 (Ipswich and Sudbury); G. H. Martin, ed., *The Ipswich Recognisance Rolls, 1294–1327: A Calendar*, SRS 16 (Woodbridge, 1973), pp. 17–18; *PSIA* 38 (1996), p. 467; *PSIA* 39 (1998), p. 218 (Debenham).

TABLE 3   Rank order of Suffolk towns in 1327 and 1334

1327		1334	
Rank order of towns	*No. of taxpayers*	*Rank order of towns*	*Taxable wealth*
Ipswich	235	Ipswich	£64 10s. 6d.
Beccles	205	Bury St Edmunds	£24
Bury St Edmunds	167	Sudbury	£18 14s.
Sudbury	167	Beccles	£14 4s. 3d.
Hoxne	123	Exning	£14 4s. 2d.
Exning	80	Dunwich	£12
Hadleigh	76	Mildenhall	£11 10s.
Mildenhall	71	Hoxne	£11 0s. 8d.
Northales (Covehithe)	71	Orford	£10
Orford	69	Northales (Covehithe)	£9

Sources: 1327 Lay Subsidy; 1334 Lay Subsidy. The entries for Exning incorporate two urban settlements, the failed eponymous borough and Newmarket.

Early fourteenth-century Suffolk contained nine boroughs and nearly twenty market towns (map 14). The number of taxpayers recorded in the 1327 Lay Subsidy, and the amount of tax paid in 1334, provide a sense of urban size and hierarchy in Suffolk at the culmination of a long period of urban plantation and expansion. Table 3 shows that Ipswich and Bury St Edmunds were comfortably the most dominant towns, followed by six medium-sized centres at Beccles, Dunwich, Hoxne, Mildenhall, Orford and Sudbury. Dunwich had suffered badly from a silting harbour and catastrophic marine inundations in the late thirteenth and early fourteenth centuries, and consequently had lost ground to Ipswich. Together these eight towns comprised the core of Suffolk's urban structure in the early fourteenth century and were evenly distributed around the county. All were 'prescriptive' markets, to use a contemporary term (i.e. were established before 1189), and thus by the early fourteenth century had been long established as trading centres.

Only three of Suffolk's towns (Ipswich, Bury St Edmunds and Sudbury) feature among the fifty wealthiest in England recorded in the 1334 Lay Subsidy, which emphasizes that its major urban centres were not large by national standards and had lost the relative importance they had enjoyed two centuries earlier. This point is illustrated by the urban tax assessments made in 1282 to support Edward I's Welsh campaign, in which Suffolk's biggest towns compared modestly to those of Norfolk: Yarmouth was assessed at £666, Norwich at £333 and Lynn at £200, compared with £266 for Bury St Edmunds, £100 for Ipswich, £60 for Dunwich and £10 for Orford. Similarly, in the early fourteenth century London was home to an estimated 100,000 people and Norwich to around 25,000 inhabitants, whereas Bury St Edmunds and Ipswich contained around 5,000–7,000 inhabitants and Sudbury about 2,500. Most of the small towns had populations of around 750–1,000 at their peak in the early fourteenth century: Lakenheath and Mildenhall probably exceeded 1,000 inhabitants, Clare not more than 600, and Ixworth perhaps 550. In 1327 Suffolk's towns contained just over 15 per cent of the county's taxpayers: although it had no large towns by national standards, it was still moderately urbanized.[22]

Ipswich and Bury exerted the widest economic influence, with hinterlands of perhaps 15 miles for basic agricultural supplies and further for more specialized mercantile activity (such as the cloth trade). No other market or fair lay within 6 miles of each town, reflecting their competitive advantage and local control over the distributive and retail trades, and, in the case of Bury, the ability of the abbey of St Edmund to suppress attempts by other landlords to found a market in close proximity. Boroughs of this size and influence had developed a variety of functions well beyond that of a local market for basic goods and services. Both Ipswich and Bury St Edmunds were centres for the manufacture and distribution of some luxury goods, judging by the number of unusual occupations recorded in both towns in the early fourteenth century, and the extent to which labour had become divided between specialists in the major industrial processes (such as dyers, weavers, fullers and shearmen in the textile trade). Ipswich contained a number of specialist tanners, and was a centre of the leather trade, while Bury St Edmunds contained specialists in luxury goods, such as bed and coverlet makers, booksellers, bell-founders and various medical practitioners. Bury's status was founded upon the presence of the abbey of St Edmund, one of the largest and wealthiest Benedictine monasteries in England (plate 8). Not only did the abbey consume a wide range and substantial volume of goods and services, but it also attracted hordes of pilgrims to one of the country's most important religious shrines (of St Edmund himself), and exercised various judicial rights and administrative duties over west Suffolk (the Liberty of St Edmund), both of which attracted much additional business to the town. It also enjoyed a reputation for the

---

[22] In 1334 Ipswich was ranked nineteenth among English towns; Bury St Edmunds was twenty-sixth. *UH*, i, pp. 124, 510; *PSIA* 12 (1906), p. 138; Gottfried, *Bury St Edmunds*, p. 54, puts Bury's population at 7,000, which implies that the taxpayers recorded there in 1327 are significantly under-numerated; Bailey, *Dunwich*, p. 3; Davis, 'Petty Traders', p. 223; Amor, 'Riding out Recession', p. 129. The proportion of urban dwellers was calculated from the taxpayers of 26 towns, namely the ten largest (table 3), plus Blythburgh, Brandon, Bungay, Clare, Debenham, Eye, Framlingham, Ixworth, Lavenham, Long Melford, Needham Market, Saxmundham, Stowmarket, Walberswick, Wickham Market and Woodbridge, using the *1327 Lay Subsidy*, and Dyer, 'How Urbanised?', pp. 173–4.

manufacture of good-quality woollen textiles. Textile manufacture was not as well established in Ipswich, which was also less important than Bury as a religious centre, although it did contain seven lesser religious houses and the popular shrine of Our Lady near the Westgate (which was sufficiently influential to attract Edward I in 1297). Ipswich's other main functions were to serve as the centre of the county's administration and system of justice, and as its major port, blessed with a safe and extensive harbour: in the early four-teenth century its main seaborne trade was in wine, ale, herrings, hides, linen and canvas cloth, wool, millstones and salt.[23]

The six next largest towns in Suffolk's urban hierarchy in the early four-teenth century (Beccles, Dunwich, Hoxne, Mildenhall, Orford and Sudbury) had populations of between 1,000 and 2,500, and the majority of their com-mercial contacts extended up to 10 or 12 miles. None of their economies exhib-its the same range and scale of activities as Bury and Ipswich, although all had specialist functions beyond their core role as a sub-regional market. Hoxne, for example, was a modest religious centre, Orford was a port and military strong-hold, Beccles and Dunwich were established in the herring trade, while Sud-bury housed a small Jewish community of moneylenders and manufactured a few luxury goods, especially woollen textiles. It is instructive – although unsur-prising – that four out of Suffolk's ten leading towns were ports, which had established contacts with merchants from the Rhineland, the Low Countries and, to a lesser extent, the Baltic. Dunwich, Orford and Ipswich all exported small quantities of wool and grain in the late thirteenth century, and the ports of Orwell and Goseford (the Deben estuary) were known for their imports of German and French wine. However, the relatively small size of Suffolk's ports indicates that the scale of this overseas trade was not very significant. In 1200 Ipswich handled a mere 0.7 per cent of England's overseas trade by value, most of which was controlled by foreign, mainly Flemish, merchants. In 1282 the overwhelming majority of ships owned by Ipswich merchants were small coastal vessels rather than larger sea-faring ships, emphasizing that the bulk of its trade – and that of the other Suffolk ports – lay in coastal shipping and fishing.[24]

---

[23] *HistA*, pp. 76–9; *VCH*, i, p. 649. For tanning in Ipswich, see *PSIA* 12 (1906), pp. 145–6, 149–53; Gottfried, *Bury St Edmunds*, p. 115; P. Bishop, *The History of Ipswich* (London, 1995), p. 39; Bacon, *Annals*, pp. 66–7; Davis, 'Petty Traders', p. 22.

[24] The population estimates are based on the lists of taxpayers recorded in the *1327 Lay Subsidy*. The entries for places like Hoxne and Mildenhall include taxpayers who lived in outlying rural settlements, which makes the size of their urban core more difficult to estimate. C. G. Grimwood and S. A. Kay, *A History of Sudbury* (Sudbury, 1952), p. 88; Mortimer, *St Bartholomew's, Sudbury*, p. 18; Lloyd, *Wool Trade*, p. 5; *UH*, i, pp. 477, 488; Ridgard, *Framlingham*, p. 84; Bailey, *Dunwich*, pp. 21–2; D. Allen, ed., *Ipswich Borough Archives, 1255–1855: A Catalogue*, SRS 43

The majority of Suffolk's small towns supplied basic goods and services to agrarian hinterlands of around 6–8 miles and also serviced the traffic along the county's thoroughfares. Botesdale and Ixworth were classic small market towns, providing basic goods and services to their immediate locality and supplying the passing trade along locally important roads: over half of the debts recorded in the Ixworth court were small (under 5s.) and involved local landholders. The occupational structure of Botesdale reflected its sole function as a local market town: it contained a significant pool of landless petty traders and semi-skilled artisans, described variously as chapmen, merchants, cooks, carters, tilers, thatchers and ironmongers. Trading enterprises were small, based on a workshop and perhaps a market stall, and trades people were neither large employers nor wealthy: few merchants lived in these small towns. The growth of small market towns into bigger and more successful places often depended upon the development of a major specialist function, or of a range of minor specialisms, in addition to this core function. For example, Brandon, Newmarket and Needham Market were situated astride important regional routeways, and provisioned the high volume of passing traffic on a daily basis; Lakenheath was an inland port and an important supplier of fenland produce, especially fish, across west Suffolk; Lavenham and Hadleigh became centres of textile manufacture; Haverhill manufactured some woollen textiles and processed horse carcasses; Woodbridge sat on the boundary of two distinctive agricultural regions, the Sandlings and High Suffolk, and possessed a fledgling port; and Clare had developed a modest reputation for woollen textile manufacture, and also housed two resident aristocratic households (based at the castle and the Augustinian friary). Consequently, Clare possessed a wider occupational base than, say, Botesdale, and contained a greater proportion of artisans associated with the textile, provisioning and building trades.[25]

Woodbridge is a good example of a small town slowly developing a wider range of discernibly urban activities and functions. It probably originated as an informal trading centre next to the river Deben, rivalling the older administrative centre of Melton a couple of miles to the north, and in the 1270s the eponymous priory formally acquired a market charter and subsequently laid out a new market square. Early fourteenth-century Woodbridge was neither large nor wealthy. In 1327 it had fewer than forty recorded taxpayers (and thus a population of perhaps 300); in 1334 it paid (together

(Woodbridge, 2000), p. xiv; *VCH*, i, p. 647; *VCH*, ii, pp. 203–4, 289–90. The largest Essex towns had hinterlands for basic goods and services estimated at 7–10 miles, R. H. Britnell, 'Urban Demand in the English Economy, 1300–1600', in Galloway, *Trade, Urban Hinterlands* (2000), pp. 7–9.

[25] Smith, 'Periodic Market', pp. 468–9; Amor, 'Riding out Recession', p. 134; *UH*, i, pp. 510, 517–18, 522–3, 525; Davis, 'Petty Traders', pp. 219–26; *PSIA* 39 (1999), p. 375.

with Dallinghoo and Hoo) a modest £4 15s. 10d. in tax; and in the 1340s its market tolls were worth around £4 per annum, indicating a steady volume of trade. Yet its port offered three quays (a public quay, and one each belonging to Woodbridge priory and the earl of Suffolk), and residents sought to provision ships mustering or sheltering in Goseford haven, at the mouth of the river Deben. Rope manufacture had begun to develop on a small scale (a specialism which was to develop further in the next two centuries), together with a little textile – including linen – manufacture. By the early fourteenth century Woodbridge possessed distinct urban characteristics, and a growing range of activities, but it had yet to develop any significance beyond local marketing.[26]

URBAN STRUCTURE AND GOVERNANCE, 1200–1500

Boroughs

Most of Suffolk's largest towns had borough status (Ipswich, Bury St Edmunds, Sudbury, Beccles, Dunwich and Orford). These places and their leading residents (burgesses) were thus set apart from the small towns and their residents. Burgesses were a privileged elite within boroughs. Few women were burgesses, and all other residents of a royal borough were deemed to be free if they resided there for more than a year and a day. The status of burgess was usually inherited by the eldest son, while others acquired it through invitation and election by the other burgesses. Burgesses constituted around one-third of the male taxpayers of early fifteenth-century Dunwich. Most of these were local men who had gained their status through birth, whereas the circle of burgesses of Ipswich was deliberately extended to include important members of the county gentry and the heads of local religious houses. Upon their admission new burgesses swore an oath of loyalty in front of their peers, and paid an entry fee to the borough coffers: the amount varied, although the standard rate at Dunwich in the early fifteenth century was 6s. 8d., and that at Clare was 2s. Occasionally more unusual terms were agreed: John Causton became a burgess of Ipswich in 1445 on condition that he maintained the borough's stages and props for its annual Corpus Christi pageant, and a local landlord elected in 1472 rendered a brace of bucks. A burgess then enjoyed his status for life unless disenfranchised for specified misdemeanours, which at Ipswich included indebtedness to the borough, certain trading irregularities, or failure to defend another burgess against physical assault:

[26] Arnott, *Suffolk Estuary*, pp. 111–14; Bacon, *Annals*, p. 71; *PSIA* 9 (1897), p. 347; SROI HD1538/394; *1327 Lay Subsidy*, p. 135; *1334 Lay Subsidy*, p. 295: see below, pp. 282–3 for its expansion after the Black Death.

Richard Kirkhouse was disenfranchised from Ipswich for 'injuries, deceits and trespasses'.[27]

All burgesses enjoyed certain liberties and privileges, although their precise nature and extent varied from place to place. The most basic privilege was to hold land on burgage tenure and to be exempt from paying tolls in the home market. Put crudely, burgage tenure was an elevated form of freehold tenure, whereby the tenant held the land for a standardized money rent, free from manorial obligations and with relative freedom to dispose of it. Ipswich women could inherit land on burgage tenure if they were the nearest heir, but few became burgesses. Burgesses in most boroughs enjoyed a further range of privileges. For example, they might possess the right to answer any legal charges against them (other than those of the Crown) in their own borough court, where they might expect to receive preferential treatment. Others, such as the burgesses of Sudbury, were exempt from paying tolls in other markets. Those at Ipswich were exempt from impositions by royal officials, permitted to run their own mercantile gild and their own borough court (and to prove their wills in it), and they were able to discharge, and elect to, the office of coroner on behalf of the Crown within the town. Crucially, these were privileges rather than inalienable rights, and most towns took the precaution of obtaining fresh confirmation of their liberties from each new monarch. A borough could have its privileges removed or suspended under certain circumstances (mainly incurring royal disfavour), or augmented under others (mainly winning royal favour). For example, Ipswich's privileges were suspended for eight years in the 1280s after a riot in the borough, and it lost them briefly again in 1344: conversely, in 1446 it acquired the additional privilege to elect its own Justices of the Peace to operate within the borough as a separate jurisdiction. Occasionally a borough might claim privileges for its burgesses that it did not possess. In the 1270s the constable of Orford would not permit the bailiff of the Liberty of St Etheldreda (within which Orford lay) into the borough to collect debts and other distraints on behalf of the king, because he claimed that right for the borough itself.[28]

Just as the precise package of personal – and sometimes arcane – privileges enjoyed by each burgess varied from borough to borough, so the extent to which the body of burgesses possessed the autonomy to run their own affairs varied from place to place. The degree of autonomy, and by extension

---

[27] Bailey, *Dunwich*, pp. 4, 7; *VCH*, i, pp. 639, 647; Davis, 'Petty Traders', p. 223; Bacon, *Annals*, pp. 54, 101, 105, 121, 132, 166.

[28] Bacon, *Annals*, pp. 87, 78, 111, 122–3; L. J. Redstone, *Ipswich through the Ages* (Ipswich, 1948), p. 56; Allen, *Ipswich Borough Archives*, pp. xx, xxii, 2–6; *VCH*, i, p. 650 (Ipswich); Bailey, *Dunwich*, p. 9; Grimwood and Kay, *Sudbury*, p. 13; *RH*, ii, p. 189 (Orford).

self-government, was greatest in royal boroughs (Dunwich, Ipswich and Orford), where the burgesses had the power to run the borough with little interference from others, in contrast to 'mesne' boroughs (held by aristocratic landlords) where manorial lords continued to exert greater control over the town's affairs. In addition, these were the only Suffolk towns eligible to send representatives to Parliament in the Middle Ages. Ipswich can justly claim to be the greatest borough in Suffolk, because its powers of self-government, and the range of privileges enjoyed by its burgesses, were more extensive than anywhere else in the county, while Lidgate represents the most humble form of borough. Its burgesses possessed no more than the most basic privileges of holding land by burgage tenure and trading in Lidgate market without paying tolls, and in all other respects they were indistinguishable from the free tenants of the manor of Lidgate. The lord of Lidgate retained control over all other aspects of the 'borough', and there is no sense in which the burgesses acted as a collective body.[29]

The autonomy to run a royal borough with little interference was greatly prized, but it carried an administrative and financial cost. Burgesses were responsible for collecting the rent from borough land and burgage tenures, administering the market, running the borough courts, and assessing and collecting rates and other levies from the townsfolk on behalf of the borough. This income went into the borough coffers to fund a range of communal activities that were largely determined by the burgesses themselves, such as the upkeep of public buildings and town defences, the expenses of borough officers on official business, pressing legal actions on behalf of the borough, and so on: Ipswich even built a barge for common use. The revenue was also deployed to meet the borough's obligations to the Crown, such as fulfilling its military requirements (providing forces, supplies and ships for campaigns), providing hospitality for visiting royal officials, and – most expensive of all – the payment of an annual 'fee-farm' (rent) to the Crown in return for the borough's autonomy and privileges. The level of fee-farm could therefore change over time, as a borough gained more privileges or as its major sources of income ebbed or flowed. The fee-farm paid by Ipswich increased in the thirteenth century as its trade boomed and it gained more privileges, while that of Dunwich declined: at its peak in the late twelfth century Dunwich's fee-farm was set at £108 a year, but was reduced to £65 by 1279 and to £14 by the early fifteenth century as coastal erosion and silting damaged the port and choked its trade.[30]

The administration of a large royal borough was too demanding and complex to be managed actively by the whole body of burgesses. In fact the

---

29 VCH, ii, p. 197; SROB E3/11/1.3 and 1.4.

30 Parker, *Men of Dunwich*, 42; Bailey, 'Per Impetum Maris', p. 195; Bailey, *Dunwich*, pp. 4–7, 14; Bacon, *Annals*, pp. 115, 129; Redstone, *Ipswich*, p. 56.

burgesses rarely met more than once a year and left the management of the borough to an elected council of 'the better sort' of burgesses, who probably met once a month to discuss pressing issues with the main officers. A council of twelve 'chief portmen' ran Ipswich, who were identifiable by their special livery, and twenty-four burgesses sat on the Dunwich borough council. The main officer in most large boroughs was the mayor, although this office never developed in Ipswich, and was discontinued in the early fourteenth century in Dunwich. Here the leading officer was the bailiff, two of whom were usually elected from and by the body of burgesses to serve for one year. The bailiffs performed the functions of an executive officer, combining the roles of finance director, managing director and president in the borough court with little obvious division of function. Although bailiffs must have been constantly involved in the borough's business, the office was honorary at Dunwich (in receipt of expenses only), and at Ipswich attracted an annual stipend of £5. The onerous demands of the office were such that very few burgesses were deemed capable or wealthy enough to fill it, which partly explains why between 1403 and 1429 only twelve men served as the bailiffs of Dunwich. The bailiff was the most powerful officer in the royal borough, and the burgesses of Ipswich occasionally passed ordinances to limit the bailiffs' powers and opportunities for personal profit. Yet authority and responsibility carried a strong sense of public duty, and bailiffs were accountable to both their peers and lesser townsfolk: the bailiff's oath in Dunwich included a commitment to provide 'justice to rich and poor alike'. Most bailiffs discharged their office with pride and high levels of competence.[31]

The bailiffs of royal boroughs were aided in their work by a range of minor officers, each of whom was assigned responsibility for a specific task or tasks. The sub-bailiffs ran the market and fair, and associated courts, and were provided with a symbol of their authority that was instantly recognizable to outsiders: at Dunwich they carried a silver sceptre, and at Ipswich they wore a gown in the borough's livery. Chamberlains were increasingly common from the fourteenth century as financial officers in support of the bailiffs, and after 1319 those at Ipswich were deliberately elected from the 'inferior sort' of burgesses. This reflects a sensible desire to create checks and balances to the activities of those borough officers drawn from 'the better sort', and, after sustained abuse of their authority by some of the leading officers of Ipswich, the burgesses decided to elect four clavigers to guard access to (and therefore verify the use of) the common seal of the town. A town clerk, often a salaried professional, acted as both scribe to the officers and personal assistant to the bailiffs. Collectors of rents, and assessors and collectors of rates, levies and taxes, were

---

[31] Bacon, *Annals*, pp. 54–5, 80, 94; Bailey, *Dunwich*, pp. 7–8, 33.

appointed as required, and provided a good testing and training ground for those burgesses seeking higher office.[32]

In practice, access to high urban office in the Middle Ages was restricted to a narrow range of individual burgesses, and consequently many boroughs were controlled by oligarchies. Civic office in early fifteenth-century Dunwich was consciously maintained within a tight circle of burgesses, and members of the town council were wealthy, often related to previous councillors, and controlled elections to the office of bailiff: hence, although twelve different people served as bailiffs between 1403 and 1429, the post was actually dominated by just three men. The twelve portmen at Ipswich represented each parish in the town and were ostensibly elected by 'common assent'. However, the bailiffs and coroners selected the electors, and the candidates themselves were drawn from the ranks of the 'better, more discreet and more influential men of the town'. This narrowing of both the electorate and candidates for civic office ensured that urban power was concentrated in the hands of the wealthy elite: in 1200 only twelve burgesses filled all twenty-six civic posts available in Ipswich. The leading burgesses in the largest towns were conspicuously wealthy, and their assets compared favourably with the upper ranks of the landed gentry. The burghal elite of Suffolk's largest towns invested heavily in both urban and rural landholdings. The Codon family of Dunwich held a number of small rural manors, and one of the greatest burgesses in fourteenth-century Bury St Edmunds, Richard Charman, accumulated significant amounts of land in the borough and surrounding vills. Merchants of such wealth were not found in the small towns, whose leading residents tended to be innkeepers or artisans.[33]

Mesne boroughs often possessed a narrower range of privileges than royal boroughs, and the freedom of their burgesses to run their own affairs was usually more restricted. The latter was particularly true if the landlord was also resident in the town, and therefore likely to assume an active interest in the town's affairs. These burgesses might have some involvement in the day-to-day administrative tasks, but most of the executive management was vested in the landlord's own officials. Likewise, the income generated by rents, market tolls and courts in mesne boroughs accrued directly to the landlord. The borough of Clare was held by the eponymous family, and by the thirteenth century its burgesses enjoyed four basic privileges: to hold land by burgage tenure, exemption from the payment of tolls and stallage in Clare market, to attend the borough court as a suitor, and to elect the officials of the borough (notably the bailiffs, constables and ale-tasters). However, their degree of collective

32 Bailey, *Dunwich*, p. 6; Bacon, *Annals*, p. 55.

33 Bailey, *Dunwich*, p. 7; Miller and Hatcher, *Medieval England: Towns, Crafts and Commerce*, pp. 315–16; *CCR, 1405–9*, pp. 314–15; Gottfried, *Bury St Edmunds*, pp. 136–8, and chap. 4.

self-government was limited, because the borough officers were answerable directly to manorial officials, not the burgesses, the lord's bailiff ran the market and market court (which regulated quality and prices, other trading offences, and public health and order issues), and the income from the borough court and rents went to the lord.[34]

The tension between burgesses and landlords in mesne boroughs could be considerable, as the former sought the autonomy to run their own affairs, and the latter remained determined to retain their authority. The burgesses of Bury St Edmunds were wealthy and numerous, and consequently harboured high expectations of obtaining greater autonomy from the abbey which controlled the town. Yet a papal bull of *c.* 1150 had stated unequivocally that the borough existed 'for the service of the church' and to support the office of the sacrist of St Edmund's abbey, a status that the abbey refused to abandon. The abbey's privileges and powers over the borough were extensive: the sacrist directly controlled the courts, the fair and market; he collected the income from land rents, pavage and stallage; and he enjoyed other rights within the borough, such as the view of frankpledge (i.e. control over petty criminal and civil cases) and control of all gild activity. The residents were also liable for a number of customary dues, including the payment of an enormous recognition fine of 100 marks (£66 13s. 4d.) on the election of each new abbot, and cash payments to the cellarer for anciently commuted labour services ('repsilver'). The senior officers of the borough, the bailiffs, were chosen and paid by the sacrist, and the burgesses were not permitted any formal structures of urban government, such as a mayor or council. Lobel stresses that control of the bailiffs was the cornerstone of the sacrist's authority in Bury. The leading townsfolk of Bury St Edmunds must have regarded enviously the privileges and autonomy of their peers in Ipswich and Dunwich, and their relationship with the abbey was notoriously fractious, erupting into riot and murder in 1327 and 1381.[35]

In January 1327 the frustrations of the leading burgesses exploded into rebellion, when, urged on by agitators from London, they attacked the abbey and imprisoned the prior and a handful of monks. They controlled the abbey for around two weeks and coerced the abbot into signing a new charter of extensive urban liberties for the borough and burgesses. The abbot then escaped to London and rescinded the charter, arguing with good reason that he had signed under duress, which provoked further riots in February and again in

---

34 Thornton, *History of Clare*, pp. 32–43.

35 Lobel, *Bury St Edmunds*, pp. 33, 61–72, 142–5; M. D. Lobel, 'The 1327 Rising at Bury St Edmunds and the Subsequent Trial', *PSIA* 21 (1933), pp. 215–31; Gottfried, *Bury St Edmunds*, pp. 169–71; M. Statham, *The Book of Bury St Edmunds* (Buckingham, 1988), p. 55–6. The tensions at Bury should be contrasted with the example of Sudbury, where the mesne lords worked through and with the leading burgesses with little sign of conflict, Mortimer, *St Bartholomew's, Sudbury*, p. 17.

May. These later riots attracted support from villeins on the abbey's manors, from the friars of Babwell, and from priests working in parish churches
appropriated by the abbey. An uneasy peace was restored, with the new king
Edward III attempting to arbitrate between the parties from a distance and
warning the townsfolk about any future misconduct. Then on 18 October a
group of monks and abbey servants launched a revenge attack on some of the
burgesses, provoking a furious and violent reaction lasting five days, in which
parts of the abbey and some of its outlying manors were burnt and ransacked.
Peace was again restored by the arrival of royal troops and the immediate trial
of the leading participants. However, the abbot – Richard de Draughton – had
been kidnapped by the burgesses and spirited away to Brabant as a bargain-
ing counter: he was eventually released in 1329, in response to which the huge
fine levied on the town was reduced. The violence of 1327 is commemorated
by the impressive abbey gatehouse, a fine stone defensive structure at the end
of Abbeygate street, which was constructed during the 1330s to replace its
destroyed predecessor (plate 11).

The legal indictment of the leaders of the rebellion in Bury in 1327 named
well over 100 people 'with a great multitude of other persons'. The majority of
these were residents of Bury St Edmunds itself, many of whom were specifically listed as trades people, but others included no fewer than nineteen chaplains and the vicars of Bradfield, Little Whelnetham, Barrow and Rougham.
The weakness of royal authority in 1327 – during the deposition of Edward II
and Edward III's accession to the throne – provided an opportunity for the
burgesses of Bury to press the abbey hard for a resolution to many of their
grievances against its urban overlordship, and their actions encouraged others
to seize the opportunity to press home their somewhat different grievances.
The vicars and priests of the abbey's rural churches were complaining about
their meagre stipends; the friars of Babwell were airing an old grievance that
the abbey had prevented them from establishing a house within the town
itself; and villeins on its rural manors were frustrated by their obligation to
render some of the most heavily burdened rent packages in the county.[36]

The abbey of Bury St Edmunds was not insensitive to the burgesses' desire
for greater self-government, and recognized that, without some concessions,
its burgesses would lose their competitive mercantile edge against those from
other boroughs, with adverse consequences for both abbey and town. The
abbey therefore permitted the burgesses to exercise more freedom than their
restricted legal position might imply: first, it could choose not to impose all
of its rights over the burgesses, a practice observed disapprovingly in the late
twelfth century by Jocelyn of Brakeland; second, it could choose to involve

---

[36] *CPR, 1327–30*, pp. 217–20; Lobel, *Bury St Edmunds*, pp. 142–5; Lobel, 'The 1327
Rising', pp. 215–31.

the burgesses in the day-to-day running of the town. The latter was a significant concession, and, for example, burgesses were permitted to establish and regulate the rules of trade for bakers and weavers within the borough, and to administer the town gates. From the twelfth century the burgesses also had a gild merchant, whose leading representative, the alderman, was often consulted by the sacrist on affairs of the borough. The office of alderman of the gild merchant in Bury St Edmunds was obviously prestigious and influential, although its exact powers are uncertain: inevitably the burgesses regarded the scope of the alderman's powers to be rather wider than did the abbey, although there is little doubt that the influence of this office increased in the fifteenth century. The important point is that the alderman had no formal standing in the government of the borough, and the burgesses had no rights to construct formal structures of government, such as a town council: they could only exercise as much authority as the sacrist's discretion allowed. The sacrist could even veto the burgesses' choice of alderman – another frequent source of dispute between these quarrelling parties in the thirteenth and fourteenth centuries.[37]

Ipswich also had a gild merchant in the twelfth century, and the involvement of gilds in the organization of urban trade and crafts was a prominent feature of the largest English towns during the eleventh and twelfth centuries. At this time few boroughs had any formal structures of government, yet the leading townsfolk needed to meet occasionally to discuss peculiarly urban issues such as trade, public order, sanitation and collective obligations to their lord. Consequently they founded religious gilds and used their regular meetings as a forum for such discussions: more overt meetings of burgesses in any other forum would have been regarded as a flagrant challenge to the lord's overall authority to run the borough. Gilds merchant considered the major issues of urban government, while craft gilds emerged with a specific interest in regulating activity in their particular trade. However, twelfth-century merchant and craft gilds were dependent for their existence upon the goodwill of their lord, and therefore had strict limits to their powers and authority, and their importance quickly waned in many boroughs with the development of formal structures of urban self-government in the late twelfth and thirteenth centuries. A borough that had received a charter of privileges from the Crown had royal authorization to exercise its powers autonomously, and its officers and council had a seal to authenticate their actions. Hence in the twelfth century the gild merchant of Ipswich acted as an informal town government, whose leading officers represented a *de facto* town council, at a time when the

---

37 Greenway and Sayers, *Jocelyn of Brakelond*, pp. 88–91; Lobel, *Bury St Edmunds*, pp. 87–90, 159–63; Gottfried, *Bury St Edmunds*, pp. 107–8, 132–5; Statham, *Book of Bury*, pp. 55–6.

borough had no formal powers of self-government. When Ipswich acquired
those powers through its royal charter of 1200, and with it the right to elect
bailiffs, coroners, and a borough council of twelve 'portman', the role of the
gild merchant in regulating the town diminished. In many large boroughs,
existing merchant and craft gilds disappeared with the acquisition of formal
powers of self-government, and new boroughs created after this time had little need to regulate trade through a merchant gild. Ipswich retained its gild
merchant after 1200, although its purpose and function changed: it became a
socio-religious club for all the burgesses, and eventually developed a prominent ceremonial function after its rededication to Corpus Christi in the early
fourteenth century.[38]

In general the role of gilds in regulating trade and individual crafts tended
to be greater in large towns where formal powers of self-government were
poorly developed. In the absence of any formal powers to run their own affairs,
the burgesses of Bury St Edmunds used the informal structures of trade and
craft gilds to organize commercial activity at arm's length from the abbey
of St Edmund throughout the Middle Ages. The weavers' and linen drapers'
gild regulated the trade in, and manufacture of, textiles within the borough
through a sophisticated body of bye-laws. These were created by gild members
and enforced by four gild wardens, who were elected annually by the membership and, predictably, approved and nominally supervised by the abbey's own
officers, the bailiffs of the borough. The bye-laws were principally concerned
to regulate the quality of both the textiles produced within the borough and
the workforce, and to punish delinquents with fines. Weavers working within
the borough had to acquire membership of the gild through either purchase or
apprenticeship, and the use of part-time and casual labour was restricted. The
bakers and shoemakers (cordwainers) of Bury St Edmunds also had their own
craft gilds, controlling their trade in a similar manner to the weavers: both
paid regular fees to the abbey in recognition of its overlordship. The bakers'
gild dates to the 1170s, when abbot Hugh permitted its foundation so that the
'mystery' of baking could be conducted within the borough 'to the profit of the
church and all of the town of St Edmund': naturally, he took the precaution of
insisting upon the right to appoint an hereditary alderman as the head of the
gild.[39]

Trade and craft gilds were very prominent in medieval Bury St Edmunds.
Its weavers' gild supported an annual pageant and procession in the town, and

---

38   Allen, *Ipswich Borough Archives*, pp. xx, xxv; for examples of the regulation of trade
within the borough of Ipswich, see Bacon, *Annals*, pp. 29–38, 54, 105, 112, 128, 141,
149.

39   Gottfried, *Bury St Edmunds*, pp. 102–3, 107–8; Lobel, *Bury St Edmunds*, pp. 72–95;
Miller and Hatcher, *Medieval England: Towns, Crafts and Commerce*, pp. 362–3.

in 1477 its status was enhanced and formalized by a royal charter. The gild merchant of Bury St Edmunds, which by the mid-fourteenth century had become known as the Candlemas gild and was based in St James' church, probably increased its influence within the borough over the next couple of centuries, and in 1472 its statutes were altered to allow it to make bequests to the town: this was an important device, because it enabled the burgesses as a collective body to provide financial support to various borough-wide activities and institutions. One of the most substantial early bequests was designed to generate enough income each year to enable the gild to pay on behalf of the townsfolk the recognition fee owed to the abbey on the election of a new abbot, at a time when the gild's alderman had acquired greater influence in the running of the borough. By the end of the fifteenth century the gild merchant had acquired sufficient legal standing to allow the burgesses of Bury St Edmunds to act as a communal body. A similar development is discernible at Beccles, where the burgesses rented the town fen from their lord (the abbey of Bury St Edmunds) for £6 13s. 4d. each year and probably ran this substantial common on behalf of the town through the gild of the Holy Ghost. Yet the prominence of gilds in regulating trade and commerce in Bury St Edmunds and, perhaps, Beccles is a direct consequence of their burgesses' subjugation to a powerful manorial overlord and their lack of formal self-government. In stark contrast, trade and craft gilds played little or no role in the governance of any of Suffolk's other boroughs after *c.* 1200, especially the main royal boroughs of Dunwich and Ipswich, where commercial activity was regulated directly by the borough's own officials.[40]

Small towns

This lengthy discussion of the organization of Suffolk's boroughs reflects both their size and their influence upon the economic and social life of the county. It also reflects the relative abundance of extant archival material from such places, because larger boroughs generated much written documentation and tended to preserve their archives as muniments. In contrast, small market towns possessed no formal powers of self-government and therefore did not generate their own archival base. Their history can be partially recovered through manorial documents, although these inevitably reflect the interests of the manorial lord, rather than those of the mercantile elite, and focus more on agriculture than commerce. This is partly due to the simple fact that agrarian activity was often more significant than commerce in small market towns, but

---

[40] Gottfried, *Bury St Edmunds*, pp. 102–3; Statham, *Book of Bury*, p. 56; Lobel, *Bury St Edmunds*, pp. 159–60; N. Evans, 'The Holy Ghost Gild and the Beccles Town Lands Feoffees in the Sixteenth and Seventeenth Century', *PSIA* 37 (1989), pp. 31–2. Also true of Clare, Thornton, *History of Clare*, p. 45.

it hinders the attempts of the historian to reconstruct their history. Consequently, we risk allowing the history of boroughs to absorb a disproportionate amount of our attention: an unacceptable risk in a county like Suffolk, whose urban structure was dominated by smaller towns which did not enjoy borough status.

It was once assumed that market towns must have been heavily constrained by the obligations of villeinage and the manorial system, but historians now recognize that manorialism was not necessarily inimical to trade. The relative absence of boroughs, and abundance of market towns, in a highly commercialized county such as Suffolk (see chapter 7) indicates that its manorial system was capable of accommodating and stimulating trade and enterprise. As we have seen, landlords nurtured trade by providing the institutional and legal framework of markets and fairs, but they also encouraged it in more subtle ways. First, tenurial arrangements for the traders who lived in market towns were often favourable, enabling them to concentrate upon commercial activities rather than diverting their time and energy into agricultural labour services on the demesne. The manor of Barking was typical of the Suffolk manors of the bishop of Ely, containing a high proportion of heavily burdened villein holdings, yet the new market settlement which sprung up on the Ipswich–Stowmarket road on the edge of the manor was characterized by lightly burdened tenures: in 1251 the 'new fees in the market of Needham' paid simply a low cash rent without any labour services. Similarly, the holdings laid out along the road at Newmarket were free tenures, lightly burdened and with little agricultural land.[41]

The second way in which landlords nurtured trade was by adapting manorial institutions to support the endeavours of those involved in commercial life. Although not much is yet known about systems of government in Suffolk's smaller towns, some landlords were pragmatic and flexible in ensuring that manorial institutions, such as the leet court or the market franchise, were well adapted to the needs of traders. For example, the market and fair of Hadleigh were first leased to a consortium of local men, and then placed in the hands of a group of trustees, who ran both franchises without any seigneurial interference and even funded the construction of a new market hall in the 1450s. At Newmarket the lay absentee landlord entrusted supervision of his manor to a steward, who in turn ensured that the lord's income and interests were protected, and that the manorial institutions – the manor, leet, market and fair courts – were robust and active. The market and fair courts dealt largely with trading disputes, especially debt recovery, the leet regulated the victualling trades and public order, and the manor court regulated land transfers and

---

[41]   See Dyer, 'Small Places'; Bailey, 'Trade and Towns', pp. 194–210; CUL EDR G3/27, f. 178; May, *Newmarket*, pp. 32–6, 39.

agricultural issues. However, the running of the courts, the weekly market and two annual fairs was entrusted almost entirely to elected manorial officials – bailiffs, aletasters and constables – who were answerable to the court juries. The latter drew heavily from local tradesmen, although the market and fair courts included jurymen from outside Newmarket. In the regular absence of the steward, close supervision of these officials was left to the jurors, who readily amerced those who failed in their duties or exceeded their powers. Yet the jurors also acted firmly against any challenges to the authority of court officials as they went about their business, and understood well that these part-timers would struggle to discharge their office without the support, trust and co-operation of the community. Indeed, the bailiffs and leading jurymen were often drawn from the more prosperous residents of Newmarket, who were locally respected and understood intimately the needs and problems of traders on the ground.[42]

The Newmarket courts were effectively run by local tradesmen for the benefit of traders, and their officials consciously tried to maintain a pragmatic balance between allowing traders to pursue their business with minimal interference and imposing their authority in cases of persistent or serious misconduct: in essence, they allowed regular traders to operate within acceptable margins of flexibility, but acted firmly against flagrant breaches and those who challenged the courts' authority. James Davis believes that the regulatory system at Newmarket provided a reliable structure that offered traders fair, affordable and effective justice that protected them against theft, fraud and prohibitive transaction costs. He argues that it may have offered a more accessible and open trading environment than many boroughs, with unobtrusive regulations and justice based on trust, co-operation and flexibility. Debt pleas constituted a very high proportion of the business recorded in the market court of Newmarket, and outsiders sometimes chose to settle their trading disputes there, which must have reflected its reputation for efficient and effective justice. Similarly, outsiders also used the manor court at Brandon to settle disputes (including one case involving a merchant from St Ives (Huntingdonshire) against one from Old Buckenham (Norfolk), implying that it too possessed a reputation for efficiency.[43]

The example of Newmarket underlines the obvious point that the local people who ran Suffolk's small towns were usually among the wealthiest residents in their own community. However, they were not as wealthy as the leading merchants in the largest boroughs, and they did not convert their wealth into

---

[42] S. Andrews and T. Springall, *Hadleigh and the Alabaster Family* (Bildeston, 2005), pp. 7–8; J. Davis, 'Administering a Fifteenth-Century Small Market Town' (unpublished paper).

[43] Davis, 'Petty Traders', pp. 288–90; Bacon Mss 295/18, 295/39, 296/2.

landed holdings: most of the leading inhabitants of late-medieval Ixworth and Woolpit held relatively small areas of land, and were taxed on their income from trade rather than agriculture. In addition, they tended to trade locally in basic commodities, rather than over long distances in luxury goods, so that the leading residents of Newmarket were innkeepers, victuallers and butchers. Small towns had few very wealthy residents, and late fifteenth-century testamentary evidence indicates that a successful textile town like Lavenham had around eight times more wealthy residents than Ixworth and Woolpit combined. Although wealth was less polarized than in the larger boroughs, small towns still contained a high proportion of poorer residents: nearly half of the inhabitants of Ixworth in 1524 were labourers and smallholders. However, these observations do not imply that the residents of small towns lacked entrepreneurial verve, because many in Newmarket acquired property and stalls in the town to sublet to poorer residents, while developing other business interests.[44]

Small towns in Suffolk were run by ordinary traders, who by the late Middle Ages had day-to-day control over the local manorial institutions and used them to run the town as they saw fit: as long as the lord's rights and income were respected, both residents and lord benefited from a thriving market town. The residents of Newmarket lacked the status and privileges of burgesses, but their rents and services differed little from those owed by many burgesses, and they exercised a good degree of *de facto* institutional control over their town, while carrying few of the burdens of burgesses. Even in a market town dominated by a conservative and powerful landlord, such as Brandon, the lord did not suppress trade but simply sought to stimulate, channel and profit from it. Although the legal jump from market town to chartered borough was short and uncomplicated, it is striking that neither lords nor tenants in Suffolk's numerous market towns attempted to elevate the status of the settlement to that of a borough. Lavenham was one of the most spectacular growth towns of the later Middle Ages, and England's wealthiest market town in the early sixteenth century, yet it never acquired burghal status: it did, however, enjoy some of the trappings of a borough after 1329, when the lord of the manor acquired for his tenants freedom from the requirement to pay tolls in markets throughout England, and permitted the town to be run by six 'headboroughs' appointed by him. This is a remarkable arrangement, effectively creating a *de facto* but not *de jure* borough.[45]

The Lavenham example provides an obvious explanation for the reluctance among the inhabitants of Suffolk's market towns to pursue full borough status:

---

44 Amor, 'Riding out Recession', p. 139; Davis, 'Petty Traders', pp. 286–8.

45 D. Dymond and A. Betterton, *Lavenham: An Industrial Town* (Lavenham, 1982), pp. 3–4.

they had acquired sufficient *de facto* freedom from the obligations imposed upon them by the manorial system to pursue their commercial interests effectively. Richard Britnell has speculated that entrepreneurial and profit-making activity was easier in small towns, because the larger boroughs imposed stricter controls on trade through their extensive regulatory frameworks of courts and officials, and became increasingly protectionist and distrustful of outsiders. The proliferation of small market towns in Suffolk, the relative absence of boroughs, and the robust yet flexible regulatory framework available in places like Newmarket all provide good support for this argument. In areas of loose manorialism and high levels of personal freedom, such as Suffolk, trade could flourish without a formal network of boroughs.[46]

TOWN LIFE, 1200–1500

Town dwellers, even wealthy merchants, did not fit comfortably into the conventional structure of medieval society, based on the three estates of knights, ecclesiastics and peasants, and consequently were tolerated rather than embraced by the established order: the church was concerned by what it saw as the avarice of the mercantile elite, and the aristocracy disdained the merchant's inability to grasp the finer points of chivalric, military or courtly behaviour. Yet in the later Middle Ages towns were dynamic and progressive places, acting as social melting-pots where the most humble serf could seek work and perhaps make his fortune. They were centres of learning and culture, and it is likely that merchants were among the most literate members of lay society. The friars established their religious houses exclusively in towns in the thirteenth century, offering radical preaching to a receptive and intellectually engaged urban audience and also charity to the long tail of poor and destitute residents. Towns offered a better means of making a living than rural communities, especially for the landless and dispossessed, and contained a high proportion of people engaged in domestic or craft work. In the 1381 Poll Tax returns for Mildenhall, 31 per cent of the adult population was engaged primarily in crafts and 51 per cent were labourers, significantly higher proportions than in rural communities.[47]

The daily immersion in commercial activity, industry and craftwork, and the reality of a dense and mobile population, set towns apart from rural settlements, and presented the people who governed them with peculiarly urban problems:

---

[46] Britnell, *Commercialisation*, pp. 177–8; R. H. Britnell, 'Morals, Laws and Ale in Medieval England', in *Le Droit et sa perception dans la littérature et les mentalités médiévales*, ed. U. Muller, F. Hundsnurscher, and C. Sommers (Goppingen, 1993), pp. 28–9; Davis, 'Petty Traders', p. 289; Bailey, 'Trade and Towns', pp. 200–5.

[47] Dyer, *Making a Living*, pp. 225–7; Powell, *Rising in East Anglia*, pp. 85–9.

in this respect the only difference between a small town and a large borough was a matter of scale. Towns were more crowded than villages, and the shortage of space meant that two-storey houses were already common urban features in the thirteenth century. Journeymen, labourers and drifters were packed into rented rooms in squalid conditions. Dense populations created problems of waste disposal, which were exacerbated by the pollution from industrial processes and by-products. Animal and human excrement littered streets, butchers and tanners failed to dispose of animal remains effectively, and obstructions in public places caused flooding and stagnant water. The leet court of Newmarket contains regular presentments against traders who obstructed roads, allowed dung to accumulate in the street, polluted public places with animal remains, or obstructed street traffic with gutters and banks. In April 1482 nine people were amerced for obstructing with dung Plumpton Lane and Dockpit Lane in Sudbury, and at various times in the fifteenth century the Mildenhall leet amerced people for piling dung, starting 'nettlefires', dumping ashes in the street, and for acts of industrial pollution in local roads and in water supplies. The need to maintain roads eroded by constant use is another peculiarly urban issue, and financial provision for their upkeep dominates bequests in the wills of fifteenth-century Lavenham and is also a feature of smaller towns such as Newmarket.[48]

The high mobility of urban populations, the regular influx of strangers and visitors, and the ready availability of alcohol in alehouses, inns and taverns fuelled well-founded concerns about public order and morality. Levels of physical violence were high in medieval towns, and cases involving assaults, affrays and drawing blood are common in their courts, prompting Gottfried to conclude that murder, larceny, burglary, robbery, rape and assault were disturbingly common in Bury St Edmunds. In 1385 fifteen assaults of various kinds were deemed sufficiently serious to be presented in the leet court of Brandon, a significantly higher number than commonly recorded in the leets of rural communities of equivalent size. An increase – or a perceived increase – in violent behaviour must explain the decision in 1404 by the burgesses of Dunwich to introduce fixed and stringent amercements for anyone found guilty of drawing a knife with intent (40d.) or malicious wounding (10s.), which were immediately enforced by the borough court. In 1447 concerns about public order issues resulted in an adjustment to the oath made by the burgesses of Ipswich to include a commitment to 'sustain and keep' the King's peace, and to 'reform and destroy' 'all routs, riots, rebellions and conjurations against the

---

48 Goldberg, *Medieval England*, pp. 110–11; Davis, 'Petty Traders', pp. 283, 291; PRO sc2/213/71 (Sudbury); SROB E18/451/5, courts held March 1462 and July 1470; E18/451/6, courts held July 1474 and July 1482; E18/451/69, ff. 45, 52 (Mildenhall); Dymond and Betterton, *Lavenham*, p. 16.

same peace'. The responsibility to keep the peace on the streets was vested in elected constables and watchmen, and towns were likely to have a greater number of watchmen on duty each night. For example, three men in Mildenhall, and four in Brandon, were required to 'maintain the vigil of the lord King' each night. Brandon appears to have been a particularly violent town, with a team of night watchmen, constables and subconstables trying to enforce the law: Alan Lakenheath, constable in 1430, was severely assaulted when he tried to arrest four men wielding swords, cudgels and pitchforks for a breach of the King's peace in Ferrystreet.[49]

By the fifteenth century concerns about public order had become closely associated with concerns about public and private morality, which encouraged town courts to regulate anti-social and immoral behaviour more actively and specifically. Some concerns focused upon the strangers who constantly drifted in and out of towns, and the people who housed them: householders were held responsible for the behaviour of anyone staying within their house for more than a day and a night. In 1482 four residents of Ixworth were fined for harbouring 'ignominious and suspicious men' and 'ryotous mytybeggars', and Henry Egle of Brandon, a regular brewer and therefore probable alehouse keeper, maintained many 'ignominious' men who were 'lecherous and suspicious'. Indictments for sexual impropriety and assaults upon women appear to have increased in late fifteenth-century Ipswich, where in 1479 all 'harlots and bawds' were banned from the town, and the existence of a street called 'Gropecuntlane' in Orford implies a favoured territory of prostitutes rather than a romantic lovers' lane: in 1479 the borough court amerced a couple for keeping a bordel house 'where they entertained the wives of their neighbours against the will of their husbands'. Retailing food and drink had always been an important element of trade in small towns, but during the fifteenth century alehouses were transformed from temporary drinking houses into permanent establishments, as standards of living and levels of consumption increased among the mass of the populace, and behaviour within them became a particular focus for manorial and urban courts. A number of references to disturbances of the peace in alehouses are recorded in fifteenth-century Clare, and the jurors of Mildenhall passed a bye-law requiring that 'no common taverns remain open after the ninth hour of the night at any time of the year'. Jurors began to target known offenders in an attempt to regulate behaviour. In 1474 William Culpy of Brandon was amerced because he 'frequents taverns at night and habitually consorts with unknown and suspicious men'. Any Dutchman or recent immigrant who had established an inn in fifteenth-century Ipswich

---

49 Gottfried, *Bury St Edmunds*, p. 217; Bailey, *Dunwich*, pp. 33, 39; Bacon, *Annals*, p. 105; SROB E18/451/3, court held July 1404 (Mildenhall); Bacon Mss 295/10, 12, 16, 26 (Brandon).

was forced to pay a special levy to the borough and required to answer for his servants annually. Yet the proliferation of alehouses and taverns also emphasizes the role of towns as places of entertainment, providing a social experience which was distinctive from that in rural settlements. The annual Assumption play in Ipswich, with its elaborate and colourful procession on the feast day of Corpus Christi, exemplifies the richness of medieval urban culture, and even a small town such as Bungay contained a troupe of players who performed at the local priory.[50]

The high concentration of alehouses and taverns, the high density of population, and the constant ebb and flow of strangers served to exacerbate other social tensions which were peculiar to, or more pronounced in, towns. First, the concentration of power and the control of urban offices into the hands of a self-perpetuating elite could create conflict between the governing oligarchy and the other burgesses, or between the burgesses and the rest of the townsfolk. For example, in 1264 a group of the younger and lesser burgesses of Bury St Edmunds led a rebellion against the abbey, which failed when the senior burgesses moved against them and sought an accommodation with the abbot; and the suspension of Ipswich's borough charter in 1283 was due to a dispute between the elite and the rank-and-file. Second, the various legal jurisdictions which often existed within a single town could sometimes create a conflict of power and authority: for example, the potential tension between the manor and borough at Clare, the lord and burgesses – or the gild and the borough – at Bury St Edmunds, and the leet and Justice of the Peace courts in Ipswich. Wherever such jurisdictions touched one another, authority could be disputed and blurred in matters of both theory and practice. Finally, the intensity of town life created a heated and quarrelsome atmosphere prone to faction.[51]

Medieval townsfolk were acutely aware of the potential for, and existence of, social tensions within their community, and so took extra steps to try to ameliorate them. Concerns about oligarchical control of towns were tempered by the acceptance of new talent into the governing elites, for urban social mobility was higher than in the countryside. In the 1410s Philip Canon became town clerk of Dunwich and later a Member of Parliament, despite modest personal wealth and no prestigious family connections in the borough. Robert Skaldar was a serf from humble farming stock who left Huntingfield

---

[50] Amor, 'Riding out Recession', pp. 139–40; Bacon, *Annals*, pp. 135, 144, 150, 159; *UH*, i, pp. 514, 517; SROB E18/451/6, court held July 1476 (Mildenhall); Thornton, *History of Clare*, p. 104, PRO SC2/203/72; Davis, 'Petty Traders', p. 261 (Clare); Bacon Ms 296/21, 23 (Brandon); Bailey, *Marginal Economy*, pp. 169–70; Bacon, *Annals*, p. 142; M. Rubin, *Corpus Christi: The Eucharist in Late Medieval Culture* (Cambridge, 1991), pp. 260, 275, 279; SROI HD1538/156/7 (Bungay).

[51] Lobel, *Bury St Edmunds*, pp. 126–32; Gottfried, *Bury St Edmunds*, pp. 218–9; *VCH*, i, p. 650; *UH*, i, pp. 529–30.

in the mid-1370s for Sudbury, and in 1380 a Brandon court complained that one Robert Skaldar, burgess of Sudbury, was attempting to procure the town's best cloth workers to settle there: it seems appropriate that an ambitious and upwardly mobile young burgess should prove his worth to his peers by undertaking dirty business on their behalf. Social tensions were also eased by the broad geographical mixing of rich and poor residents within towns: although the wealthier residents tended to live around the marketplace and the poor in the suburbs, there is little evidence of the social zoning that characterized late Victorian towns. Finally, religious gilds offered confraternity and a sense of belonging, and could therefore play an important role in integrating newcomers into late medieval towns. It is significant that such gilds were especially numerous in towns, especially after the mid-fourteenth century, and Bury St Edmunds had at least eighteen by 1389. They filled a social as well as a religious need, providing friendship, communal activities and a sense of belonging to both established residents and newcomers. In binding its members together in confraternity, gilds promoted peaceful and amicable relations among townsfolk and took an active role in resolving disputes.[52]

The various borough courts also sought to promote harmonious relations between residents by their provision of cheap, ready and reasonably efficient justice, and jurors in Romford (Essex) sought to mediate between antagonists to promote informal settlements to disputes. These arguments appear to apply equally well to Suffolk towns. The burgesses of Dunwich intervened when a feud had apparently developed between two small groups of Dunwich burgesses, who were consequently bound over to keep the peace against each other. Both groups were threatened with a £20 forfeit if they broke the agreement, which was formally recorded in the town minutes for good measure. A spirit of conciliation and compromise was necessary in small, densely populated, communities: after all, they had to live with one another in a world without a professional law-enforcement agency.[53]

CONCLUSION

The urban characteristics of medieval Suffolk were very distinctive. First, it was relatively urbanized, especially at the beginning and end of our period. In 1086 three of the most important towns in England were situated in Suffolk. By 1300 over 15 per cent of its population lived in towns (compared with a national average of about 20 per cent), and by *c.* 1500 perhaps 30 per cent were

---

[52] Bailey, *Dunwich*, pp. 8–9; CUL Vanneck Ms, box 5; Bailey, *Marginal Economy*, p. 180; *PSIA* 12 (1906), pp. 24–7.

[53] M. K. McIntosh, *Autonomy and Community: The Royal Borough of Havering, 1200–1600* (Cambridge, 1986), chap. 5; Bailey, *Dunwich*, p. 60.

urban dwellers (with a national average still around 20 per cent). In *c.* 1300 nearly thirty settlements in Suffolk could be described as a town, and by *c.* 1500 well over thirty places. Only two other English counties possessed a higher density of small towns. Second, after *c.* 1200 none of its towns was particularly large or wealthy by English standards. In 1334 only five Suffolk towns feature in the wealthiest hundred towns in England, compared to nine in Norfolk, and Ipswich was barely a quarter of the size of Norwich, and less than half the size of either Yarmouth or Lynn. Third, few of Suffolk's urban centres were boroughs, and the majority were manorial market towns containing between 300 and 1,500 inhabitants. The density of foundations of weekly markets and fairs – many of them dating from the thirteenth century – was higher in Suffolk than anywhere else in England.

The extent of urbanization reflects the relatively high population densities recorded in medieval Suffolk, but also indicates that its economy was geared towards trade and commerce to a significant degree (chapter 7), and became increasingly industrialized (chapter 11). In this context, the relative absence of very large and wealthy towns is more difficult to explain. The greatest cities of medieval England were located on navigable rivers and fulfilled a wide range of important functions, including the administration of religious and civil affairs. Rivers in Suffolk were not navigable for any great distance from the coast, and most of their estuaries were shifting or narrow. Ipswich possessed the best harbour and most accessible estuary, and was an important port, but it failed to compete with London or Yarmouth as a centre of international trade. Similarly, its role as the county town was diminished by the 'privatization' of royal administration and justice across large areas of west Suffolk (the Liberty of St Edmund) and parts of east Suffolk (the Liberty of St Etheldreda), which reduced the size of the geographical area over which it had jurisdiction. Without these peculiar jurisdictions, Ipswich might have become larger and more important than Norwich.

The proliferation of small towns and the foundation of large numbers of rural fairs and weekly markets in the twelfth and thirteenth centuries was initially a response to the increasing but essentially localized demand across the county for basic goods and services from farms and rural households. The collapse of population after the Black Death in 1349 reduced this demand, and therefore threatened the economic viability of small towns and markets, but it also opened up new opportunities for the production of specialist goods and wares by professionals (chapter 11). Medieval boroughs have been dubbed free islands in feudal seas, because they provided their leading residents with the legal means to pursue trade free from the shackles of feudal lordship. Yet their relative absence in Suffolk indicates that the county's social, and especially its manorial, structure was not inimical to trade and commerce. The loose social structure, the success of manorial institutions in providing an effective regulatory framework for commerce, and the personal freedom of most Suffolk folk all explain why small market towns, rather than boroughs, dominated its urban scene.

– CHAPTER 7 –

Commerce, Crafts and Industry

ENGLAND's economy and society became significantly more commercialized during the course of the Middle Ages. This is reflected in an expansion in the supply of money, the provision of smaller denominations of coin,
the emergence of credit markets, and the growth of towns, weekly markets
and seasonal fairs (chapter 6). The existence of more formal markets and fairs,
with legal structures to enforce the rules of trade, reduced the costs and risks
associated with commerce, and therefore encouraged more people to produce
goods and services for consumption by others rather than for themselves. The
economy of Suffolk was strongly influenced by this growth in commercial
enterprise: its proximity to London and the Continent, its high population
density, the high degree of commercialization of agricultural production on
many farms, and its exceptionally high density of market and fair foundations
are indicative of the strength of commercial opportunity and activity.[1]

The commercialization of agriculture was paralleled by the growing sophistication of the labour market and the development of crafts and services. The
range and availability of these employment opportunities grew during the
twelfth and thirteenth centuries, providing supplementary income for the
high proportion of the population with insufficient land to sustain themselves.
Much of this employment was geared to servicing the basic needs of farming
(e.g. metal working, carting, carpentry), or involved the processing and retailing of food and drink (e.g. baking, brewing, cooking, fishing) or the processing of natural and renewable resources (e.g. providing fuel from woodland,
turf and bracken). However, other activities involved more specialist skills, a
greater division of skilled labour during the manufacturing process and some
capital investment (e.g. textile manufacture and shipbuilding).

The purpose of this chapter is threefold. The first is to consider the range
of employment opportunities available in Suffolk: changes in the fortunes and
scale of particular by-employments, crafts and industries – such as the extraordinary growth of woollen textile manufacture after the mid-fourteenth century – are considered in chapter 11. Second, to assess the extent to which the
labour force was geographically mobile. And, finally, to explore the efficiency
of the local transport network and to identify the principal markets for Suffolk
produce and manufactures.

[1] For a general background, see Britnell, *Commercialisation*.

BY-EMPLOYMENTS, CRAFTS AND INDUSTRY

The overwhelming preponderance of smallholdings in medieval Suffolk increased the relative importance of activities such as labouring, servant-hood and the petty craft and retail trades. The wide availability of this work is reflected in the presence in almost every rural parish of craftsmen plying basic trades, such as smiths, leather workers, tailors, carpenters and thatchers. Their presence implies that some aspects of metal-working and house-building (such as construction of the frame and roof) were routinely undertaken by paid specialists and that ordinary people also looked to professionals to supply some of their clothes. Similarly, almost every village contained people who were employed in processing food for local purchase and consumption, such as bread, meat joints, cheese, butter, puddings, ale and pies, and in supplying fuel. Most workers in these trades worked in small units of production (often in a domestic setting), and were personally involved in most stages of production, from obtaining the raw material to selling the final product. By extension, the quality of the finished product was modest in most cases. This was especially true of the period *c.* 1200–1350, when such work tended to be occasional and poorly paid, and when many workers turned their hands to a diverse range of activities. After 1350 work was better paid and more persistently available, which encouraged greater specialization among the workforce and the production of higher-quality manufactures.[2]

The existence and importance of petty crafts and by-employments in medieval England is too well documented to merit detailed repetition here. The key questions are whether the range of such opportunities was wider in Suffolk than in other areas of the country, and, if so, whether certain trades were especially prominent. Inevitably, the nature of the sources does not permit a definitive judgement on this issue, but the very high proportion of smallholdings was possible precisely because the availability of non-farm employment was greater here than elsewhere. The incomplete Poll Tax returns of 1381 provide the clearest indication of the importance of by-employments within individual rural communities. Those for Thingoe hundred reveal that 39 per cent of the adult population were labourers, 41 per cent servants and 12 per cent artisans (i.e. craft workers) of various kinds. Of course, these categorizations indicate the *primary* source of employment, and in reality workers secured employment from a number of sources. A labourer may well have occupied a smallholding and turned his hand to a variety of pursuits, while 'servants' may well have been involved in various forms of craftwork, retailing and domestic chores in the home of their employer. In a few places the proportion of artisans – those whose primary employment was earned from skilled or semi-

---

[2] Dyer, *Making a Living*, pp. 168–73.

skilled craftwork – was even higher. This was obviously true of small towns and textile manufacturing centres, but also of some rural settlements: in 1381 20 per cent of adults in Buxhall were artisans, including weavers, cloth cutters and skinners.[3]

Three broad observations offer further support to the assertion that the proportion of labourers, servants and artisans was high in Suffolk's rural communities. First, accidents of geology have resulted in a variety of soil types over relatively short distances in Suffolk, which produced an unusually diverse resource base. Local communities then exploited the various products of these different resources with great intensity and ingenuity, judging by the extraordinarily high values attached to non-arable resources in *c.* 1300, especially for woodland, marshland and even heathland. Fuel was intensively prepared and sold, not just in those areas of the county well stocked with woodland, such as south-west Suffolk, but also in places where hardly any woodland existed, such as the Sandlings (using bracken) and Fenland (peat). Fenland marshes yielded a wide range of natural resources, which in turn provided much employment in preparing and selling products such as sedge, turves, baskets and eels.[4]

Second, the high density of markets and urban outlets, and the commercialized nature of the Suffolk economy, widened the scope for involvement in non-farm activities. At least six different types of craft could be found in most market settlements, and small towns often boasted around fifteen to twenty different trades. In 1304 tradespeople (barkers, fullers, ditchers and smiths) dominated the 'new tenancies' recorded in the expanding town of Hadleigh. The numbers of people involved in the main retail trades in small towns could be impressively large. For example, in the 1340s around forty-nine brewers were amerced each year at Mildenhall, thirty at Lakenheath and twenty-one at Brandon, perhaps representing one-quarter of all local households. Around twenty people were amerced each year in the Brandon court rolls for illegal peat cutting, and many more did so legally. Carters plied the county's highways, and boatmen its waterways, carrying goods to and fro. The labour market was sufficiently fluid and active to attract the attention of middlemen, who probably acted more like gangmasters than employment agents. Labourers enjoyed contacts far outside their home village, often journeying up to 15 miles for employment, and they turned their hand to a variety of activities, from petty craftwork to unskilled labouring on other people's farms. The proliferation of small demesnes with no servile labour force would have increased the opportunities for wage labouring, and labourers were also hired to work on peasant holdings. For example, William le Wolf of Aldham contracted William Carter to plough 7 acres of his land during the winter of 1343–4 for 2s. 10d., and also

3 Powell, *Rising in East Anglia*, pp. 92–4, 122.

4 Bailey, *Marginal Economy*, pp. 163–5.

employed Alice Goodrich to undertake unspecified work on his behalf for six months, probably tending animals: unfortunately, le Wolf failed to pay either of them and was outlawed for various felonies two years later.[5]

The third and final point to support the argument that the range of by-employments was greater in medieval Suffolk than in many other parts of England is the presence of three major specialist activities: marine fishing, leather working and commercial textile manufacture. Just as the Fens and the freshwater waterways of north-west Suffolk provided supplementary produce for local residents, so the tidal rivers and the sea provided an important harvest for residents of east Suffolk. Unlike vast stretches of the Cornish and north Yorkshire coastlines, where towering cliffs restricted access to the resources of the sea, the Suffolk coast was readily accessible through its extensive shingle beaches and shallow tidal rivers. The latter were a major source of oysters, then a cheap and abundant food rather than the delicacy of modern times. The farming of oyster beds has left remarkably little evidence in the documentary sources, but it must have been significant if the chance reference to a single consignment of 32,600 oysters, due from an Ufford boatman to a Yarmouth merchant in 1367, is typical. Oysters were removed in large quantities from the river Alde in the fifteenth century, and fertile oyster beds may well explain the high value of 'marshland' around Butley creek. Casual fishing along these rivers and off the coast was commonplace, and a Parliamentary petition complained about the congestion created by small boats operating around the mouth of the river Alde. The areas between the high and low watermarks on estuarine rivers were strewn with wattle weirs to trap fish at every tide; the weirs were owned, hired and worked by fishermen who paid highly for them. At least twenty-five were located on the Felixstowe side of the river Deben, and in 1396 the sale of three large weirs raised the huge sum of £15 in entry fines.[6]

Boatbuilding was usually a specialism of the larger ports, and featured prominently at Dunwich in the twelfth and thirteenth centuries. Wreckage and beachcombing could offer some occasional but worthwhile financial rewards. Timber and barrels of iron, processed food, wine and beer were regularly found floating on the sea or washed upon the foreshore at Sizewell,

5 Smith, 'Periodic Market', pp. 468–78; *PSIA* 11 (1903), pp. 169–71; Bailey, *Marginal Economy*, pp. 261–2; Bacon Mss 291/14, 16; A. R. DeWindt, 'Defining the Peasant Community in Medieval England', *Journal of British Studies* 26 (1987), p. 189; CUL Vanneck Ms, box 1, courts held March 1344, October 1345 and December 1346 (Aldham).

6 This section on fishing draws heavily upon Bailey, 'Coastal Fishing', and Bailey, *Dunwich*, pp. 15–19. See also *VCH*, ii, pp. 203–7; Arnott, *Alde Estuary*, pp. 41, 49–50; Bacon, *Annals*, p. 125; BL Add. Rolls 40712–40722 (Dunwich smokehouses); and Arnott, *Orwell Estuary*, pp. 70–5, 89–92.

Thorpe and Felixstowe, and clothing and personal effects were not uncommon. The 10d. earned in 1385 by Henry Hudde for the clothing he stripped from a shipwrecked corpse lying on the shingle at Sizewell indicates the income to be squeezed from unusual sources, as well as providing a stark reminder of the danger of maritime pursuits in the Middle Ages. Occasional acts of piracy, particularly against foreign ships, presented another source of income, as exemplified in 1404 by an attack against two Flemish ships off Felixstowe co-ordinated by a small group of established local fishermen: the booty earned a few shillings each for scores of men, some living as far away as Earl Soham, Framsden and Debenham.

The herring and sprat fisheries greatly enhanced the importance of the sea to the Suffolk economy. Both species spawned off the northern part of the Suffolk coast during the summer and autumn, and were caught in huge quantities. Herring rents and dues were recorded in 1086 in a number of coastal settlements between Gorleston and Dunwich, reflecting their local importance at this early date, after which the industry expanded until it peaked around 1300, by which time Great Yarmouth dominated the English trade. Processed herrings and sprats offered a cheap and nutritious source of food, particularly when grain prices were high, and were caught, cured, barrelled and consumed in vast quantities throughout England and north-west Europe: at its peak, the Yarmouth fleet alone caught in excess of perhaps 10 million herrings each year. There is no doubt that some of the herring passing through Yarmouth was caught by fishermen drawn from Suffolk. Northales, Kessingland and Kirkley all had established fishing fleets, the rise of Gorleston in the early fourteenth century caused concern in Yarmouth itself, and boats from as far south as Thorpeness caught herring. The herring season tended to be dominated by fishermen from the larger ports, partly because the bigger boats necessary for the deeper sea voyages associated with this trade were concentrated there. Casual fishermen and those operating from smaller coastal settlements – such as Aldeburgh, Sizewell and Thorpeness – tended to stay closer to the coast and to concentrate upon sprats and line fishing.

It is impossible to know the size of the fishing fleets operating from any given centre at any one time, and most of the direct evidence dates from the later Middle Ages when the herring industry had passed its peak. In the late fourteenth century around ten to twelve small boats regularly worked the herring and sprat shoals from Sizewell and Thorpe; in the early fifteenth century the Dunwich fishing fleet comprised between twenty and thirty boats; and in 1451 that at Walberswick comprised twenty-two boats of various kinds. The larger boats could gross £10–30 per annum from the herring season, and smaller boats £5–10. Deep-sea voyages to the Icelandic fishing grounds were rarer, but could generate ten times these sums. Such earnings were subject to tithe payments to the parish church (one-tenth of the catch), and to further deductions by town authorities or local lords as a fee for mooring and landing: whatever was left was split among boat owner, master and crew according to a customary share system. Boat owners, usually the wealthier residents of the bigger ports, reaped the major share of the profit, although owner/masters could earn a comfortable living from the sea. The majority of boat masters and crew are unlikely to have earned anything more than a supplementary income from fishing. Crews were often residents of coastal and river settlements, although some were drawn from villages further inland. Most sea fish was cured (usually smoked or salted) and barrelled as soon as the boats returned to shore, which provided an additional source of employment, mainly for women: fishermen did not often involve themselves in the processing of fish, although their wives and daughters usually did. Tens of thousands of herrings and sprats were caught by Dunwich fishermen each year, most of which were then smoked in 'fumigars' located within the borough. These were small smokehouses, flimsy constructions which were readily assembled in courtyards and gardens (and on one occasion in the abandoned churchyard of St Nicholas). Many leading residents of Dunwich owned smokehouses and rented them to poorer residents.

The predominantly mixed nature of Suffolk farming, and the local importance of dairy herds and sheep, created regular work preparing animal hides and skins. Yet tanning and leather working remain one of those 'forgotten' industries, mainly because they have left hardly any impression upon the surviving documentary sources: contemporaries took leather for granted, and so historians have tended to ignore it. Surname evidence indicates that barkers and tanners were fairly common throughout early fourteenth-century Suffolk, although they tended to congregate in towns where they had ready access to butchers and knackers, and to the decent water supply required for the tanning process. In 1282 eleven tanners were wealthy enough to be taxed in Ipswich, although their tanneries were not very valuable, rated at around 20s. each, and the markets at Ipswich, Bury and Newmarket had rows of stalls devoted to leather trades. In general, tanners were not wealthy, and they featured heavily among the poorest trades people in Bury St Edmunds, judging from the size of bequests they made in their wills.[7]

By the end of the thirteenth century a few places in Suffolk had become established as specialist manufacturers of woollen textiles, whose cloths were sold well beyond the immediate locality. In addition, some linen textiles were

7 L. A. Clarkson, 'The Leather Crafts in Tudor and Stuart England', *AgHR* 14 (1966), p. 25; *HistA*, pp. 144–5; *VCH*, i, p. 649; *PSIA* 12 (1906), pp. 145–6, 149–53; Gottfried, *Bury St Edmunds*, pp. 111, 117–19; *1327 Lay Subsidy*, pp. 227, 293–4; Denney, *Sibton Abbey*, p. 112; see also Britnell, *Colchester*, pp. 14–15.

produced in the Waveney valley, and parts of east Suffolk produced some sail-cloth. The manufacture of higher-quality textiles, which were sold in more distant markets and were sought by wealthy mercantile and aristocratic households, was characterized by a greater division of labour in the production process, which involved the application of either more specialist skills or simply more labour inputs, and perhaps a greater investment in capital equipment. Spinning and, to some extent, weaving required limited skill and capital, and were therefore easy by-employments to enter and leave. Wool was usually spun into yarn by hand, often by women within the household, and then woven into cloth on an upright loom by men: most looms were located in a domestic setting. Increasing use was made of the horizontal loom, which was more expensive and demanding of labour but which produced a tighter and finer cloth, and was therefore largely confined to specialist rather than casual weavers. The cloth was then fulled, sometimes manually but often in mechanized fulling mills, stretched, sheared and dyed. Fulling was a more structured and less casual business than spinning or weaving, and the lessees of fulling mills handled a high volume of cloth through teams of hired and semi-skilled workers. Depending upon the style of the cloth and the amount of labour input, the finished product might be coarse and undyed or very fine and brightly coloured. However, units of production were small at every stage of the manufacturing process and usually located in domestic settings.

In 1200 Bury St Edmunds and Sudbury were ranked in the second league of English cloth-manufacturing towns, and by *c.* 1300 the manufacture of textiles had spread to Clare, Ipswich and a few rural settlements in south Suffolk, such as Hadleigh and Lavenham. Even outside these core locations, the volume of manufacture was already sufficiently high to justify the capital investment required to construct water-powered fulling mills in places such as Blakenham, Orford and Ufford, and along the river Lark. Although Suffolk was not yet at the forefront of English textile manufacture, its industry gained further momentum in the second quarter of the fourteenth century, when rising real wages, expanding orders for the military, the addition of a excise duty on the export of English wool to the Continent, and political difficulties in the Flemish textile towns all combined to favour indigenous textile manufacture. The traditional view that an influx of Flemish weavers at this time boosted Suffolk production is a myth, because the few Flemings living in Suffolk tended to be involved in other trades. The growth in economic activity in Clare in the 1340s – based principally upon its expanding textile trade – is particularly striking. Thus the woollen textile industry was already well established by *c.* 1300 in small pockets scattered across south and west Suffolk, and then it expanded even further in the late fourteenth century. Indeed, Dymond reminds us forcefully that medieval Suffolk was, by contemporary standards, an *industrial* county.[8]

To what extent was work in medieval Suffolk sex-specific? Of course, some overlap occurred in all aspects of working life, so that women helped out with menial tasks on the farm at critical times of the year, such as the harvest and the haymaking, and a few took over the running of farms and businesses after the death of their husbands. However, it is possible to identify certain activities which were mainly undertaken by women. The most obvious were household tasks, such as cleaning, childcare, preparing meals, tending to the fire, and drawing water from the well. Similarly, women attended to the necessary tasks of recycling domestic goods and utensils, stitching clothes and maintaining furnishings. The shortage of direct evidence for women working in other activities is frustrating, but certain agricultural tasks were principally the preserve of females, most notably tending to livestock in general and dairy herds in particular: they were usually in charge of keeping poultry, tending the garden, milking cows and ewes, and making butter and cheese. Hence women dominated dairying, one of the most important components of Suffolk's agrarian economy, whether tending to the family's own cow(s) or as live-in servants on someone else's dairy farm. This point is powerfully illustrated by Katherine Dowe, who managed the abbot of Sibton's large herd of cows without any male assistance: indeed, the scale of, and income from, the dairy increased impressively under Dowe's skilful direction. Her team included Alice Harys and three other female servants, who in 1510 produced 80 weys of cheese and over 330 gallons of butter. Women also appear to have dominated the cutting and processing of heathland products, either to sell as fuel or to make into brooms, as evidenced by the dominance of females among the lessees of parcels of heath at Easton Bavents, and of those cutting broom at Walton.[9]

The example of Katherine Dowe provides other insights into the involvement of women in 'industrial' work, because her team of dairy hands also spent some of their time spinning wool and flax. Spinning is well known as a female

---

[8] This survey draws upon G. Unwin, *Essays in Economic History* (London, 1927), pp. 262–4; B. McClenaghan, *The Springs of Lavenham* (Ipswich, 1924), p. 3; Thornton, *History of Clare*, pp. 142–6; Bailey, *Marginal Economy*, pp. 171–82; Dymond and Betterton, *Lavenham*, pp. 95–6; L. R. Poos, *A Rural Society after the Black Death: Essex, 1350–1525* (Cambridge, 1991), pp. 65–9. For fulling mills, see Davis, 'Petty Traders', p. 221 (Clare), SROB E3/2/7, court held December 1387 (Layham); PRO SC6/1003/3 (Orford); SROI HD1538/395/1 (Ufford); *HistA*, p. 140; Arnott, *Alde Estuary*, p. 40; Holmes, *Higher Nobility*, p. 93; Britnell, *Colchester*, pp. 21–2.

[9] For useful general surveys, see M. E. Mate, *Women in Medieval English Society* (Cambridge, 1999), pp. 27–56, and Rigby, *English Society*, pp. 243–83. Denney, *Sibton Abbey*, pp. 38–9.

task in the Middle Ages, and its importance in feeding the expanding and productive textile looms of late medieval Suffolk is self-evident. The preparation of flax and hemp, as part of the process of making linen cloth and rope, was an important yet under-recorded activity. The tasks of growing these plants, and then retting, drying, breaking and heckling them for industrial use, were time consuming but – once again – they could be undertaken in and around the home, and were readily combined with other domestic or farm work. Women must also have been prominent in preserving the hundreds of thousands of herrings and sprats caught each year off the Suffolk coast, particularly in the key processes of gutting, smoking and salting the fish.[10]

Brewing was the third major 'industrial' task dominated by women, at least until the fifteenth century. Although manorial court rolls often amerced males for brewing, this simply reflected their status as the head of the household, and, in reality, it was their wives, daughters and/or servants who were brewing the ale in domestic settings: indeed, the courts of Earl Soham variously list husbands and wives, while those of Dunwich record mainly women. In small towns, such as Newmarket, many regular female brewers were innkeepers in partnership with their husbands, whereas those in early fourteenth-century Redgrave were often single, destitute and selling their ale by the jug to passing trade. Other poor women often bought up small quantities of ale and bread from other producers, and hawked these basic refreshments around the streets or the marketplace, or sold them through windows. Women in early fourteenth-century Lakenheath also occupied other niches in the retail trades. They organized the preparation and then sale of hot pasties to hungry traders and boatmen, and they also dominated the presentments of those who helped themselves illegally to peat turves from the piles of other residents drying in the marshes, indicating their role in retailing rather than digging fuel. In general, the precise and full contribution of women to the medieval economy is seldom reflected in the extant sources, but it is clear that their backroom contribution to three of the most important activities in Suffolk – in curing saltwater fish, spinning yarn for textile manufacture, and making cheese and butter – was immense.[11]

[10] Denney, *Sibton Abbey*, p. 39; N. Evans, *The East Anglian Linen Industry: Rural Industry and Local Economy, 1500–1850* (Aldershot, 1985), pp. 22–35.

[11] J. M. Bennett, *Ale, Beer and Brewsters in England: Women's Work in a Changing World, 1300–1600* (Oxford, 1996), p. 175; BL Add. Rolls 40710, 40722 (Dunwich); Mate, *Women*, pp. 38–46. The Lakenheath examples are from CUL EDC 7/15/11/1/2, court held June 1310; 7/15/11/1/5, court held May 1314; and 7/15/11/1/8, mm. 3, 19, 7/15/11/1/10, m. 3 (peat turves).

GEOGRAPHICAL MOBILITY

The establishment and growth of towns in the thirteenth century depended heavily upon a mobile and migratory workforce: likewise, the response of many non-inheriting sons and poverty-stricken people to rural economic hardship was to seek employment opportunities wherever trades people congregated. Unfortunately, manorial courts in the pre-plague era paid little attention to out-migration from their overpopulated manors, thus depriving historians of a mine of detailed information. Surname evidence offers some general insights into the patterns of local migration before 1349. McKinley's study of locative surnames concluded that Suffolk's population was given to frequent moves over limited distances, longer migrations were quite common, and high levels of permanent movement occurred within 20 miles of the home village. An analysis of the information contained in the 1327 Lay Subsidy reveals that both Bury St Edmunds and Ipswich acted as magnets to migrants within a 10-mile radius, and Gottfried shows that 60 per cent of immigrants to Bury originated within 20 miles of the town. In addition, east Suffolk provided many migrants to Norfolk and London.[12]

The most precise information about geographical mobility comes from the record of the payment and evasion of chevage in manorial courts. Landlords had been largely indifferent to out-migration from their manors in the over-crowded conditions of the early fourteenth century, but they became much more sensitive after the Black Death, when tenants and labourers were in short supply. Consequently, their courts recorded more chevage cases, and included more detail on the whereabouts of flown serfs, which helps to create a clearer picture of patterns of migration.

The evidence contained in table 4, featuring migration patterns from a sample of ten manors located across the county, indicates that over half of Suffolk migrants moved to a settlement within 10 miles of their home manor, and over three-quarters settled within 20 miles. Long-distance migrants were a clear minority, although a sizeable one in coastal settlements with wider trading contacts. For example, migrants from Dunningworth (located on a navigable stretch of the river Alde near what is now Snape Maltings) settled almost exclusively in ports along the East Anglian coast, such as Southwold, Orford, Aldeburgh, Northales (Covehithe), Yarmouth, Ipswich and Colchester. The residents of Walton, sandwiched between Goseford and Orwell havens, had established trading contacts over greater distances than those of Dunning-worth, and consequently their migrants displayed an even greater propensity

---

[12] R. A. McKinley, *The Surnames of Norfolk and Suffolk in the Middle Ages* (London, 1975), pp. 76–7; *HistA*, pp. 84–5; Dymond and Northeast, *History of Suffolk*, p. 44; Gottfried, *Bury St Edmunds*, pp. 69–70.

TABLE 4   Distance of permanent migration by serfs from selected manors

Manor	Period	Sample size	1–10 miles	11–20 miles	20+ miles
Aldham	1371–1468	26	38%	54%	8%
Cratfield	1417–92	25	60%	16%	24%
Dunningworth	1359–1470	29	67%	17%	16%
Fornham	1354–1423	16	56%	19%	25%
Harleston	1415–59	12	42%	8%	5%
Lakenheath	1387–1418	17	24%	52%	24%
Lidgate	1394–1470	25	48%	36%	16%
Thorpe Morieux	1403–10	7	71%	29%	0%
Ufford	1370–1433	22	86%	9%	5%
Walton	1382–99	43	14%	21%	65%

Sources: CUL Vanneck Ms, box 1 and SROI HA85/484/315 (Aldham); CUL Vanneck Ms, box 3 (Cratfield); SROI HD1538/207/2–8 (Dunningworth); SROB E3/15.17/1.8 – 1.15 and E3/15.6/1.11 – 1.18 (Fornham); SROB E3/15.17/1.1 (Harleston); CUL EDC 7/15/11/box 2/22 (Lakenheath); SROB E3/11/1.1 – 1.5 (Lidgate); SROB 1700/1/3 (Thorpe Morieux); SROI HD1538/394/1–5 (Ufford); SROI HA119/50/3/17–19 (Walton).

to settle afar. For example, in 1394 eighteen men paid chevage at Walton, of whom two were reported to be living in London, three in Norwich, one in Bristol, four in the Yarmouth/Lowestoft district, one in Cley (Norfolk), three in Dunwich, and three in Ipswich.[13]

The personal reasons for migration are never stated in the terse court roll entries, but the main forces pushing an individual from the home manor, or pulling to another location, were economic. Many migrants moved to secure a family holding or a more attractive tenure, which enabled them to construct a bigger or better livelihood, while others sought jobs in trade or industry. Walter Mengy moved from Dunningworth to neighbouring Blaxhall in the late 1420s to occupy a landholding; then he acquired more land back in Dunningworth in 1430 before eventually moving to Orford in 1443, where he died fourteen years later. The lure of urban streets, popularly assumed to be paved with gold, proved too strong for John Miles, who left Dunningworth in 1451 at the age of thirteen to become an apprentice to John Burre, a burgess of Ipswich. By 1461 he had obviously served his apprenticeship and moved on, so the Dunningworth court noted with concern that his whereabouts was now unknown. Yet by 1471 the court had established that John, now aged thirty-three, had settled in Dedham (Essex), an established centre of textile manufacture.

[13] The following Dunningworth examples are from SROI HD1538/207/4–8; SROI HA119/50/3/17, m. 54 (Walton).

He was clearly thriving, and a fast worker, because the court of 1477 noted dryly that he now had five children. The desire for occupational advancement was a family trait, for in 1470 John's cousin or nephew, Nicholas Miles, left Dunningworth to be apprenticed to Thomas Grubbe of Ipswich.

All of these examples emphasize the primary importance of familial and neighbourhood links in finding work or establishing introductions for land tenancies in new places. Various members of the Gille family moved from Lidgate to either Kedington or Cavendish, and a branch of the Batchelor family migrated to Fordham (Cambridgeshire); similarly, many Krembylls from Aldham settled around Bredfield, Dallinghoo and Woodbridge, while others moved to nearby Hadleigh. Other migrants had strong personal reasons for leaving their home manor. One of these was William Oxe, who left Blaxhall to enter the household of his lord, the duke of Norfolk, at Framlingham castle. Oxe's devotion to the service of his lord would not have impressed William Dawys of Tunstall, whose motives for moving to Yarmouth in 1428 included a desire to conceal his servile status by changing his surname. In his new neighbourhood ('near the bridge in Yarmouth'), William was known as 'William Smyth, shipman', and his choice of a humdrum and ubiquitous alias reflected a determination to shed a surname that, on his home manor, pointed damningly to servile origins.

The record of female migration is poor, because manorial courts had no interest in females once a merchet had been paid for their marriage, unlike married servile males, whose departure represented an erosion of the capital asset base of the manor and whose whereabouts was consequently recorded for many years after their departure. Some women sought occupational advancement, especially when labour was short after the Black Death, but the majority sought either domestic service, or accompanied their migrant family, or went in search of marriage partners elsewhere. Occasionally, the court entries are less terse and provide some details about women's personal circumstances. For example, Catherine Miles was enticed away from Dunningworth in early 1403 without the lord's permission by one Luke Companion, although the jurors who presented the case understood exactly the type of companionship Luke had in mind. Consequently, in September 1404 a handsome marriage licence of 6s. 8d. was paid to the lord, and Catherine disappears from the historical record.

TRANSPORT

Transport is an essential component of a commercialized economy, and in medieval England passage by boat significantly reduced the cost of transporting bulky agricultural goods and building materials. The tidal creeks and rivers which cut into the coastline of east Suffolk increased the number of rural producers capable of accessing boat transportation and therefore of reaching distant markets profitably. The river Waveney was navigable as far as Beccles, the Blyth to Blythburgh, the Alde to Snape bridge, the Deben to Wilford Bridge, the Gipping to just beyond Ipswich, and the Stour to Cattawade bridge. Furthermore, the navigability of the Ouse river system connected parts of north-west Suffolk to the east Midlands and Lynn. The river Lark was navigable as far as Mildenhall, and the Little Ouse to Thetford, which enabled small boats to reach rudimentary docking facilities at Mildenhall, Lakenheath, Santon Downham and Brandon. Goods, livestock and people were routinely transported around the fens by boat, and traders came from Cambridge, the east Midlands, Lynn and even York to the riverine ports of north-west Suffolk. Millstones, tar and timber from the Baltic, coal from Newcastle, and ashlar from Northamptonshire were shipped as far as Brandon, Lakenheath and Mildenhall, and then carted to destinations in west Suffolk.[14]

Little evidence has remained of the boats used to convey goods along Suffolk's rivers and around its coast, but they were ubiquitous and versatile. The most common was the *batella*, a generic term covering a variety of types of smaller craft. It was unlikely to have been longer than eight metres, or to have carried more than five crew, and was small enough to be dragged onto shingle beaches at places like Aldeburgh, Sizewell and Thorpe. The assumption that the word *batella* describes the smallest type of boat is supported by the use of others to describe larger craft found in the deeper-water ports. Craft operated by local fishermen visiting Dunwich haven were described as *batella*, whereas a Dutch visitor there owned a *navus*. The Little Ouse at Brandon was deep enough to accommodate a 'keel' valued at more than £5, and at Dunwich the *farcost* was deployed both in deeper sea-fishing operations and as a coastal trader, and was clearly larger (and more numerous) than the *batella*, which was used mainly for in-shore trading and fishing. Larger ships – barges, hulks, cogs, '*naves*', and 'grete botes' – are recorded in the deeper havens of Dunwich, Walberswick, Orwell, Lowestoft and Goseford, and were probably variations of two- or three-masted ships of up to 200 tons capable of sustained deep-sea voyages. In *c.* 1500 it was known that the 'creeks' of Northales, Sizewell and Thorpeness could accommodate boats over 10 tons, while the ports of Southwold, Walberswick and Dunwich could handle those over 60 tons.

[14] Bailey, *Marginal Economy*, pp. 147–55; Bacon Ms 295/18; Stone, 'Hinderclay', p. 616; Amor, 'Late Medieval Enclosure', p. 190, suggests that the Gipping might have been navigable to Stowmarket; Ridgard, *Framlingham*, p. 96; Amor, 'Riding out Recession', p. 134.

However, the largest Suffolk ships were notably smaller than those operating from London and the Cinque ports.[15]

Quays, jetties or hithes were built and maintained by landlords or urban authorities in river and coastal ports to facilitate and attract water-borne transport, which in the largest places included rudimentary cranes and lifting gear. Most ports had an area of 'common' quay, a place where residents could dock and load their boats with nominal charge, but many also had a number of quays in private ownership, which charged for usage. For example, the common quay in Ipswich lay next to one belonging to the earl of Norfolk and another called 'Harney's Quay'. The common quay at Woodbridge was supplemented by at least three others, one held by the eponymous priory, another by the earl of Suffolk (which carried rights over 'all anchorage and groundage with other charges and profits from ships, boats and merchandise there'), and in November 1437 the lord also permitted Geoffrey Kempe 'to occupy a quay of his own, for his own ships, boats, goods, chattels and merchandise, and not those of outsiders'. Access to the wharves of Suffolk's lesser ports could be precarious, as illustrated by a case at Woodbridge in December 1377, when 'a ship was moored at the quay at Woodbridge because its crew had unloaded clay and stone [i.e. building materials]: then a tide swelled by high winds carried this clay and stone into le Flete next to the Quay, which prevented boats from mooring at the quay to the grave damage of the lord and his tenants. And the aforesaid men were resting in the taverns of William Cook and William Kech when the ship was aroused.' The rights attached to quays were lucrative – the common quay in Ipswich was leased for £17 per annum – and were carefully enforced in local courts: in 1365 four 'ships' and five 'boats' were amerced for illegal use of the earl's quay in Woodbridge, and two years later the crew of a Flemish ship was amerced for helping themselves to shingle from the foreshore to provide ballast for their return journey.[16]

Overland travel was not easy in the Middle Ages, although its speed and efficiency was greatly improved during the thirteenth and fourteenth centuries by the construction of wooden bridges across fording points and the replacement of wooden with stone bridges on major routeways. A wooden bridge was built in the early thirteenth century to replace a ferry across the Little Ouse at Brandonferry, and certain tenants, called Briggemen, were made responsible for its upkeep and maintenance. This bridge almost certainly stood on the

[15] Bailey, 'Coastal fishing', p. 104; Bailey, *Marginal Economy*, pp. 153–5; BL Add. Roll 40712; Bailey, *Dunwich*, p. 17; Arnott, *Alde Estuary*, pp. 49–50; J. Middleton-Stewart, *Inward Piety and Outward Splendour: Death and Remembrance in the Deanery of Dunwich, 1370–1547* (Woodbridge, 2001), pp. 17, 82; *VCH*, ii, p. 211.

[16] Bacon, *Annals*, pp. 71, 112; SROI HA119/50/3/19, mm. 73, 102 (Ipswich); SROI HD1538/394/1, 2 and 395/1 (Woodbridge); Arnott, *Suffolk Estuary*, p. 113.

site of the present one, a short distance up-stream from the hithes of Brandon (on the south bank of the river) and Oteringhithe (on the north bank), and its construction must have undermined the attractiveness of Thetford to traders, 9 miles up-stream. This wooden bridge was then replaced by a stone construction in the 1330s, built at the great cost of over £200 by the lord of the manor, the bishop of Ely. The bridge may well have reduced the subsequent volume of river traffic to Thetford, and certainly confirmed Brandon's position ahead of Thetford as the major crossing point of the Little Ouse for overland travellers in the western areas of Norfolk and Suffolk: by the fifteenth century it was firmly established on the pilgrimage route to the important Shrine of Our Lady at Walsingham. Evidence of other stone bridges dating from the fourteenth century has survived at Cavenham, Kentford and Moulton (plate 10), implying that this was an important period in such construction, and many others must have also once existed. Bridges were particularly important in creating efficient transport links across the river-pierced coastline of east Suffolk, and bridge construction and upkeep attracted considerable attention from local people in their wills.[17]

The attention paid to bridges, no less than the success of new towns established on major routeways, underlines the significance of overland transport to the economy of medieval Suffolk. As the quantity of extant wills increases during the later Middle Ages, so they reveal the significant sums of money expended upon the upkeep of local roads through charitable bequests, which in turn reflects the importance of roads to economic well-being and the creation of individual wealth. William Forthe, the great Hadleigh clothier, left £66 13s. 4d. in his will to repair and maintain roads within 6 miles of Hadleigh, and John Motte of London, with interests in Bildeston, bequeathed a staggering £240 to maintain the roads and bridges from Bildeston to Semer, Rattlesden, Ipswich, Colchester and London. The traditional image of impassable roads clogged by mud is exaggerated, because road upkeep was closely regulated by courts and funded by charitable bequests, although winter passage across the clays of north-east Suffolk could test the patience of regular travellers. In general, road travel appears to have been relatively fast and safe compared with more isolated areas of the country. Only the area around Newmarket, with its expanses of lonely heathland and high volume of traffic on the main east–west route into East Anglia, gained a sustained reputation for danger among travellers, although even there the concentration of complaints during the third quarter of the fourteenth century may reflect the nefarious activities of particular gangs: for example, a royal commission in 1356 found

[17] D. F. Harrison, 'Bridges and Economic Development, 1300–1800', *EcHR* 45 (1992), pp. 240–61; CUL EDR G27/3, f. 192 and PRO E101/543/4 (Brandon); *PSIA* 21 (1933), pp. 111–15; Middleton-Stewart, *Inward Piety*, p. 81.

that these heaths drew 'large numbers of felons and evildoers' who 'hold the passes there and commit numerous [felonies] on those passing through those parts'.[18]

The other main indicator of the importance of road transport is the prevalence of carts. The two-wheeled cart (*carecta*) was a ubiquitous and extremely common form of light haulage in medieval Suffolk, capable of carrying a ton of goods, and was widely deployed to carry grain short distances and expensive goods much farther. Wine from Ipswich was regularly carted to Lakenheath then shipped to Ely; the burgesses of Dunwich shifted barrels of wine and herring to various parts of East Anglia by the same means; fish was routinely carted to Clare castle from Yarmouth and Bury St Edmunds; and manorial officials of Mildenhall hired a local carter to fetch millstones from Ipswich. Carters from outside Dunwich were charged a fee for operating in the market, which was the borough's cut from either their haulage profits or sales. Horses and carts were routinely hired out. One Lakenheath resident hired a horse and cart from the manor to conduct business in Bury St Edmunds, and another borrowed a horse to visit Ipswich, over 40 miles away. Lords leased their demesne carts to local people when not required for the lord's business, an early form of rent-a-van. On one occasion the manor of Aldham charged a rental fee of 16d. per day for seven days, and John Wodebite of Walsham was reprimanded for using the demesne carts for private business for two days. A run of cases in the borough court of Clare involved damages against lessees who had worked their hired horses too hard; one case concerned a man who had driven to Norwich in a day to collect some goods.[19]

Carts were exclusively horse-driven. John Langdon has established that both horse hauling and horse ownership increased markedly during the course of the thirteenth century. Although horses were more expensive to keep than oxen, they could haul twice as fast and work for longer, enabling producers to supply wider markets. Consequently, the extent of horse ownership, and the timing of changes in that ownership, says something significant about the level of commercialization in the local economy. The density of cart horses – which were more powerful than other types of horse – per 1,000 sown acres

---

[18] N. Amor, 'Merchant Adventurer or Jack of all Trades? The Suffolk Clothier in the 1460s', *PSIA* 40 (2004), pp. 426–7; W. R. Childs, 'Moving Around', in Horrox and Ormrod, *Social History* (2006), pp. 263–4; Middleton-Stewart, *Inward Piety*, pp. 81–2, 85; *CPR, 1354–8*, p. 446; *CIM, 1348–77*, p. 252; *CPR, 1364–7*, pp. 149–50; *CPR, 1367–70*, p. 75; *CPR, 1370–4*, p. 185; *CPR, 1381–5*, p. 260.

[19] Langdon, *Horses, Oxen*, pp. 116, 142–9, 221–5; Bailey, *Marginal Economy*, pp. 156–7; Bailey, *Dunwich*, pp. 57, 60, 70; Davis, 'Petty Traders', p. 254; BL Add. Roll 53127 (Mildenhall); BL Add. Roll 40717 (Dunwich); CUL Vanneck Ms, box 1, court held October 1381 (Aldham); Lock, *Walsham*, i, p. 100; R. C. Palmer, *English Law in the Age of the Black Death, 1348–1381* (London, 1993), p. 208.

was as high in Suffolk as anywhere else in the country, although most working horses were affers (a small versatile horse). By *c.* 1300 the horse comprised
more than 75 per cent of all draught animals owned by Suffolk peasants, compared to the national average of 45 per cent. The prevalence of horse-owning
farmers was higher in Suffolk – with the possible exception of Norfolk – than
any other English county, and they must have supplemented their agricultural
income with work as jobbing light haulers. Their existence in such numbers
reflects the importance of carting and the high degree of commercial activity
in medieval Suffolk.[20]

MARKETING NETWORKS

By *c.* 1300 much of the agricultural output of Suffolk was strongly influenced
by market forces. However, the scale of this marketing and the extent to
which it was driven by urban demand will always remain uncertain, because
records of sales in manorial accounts or of debt disputes in court rolls seldom
state the destination of produce. The result is an interesting debate among
historians, some of whom argue that by *c.* 1300 commercial activity in England was relatively well integrated into a rudimentary national market, cen-
tred on the fifty or so largest English towns. This line of argument would
imply that Suffolk's weekly markets and fairs were principally collecting
points for the larger urban centres, rather than centres of consumption themselves, and therefore places such as Beccles, Bury St Edmunds, Dunwich,
Ipswich and Sudbury must have driven and shaped the marketing of agricultural produce in medieval Suffolk. Yet other historians are sceptical of such
claims, arguing that urban demand was still relatively weak at this time, and
most commercial activity was driven by localized demand generated by small
towns and swollen rural communities. The differences between these inter-
pretations are significant, because they embody contrasting views on the level
of sophistication achieved by the medieval economy. The belief that England
possessed a loosely integrated national system of marketing before the Black
Death implies an advanced level of economic development, whereas the
notion that marketing networks remained mainly localized assumes something more modest. As Suffolk was one of the most commercialized areas in
medieval England, a survey of the *direct* evidence of the markets for its agricultural produce would contribute usefully to this debate.[21]

---

[20] Campbell, *English Seigneurial Agriculture*, pp. 127–8; Langdon, *Horses, Oxen*,
    pp. 143, 198, 205, 222–3, 264, 273–4.

[21] J. Masschaele, *Peasants, Merchants and Markets: Inland Trade in Medieval England,
    1150–1350* (Basingstoke, 1997); Britnell, 'Urban Demand', pp. 2–9; see also Hatcher
    and Bailey, *Modelling the Middle Ages*, pp. 121–73.

There is no doubt that some of the grain produced in Suffolk was drawn into regional, national and international trade. Grain was expensive to transport overland in the Middle Ages, because it was low in value relative to its weight, and consequently the commercial horizons of land-locked farms were restricted to 10 miles or so (except in years of great scarcity). In contrast, the costs of moving grain by boat were significantly lower, and so farms which were readily accessible to a navigable waterway could transform their commercial potential. The navigability of the Ouse river system, and the river-pierced coastline, meant that producers east of a line running roughly from Nayland, Hadleigh, Needham Market, Framlingham to Bungay, and those west of a line running from Market Weston, through Ixworth to Newmarket, could contemplate shipping their grain to distant markets without incurring prohibitively high transport costs. Hence grain from a landlocked place such as Hoxne was carted to Beccles for boat carriage to Great Yarmouth, and sea-faring ships laden with barley are recorded at Snape bridge.[22]

Some of this grain was exported overseas, mainly through Ipswich, Lynn and Yarmouth, although very occasionally through the smaller ports. Lynn's grain trade was mainly conducted with Norway and the Baltic, which increased in frequency and volume during the course of the thirteenth century and drew upon some supplies from producers in north-west Suffolk. In the twelfth century Dunwich had dominated exports of corn from Suffolk before losing out in the thirteenth to Ipswich, whose international grain trade focused on Flanders, especially Bruges and Damme, although the quantities exported from Ipswich were very small by national standards. Rye comprised the bulk of its international grain shipments, even though it was not widely grown across the county nor featured as a major cash crop. However, rye production did feature most prominently in the vicinity of Ipswich, where the demesnes of Harkstead, Loudham, Melton and Tattingstone all sold significant proportions of this crop. Thus the production of Suffolk's major export grain was largely confined to the vicinity of Ipswich.[23]

The exact proportion of the grain produced in Suffolk which was exported to the Continent is unknowable, but it was unlikely to have constituted more

---

[22] Campbell, *English Seigneurial Agriculture*, p. 268; SROI HD1538/207/3, court held January 1389 (Snape).

[23] B. M. S. Campbell, J. A. Galloway, D. Keene, M. Murphy, *A Medieval Capital and its Grain Supply: Agrarian Production and Distribution in the London Region c. 1300*, Historical Geography Research Series 30 (1993), p. 181; N. Hybel, 'The Grain Trade in Northern Europe before 1350', *EcHR* 55 (2002), pp. 219–47; *VCH*, ii, p. 203; SROI HD1538/295/4 (Loudham); SROI SI/10/6.6 (Harkstead); CUL EDC 7/16/11/6–9 (Melton); SROI HB8/1/821, 828 (Tattingstone); *VCH*, ii, p. 203; Bailey, *Dunwich*, p. 21, although Dunwich retained contacts with Flanders, northern France and Gascony, PRO SC6/995/30; *PSIA* 9 (1897), p. 348.

than a few per cent of the overall output. However, a slightly higher proportion found its way into regional markets and to the larger urban centres. Again, the evidence is anecdotal and random, not quantifiable: for example, some wheat from Woodbridge was sold in Kent, and large consignments of malt from Cavenham were bought by a merchant operating from Saffron Walden, probably with London in mind. The Suffolk coastal areas lay just within London's wheat-producing region, and producers further inland could supply the London market profitably during years of high prices. Grain from the larger demesnes was sometimes sold in bulk ('*in grosso*') to a single merchant, which is strongly indicative of provisioning for urban markets, and the villeins of Hartest could be called upon to cart demesne produce to Colchester and Ipswich. On one occasion some producers in Mildenhall carted their grain to Cambridge, and surpluses of oats from the demesne of Staverton were sometimes sold in Ipswich. Yet, in general, such explicit evidence for the sale of grain to distant and urban markets is rare, and bulk sales are usually only found on the largest demesnes of the great landlords. In the light of these findings, it is significant that Suffolk producers did not feature prominently among the recorded contacts of London cornmongers, unlike those of eastern Norfolk.[24]

The direct evidence from local sources reveals clearly that in *c.* 1300 most grain in Suffolk was sold and consumed locally, i.e. within 10 miles of the farm of origin (roughly equivalent to a day's journey by cart). As we have seen, none of the leading towns was sufficiently large to create concentrated urban demand. Yet the prominence of smallholdings, the high density of the rural population, and the extent of landlessness all heightened the rural demand for agricultural produce. The importance of local sales is strongly evident. Hartest villeins were usually required to carry their lord's grain to Bury St Edmunds, Clare, and Sudbury, all situated within 10 miles, and those of Blakenham were required to carry demesne corn 5 miles to Ipswich. The Hinderclay demesne sold some grain in Thetford and Bury St Edmunds, but most was sold locally. In 1385–6 much of the wheat bought for the duke of Norfolk's household at Framlingham was acquired from a variety of local suppliers in Framlingham itself, and nearby Cratfield, Cretingham, Easton, Fressingfield, Heveningham and Huntingfield, and its suppliers of oats were simply too numerous to be listed separately in the main account, which is suggestive of manifold local sources. The manors of the earls of Clare disposed of produce locally; Sibton abbey sold small lots of grain in local markets; Hoxne priory routinely

---

[24] *VCH*, ii, p. 203; Arnott, *Suffolk Estuary*, p. 113; PRO sc6/1117/12 (Cavenham); Campbell *et al.*, *A Medieval Capital*, pp. 60–3; Bailey, *English Manor*, p. 51; SROB E18/451/69, f. 42 (Mildenhall); PRO sc6/1005/10–12 (Staverton); *AHEW*, iii, p. 373; Lee, 'Feeding the Colleges', p. 261.

disposed of its surpluses in Hoxne and nearby Denham; and in the autumn of 1331 Staverton manor sold small batches (around 2 bushels each) of peas locally. The overwhelming majority of demesne sales comprised small batches of a few bushels of grain, which is highly indicative of local sales. Sometimes the purchaser is named, implying that he or she was known locally, and some sales are specifically described as *in patria* ('in the locality'): in 1323 the Mildenhall demesne thus disposed of maslin and barley. Tattingstone manor regularly sold its grain in small batches to men in the village and its vicinity, such as Bentley, Brantham, East Bergholt, Holbrook, Stratford St Mary and Stutton.[25]

Livestock and pastoral produce was marketed over longer distances than grain, the former because it could be walked to market and the latter because it was higher in value relative to its weight, and thus could absorb higher transport costs. In addition, the concentration of wealth in urban centres generated greater demand for more expensive goods such as meat and leather, and so the trade in pastoral produce was more likely to be influenced by urban demand. The fleeces of Suffolk sheep were lightweight, and therefore cheap, by English standards, and did not feature heavily in the exports of English wool to the Continent. Indeed, major ports such as Dunwich and Orford exported hardly any wool, and the small quantities exported from Ipswich usually belonged to merchants from London or Stamford who were only using the port for convenience. Merchants from Bury St Edmunds, Colchester, Ipswich and Norwich sometimes bought wool from Suffolk demesnes, but it is not known what then became of it. The likelihood is that most of Suffolk's wool was used within the region to make cheaper lightweight textiles. For a number of years the whole clip from the Tattingstone flock of around 300 sheep was sold as a single lot to a succession of different merchants, including one from Ipswich. Then, after 1403, the clip was sold each year to John Bryan of Hadleigh, and after 1410 to John Longman of East Bergholt, rare confirmation that some Suffolk fleeces went directly to local textile centres.[26]

[25] *AHEW*, iii, pp. 361–6; Chibnall, *Select Documents*, pp. 94, 174–85; Chibnall, *Compotus Rolls*, pp. 81, 106–7, 134–5 (Blakenham); Bailey, *English Manor*, p. 51 (Hartest); SROI HD1538/357/1, m. 5 (Staverton); Stone, 'Hinderclay', pp. 618–19; Ridgard, *Framlingham*, pp. 94–5; Holmes, *Higher Nobility*, p. 89; Denney, *Sibton Abbey*, pp. 113–15; NRO DC 2/6/3 (Hoxne); Bodleian Suffolk Rolls 23 (Mildenhall); SROI HB8/1/823–828 (Tattingstone).

[26] Bailey, *Marginal Economy*, p. 149; Richmond, *John Hopton*, pp. 79–80; PRO SC6/1117/12; Davis, 'Petty Traders', p. 222; Bacon Ms 295/18; P. Nightingale, *A Medieval Mercantile Community: The Grocers' Company and the Politics and Trade of London, 1000–1485* (London, 1995), pp. 99, 103; Lloyd, *Wool Trade*, pp. 69, 254; SROI HB8/1/823–840 (Tattingstone); the Melton wool clip was sold to a Norwich merchant, CUL EDC 7/16/11/9.

The markets for livestock and dairy produce were more integrated than that for grain, with rudimentary regional, and perhaps even national, networks. We do not know the predominant style of the cheese made in Suffolk's medieval dairies, although in the early modern period it was hard, highly durable, and rated among the best in England. If this was also true of the medieval period, then Suffolk cheese would have been ideal for supplying distant urban, and even overseas, markets: in which case it might be significant that cheese and hides feature in the export trade between Ipswich and the Low Countries and Brittany. Cattle from northern England appear increasingly on Suffolk pastures, and buyers attended distant fairs to purchase stock originating from across, and outside, East Anglia. In 1386 Framlingham castle acquired livestock from the fairs at Clare, Diss, Loddon and Newmarket; manors in west Suffolk often sent officials to Ely, Stourbridge (Cambridge) and Thetford fairs to buy stock; people from north Essex sought cattle and horses at Haverhill and Newmarket; and cattle fattened around Darsham and Sibton was driven for sale to Norwich and Bungay. Rabbits from Easton Bavents, Walberswick and Brandon were sold in London. Of course, much livestock and deadstock was also acquired and consumed locally. Framlingham castle obtained other supplies of livestock from nearby Charsfield, Framlingham, Rendham and Woodbridge; the Loudham demesne bought fourteen cows in 1372 from local men, including two from the parson of Ufford and four from dealers in Woodbridge; and the Tattingstone demesne invariably turned to local suppliers to supplement its herds and flocks. Butchers were prominent in Suffolk's small towns, indicating a sustained local urban demand for meat. The Tattingstone demesne often supplied butchers in nearby Bergholt, Lawford and Manningtree, and butchers from Haverhill and Stoke-by-Clare were active along the Stour valley.[27]

Mature 'timber' was marketed over significant distances, reflecting its scarcity and high value, and fast-growing hardwood was imported from the Baltic through many East Anglian ports. In contrast, the marketing of fuel (especially of 'wood') was unquestionably localized and poorly integrated. Hence mature oaks grown in Lidgate park were often sent to Cambridgeshire, while its other produce, such as faggots, does not appear to have been sold any further than nearby Exning. Sibton abbey disposed of most of its faggots in local places such as Westleton, Wenhaston, Kettleburgh and Bruisyard, the produce of Walsham wood was routinely sold to local inhabitants, and Thetford priory sourced its fuel from nearby Barningham, Euston,

27 G. E. Fussell, *The English Dairy Farmer, 1500–1900* (London, 1966), pp. 223, 250; Redstone, *Ipswich*, p. 31; *AHEW*, iii, pp. 384, 391; Ridgard, *Framlingham*, p. 97; Denney, *Sibton Abbey*, pp. 113–15; Bailey, 'Rabbit', pp. 13, 15; Richmond, *John Hopton*, pp. 39, 89; SROI HB8/1/817–840 (Tattingstone); SROI HD1538/295/2 (Loudham).

Fakenham, Hepworth, Rougham, Stanton and Thelnetham. Faggots produced at Hoxne and Hundon were overwhelmingly consumed locally; wood from Melton was invariably destined for Woodbridge; and most faggots from Chevington went to Bury St Edmunds. Only producers in some parts of west Suffolk – mainly in Haverhill, the Bradleys, Cowlinge, Newmarket and the Wrattings – were able to break out of the highly localized market for fuel by supplying Cambridge, although this exception to the local rule reflected the acute shortage of woodland in the university town's immediate vicinity.[28]

Links between Suffolk and London were so well established as to be commonplace, although they were not solely a function of some trade in agricultural produce. John King was a London grocer as well as a clothier with a particular interest in Shelley, and John Stansby and John Motte, Londoners who controlled cloth production in Bildeston in the 1460s, were both stockfishmongers, channelling dried cod from the Baltic as far as the Mediterranean. London drew the county's social elite for social, political and legal purposes, as well as for the consumption of luxury goods. Representatives of Dunwich regularly conducted business in the capital on behalf of the borough, and members of the earl of Norfolk's household at Framlingham had much contact with the city. In the early fifteenth century people living in south and north-east Suffolk were especially well represented among the capital's main trading contacts, reflecting the growing importance of the trade in woollen textiles and pastoral products, and wealthy Londoners bought land in Suffolk. Many resident clothiers were regular visitors to the capital, where they owned property and nurtured social contacts as well as pursuing their business interests. Contact with London extended down the social scale. In 1341 the bailiff of Icklingham was sent to London on manorial business, and in 1327 and 1381 political agitators from London were blamed – perhaps conveniently – for stirring up rebellion in Bury St Edmunds. East Anglia was the most important source of migrants to London after the Home Counties (the family of Geoffrey Chaucer originated from Ipswich), and a number of individuals migrated from Walton to the capital in the hope of making their fortunes. The reality, of course, was usually very different, although few migrants were as unfortunate as John de Bois, a leather

---

[28] *AHEW*, iii, pp. 409–11; J. Galloway, D. Keene and M. Murphy, 'Fuelling the City: Production and Distribution of Firewood and Fuel in London's Region, 1290–1400', *EcHR* 49 (1996), p. 467; SROB E3/11/1.2, court held July 1420, and E3/11/1.4, mm. 7, 8 (Lidgate); Denney, *Sibton Abbey*, pp. 113–14; SROB HA504/3/5–10 (Walsham); Dymond, *Thetford Priory*, pp. 32, 35; PRO sc6/999/27 to sc6/1000/1, sc6/999/19 (Hundon); NRO 95/20 (Hoxne); CUL EDC 7/16/11/19, 32 (Melton); SROB E3/15.3/2.20b – 2.35 (Chevington); Lee, 'Feeding the Colleges', pp. 250, 254.

worker from Suffolk who fell to his death from a first-storey window in Cheapside.[29]

CONCLUSION

The range of employment opportunities was unusually wide in medieval Suffolk, reflecting the diversity of its resource base – including the produce of the sea – and the variety of work in crafts, petty retailing and wage labouring. Unfortunately, the absence of peasant household accounts means that we cannot calculate the relative importance of these various sources of income, or reconstruct peasant budgets. However, the range of work, when coupled with the higher levels of land productivity on peasant holdings and the importance of livestock and poultry, suggests strongly that a smallholder with 5 acres of land in Suffolk was better able to feed a family of five than a similar smallholder living in other parts of England where the resource base was less accommodating and the labour market was less active.

The evidence for marketing networks in contemporary documents is sporadic, rather than systematic or fulsome, which fuels speculation about the structure of internal markets in England in *c.* 1300 and also explains this rather anecdotal analysis of those in Suffolk. It is, however, sufficiently reliable to permit two general conclusions. First, Suffolk was one of the most commercialized areas of medieval England. It possessed the highest recorded density of markets and small towns in the country, and production was strongly geared towards the market at all levels of agriculture. On demesnes the majority of barley and wheat was sold as a cash crop, and, excepting the requirements for manure and traction, much of the animal produce was sold. Fuel production was also highly commercialized. The most strongly commercialized manors in Suffolk tended to be located around the county's largest towns and navigable rivers, and in the lower to middle reaches of the Stour valley, but manors in land-locked locations still produced grain for local markets. The evidence from tenant holdings indicates that agricultural production was even more commercialized, although it is less certain that these farmers entered the market on terms favourable to them. Pastoral production in Suffolk was probably as commercialized and as intensive as anywhere in medieval England. Arable

---

[29] Richmond, *John Hopton*, p. 49; Bailey, *Dunwich*, pp. 57, 61, 63, 68, 70, 78, 80; Ridgard, *Framlingham*, p. 84; Lobel, 'The 1327 Rising', p. 216; D. Keene, 'Changes in London's Economic Hinterland as Indicated by Debt Cases in the Court of Common Pleas', in Galloway, *Trade, Urban Hinterlands* (2000), tables 4.1 and 4.4; Amor, 'Jack of All Trades', p. 427; NRO Ms 13196 (Icklingham); SROI HA119/50/3/18–19 (Walton); McKinley, *Surnames*, p. 78; Nightingale, *Medieval Mercantile Community*, pp. 99, 103; Dyer, *Making a Living*, pp. 193–4; Redstone, *Memorials*, pp. 244–60 for the Chaucer family.

production was commercialized, but seldom as intensive as on demesnes in north-east Norfolk, where the level of both rural and urban demand was greater.[30]

Second, the majority of produce entering the market was consumed locally. Certainly, some entered regional or national marketing networks, particularly wool, cheese and livestock: even quantities of grain were exported abroad or sold elsewhere in East Anglia and south-east England. However, the direct evidence reveals clearly that grain was usually consumed within 10 miles of the farm of origin; large quantities of livestock and dead stock were sourced and consumed locally; and the market for fuel was highly localized. In this context, the large numbers of markets, fairs and small towns in Suffolk must have existed primarily as centres of local trade rather than as collecting centres for regional and national trade. The high density of population, the proportion of smallholdings, and the proliferation of crafts and by-employments all meant that by *c.* 1300 levels of demand for basic foodstuffs, goods and services in the Suffolk countryside were unusually strong. At this time rural, not urban, demand provided the primary stimulus to the commercialization of its economy, in contrast to counties such as Hertfordshire and Norfolk, where the influence of urban demand was stronger.

The example of Suffolk must illustrate something important about the essence of medieval commerce. The trade in basic agricultural produce was not only localized, but it was also insufficient to sustain more than a couple of daily markets within the county: the overwhelming majority of formal marketing outlets were periodic, in the sense that they were either weekly (markets) or seasonal (fairs). Farm production was reasonably specialized, but it had not yet thrown off all the shackles imposed by either the consumption needs of the household or the constraints imposed by the nature of local soils. Finally, the hair-trigger sensitivity of grain prices and the land market to harvest failures around 1300 indicates the heavy reliance of Suffolk's rural population upon localized grain markets, which were highly prone to disruption. Medieval commercialization was not the same as modern commercialization, nor was it always entirely beneficial to the economy: by *c.* 1300 it enabled a greatly swollen population to be sustained at a low standard of living, but with the result that smallholders were brutally exposed to the vicissitudes of the weather and economic disruption.

---

[30] Campbell, *English Seigneurial Agriculture*, p. 211; Bailey, 'Peasant Welfare', pp. 235–8.

CHAPTER 8

Pestilence, Rebellion and the Decline of Villeinage, 1349–1500

THE BLACK DEATH

The Black Death erupted in southern England during August 1348 and had reached London by September. Using the internal evidence of manorial court rolls (which record the death of tenants) and bishop's registers (which record the appointment of beneficed clergy to a parish), Jessopp concluded that the pestilence first reached East Anglia during the spring of 1349. His pioneering work was largely based on Norfolk, where some coastal communities were first hit in March and others closer to Norwich were struck in April and May: the pestilence was raging in central Norfolk in the high summer and early autumn, when it was also most active in Lincolnshire. More recently Benedictow has argued that the disease was already present in the Stour valley at the very end of 1348, but took another five weeks or so to develop into epidemic form in local communities. The earliest recorded outbreak of the epidemic in Suffolk occurs in January 1349, and it had largely passed by July, during which time it killed around one-half of the population. Contemporaries did not call this lethal disease the Black Death or plague: to them it was simply 'the pestilence'. As a bald statement announced at the head of a manorial account for 1348–9 from Easton Bavents: 'in which year the pestilence of men raged in England'.[1]

Our knowledge of the local spread of the Black Death is still partial. Manor court rolls provide a sound basis for establishing the approximate date of the epidemic's arrival in, and departure from, a locality, but complete series of courts from 1349 are uncommon. The manorial court held at Lakenheath on 11 February 1349 records the deaths of almost twenty tenants, and many more in the next court session in May. Similarly, one death is recorded in the January court at Worlingworth, eleven in the session on 30 April, forty-one on 8 July, and five in October. While it is not possible to date the arrival and passage of the epidemic precisely from such evidence, it is likely that it had arrived in late

---

[1] For a general introduction, see R. Horrox, ed., *The Black Death* (Manchester, 1994). A. Jessopp, *The Coming of the Friars* (London, 1889), pp. 199–205; O. Benedictow, *The Black Death, 1346–1353: The Complete History* (Woodbridge, 2004), pp. 123–38; SROI v5/19/1.3 (Easton).

January at Lakenheath, raged during the spring and had passed by the early summer, while at Worlingworth it probably arrived in April and had passed by the end of July. The Black Death had certainly penetrated the lower reaches of the Deben and Stour valleys by February 1349, because exceptional deaths are recorded in courts held that month at Eyke, Aldham, Layham and Stoke-by-Nayland, where it continued to rage until the end of April. It did not reach Cornard and Clare, located further along the Stour valley, until March, and stayed there until June. Similarly, places higher up the Alde and Deben valleys – such as Bredfield and Sweffling – were not afflicted until April. Fornham and Walsham in west Suffolk were first hit in late March or April and the epidemic then lasted throughout May and June. Every surviving manorial document from 1349 reveals evidence of the visitation of pestilence, indicating strongly that nowhere escaped its grip.[2]

Bishop's registers record the institution of the beneficed clergy to a new parish, and survive for the whole of 1349 for the diocese of Norwich. The rapid climb in the number of institutions of new priests in the diocese, from an average of three each month in 1348, to five in January 1349, seventeen in February, seventy-three in May, to a peak of 222 in July, testifies to the ferocity and passage of the disease. However, this source is not as accurate as a good series of manorial courts in plotting the progress of the Black Death, because the time lag between the death of an incumbent and the appointment of a successor was highly variable, nor, of course, can we know whether the death of the parish priest occurred early or late in a local epidemic.[3] Map 15 attempts to chart the early progress of the Black Death in Suffolk by plotting every parish to which a new priest was instituted between 1 February and 31 May 1349, together with the evidence for its arrival contained within some manorial court rolls. The resultant picture contains some paradoxes and anomalies, but it does provide a clear indication that the disease penetrated Suffolk simultaneously through four main points of entry. First, the Stour valley was a major and early routeway for the Black Death, which by the end of May had

---

[2] CUL EDC 7/15/11/2/17, mm. 9–13 (Lakenheath); Ridgard, 'Worlingworth', p. 184; SROI HD1538/357/3, mm. 10–13 (Eyke); SROI HA68/484/135 (Aldham); SROI E3/1/2.2 (Layham); SROI HA246/A10/1–2 (Nayland); NRO Walsingham XXXIV/5, ff. 14–15 (Cornard); Thornton, *History of Clare*, pp. 107–8; SROI HA91/1, mm. 61–2 (Bredfield); SROI V5/15/1 (Sweffling); SROB E3/15.6/1.12 (Fornham); Lock, 'Black Death', pp. 316, 321; Jessopp, *Coming of the Friars*, pp. 204–5.

[3] P. E. Pobst, ed., *The Register of William Bateman, Bishop of Norwich, 1344–1355*, part 1, Canterbury and York Society 84 (Woodbridge, 1996), pp. xxx–xxxi. Pobst emphasizes the variability of the time lag between the death of an incumbent and the appointment of a successor, while Benedictow, *The Black Death*, pp. 123–6, is more confident that it was usually around five weeks. His optimism is implausible, because the speed of reporting and, in particular, the identification of a suitable successor would vary markedly under the pressure of the epidemic.

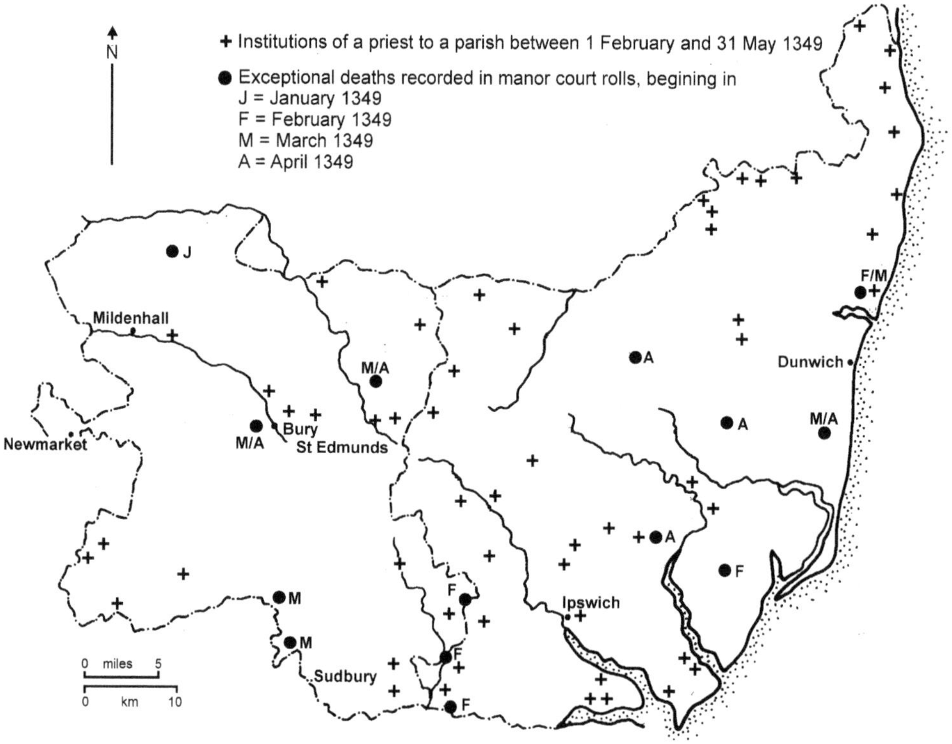

MAP 15 Appointments of new priests to parishes between 1 January and 31 May 1349

already claimed the lives of two successive priests of Holbrook. The second routeway was through Lakenheath into north-west Suffolk, probably from Lynn and down the river Ouse.[4] Third, it penetrated along the lower reaches of the rivers Orwell and Deben (although not initially the Alde valley). Finally, it entered through the ports of north-east Suffolk and up the Waveney valley. The importance of navigable rivers, and the coastal trade from London, in the spread of the disease is strongly evident. The pestilence in Suffolk was largely confined to the first six months of 1349, reaching central areas in April and May, and, after establishing itself in epidemic form, usually remained active within a settlement for three to four months. This chronology helps to explain the movement of the bishop of Norwich during the pestilence, who left the city in July to reside at Hoxne for three months: the epidemic was still raging around Norwich in July, but by then had probably passed through Hoxne.[5] Its geographical spread was remarkably complete and it generated tragically high mortality rates: this disease was both highly infectious and lethal.

---

4 Pobst, *Register of William Bateman*, 1, pp. 85–6, 91 (Holbrook); Benedictow, *The Black Death*, p. 134.

5 Jessopp, *Coming of the Friars*, pp. 214–15.

1. Wingfield castle. During the twelfth and thirteenth centuries moats became popular among manorial lords and leading freemen as a fashionable status symbol, rather than for their defensive capabilities. A splendid flint gatehouse dominates the edge of this large moat, signifying the high social standing of the owner. Built in the 1380s, Wingfield castle provided a Suffolk residence for the De La Poles, earls of Suffolk, and its living accommodation was more comfortable than that available in earlier castles such as Orford (plate 9).

2. Clare castle. The motte was hastily constructed after the Norman Conquest of 1066, and now supports the remains of a small stone keep. This photograph is taken from the extensive inner bailey, where by the 1330s Lady Elizabeth de Burgh – one of the wealthiest aristocrats in England – had established her principal residence. The traces of her commodious and comfortable accommodation, and her elegant gardens, have long disappeared, but the presence of an important household contributed to the economic success of Clare, which peaked around this time.

3. Early aisled-hall house, Purton green, Stansfield. This house was originally constructed in the thirteenth century, when it comprised an aisled hall of two bays measuring 10 × 5 m, and featured wooden shutters rather than glass windows. It would have been built and occupied by a relatively prosperous peasant family. In the mid-fifteenth century its hall was raised and wings were added at each end to provide separate chambers and rooms, both common features of later medieval houses.

4. All Saints green, South Elmham. Population growth in the twelfth and thirteenth centuries encouraged the spread of settlement around the edges of communal greens, which were often situated on patches of waterlogged clayland or near parish boundaries. Greenside development transformed the settlement pattern of the Elmhams during this period, as illustrated by this aerial view of All Saints green. Houses are still scattered around its fringes, yet the empty plots and earthworks between them indicate the size of this settlement at its peak in the early fourteenth century.

5. Lidgate castle and bailey, from the north. One of the most fascinating, but least known, sites of medieval Suffolk. The castle was hurriedly constructed during the civil war of the mid-twelfth century and remained operational until demolished in the 1260s on the orders of Henry III. The keep was positioned on the square mound in the centre of the earthworks (**1**), surrounded by deep moating (**2, 3**). The parish church is visible within the northern end of the original bailey, whose roughly rectangular shape is traced by the dotted line. Burgage plots and a market place were established on the bailey in the late thirteenth century, but this attempt at urban plantation was not successful, and the market ceased to operate after the 1420s.

6. The Westgate, Ipswich, *c.* 1770. The formidable edifice of the Westgate (from a late eighteenth-century engraving) guarded the main routeway into Ipswich. The lower section, faced with ashlar, dates from *c.* 1200, while the upper section is probably fourteenth century: the latter was partially rebuilt in the 1440s and used as a gaol. It was demolished in 1782.

7. Market shambles, Mildenhall. The medieval shambles in the market square, with the fine parish church in the background, provided a focal point for trade in one of Suffolk's largest towns. A formal weekly market was first obtained here in 1220, but a subsequent grant in 1413 switched the market day from Tuesday to Saturday. This change was intended to revive the flagging franchise, and the manorial lord also commissioned the construction of new stalls and a shambles to complete the facelift. It proved moderately successful, although not even this venture could arrest the economic decline of Mildenhall during the fifteenth century.

8. Bury St Edmunds, from the east. The great enclosure of the abbey of Bury St Edmunds, with the ruins of its great cruciform church (**1**) and various monastic outbuildings, is clearly evident in the middle foreground, and dominated the eastern area of the town. The borough's rectilinear street plan – a superb example of medieval town planning – was laid out in the late eleventh century, with the two central east–west streets leading directly to the two main entrances of the abbey, the Norman Tower and the Abbey Gate (plate ɪɪ). The Angel Hill (**2**), the likely site of Bury's annual fair, is identifiable as the open space in front of the Abbey Gate, while the large market square was situated at a discreet distance from the abbey at the western end of Abbeygate Street. The subsequent infilling of the square by permanent shops along the line of former stalls is clearly apparent (**3**).

9. Orford castle and town. The royal borough of Orford was established in the 1160s as part of Henry II's hasty redevelopment of the site as a military stronghold to counter the powerful but unruly Bigods, earls of Norfolk. A large rectangular market place and distinctive grid pattern of streets were laid out between the innovative castle and the church. The property boundaries of some of the original, regular-sized, burgage plots are still recognizable in this aerial photograph. In the 1160s Orford stood near to the mouth of the river Alde, visible top right, and enjoyed early success as a port. Thereafter, it declined at the expense of Aldeburgh and Woodbridge, as its harbour deteriorated through the inexorable growth of Orford Ness and its military significance dwindled.

10. Moulton bridge. Bridges were essential to the efficient transit of people and goods in a commercialized region, and this is the best preserved of the many which were built in Suffolk during the thirteenth and fourteenth centuries. It stood on one of two competing routeways between Bury St Edmunds and Newmarket, and was designed to accommodate small horse-drawn carts rather than pack horses. Stone bridges such as this were very expensive to build, and therefore required substantial capital investment from a wealthy manorial lord, although subsequent maintenance costs were supported by public donations.

11. The Abbey Gate, Bury St Edmunds. The Abbey Gate, completed in the 1340s, symbolizes medieval Bury St Edmunds. Its ornate features, elegant grandeur and redoubtable ashlar stone reflect the power and status of the wealthy abbey whose vast enclosure it defends. Yet it was built to replace an earlier gate that had been comprehensively destroyed in the ferocious town riots of 1327, in which the burgesses had attempted to obtain greater freedom from the abbey's control during a period of national political turmoil. They failed, but gained some leverage and pleasure by kidnapping the abbot and holding him captive for nearly two years at a safe house in Flanders.

12. Lavenham church. This superb example of perpendicular gothic architecture exemplifies the impressive wealth generated after the mid-fourteenth century in a number of communities in south Suffolk by the manufacture of woollen textiles. Its construction was completed during Lavenham's heyday (1480–1520), by which time the town had become Suffolk's foremost centre of cloth manufacture. It was also the home of one of the richest men in England, Thomas Spring III, who contributed handsomely to the completion of the porch and tower.

13. Market hall, Hadleigh. Built in the mid-fifteenth century, at which time the western range on the right originally extended to three storeys, while the original eastern section was demolished in the late eighteenth century and replaced with the brick apse on the left. This stunning building separated the parish church (its cemetery is in the foreground) and the market place (behind the building). Its size and architectural quality reflect the wealth and civic pride of one of Suffolk's leading towns. The ground floor originally contained a row of shops, all of which opened onto the market place, but not the churchyard.

14. St Andrew's church, Northales (Covehithe). The original size and quality of the medieval church reflects the wealth and importance of this coastal port, while its dilapidated condition symbolizes the town's subsequent decline. Northales possessed a sizeable natural harbour situated to the south of the church, which sheltered one of the largest fishing fleets in north-west Suffolk. Its market had been granted in 1298, and by the 1330s it was about the same size as Orford and ranked among the top ten towns in Suffolk. Yet it declined over the next two centuries, possibly because of coastal erosion, but certainly due to competition from Lowestoft and Southwold, which rose rapidly during the same period. Little remains of the medieval port and town of Northales.

15. Fifteenth-century houses, Fore Hamlet, Ipswich. This range of fifteenth-century buildings is one of the few secular survivals from medieval Ipswich. It occupies a prime location close to the main quay – at the time one of the most densely populated areas of the medieval town. All were built by wealthy merchants. The house on the far right, recently restored, incorporates, at right angles to the frontage, a superb range of outbuildings extending down towards the quay, which once contained warehousing and a shop.

16. Dunwich, from the south. At its peak in *c.* 1200 it was one of England's premier ports, and the only Suffolk town to rank among the top ten nationally. Yet between 1280 and 1340 more than six parishes and hundreds of buildings were washed away by successive marine inundations and, perhaps, tsunami caused by landslides on the bed of the North Sea. All that remains of its large harbour (**1**) is the marshland to the left of the shingle bank which dominates the top half of the photograph (taken in 1951). Just to the south of marshes in the centre-ground lie the ruins of the Greyfriars monastery (**2**), now dominating the site above the cliff line, although its eastern boundary wall (above the woods) followed the landward defences of the medieval borough (**3**, **4**). The east–west track visible within the woods led to the main entrance to the medieval town, the Middle gate, whose site is about to disappear over the cliff. Dunwich is still evocative for the presence of absence.

There are no mortality figures extant for the population at large from medi-eval England, but the evidence for death rates among tenants on a few manors and the clergy – which are assumed to be broadly representative of the wider populace – is uniformly high. Priests were especially vulnerable, as they tended to the sick and dying, and in 1349 more than 800 parish priests died in the dio-cese of Norwich (in which Suffolk lay), a death rate of around 60 per cent, and nearly 100 parishes lost at least two priests during the epidemic. All the breth-ren of the small monastic houses of Alnesbourne and Chipley priories per-ished, and the complement of monks at Bury St Edmunds abbey probably fell by 40 per cent. Around 60 per cent of tenants in Redgrave, 43 per cent of adult males in Worlingworth, and around half of the population of Walsham died. Urban mortality rates are difficult to assess, but those at Bury St Edmunds appear to have been similar. Significantly, the death rates recorded among live-stock on demesnes in 1349 were not abnormal, underlining the point that the Black Death afflicted humans only, and therefore could not have been anthrax, as Twigg once asserted.[6] Yet it is also apparent that this disease spread faster and was more virulent than modern forms of bubonic plague.

The dry entries in manorial records reveal nothing of the terror, pain, help-lessness and anguish generated by the Black Death. Terrified communities knew that it was approaching and consequently some individuals arranged their personal affairs as best they could. The land market was exception-ally active in the February court at Dunningworth (although no deaths are recorded), implying a deliberate redistribution of property in advance of the epidemic, and many leases of marsh pasture were (unusually) terminated in the late winter at Easton Bavents in anticipation of the onslaught ahead. Court rolls provide many examples of families devastated by the pestilence and of orphaned children taken into care by relatives or neighbours, such as one year-old Agneta Reynold of Iken. While the Clevehog and Robhood families of Walsham survived almost unscathed, no males survived in the de Cranemere family, the Rampoyles were almost wiped out, and twenty-one families in Little Cornard were all killed. Looting of abandoned houses is recorded in Brandon and Fornham, and some residents of Iken plundered

[6] Dymond and Northeast, *History of Suffolk*, p. 48; C. Harper-Bill, 'English Religion after the Black Death', in *The Black Death in England*, ed. W. M. Ormrod and P. Lindley (Stamford, 1996), p. 85; C. Rawcliffe, 'On the Threshold of Eternity: Care for the Sick in East Anglian Monasteries', in Harper-Bill *et al.*, *East Anglia's His-tory* (2002), pp. 51–2; Gottfried, *Bury St Edmunds*, pp. 54–5, 70; Ridgard, 'Worling-worth', p. 186; Lock, 'Black Death', p. 321. The lack of significant livestock deaths is evident at Easton, SROI v5/19/1.3; Fornham, SROB E3/15.7/2.4; and Rickinghall, BL Add. Roll 63526, where the pestilence still struck the human population, and provides a powerful counterargument to Twigg's belief that the pestilence was anthrax, G. Twigg, *The Black Death: A Biological Reappraisal* (London, 1984).

the marshland fisheries using illegal nets. The harvest of 1349 was diminished by the reduced supervision of fields and farms, and disrupted by shortages of labour: wage rates for ordinary workers doubled during the summer in Clare, and twenty-one tenants of Staverton were amerced in the manor court for performing harvest labour services badly or not at all. The abandonment of holdings meant that rental revenues slumped almost everywhere, and consequently landlords experienced a dramatic fall in their household income: the revenue received by Elizabeth de Burgh's household at Clare fell from around £3,500 per annum in the 1340s to £2,300 in 1349–50.[7]

Yet, for all the tragedy and disruption, the most remarkable aspect of the pestilential year is the resilience of institutions and people. The administration of many estates stood firm in most places, and regular courts were held throughout the year at Aldham, Layham, Staverton, Walsham and Worlingworth: indeed, the hapless reeve of Walsham was amerced in the court for relatively minor, and entirely understandable, administrative lapses. The great courts of Ipswich were held each month, although a number of cases in the summer were postponed due to a shortage of jurors; the September fair was held as usual at Clare, and the lease of its market produced the required income; and willing lessees could be found for the corn and meat markets in Ipswich, although no interest was expressed in leasing the fish and small markets. Other lords temporarily suspended sessions of their manor courts: no courts were held in Brandon until December 1349; the first post-Black Death court at Iken was delayed until December; and only two courts were held at Easton Bavents that year. The quality of the handwriting in the court rolls of Clare, Layham and Horham deteriorated markedly in 1349, implying difficulties finding a good scribe.[8]

Once the wave of pestilence had passed, landlords were faced with the problem of finding new tenants as quickly as possible within the context of a fall in the value of property. In some cases, heirs or their guardians readily identified themselves and took over their land, eager to harvest the crop and maintain the holding in good condition. At Walsham all but one of the abandoned land parcels had been regranted by the end of the year. However, in most places heirs proved difficult to identify or reluctant to take up their inheritance for a variety of reasons. The majority of the land abandoned by the

---

7   SROI   HD1538/207/2   (Dunningworth);   SROI   v5/19/1.3   (Easton);   SROI HD32/293/390, mm. 23–4 (Iken); Lock, 'Black Death', pp. 327–8; Jessopp, *Coming of the Friars*, p. 201; Bailey, *Marginal Economy*, p. 223; SROB E3/15.6/1.7 (Fornham); Holmes, *Higher Nobility*, pp. 91, 149; SROI HD1538/357/1, m. 11 (Staverton).

8   Lock, 'Black Death', pp. 323–4; Holmes, *Higher Nobility*, p. 57; SROI c5/6 (Ipswich); Bacon 291/16, 17 (Brandon); SROI HD32/293/390, mm. 23–4 (Iken); Thornton, *History of Clare*, pp. 107–8; SROB E3/1/2.2 (Layham); SROI HA68/484/80 (Horham).

victims of the Black Death remained unwanted for most of the year in Brandon and Timworth; 55 per cent of abandoned land parcels were still untenanted in September 1349 at Horham; and by November heirs been admitted into only 18 per cent of such land parcels in Cornard Parva – although heirs had been identified and ordered to take up their inheritances in 36 per cent of cases, no heirs or tenants could be found for the remainder. Manorial officials exerted pressure on heirs where they could, and accepted financial offers from other people to harvest and work this land on a temporary basis (known as *de exitus* payments), but a significant proportion of tenant land remained unoccupied in 1349: consequently some crops rotted in the field in the summer and autumn, and weeds proliferated.[9]

Difficulties in finding some heirs or tenants often extended into the early 1350s. In 1350 over 450 acres of villein land were still lying *frisce* and untenanted in Brandon; a significant amount of land in Iken was still unoccupied in October 1350; land abandoned in 1349 was still being leased on an *ad hoc* basis in 1351 in both Iken and Layham; and some heirs in Sweffling did not occupy their landed inheritances until 1353. The reluctance of tenants to acquire customary land was exacerbated by the problems of fulfilling labour services after such appalling mortality. Landlords recognized this reluctance and some were prepared to waive labour services for a short period as a concession. For example, in 1353 the steward of Aldham respited some of the services owed by the villeins for three years after complaints that shortages of family labour had greatly reduced their capability to perform them, while labour services were waived for the year in Walsham on condition they were performed the next. Such temporary concessions to existing tenants were innovative, but they were unlikely to entice many new tenants into accepting the most heavily burdened villein holdings. After a year or two lying uncultivated these holdings needed a considerable amount of hard labour to prepare them for a new crop, and consequently prospective tenants sought more favourable terms to reflect their higher start-up costs. By the mid-1350s many landlords had accepted this reality and offered some untenanted customary land on leasehold contracts, in which the tenant simply paid a cash rent and owed none of the other services and dues associated with villeinage. The abbey of Bury St Edmunds adopted this policy widely on its estates: in the early 1350s land at Risby was offered on very low rents for short terms of two or three years to entice tenants, although on the expiry of each lease both the rent charge per acre and the length of the term were increased; and in 1352 six vacant villein *tenementa* at Fornham All Saints were converted to leasehold. Other landlords addressed the same issue in similar ways. In 1350 over 58 acres of customary land were leased in

---

[9] Lock, 'Black Death', pp. 323–4; Bailey, *Marginal Economy*, pp. 223–4; NRO Walsingham xxxiv/5, ff. 14–15 (Cornard).

various parcels in one court session in Lakenheath, in 1352 various parcels of abandoned land were granted in fourteen separate leases at Iken, and in 1357 some customary holdings at Horham were leased for terms of five to seven years with straight cash rents of about 12d. per acre: ingeniously, the lease of a toft and 8 acres of land to Angus le Brown also required him to serve as a carpenter whenever required by the lord or his bailiff.[10]

By the early 1360s land occupancy and rental income had recovered remarkably well. This recovery owed something to the pragmatic concessions on rents, but much to the sustained buoyancy of grain prices in the 1350s and 1360s, and to the high proportion of landless or near-landless people who now sought to acquire or extend a smallholding. The sudden increase in the availability of land presented clear opportunities for enterprising farmers. In the 1350s John Dousing accumulated a significant amount of property in Worlingworth, although ironically he succumbed to the second outbreak of pestilence in 1361. In 1352 John Albred entered into five separate lease agreements with the manor of Risby, securing at least 39 acres of arable land, and he continued to take on other leases over the next decade.[11]

The epidemic of 1349 caused a fundamental shift in the economic ground: it was primarily responsible for changes in relative factor prices, especially land and labour, in the balance of power between lords and tenants, and in patterns of demand. These new economic conditions increased both the opportunity and the ability of individuals and whole families to move in search of land and/or work. The under-supply of tenants, lower rents, and easier land tenures all encouraged mobility, yet the incentive for Suffolk residents to migrate was enhanced by the rapid growth of new industrial activities. The government reacted sharply to the greater mobility of the post-plague workforce, passing the Statute of Labourers in 1351 in an attempt to restrict movement and to fix labour contracts and wages on pre-plague terms. This was a highly ambitious piece of legislation, because it attempted to overturn the forces of supply and demand in the labour market, and it was most strongly enforced by royal justices in the third quarter of the fourteenth century in East Anglia and the Home Counties. The shortage of tenants awakened seigneurial interest in the illicit departure of serfs, because the number of chevage cases recorded in court rolls increased sharply in the 1350s. Some manors presented instances of

---

[10] Bailey, *Marginal Economy*, pp. 224, 228–9; SROI HD32/293/390, mm. 24–5, 28, 35 (Iken); SROB E3/1/2.2 (Layham); SROI v5/15/1 (Sweffling); Horrox, *Black Death*, pp. 286–7; Lock, 'Black Death', p. 324; SROB E3/15.6/1.10 and 2.21 (Fornham All Saints), and similarly, in 1357 a number of new leases were granted to clear a stack of abandoned land in Fornham St Martin, SROB E3/15.6/1.3 (St Martin); CUL EDC 7/15/11/2/17, m. 15a (Lakenheath); SROI HA68/484/79 (Horham).

[11] Ridgard, 'Worlingworth', p. 192; SROB E3/15.13/2.21 – 2.30b (Risby); Bailey, *Marginal Economy*, pp. 226–8.

illegally flown serfs to the leet court – rather than the lord's court baron – after new legislation was passed in 1352, which increased landlords' legal powers to recapture them. The Bredfield leet ordered the bodily seizure and return of two serfs living in Alderton and Boulge, the payment of chevage from seven others, and questioned whether the Gerold family of Grundisburgh was free.[12]

Many places suffered a second visitation of pestilence in 1361, although the number of deaths was smaller than in 1349, reflecting a lower mortality rate of perhaps 10 per cent: this second epidemic appears to have struck mainly at children, whose deaths are not recorded in court rolls. The deaths of three tenants were recorded at Iken, nine in Cornard, and six each at Layham and Yoxford. The season of death was also markedly different to 1349, with no evidence for the presence of pestilence in spring or early summer: in all cases, the mortality was confined to late summer and autumn, which conforms to the season usually associated with bubonic plague. The 1361 outbreak jolted the economy, causing a temporary fall in both the level of leasehold rents per acre and the performance of labour services in many places. In contrast, manorial documents reveal little evidence for the presence locally of the third epidemic in 1369. Outbreaks of epidemic disease occur frequently thereafter, although they tended to be localized and nothing like as devastating as 1349 or 1361: only an epidemic in 1479 appears to have been both severe and widespread in Suffolk.[13]

The Poll Tax returns of 1377 record nearly 63,000 taxpayers in Suffolk. Most historians would accept a multiplier of 1.9 to convert this figure into the actual level of population, which produces a figure of about 120,000 people. This is broadly compatible with an estimated population of 225,000 in the 1320s and the subsequent loss of around half the population through pestilence. The level of population did not change greatly for the next century or so, judging by the sparse direct demographic data and the indirect economic indicators of grain prices, land values and wages. The 1524 Lay Subsidy records 17,299 taxpayers in Suffolk, although converting this raw figure into the actual number of people is fraught with difficulties. Cornwall favoured a multiplier of 5, yet Campbell – using evidence from Babergh hundred – prefers 4, while Alan Dyer advocates 6. These different multipliers generate a population in the range of 70,000–100,000, with the most likely figure towards the upper end: English population as a whole probably fell by roughly 20 per cent between 1377 and

---

[12] SROI HA91/1, m. 77.

[13] SROI HD32/293/390, m. 34 (Iken); NRO Walsingham XXXIV/5, ff. 14–15 (Cornard); SROB E3/1/2.2 (Layham); SROI HA30/50/22/13/12/2 (Yoxford); Gottfried, *Bury St Edmunds*, pp. 63–4. There were also four deaths at Walsham between July and October, and five in the autumn at Aldham, Lock, *Walsham*, ii, pp. 59–6, SROI HA68/484/135.

1524. The decline in population between *c.* 1380 and *c.* 1520 is usually attributed to a dismal combination of high mortality and sluggish fertility rates. Gottfried argues that plague epidemics struck late medieval East Anglia in cycles of five to ten years, and after the 1420s they combined with outbreaks of influenza and dysentery to produce calamitously high mortality rates of around forty deaths per thousand. He also claims to have identified seven distinct sub-regions of Suffolk where lethal diseases had become endemic, although the methodology is flawed and his claims are speculative.[14]

THE PEASANTS' REVOLT OF 1381

The Black Death shook English society to its roots. It undermined the authority of both the church, which was supposed to protect the populace against wrathful acts of God, and of the wider ruling elite, who initially acted as though nothing decisive or enduring had happened. It fuelled greater expectations of economic and social improvement among the mass of the populace, once they realized that the balance of economic and social power had shifted in their favour. Lords had acknowledged this shift in the early 1350s by making some concessions on rents and services, but in the 1360s and early 1370s the combination of economic recovery, repressive regulation of the labour market by the government, and some clawing back of earlier concessions had encouraged them to suppose that pestilence had triggered a short-term crisis rather than any irreversible change. The initial success of the labour legislation encouraged central government to extend its statutory powers further to regulate life in the localities, and it continued to pursue wars and raise taxes as it had done before the pestilence. Thus the heightened expectations of the populace were frustrated in the 1360s and 1370s, which exacerbated social tensions. Local acts of petty resistance and insubordination increased, as tenants and labourers sought to evade labour services, onerous rents, and unjust levies and restrictions upon their labour. Not surprisingly, the fourteenth century was characterized by a succession of popular rebellions, which reflected widespread disaffection with both central and local government, the unpredictable nature of justice and the growth of corruption among officialdom.[15]

The catastrophes of 1349 and 1361 did not immediately precipitate substantial social change. By the early 1370s people could certainly acquire land more

---

[14]   Powell, *Rising in East Anglia*, p. 123; *1524 Lay Subsidy*, pp. xxiv; J. Cornwall, 'English Population in the Early Sixteenth Century', *EcHR* 23 (1970), pp. 38–42, and the other arguments are skilfully reviewed by S. H. Rigby, 'Urban Population in Late Medieval England: The Evidence of the Lay Subsidies' (forthcoming); Gottfried, *Bury St Edmunds*, pp. 63–4; R. S. Gottfried, *Epidemic Disease in Fifteenth-Century England: The Medical Response and the Demographic Consequences* (Leicester, 1978).

[15]   *AHEW*, iii, pp. 744–50.

easily, but not at vastly discounted or favourable rents. Labourers could obtain more work, and good workers found their disposable incomes improved quickly, but they were irritated by attempts to depress wage rates below free market levels through the new labour legislation. Most prosecutions under the Statute of Labourers were against either job agents ('procurers of labour') or labourers for accepting wages in excess of those proscribed in the statute. The court of the King's Bench was especially active in prosecuting labour cases in the 1360s and 1370s in East Anglia, backed by teams of local officials responsible for deciding which cases to prosecute and ensuring that the defendants attended the court. Hence when Geoffrey Speed of Somerton had agreed to work as a ploughman for Nicholas Pickard of Rede, but was then enticed to work elsewhere by Adam de Gatebury, the bailiff of Risbridge Hundred was charged with ensuring their appearance before the next local sessions of the King's Bench. Most of these cases were directed against agricultural workers, and the most hardened offenders came to regard the financial penalties they incurred as part of their business expenses. In fact, the number of successful prosecutions under the Statute represented only a small proportion of total hirings, but the legislation created resentment beyond its direct economic impact. Freemen were not used to restrictions upon their labour, particularly in a region where wages were an important component of household income, and the general sense of injustice and outrage at legislation which denied them the full worth of their scarce labour was exacerbated by the fact that the landlords who willingly *paid* such excessive wages – and sought the services of agents in their desperation for workers – escaped punishment entirely.[16]

The mounting frustration with the labour legislation was exacerbated by other tensions in Suffolk society which surfaced during this period. Villeinage was neither widespread nor onerous, but the heavy weight of week works borne by a sizeable minority of villein tenants on the estates of the greatest landlords seemed especially onerous when contrasted with the personal freedom and less demanding lordship around them, particularly when many lords continued to call upon them in the 1360s and 1370s. Similar contradictions frustrated the townsfolk of Bury St Edmunds, who traded under the shadow of a powerful and conservative landlord in a county where seigneurial influence over towns was limited. The restlessness of the county's inhabitants was fuelled by their high degree of political awareness and legal consciousness, not least because of their wide trading connections and their geographical proximity to the centre of royal justice. Periods of perceived weakness at the centre of English government, such as 1327, tended to encourage rebellious behaviour,

[16] *AHEW*, iii, pp. 757–9, 770; B. H. Putnam, *The Enforcement of the Statutes of Labourers, 1349–1359* (London, 1908), pp. 179–83, 221, 410.

because at such times activists believed that they might achieve something by their actions.[17]

The participation of rebels from Suffolk in the revolt of 1381 was extensive and violent. The course of events is well documented, and John Ridgard, who has devoted a lifetime's research into the local incidents and participants, will eventually provide a detailed analysis of its causes and nuances. Suffolk is particularly worthy of close study, because some of the most violent acts of the Revolt were perpetrated here, including around twenty deaths on both sides, and hundreds of people were subsequently indicted as a result of their actions. The rebels were most active during the period 12–18 June 1381; the main flashpoints occurred in centres of government and trade: in particular, Bury St Edmunds – culminating in the ransacking of the abbey, the assassination of the Lord Chief Justice, John de Cavendish, and the murder of a number of monks (including de Cavendish's close friend, and acting head of the abbey, John de Cambridge) – Ipswich, Lowestoft, Melton (the administrative centre of the Liberty of St Etheldreda) and Sudbury. The rebellion in west Suffolk was largely quelled on 23 June by the arrival of the earl of Suffolk in Bury St Edmunds with 500 royal lancers, although unrest still simmered during July in parts of east Suffolk.[18]

The ferocity of the events of 1381 in Suffolk indicates that they drew upon deep and gnawing sources of discontent, which had been stirred to boiling point in the generation after the Black Death. These causes can be usefully illustrated by reconstructing a series of flashpoints which occurred in the 1370s in Lakenheath, culminating in 1381 in the murder of John de Cavendish. The first documented incident came in late 1370, when some inhabitants of Lakenheath refused to co-operate with royal officials sent to the town to collect money due to the Crown. Consequently in January 1371 three more senior royal officials, led by John Bole, were dispatched by the Crown with writs to enforce payment, and to require the recalcitrant individuals to appear at a future meeting of the hundred court to answer for their actions. When these royal officials again met with refusals to pay, they decided to seize personal belongings from the debtors as distraints. This act of seizure immediately inflamed local opinion, and an angry group of at least thirty people quickly gathered and confronted Bole and his two associates. The mob assaulted them, symbolically seizing Bole's staff of royal office and breaking it into a number of pieces, reclaimed the distrained chattels and then triumphantly ejected the officials from the town, warning them against any further attempts to return. Later that day, mindful of his duty and outraged at his treatment, Bole returned to the outskirts of Lakenheath, only to be

---

[17] Schofield, *Peasant and Community*, pp. 173, 182–3; Lock, *Walsham*, i, p. 19.

[18] *HistA*, pp. 90–1; Powell, *Rising in East Anglia*, pp. 24–5.

threatened once again by the 'warlike' mob. He wisely opted for discretion over valour.[19]

The escalation of this conflict into violence, and the inhabitants' refusals to pay the Crown its due, inevitably drew a firm response from the highest level of government. On 30 January 1371 Edward III formally dispatched a judicial commission to Lakenheath, made up of four of his most effective law enforcement officers in East Anglia: William de Wichingham, Roger de Boys, John de Cavendish and Reginald de Eccles. This bristling display of royal authority proved effective at eliciting payment and restoring, albeit temporarily, the Crown's authority in Lakenheath, for there is no record of any hostile response to the commission or its findings. The protestors had made their point, and had pressed it as far as prudence dictated. Indeed, this was no crude and ignorant mob formed by some medieval underclass, but was led by some of Lakenheath's most respected inhabitants: Simon, the vicar of Lakenheath, and members of his household, leading tenants, manorial jurors, several women and two men, John Carter and John Mayhew, who were destined to become constables of Lakenheath within ten years.

The underlying cause of this conflict is not as clear to the historian as it was to the inhabitants of Lakenheath, but the most likely answer lies in heavy-handed or corrupt behaviour by local officers of the Crown exacerbated by inflexible local lordship. The tensions that corruption could generate at this time are exemplified by a notorious and contemporaneous case from the other side of the county, where in 1370 the constables of Blything and Hoxne hundreds had been charged with extortion and corruption. Their crimes provoked outrage: they were accused of capturing felons, but then releasing them on the payment of a ransom; arresting known innocents and demanding money for their release; and offering corrupt assessments of moveable wealth to local freemen, which would reduce their liability for a financial contribution that year to an array-of-arms. (The levying of arms, soldiers and cash for national defence itself was triggered by the resumption of war with France in 1369.) In the absence of any other clear motive, it is not inconceivable that the people of Lakenheath were reacting to similar injustices by local officials of the Crown. Whatever the reason, the events of 1370 were merely the beginning of a decade of violence in the town, culminating in an infamous murder.

In 1371 the Crown, to ease its insolvency in the face of renewed hostilities with France, experimented with a new form of taxation known as the Parish Tax. This was agreed by Parliament in February 1371, and collected by specially appointed commissioners from March onwards, and parishes in Suffolk and

[19] The following reconstruction draws upon Powell, *Rising in East Anglia*, pp. 12–23; Dyer, 'The Rising of 1381', pp. 274–87; Bailey, 'Lakenheath', pp. 16–19; *CPR, 1370–4*, pp. 100–1.

Norfolk were required to pay a proportionately higher rate than most other areas of the country. In addition, richer parishes were expected to support poorer ones in meeting their contributions: predictably, some East Anglian hundreds refused to collect the tax, and most of the others were extremely slow. Again, it seems reasonable to speculate that this fiscal experiment – never repeated – further exacerbated the general sense of disquiet about the government's intervention in the politics of the locality in a large and wealthy parish such as Lakenheath.

The next noteworthy episode occurred between October 1377 and the spring of 1379, when a fire caused extensive damage in the northern part of Lakenheath. The event cannot be dated more precisely, but its effects are recorded in the manorial account of 1378–9. At least twenty-five, possibly as many as forty, houses and cottages of various kinds were utterly destroyed, together with several stalls in the marketplace, and – most significantly – the manorial complex of the prior and convent of Ely was extensively damaged: the dovecote and grange were obliterated, and the latter had to be rebuilt at the enormous cost of £60. The rental income from land and property collapsed from £15 in the mid-1370s to a mere £5 in 1378–9, and never fully recovered. In subsequent years the manorial court gave repeated orders to the tenants of the damaged properties to rebuild their houses, but with little success. It is apparent that the great fire of Lakenheath caused more distress to the manorial lord than to the inhabitants: indeed, their staunch refusal to rebuild the lost properties seems to have been a source of defiant pleasure to them. This might raise suspicions about the cause of the fire, which could well have been arson. The explanation for this possible arson attack on the prior's manorial complex is elusive, although the end of Edward III's reign in 1377 and the minority of Richard II created a weakness at the centre of English government which fanned the flames of political unrest.

Within months of the fire, the political temperature in Lakenheath once again rose dangerously high. In 1379 the court of the King's Bench sat at both Thetford and Bury St Edmunds dealing with a range of cases, many of which probably involved the prosecution of local workers under the Statute of Labourers. The royal justice leading these sessions was none other than John de Cavendish, one of the commissioners on the Lakenheath inquiry of 1371 and now a well-known enforcer of the Crown's will – and the Statute of Labourers in particular – in Suffolk and Essex. Furthermore, the bailiff of Lackford hundred in 1379, who was responsible for both oiling the mechanisms of royal justice in north-west Suffolk and the local enforcement of the decisions of the King's Bench, was none other than John Bole, the other central figure in the events of 1371. This coincidence proved too much for John Carter and John Mayhew, rebels in 1371 and now constables of Lakenheath in 1379, and therefore duty-bound to follow any orders from de Cavendish and Bole. They refused to do so, and were predictably indicted for their failure 'to answer for certain articles' to the King's Bench. Their stance attracted widespread support in Lakenheath, because the vill pointedly declined to pay its common fine in 1379. In effect, the town was refusing to uphold the local administration of the Crown as represented by two of its old enemies.

The local antipathy to John de Cavendish was heightened by his close association with both the prior and convent of Ely and the prior of Bury St Edmunds, and the close interconnections between local government and local lordship were another potent element in the decade of unrest at Lakenheath. The prior and convent of Ely proved an uncompromising and unpopular landlord at Lakenheath in the 1350s and 1360s, not least because of their refusal to convert many villein tenures to leasehold. This unpopularity was heightened after the riot of 1371 by the prior's decision to relieve one of the ringleaders, Simon the vicar of Lakenheath, of his parochial responsibilities at an early opportunity: he was transferred to the living at Littleport in 1373. The deteriorating relationship between the prior and his tenants in the 1370s is evident in the latter's refusals to maintain fenland waterways, their persistent challenging of the prior's fold rights (most notably by another 1371 rebel, William Bishop), their failure to pay almost half of the penalties levied in the Lakenheath manorial court in the late 1370s and early 1380s, and the refusal of forty-three tenants to attend the lord's manorial court in September 1380. The antagonism was mutual: during the 1370s the prior periodically ordered rabbits (a prized delicacy and an unpopular seigneurial monopoly) to be sent from his warren at Lakenheath as a gift to John de Cavendish. Since his manorial tenants were required to transport these rabbits to de Cavendish, the prior appears to have been provoking his Lakenheath subjects. Even if this suggestion seems a little fanciful, it is clear that de Cavendish was strongly identified with the interests of their unpopular lord, and therefore, in their eyes, incapable of exercising disinterested justice.

Finally, the prior's steward of estates in west Suffolk was Edmund de Lakenheath, a member of the county gentry who lost property in the Lakenheath fire of *c.* 1378. Edmund was responsible for enforcing the prior's unpopular estate management policies at Lakenheath and also had close links with the abbey of St Edmund, serving as constable to the Liberty of St Edmund and therefore experienced at petty law enforcement in west Suffolk. He was widely known as both a land and legal agent, and his unpopularity is reflected in the ransacking of his Suffolk properties in the Revolt of 1381 at Lakenheath, Gislingham, Herringswell and Stoke-by-Clare. Edmund himself only escaped capture by a pursuing mob in east Suffolk by putting to sea, where he was promptly seized by a Flemish ship and ransomed for his freedom.

The coalescence of local events and personalities, and the complex inter-weaving of national politics and local lordship, were especially powerful and prolonged in Lakenheath during the 1370s, and explain the extraordinary events in the town during the Peasants' Revolt in June 1381. On Wednesday 12 June, when the Kentish rebels massed at Blackheath, a small band of Essex rebels under John Wrawe (formerly the priest of Ringsfield) attacked proper-ties in Cavendish and Sudbury, and the next day entered Bury St Edmunds – which they controlled for the next eight days – with a greatly swollen band. On Friday 14 June John de Cavendish, now Lord Chief Justice and, to local people, the personification of the abuse and perversion of royal justice in the localities over the previous two decades, was betrayed to the rebels near Newmarket and pursued by a murderous band to Lakenheath. De Cavendish knew well from his earlier visit that Lakenheath was an inland river port, and therefore offered the prospect of requisitioning a boat to escape across the fens to Ely, where the prior and convent could provide protection. As he ran along the town's rudimentary wharves, he spotted a single boat tied to a stake. Unfortunately, his intentions were transparent to one Catherine Gamen, who was working close by and had (significantly) both recognized de Cavendish and grasped the implications of the unfolding events. She untied the boat and pushed it away from the wharf as de Cavendish approached, thus effectively sentencing him to death: trapped, he was overwhelmed by the pursuing rebels and summarily executed. It took seven hacks to remove his head from his torso, whence it was transported gleefully to Bury St Edmunds and paraded upon a pike.

The events in Lakenheath exemplify admirably the complex interweaving of grievances and motives that lay behind the Peasants' Revolt in Suffolk in June 1381. Frustration and discontent, which had been simmering for a number of years among the lower orders of society, were seriously inflamed in May 1381 by the attempts of new commissioners to collect a second instalment of the third Poll Tax in four years. The Poll Tax itself was an exceptional form of taxation, demanded by a weak government whose legitimacy, competence and honesty were disputed, and it was levied towards the end of a period when the power and authority of royal officials and justices in the localities had been extended, and with it the potential for corruption and bias. Discontent with the local administration of the Crown spread during the 1370s, especially in areas close to London, where the exercise of royal authority was most strenuous and political awareness strongest, and it forged a common sense of injustice and unfairness across a wide range of disparate social groups. The sense of grievance at political and judicial issues is clearly reflected in some of the targets of the Suffolk rebels, which included people who had sat as Members of

Parliament since 1376, local government officials, royal justices and Poll Tax commissioners.[20]

Yet the ferocity of the attack on the abbey of Bury St Edmunds, the burning of manorial documents, and miscellaneous assaults on landlords indicates that, once it had started, the Revolt also served as a bandwagon for parading a broader range of local and personal grievances. Herbert Eiden's research on the Revolt in Norfolk and Essex highlights the prominence of 'political' targets, but he also emphasizes that the rebels targeted the unjust and bad exercise of lordship at whatever level. Both Bury St Edmunds abbey and Edmund de Lakenheath epitomized this general notion of 'bad lordship'. The abbey had long antagonized the burgesses of Bury by its restrictive management of the borough, it wielded considerable judicial clout across west Suffolk through the Liberty of St Edmund, and to radical priests it embodied the extreme wealth and conservatism of the established church. Furthermore, and despite the rapidly changing economic and social climate, it had stubbornly maintained onerous week works and other labour services on its estate in this largely free and fluid region, and consequently its rural manors as far away as Norfolk were attacked and their documents destroyed. Edmund de Lakenheath's activities across Suffolk in the 1370s were typical of the way in which royal justice and seigneurial lordship had become closely intertwined, because he served as both a law enforcement officer for the Crown and as an estate steward for two conservative and unpopular landlords.[21]

Both Ridgard and Dyer have identified a number of significant features of the Revolt in Suffolk. Ridgard notes the widespread burning of manorial documents and the attacks on major ecclesiastical targets, reflecting the dissatisfaction of many villeins and parish priests with elements of the established order, the symbolic cancellation of debts and obligations, and the destruction of the formal records on which lords legitimized their exactions. When the London rebels demanded rents fixed at 4d. per acre and an end to villeinage, they were actually seeking the best of both worlds: the removal of labour services and other servile dues, but the retention of cash rents fixed at the artificially low levels on customary holdings. Dyer emphasizes that the rebels saw themselves as taking charge of government, rather than overthrowing it *per se*, as illustrated by their instruction to the constable of Hoxne hundred to muster archers for the rebel cause (for which the rebels were prepared to pay the standard daily rate) and by the claim that the rebels in Brandon 'assumed to themselves the royal power'. Indeed, Edgar Powell points out that the rebels

[20] *AHEW*, iii, pp. 770–2; Powell, *Rising in East Anglia*, pp. 10, 14, 21, 23, 63; *PSIA* 9 (1897), p. 350.

[21] H. Eiden, 'Joint Action against Bad Lordship. The Peasants' Revolt in Essex and Norfolk', *History* 83 (1998), pp. 22, 29; Powell, *Rising in East Anglia*, pp. 21–2.

frequently used the king's name as a justification for their actions during the insurrection, although this was a prudent tactic at a time when overt challenges to the king were treasonable. The election of Robert Westbrom as the 'king of Suffolk' at Bury on 15 June was a conscious act of both irony and symbolism. These actions imply a good deal of organization and co-ordination among the rebel bands in East Anglia, who probably communicated with each other through couriers on horseback, and a high degree of political awareness. In this regard it is significant that many of the leaders of the Revolt in Suffolk were prominent peasants and artisans – not marginal elements of society – who had considerable experience in manorial government and were well established locally. Their frustrations with the ineptitude of the local officers of the Crown, with bad lordship, and with the frustrating effects of agrarian depression after 1375, were especially hard to bear during a period of rising expectations, and they were most able to articulate the source of their discontent and to link political grievances with the resentment against landlords. The result was the most famous, widespread and violent episode of rebellion in Suffolk history.[22]

The political achievements of the Revolt were limited. Although the experimental Poll Tax was abandoned, royal power and authority were quickly restored, the leading rebels were tried and executed, and no immediate and direct concessions on land tenures are discernible. Yet the Revolt sent a powerful signal to lords about the possible consequences of 'bad lordship', and within twenty years most vestiges of serfdom and villeinage had disappeared from much of Suffolk. Nor did the suppression of the Revolt eradicate protest or dissent. Petty and localized outbreaks of rebellion, drawing upon some of the grievances of 1381, are recorded throughout the 1380s and 1390s, and were increasingly interwoven with the spread of religious dissent. Larry Poos has linked a persistent strain of religious nonconformity with political volatility in late medieval Essex, perhaps drawing upon the type of anti-authoritarian tendencies that characterized Suffolk society. Anti-clericalism and Lollard sympathies became widely established among ordinary people in the cloth-making areas of south Suffolk, and also in north-east Suffolk, emphasizing the links between political and religious radicalism, and areas of rapid economic change. Disaffected textile workers feature prominently among supporters of Cade's rebellion of 1450, an overtly political movement which attempted to overthrow Henry VI's government. It is possible that Cade himself was in Bury St Edmunds in May 1450, shortly before moving onto London, and –

---

[22] Powell, *Rising in East Anglia*, pp. 21, 58; C. Dyer, 'The Social and Economic Background to the Rural Revolt of 1381', in *The English Rising of 1381*, ed. R. H. Hilton and T. H. Aston (Cambridge, 1984), pp. 15–17, 38; Dyer, 'The Rising of 1381', p. 280; *HistA*, pp. 90–1.

just as in 1381 – connections between rebels from Bury, south Suffolk and Kent were strong. Political conspiracies and unrest fermented throughout 1450–1 in Suffolk, featuring uprisings in Hadleigh and Beccles and a politically motivated murder in Alderton, after the overthrow of the earl of Suffolk sparked a national political crisis. These flashpoints were probably fuelled by economic distress following a slump in the textile trade, but the underlying theme of political, social and religious dissent is clearly apparent.[23]

THE DECLINE OF SERFDOM AND VILLEINAGE

Personal servility and villeinage were neither prominent nor heavily enforced in Suffolk before the Black Death, but in the second half of the fourteenth century the management of villein tenures and the treatment of serfs became an issue of heightened significance. After 1349 the relative abundance of land encouraged tenants to be increasingly choosy about the terms on which they entered the land market, and they were especially reluctant to hold villein land on the old terms, because its associated rent package of customary dues (particularly labour services) were regarded as onerous and demeaning in a county where free tenures dominated. Yet, conversely, some landlords wished to uphold villeinage, precisely because it provided them with a secure source of labour in an era of acute labour shortages. These widely divergent expectations in the second half of the fourteenth century exacerbated social tensions between some landlords and their tenants, to the extent that the abolition of serfdom constituted one of the main demands of the rebels in 1381. Although the Peasants' Revolt did not succeed in achieving this aim, serfdom and villeinage ultimately proved unsustainable in the economic conditions of the last quarter of the fourteenth century. The fall in the profitability of grain farming after the mid-1370s exacerbated the difficulties of landlords in finding tenants, and thus they had little option but to improve the terms and conditions upon which villein land was held. Personal serfdom proved more durable, but after *c.* 1400 the ability and preparedness of most landlords to enforce it diminished. As a result, villein tenure and serfdom gradually disappeared from most of East Anglia, a development which some historians believe had a transforming effect on patterns of landholding and, by extension, the social order.[24]

---

[23] *HistA*, pp. 90–1; Powell, *Rising in East Anglia*, pp. 24–5; Poos, *Rural Society*, chap. 12; N. P. Tanner, ed., *Heresy Trials in the Diocese of Norwich, 1428–31*, Camden Society, 4th series 20 (London, 1977), pp. 25–30, and 107, 119 and 133 where a high proportion of lollards from Beccles were involved in the leather trades; I. M. W. Harvey, *Jack Cade's Rebellion of 1450* (Oxford, 1991), pp. 17–28, 115–20.

[24] Whittle, *Agrarian Capitalism*, pp. 37–40, 302–7; M. Bailey, 'Blowing up Bubbles: Some New demographic Evidence for the Fifteenth Century?', *Journal of Medieval History* 15 (1989), pp. 349–53.

The chronology of the decline of serfdom and villeinage varied from manor to manor. In some places – usually small lay manors with a very large proportion of free land – villein tenure and serfdom appears to have disappeared completely within a generation of the Black Death. For example, all labour services had disappeared by the early 1370s from lay manors in Cretingham, Horham, Loudham and Tattingstone, after which there is no evidence that any other servile dues were being collected. The lords of these manors possessed neither the power nor the inclination to uphold the remnants of villeinage in an era when tenants were scarce and the local land market was awash with both free tenures and demesne land on leasehold.[25]

Yet circumstances were different on other manors, usually held by aristocratic landlords, where villeinage had been more prominent before the Black Death. Here neither villeinage nor serfdom showed any sign of disappearing in the third quarter of the fourteenth century: on the contrary, many landlords looked to enforce the obligations associated with them more rigorously. The ploys designed to entice prospective tenants in the early 1350s, such as the temporary waiving of labour services and widespread conversions of villein tenures to leasehold, soon disappeared. By the 1360s fewer new leases were being created, and many existing leases were withdrawn upon the expiry of their term, so that once again most customary holdings were being held on villein tenure under the old terms.[26] In the 1360s and 1370s labour services were still extensively enforced on a good number of demesnes, including those of some lower-status landlords (such as those at Boulge and Thelnetham, see table 5) who felt the shortages of labour acutely. Individual refusals to perform labour services as an act of personal defiance attracted punitive responses. One Walton tenant was isolated as a 'rebel' for a flagrant refusal to perform his ploughing service, and in 1363 a tenement called 'Cukhus' in Horham was seized from William le Clerk after he had detained labour services.[27]

Some landlords were aggressive in upholding other aspects of villeinage in the 1360s and 1370s, a calculated policy encouraged by the sustained buoyancy

[25] SROI HA68/484/318 (Horham); SROI HB8/1/817 (Tattingstone); SROI HA10/50/18/4.4 (8) (Cretingham); SROI HD1538/295/3 (Loudham).

[26] The only collective waiving of labour services after the early 1350s I have discovered is recorded at Holbrook in 1382 (SROI S1/10/9.1), although some lords might still respond sympathetically to individual circumstances: in 1367 Matilda Regge of Aldham negotiated the removal of week works from her customary holding in return for an enhanced cash rent because of her 'impotence and poverty', SROI HA68/484/135; Bailey, 'Lakenheath', pp. 10–11.

[27] D. Stone, 'Managerial Problems and the Crisis in Demesne Farming after the Black Death' (unpublished paper); Stone, *Decision-Making*, p. 252; SROI HA119/50/3/17, mm. 6, 40 (Walton); SROI HA48/484/79 (Horham). For other examples of collective protests, see Dyer, 'The Rising of 1381', p. 278.

TABLE 5
Percentage of week works performed on selected manors, 1350–1400

Manor	Year	Winter works performed	Summer works performed	Week works performed*
Akenham	1391–2			5%
Boulge	1373–4	85%		
Earl Stonham	1394–5			0%
Dunningworth	1392–3			0%
Glemham	1356–7			27%
Hargrave	1376–7			64%
Horham	1371–2			0%
Kelsale	1356–7			19%
Lackford	1400–1			0%
Lakenheath	1394–5	0%	56%	
Lawshall	1394–5			0%
Melton	1398–9	0%	0%	
Mildenhall	1388–9			5%
Risby	1384–5			0%
Thelnetham	1375–6	75%		

* Some manors simply record week works rather than distinguishing explicitly between winter and summer works.

Sources: SROI (Akenham); SROI HD1538/139/1 (Boulge); SROI HD1538/364 (Earl Stonham); SROI HD1538/206/6 (Dunningworth); SROI HD1538/238/1 (Glemham); SROB E3/15.10/2.20 (Hargrave); SROI HA68/484/318 (Horham); SROI HD1538/279/2 (Kelsale); SROB E3/15.12/2.3 (Lackford); CUL EDC 7/15/1/xx (Lakenheath); *PSIA* 14 (1912), p. 121 (Lawshall); CUL EDC 7/16/11/26 (Melton); BL Add. Roll 53119 (Mildenhall); SROB E3/15.13/2.20 (Risby); SROI HD1538/380 (Thelnetham).

of grain prices and the consequent resilience of the land market. The level of entry fines charged on inheritances rose after the Black Death on some manors, such as Drinkstone and Fornham, and in 1387 the manor of Walton seized all the land of a tenant who had refused to accept another holding on villein tenure. Chevage was enforced more rigorously almost everywhere, and landlords became particularly active against those serfs who claimed to be of free status, because both 'offences' were easy to prove and were deemed to challenge seigneurial authority explicitly. From the 1350s the incidence of chevage recorded in manorial courts increased markedly. For example, scarcely ten people had been pursued for chevage at Walsham between 1314 and 1348, but in 1361 seven were recorded in a single court. The information given in chevage cases also became more detailed, usually stating explicitly the whereabouts and name of the departed serf. Offending emigrants could now be amerced higher fines for chevage – as opposed to the odd penny that comprised the standard charge before the Black Death – or their families threatened with substantial penalties if they did not return. In 1363 Thomas Wolnoth was charged 6s. 8d. for leaving Dunningworth; in 1354 William Carter was threatened with a 20s. amercement by the Aldham court if he did not return from Hintlesham; and in 1377 the father of two emigrants from Drinkstone was amerced 20s. for failing to persuade them to return.[28]

In the second half of the fourteenth century a rise in claims by serfs to be personally free represented the most direct and overt challenge to seigneurial jurisdiction, and lords levied punitive amercements upon transgressors, because they regarded such behaviour as both contemptuous and contrary to the natural social order. In 1360 two serfs were placed in the stocks at South Elmham for asserting their freedom. Migrant serfs who had become conspicuously wealthy received special attention. Robert Hardekyn had left Felixstowe soon after the Black Death to make a profitable living as a trader in Manningtree, and subsequently the manor court of Walton made a number of attempts to seize his various shops, other properties and land, much of it held on free tenure. In 1394 Thomas Payn denied his status as a serf in a court session at Dunningworth, stating on oath that he was a freeman, and was promptly amerced a hefty 13s. 4d. 'for contempt'.[29]

The more vigorous targeting of villeins and serfs by manorial courts in the aftermath of the Black Death reflects the sensitivity of landlords to the sudden shortage of tenants and their eagerness to assert their authority in the face of rapid social and economic change. Villein families who had built up decent-sized farms presented landlords with the easiest targets for extracting payments, because they had a strong economic stake in remaining on the manor and were therefore most reluctant to liquidate their assets and depart. The exploitation of established farming families was evident on the estates of Bury St Edmunds abbey. For example, the level of entry fines charged upon a villein inheriting one of the 8-acreware customary holdings in Fornham All Saints was increased from a set fee of around 3s. 4d. in the 1340s to 6s. 8d. in the 1370s, although higher charges did not deter the three West brothers from entering their father's holding in June 1371. Yet over the next decade or so various members of the extended West family were doggedly pursued for childwite, chevage and merchet, and a substantial heriot payment of one cow

[28] SROB E7/10/1.2 (Drinkstone); SROI HA119/50/3/17, m. 22 (Walton); Lock, *Walsham*, i, and ii, pp. 61, 79; SROI HD1538/207/2 (Dunningworth); SROI HA68/484/135 (Aldham); Dyer, 'The Rising of 1381', p. 279; Dyer, 'Social and Economic Background', p. 24.

[29] Dyer, 'The Rising of 1381', p. 279; Dyer, 'Social and Economic Background', p. 24; Lock, *Walsham*, ii, pp. 146–62; SROI HD1538/207/3 (Dunningworth).

worth 6s. 8d. was demanded from Alice West when her husband died holding a solitary acre on villein tenure. When one of the brothers co-holding the 8-acreware *tenementum* died in 1386, the other two decided that they had tired of the regime, abandoning all the remaining land with crops still on the ground and immediately fleeing the manor, one to Lopham (Norfolk) and the other to (King's) Lynn.[30]

Many villeins resented the increased assertiveness of landlords, regarding such actions as a targeted move to frustrate their reasonable expectations. Their inferior social and legal status did not present an obstacle to accumulating greater wealth and improving their economic status, and many enjoyed a marked improvement in standards of living, as work became better paid and land became more freely available. Villeins at Walton appear prominently among the lessees of the manorial demesne and others at Huntingfield accumulated substantial land holdings.[31] The sharply contrasting expectations of landlords and villeins in this period raised social tensions. For example, fifteen villeins at Thurston refused to render their rents and services for three years after the Revolt of 1381, and in 1385 they were found guilty by the king's justices of 'being bound together by words and in clubs'. In 1379 Walter and Alice Skacer of Leiston refused to perform their harvest labour services for the eponymous abbot, working instead in the fields of another village. Their motive was partly financial, for they could receive better pay elsewhere, but they were also making a calculated protest against servility, because Walter's defiance had followed an express warning from the bailiff about the consequences of such actions: the court roll pointedly recorded Walter's status as a *nativus* and he received a sizeable amercement of 10s. In 1371 Nicholas Mervyn was forced to swear an oath to 'serve the lord as he wishes' after his departure from Aldham, and another serf had to return each harvest to work on the Aldham demesne.[32]

By the last quarter of the fourteenth century the enforcement of villeinage and serfdom waned sharply on many manors. The Peasants' Revolt provided a chilling warning of the possible consequences of aggressive lordship, and after the late 1370s the marked decline in grain prices deflated the land market. Even on the estates of aristocratic landlords, the managerial hassle of supervising a reluctant customary labour force, the falling area under demesne cultivation, and – in some places – the decision to lease much of the demesne resulted in a dramatic decline in the utilization of labour services in general

30 SROB E3/15.6/1.5, and E3/15.6/1.15 – 1.18 (Fornham).

31 Dyer, 'Social and Economic Background', pp. 21–2; Bailey, 'Blowing up Bubbles', p. 355.

32 Powell, *Rising in East Anglia*, pp. 64–5; CUL Vanneck Ms, box 9 (Leiston); Dyer, 'Social and Economic Background', pp. 24–5.

and week works in particular. By *c.* 1400 week works – the most onerous and disliked of Suffolk's labour services – had disappeared from almost every Suffolk manor. Harvest labour services were more useful to landlords, because they provided workers at a key time of the agrarian year, and consequently they lasted longer, although – once again – their uptake declined during this period. By the middle of the fifteenth century few if any labour services were utilized in Suffolk.[33]

By *c.* 1400 other collective dues associated with the old villein tenures had mostly dissolved. The decline of millsuit is evident in the falling revenues or abandonment of demesne mills (especially from the 1380s) and the disappearance of millsuit violations from manor courts. Millsuit is scarcely found on any Suffolk manor after *c.* 1400.[34] By the early fifteenth century tallage and recognition payments had also largely disappeared, despite enduring until the mid-fifteenth century on many estates in midland and south-west England.[35] In general, collective dues were easier to resist than personal ones, because collective acts of resistance, however low key, were harder for landlords to overcome, whereas individuals acting in isolation were more vulnerable to seigneurial threats and coercion. This explains why personal dues such as heriot, merchet, chevage and election to manorial office tended to survive longer. Elections to petty manorial offices – such as warrener, woodkeeper and parker – had largely ceased after the mid-fourteenth century, and some manors soon disposed of the major offices too: the offices of claviger and reeve had disappeared from Hinderclay by the 1380s, because of difficulties in finding willing tenants of suitable calibre. But other manors persisted with the election of the key officers of reeve and messor for much longer, sometimes until the late fifteenth century. Dunningworth continued to elect reeves episodically until the 1430s and messors until the 1460s, and both officers were routinely elected at Walsham until the 1480s. Such elections were largely nominal by this date. The continued election of reeves offered few operational benefits to lords, because professional bailiffs and rent collectors had now supplanted the traditional work of the reeve. As more and more of the old villein *tenementa* were converted to contractual tenancies, or lay abandoned in the lord's hands, so the pool of liable tenants dwindled. Lords routinely accepted a standard fine to exonerate elected tenants from fulfilling their office, so that, in reality, the system of elections continued

---

33 Bailey, 'Decline of Villeinage'.

34 For references and broader context, see pp. 233 4; R. Holt, *The Mills of Medieval England* (Oxford, 1988), pp. 165–6; SROI HA119:50/3/17, m. 63 (Walton); Lock, *Walsham*, ii, pp. 185, 204, and SROB HA504/1/10–17 (Walsham); Langdon, *Mills*, pp. 284–6; SROB E3/11/1.2 (Lidgate).

35 Bailey, 'Decline of Villeinage'.

as a useful seigneurial money-spinner rather than as an operational reality.[36]

Childwite failed to survive the fourteenth century, reinforcing Bennett's belief that it was deployed as a discretionary levy to regulate childbirth among poor servile women when demographic pressure peaked before the Black Death.[37] Merchet and chevage disappeared on many manors during the early fifteenth century: even where it survived, it was usually restricted to a small number of serf families. The last case of merchet at Walsham was recorded in 1398, the last case of chevage in 1439, and the last case of heriot in 1438. No levies for heriot, merchet or chevage are recorded by the mid-fifteenth century at Badwell Ash, Cretingham, Cornard Parva (Caxtons), Cotton, Layham, Leiston, Preston, Thorney Hotot or Withersfield.[38]

The declining incidence of the obligations associated with serfdom and villeinage was accelerated by the growing tendency after *c.* 1380 to convert large areas of villein land into contractual leasehold tenancies. Leaseholds were less secure than villein tenures, in that they were only granted for a fixed term, and they attracted higher cash rents per acre, but they provided flexibility for those tenants keen to acquire and shed land according to their personal circumstances, and they were formally free of the miscellaneous dues and services attached to customary tenure. The quantities of arable land held on leasehold had been very small in the early fourteenth century, but by the 1390s most customary land had been converted to 'leasehold' on the manors of Icklingham Berners, Lackford, Lawshall, Layham and Scotland Hall, Nayland.[39] Even on

---

36 SROB E3/15.7/1.9a (Fornham); SROI HD1538/207/4, court held October 1400, and /6–8 (Dunningworth); SROB HA501/4/12.1 – 12.22 and 15.20 (Walsham); SROB E7/1/1 (Cotton); SROB E7/10/5 (Preston).

37 Bennett, 'Writing Fornication', pp. 152–3; Bailey, 'Decline of Villeinage'; SROI HD1538/394/1–2 (Ufford).

38 SROB HA504/1/12.22, 13.11, and Lock, *Walsham*, ii, p. 203; SROI HA10/50/18/5.1 (Cretingham); NRO Walsingham XXXIV/1 (Cornard); SROB E7/1/1 (Cotton); SROB 1825/1/1–6 (Badwell); SROB E3/2/8 (Layham); CUL Vanneck Ms, box 9 (Leiston); SROB E7/10/5 (Preston); Amor, 'Late Medieval Enclosure', p. 191; SROB E3/15.6/1.3 (Withersfield); SROB E3/15.7/1.15 (Fornham) SROI HD1538/394/5 and 395/1 (Ufford); SROB E3/11/1.4 and 1.5 (Lidgate); SROB HA504/1/12.22 ff. (Walsham); SROB E3/15.17/1.1 (Harleston); CUL Vanneck Ms, box 1 (Aldham). This decline contrasts with the waves of chevage enforcement in the first half of the fifteenth century on the Ramsey abbey estates, J. A. Raftis, *Tenure and Mobility: Studies in the Social History of an English Village* (Toronto, 1974), pp. 153–66.

39 The unimportance of leaseholds before 1350 is evident across the county. See, for example, Denney, *Sibton Abbey*, p. 17, and the example of Lakenheath, where in 1347–8 only four grants of leasehold are recorded, CUL EDC 7/15/1/14; NRO Ms 13201 (Icklingham); SROB E7/17/10 (Lawshall); SROB E3/2/7 (Layham); SROI HA246/A8/13 (Nayland); SROB E3/15.12/2.3 (Lackford); P. R. Schofield, 'Tenurial

manors where villein tenures had remained important in the third quarter of the fourteenth century, such as Lakenheath and Melton, a major swing to leasehold occurred between 1380 and 1420. At Lidgate the decision to lease the demesne in the early fifteenth century coincided with a sudden increase in grants of customary land on leasehold, such as the eight new grants in one court in 1414.[40]

Customary land which was not converted to leasehold gradually shed the labour services, dues and obligations that had previously constituted its rent package, leaving just an annual cash rent, an entry fine and perhaps the odd labour service in the harvest. In addition, it came to be held on contractual tenancies whose status was not defined too closely: they were contractual in the sense that the terms were as stated (however imprecisely) in the court roll entry which recorded the grant. The logical extension of this process was to provide the tenant with a physical copy of the court roll entry recording the terms on which the land was held and, during the course of the fifteenth century, manorial courts increasingly refer explicitly to a grant of land made 'per copiam'. The use of court roll entries as proof of title to land was already established at Stowmarket by 1356, and a rental of Aldham in 1476 describes the overwhelming majority of customary land as 'held by the rod', together with the date of the manor court in which each grant had been made. By these means villein tenures gradually transformed into copyholds. Copyholds were well established on Netheralls manor in Pakenham by the early fifteenth century, and at Ixworth by mid-century; in the 1440s some of the old customary virgates in Lidgate were granted to new tenants on copyhold; by the 1470s copyholds for lives, rendering only a fixed cash rent and an entry fine, were common in Stanningfield; and by the mid-sixteenth century references to the old villein tenures had disappeared entirely from Brandon, where land was now categorized as either demesne, freehold or copyhold.[41]

Although personal serfdom had disappeared on most manors by the middle of the fifteenth century, it proved most resilient on the estates of aristocratic landlords: hence the rate at which it disappeared depended directly on the

Developments and the Availability of Customary Land in a Later Medieval Community', *EcHR* 49 (1996).

[40] CUL EDC 7/16/11/17–26 (Melton); SROB E3/15.13/2.20 (Risby); CUL EDC 7/15/1/33, 35 (Lakenheath); SROB E3/11/1.2, courts held April 1414, July 1418; E3/11/1.4, mm. 17, 19; and E3/11/1.5, court held April 1462 (Lidgate).

[41] SROI HA1/CC1/11 (Stowmarket, thanks to Nick Amor); CUL Vanneck Ms, box 1 (Aldham), see also court held October 1418 for customary land converted to contractual tenures; SROB E7/19/1, f. 32 (Pakenham); Amor, 'Ixworth', p. 22; SROB E3/11/1.4, mm. 17, 19 (Lidgate); SROB E7/10/10 (Stanningfield); SROI v11/2/1.1 (Brandon), and Bacon 295/46 for an earlier copyhold grant; Whittle, *Agrarian Capitalism*, p. 46.

attitude of the lord and the resolve of his estate administrators. This process is well illustrated by the example of Aldham (held by the de Veres, earls of Oxford), where the management of serfs alternated between periods of striking indifference (for example, the later 1370s) and zealous enforcement (the 1430s). Even here, personal serfdom had disappeared by the 1470s. It survived until the sixteenth century only upon the estates of the dukes of Norfolk and the Crown, due to a consistent and centralized estate policy, sustained by manor courts through the robust direction of successive estate stewards. Merchet and chevage were still levied towards the end of the fifteenth century at Cratfield, Dunningworth and Staverton (dukes of Norfolk), and estate officials compiled family trees to aid the identification, and thus control, of liable serfs. However, even on these estates the incidence of merchet and chevage diminished markedly in the second half of the fifteenth century as the numbers of serfs declined, as flown villeins evaded chevage where it suited them, and as the proportion of land held on villein tenure dropped further. For example, only five merchets were levied in the Dunningworth court between 1438 and 1469, compared to six in the period 1378–81; after the 1470s the record of chevage at Sutton related exclusively to one serf family, and chevage and merchet disappeared at Cratfield in the 1490s.[42]

Serfdom withered on the vine. It decayed as serf families either died out or migrated, as the trouble and costs of regulating the remaining serfs no longer justified the returns, or – as the earls of Oxford discovered – as fifteenth-century jurors refused to recognize an outmoded social status. Manumission – the formal purchase of freedom – does not appear to have been a significant factor in its decline in Suffolk. Hence by the middle of the fifteenth century the overwhelming majority of the tenants on Suffolk were free, either *de jure* or *de facto*. When in 1325 the tenants of the manor of High Hall in Walsham were required to perform fealty to their new lord, twenty were described as free and seventeen as villeins; yet, when fealty was performed in 1379, only eight were free, two were villeins and ten others failed to attend the court. In 1441 only three serfs were recorded among the tenants of Ufford. No attempt was made to distinguish the status of the tenants when new lords acceded to the manors of Cretingham, Felsham, Layham and Sutton in the fifteenth century, and contemporary documents of Sibton abbey do not bother to distinguish free from unfree.[43]

42 Bailey, 'Blowing up Bubbles', pp. 350–5; *EAM*, 1907–8, pp. 54–5; CUL Vanneck Ms, box 3 (Cratfield); SROI HD1538/207/7–8 (Dunningworth); SROI HD1538/357/6 (Staverton); SROI HD1538/395/1 (Ufford); SROI HB10/427/4/1 ff. 46–7, 400–9 (Sutton); SROI HD1538/207/3, 7, 8 (Dunningworth).

43 Lock, *Walsham*, i, pp. 13–14, 96, and ii, p. 136; SROI HA10/50/18/5.1 (Cretingham); SROB 1700/1/1.4 (Felsham); SROB E3/2/7 (Layham); SROI HD1538/401 (Ufford); Denney, *Sibton Abbey*, p. 19.

CONCLUSION

Villeinage and serfdom were locally significant in *c.* 1300, but in the aftermath of the Black Death some manors – particularly smaller lay manors – converted most of their customary holdings to leasehold. Yet on many manors held by aristocratic and ecclesiastical landlords few permanent concessions were made on villeinage in the third quarter of the fourteenth century. The reinstatement of many of the old villein tenures in the 1360s on the estates of the abbeys of Bury St Edmunds and Ely represents a remarkable achievement, given the dramatic changes to the post-Black Death economy. Furthermore, certain aspects of personal servility were imposed more widely and forcefully. Chevage, in particular, was charged more frequently, attracted larger fines, and the personal details of flown serfs were recorded more systematically in manorial courts. Such management policies were confrontational in the new economic climate and raised social tensions. The flames of discontent were fanned more widely by the new labour legislation, which was inequitable and increased the ability of royal officials to meddle in local life. The second half of the fourteenth century may have been the most tumultuous and dramatic period in Suffolk's history, as rising tensions and rapid economic change created extreme social pressures. The violent actions of the Suffolk rebels in the Revolt of 1381 reflected their frustration at the slow pace of social change, and drew upon the strong political awareness and robust sense of individualism which characterized medieval Suffolk society. Yet they were also a direct response to the dogmatic and self-regarding manner in which the Crown and certain prominent landlords had managed the dramatic changes to the post-Black Death economy.

The Peasants' Revolt did not end villeinage and serfdom, but it did mark the conclusion of a thirty-year period in which some landlords had used their seigneurial power to impose certain elements of serfdom more aggressively. It coincided with a severe decline in the profitability of grain farming after the late 1370s, and a sustained fall in land values, which also helped to undermine seigneurial power. After *c.* 1380 the shift in market forces was so pronounced and enduring that villeinage and serfdom was unsustainable in a county where the overwhelming majority of the populace and tenures were free. By the beginning of the fifteenth century villein tenure had largely dissolved. Personal servility survived longer on those few estates where it had once been prominent, and whose administrators possessed the authority and resolve to enforce its key dues, but by *c.* 1400 it too was already waning fast on most Suffolk manors.

The disappearance of villeinage and serfdom removed the stigma once associated with holding customary land, and increased the freedom of action of scores of former serfs, and consequently represents a development of real importance to such people. Yet its wider significance is less clear. Jane Whittle concluded her impressive study of eastern Norfolk with the claim that the disappearance of serfdom and villeinage transformed the structure of landholding. She argues that because serfdom had constituted a form of economic and social segregation, its dissolution had a liberating effect upon the land market in three ways: it lifted the restrictions on the acquisition of land by serfs; it considerably augmented the local stock of land by forcing lords to abandon the direct exploitation of their demesnes (and by extension to lease it to tenants instead); and it increased the accessibility and desirability of customary land. This in turn led directly to the emergence of 'capitalist' landholding and occupational structures.[44] However, this argument does not fit comfortably with the Suffolk evidence. First, it is an exaggeration to describe the operation on the ground of villeinage and serfdom in *c.* 1300 as a form of economic segregation. Second, the decline of demesne farming was precipitated by a mix of economic and social forces, and it was as much a cause as a consequence of the decline of serfdom. Third, and most important, it is difficult to ascribe so much significance and transformational power to a social institution which, even at its peak, affected no more than one-fifth of the population and about the same proportion of tenant land. The decay of villeinage certainly contributed to the broad changes in the landholding structure, and by extension late medieval society, but it was only one of a number of causes.

---

44 Whittle, *Agrarian Capitalism*, pp. 302–7.

CHAPTER 9

The Rural Economy, 1350–1500

T HE Black Death sent a seismic shock through the economy, whose consequences were profound and far-reaching. The loss of half the workforce
in 1349 could not be absorbed without major adjustments in an economy
where land and labour were the main factors of production. The agrarian
economy contracted markedly, although the extent of its decline was not as
great as the fall in population, because productivity – output and consumption per capita – rose. Labour had suddenly become scarcer; work was easier
to find; and the survivors of the Black Death discovered that land was more
readily available. These changes resulted in a rise in wages and earnings,
which improved the purchasing power and economic condition of the lower
orders of society, although it contributed to a decline in both land values and
the profitability of many sectors of farming. Reconstructing the dramatic
shifts in patterns of consumption is one of the most fascinating aspects of
the post-Black Death world, and provides the key to understanding changes
in the rural economy. Ordinary people now spent more on food and drink,
becoming disdainful of the coarse bread, thin ale and bland pottage that had
once constituted their staple diet, and they dressed in higher-quality clothes,
replaced their shoes more often, and became more responsive to fashions.
This stimulated demand for meat, dairy produce, wool and hides, and created
more work in the textile and leather trades. For Suffolk's commercially
aware producers, capable of accessing distant markets, the massive economic
jolt created by the Black Death presented both severe challenges and new
opportunities.[1]

ARABLE FARMING

The low living standards of the mass of the populace before 1349 had placed
a premium upon the production of grain, especially the cheaper crops of
rye and oats. The collapse in population after the Black Death reduced this
premium, and meant that a sizeable proportion of the arable land previously
devoted to crops was now surplus to requirements. The range of crops available to medieval farmers was narrow, so they were unable to compensate much

---

[1] Dyer, *Making a Living*, pp. 293–7; R. H. Britnell, *Britain and Ireland, 1050–1530:
Economy and Society* (Oxford, 2004), pp. 395–401.

by diversifying the types of crops grown. Grain farming was highly labour intensive at key points of the year and its profitability was diminished by the rising costs of that labour. In short, grain production bore the brunt of the contraction in the agrarian economy in the later Middle Ages, as evidenced by a fall in land values, a contraction in the area under cultivation, a slump in output, and the abandonment of some land under the plough.

The exact pace and extent of this contraction varied from place to place, although the information from demesnes contained in manorial accounts provides the most precise and detailed evidence of this process. In the third quarter of the fourteenth century the area under cultivation recovered impressively from the disruption of 1349, as the sown area on many demesnes returned to something approaching previous levels. This phenomenon has been dubbed the 'Indian Summer' of demesne agriculture, and was widely experienced in Suffolk. For example, by the 1360s and early 1370s the sown area had recovered to within 10–15 per cent of immediate pre-plague levels on demesnes such as Lakenheath, Fornham All Saints, Horham, Mildenhall and Worlingworth: at Melton, exceptionally, the area under cultivation was 17 per cent higher in the 1370s than in the 1330s. In many parts of England the sown area fell by nearly 30 per cent over the same period.[2]

This recovery owed much to the relative buoyancy of grain prices between *c.* 1355 and *c.* 1375, but thereafter the underlying decline in the demand for grain was reflected in a sustained fall in grain prices relative to wages and a consequent decline in profits. Declining profitability is especially noticeable in the 1380s and 1390s, again in the 1410s, and then finally in the 1440s and 1450s: the 'Great Slump' of the mid-fifteenth century represented the nadir. The deteriorating economic conditions led to a further contraction in the area devoted to crops on every Suffolk demesne after the mid-1370s, with further falls recorded in the early and mid-fifteenth century. The evidence for decline is overwhelming: in the last quarter of the fourteenth century the mean area under demesne cultivation at Easton Bavents was 72 acres (four accounts), a fall of 30 per cent on the 1340s, a mere 63 acres in 1429–30 (down 39 per cent), and then 51 acres in 1436 (51 per cent); between the 1380s and 1420s the area sown at both Mildenhall and Lakenheath fell by around 40 per cent, that at Fornham All Saints fell by over 20 per cent between the 1410s and 1420s, and by over 20 per cent at Chevington between the 1390s and 1420s. The decline in sown area corresponded with a reduction in the intensity of cultivation, reflected by a sharp reduction in the labour inputs deployed to prepare the land and to harvest the grain. The scythe was increasingly used to

---

[2] Bailey, *Marginal Economy*, table 4.2; SROI HA68/484/318 (Horham); Ridgard, 'Worlingworth', p. 215; CUL EDC 7/16/11/8–10, 19, 22 (Melton); Britnell, *Britain and Ireland*, p. 389.

reap grain in late fourteenth-century Hinderclay – it saved on labour but was less effective than the sickle – dung was not spread on the fields and weeds proliferated. Hedges everywhere were allowed to overgrow and ditches were not properly scoured, causing localized flooding. Quite simply, falling profits and high costs did not justify more careful arable husbandry.[3]

In the post-plague era the greater landlords faced particular difficulties in exploiting their arable demesnes, because for them the squeeze on profits was exacerbated by the peculiar managerial problem of running a large farm through local agents and using labour services. Customary tenants became more reluctant to serve as reeves and to work as labourers on their lord's demesne, particularly when they had the opportunity to build bigger farms themselves, and consequently the manor of Hinderclay discontinued the office of reeve in the 1380s after experiencing sustained difficulties in securing reliable people to hold the office. The reluctance of villein tenants to perform labour services resulted in both a marked slump in the total number of labour services performed, and a dramatic fall in the efficiency of those who did work. Such problems were widespread, which eventually encouraged many of the greater landlords to abandon direct exploitation of their arable demesnes and lease them to local farmers instead.[4]

The swing away from the direct exploitation of manors on the estates of the greater landlords was most apparent between 1380 and 1420, although in Suffolk the precise nature and format of manorial leasing was subtly and impressively varied. Some landlords simply leased the whole manor; some retained direct control over the collection of rents and the manor court, while granting the entire arable demesne on a single lease; others carved up the demesne into a multitude of short leases to many different tenants; and others leased part of the demesne to various tenants, while reserving the remainder for direct exploitation. The administration of numerous short leases held by many different tenants was time-consuming and complicated, and short-term tenants had little interest in practices essential to the long-term sustainability of the land, such as deep ploughing and maintaining ditches, and consequently landlords increasingly preferred the simplicity of leasing large chunks of the demesne on fewer, long-term tenancies. For example, in the 1340s only a few slivers of the enormous Brandon arable demesne were leased, but in 1386 158 acres were cultivated directly by the manor, while 75 acres were leased in eight separate lots to tenants: this practice ceased abruptly in 1395, when the whole arable demesne was granted in a single lease to two local men for ten years. In the 1360s the prior and

---

3 SROI v5/11/1.1 – 1.14 (Easton); Bailey, *Marginal Economy*, table 4.2; SROB E3/15.3/ 2.20b and 2.30 (Chevington); Stone, *Decision-Making*, pp. 121–55.

4 Stone, 'Managerial Problems'.

convent of Ely cultivated the whole of the Melton arable demesne directly, but by the 1390s it was leased entirely through numerous individual leases of a few acres each; in 1393 over 200 acres of the Lawshall demesne were leased to fifteen tenants; and in 1400 the earl of Oxford split the Aldham demesne into two separate leases, allocating the manor's main agricultural buildings to one of them in the process.[5]

The readiness of lessees to accept the challenge of running all or most of an arable demesne is a sure sign that some profits could still be made from large-scale grain farming after the late fourteenth century. The two Aldham lessees in 1400 – Edmund Chattisham and Thomas Goodman – are typical of the people who were willing to accept such a challenge: they were experienced and established peasant landholders, with strong knowledge of local farming conditions. The consortium of eight people who leased the Walton demesne in 1400 largely comprised local villeins who had previously served as reeve or messor there, and so possessed intimate knowledge and direct experience of running a large arable operation. The scale of this enterprise was reflected in the high level of the lease (£13 6s. 8d. per annum), but the device of a consortium helped to spread the risks among a number of farmers. They must have been successful, for the rental was raised to £15 per annum when the lease was renewed in Easter 1412 for a further six years. Similarly, Peter Poye, who leased most of the Walsham demesne for £9 in the mid-1420s, had previous experience of running an operation of this size as a bailiff on other local manors. These were precisely the type of people whose expertise as reeves had been essential to the successful exploitation of demesnes by landlords under more propitious economic circumstances, and who now saw a clear opportunity to obtain direct financial benefit for themselves.[6]

The business skills of even these canny farmers were stretched and challenged by the continued fall of grain prices in the first half of the fifteenth century, culminating in a agrarian depression in the middle decades of the century. The difficulties faced by lessees are evident in the fall in rental values of arable demesnes and mounting arrears of rent, which reveal graphically the extent and depth of the problem. For example, the rental value of the Huntingfield demesne fell from £8 0s. 5d. in 1420–1 to £6 10s. 4d. in 1434–5, at Blythburgh by over 30 per cent during the 1420s, at Wetheringsett

---

5 CUL EDC 7/16/11/16–26 (Melton); PRO sc6/1304/23 and Bacon Mss 652, 660 (Brandon); *PSIA* 14 (1912), pp. 122–34 (Lawshall); CUL Vanneck Ms, box 1, court held December 1400 (Aldham), where Edmund Chattisham acquired the sheepcote on his lease, and Thomas Goodman the dairy house, carthouse and stables on the other; Holmes, *Higher Nobility*, p. 154.

6 SROI HA119/50/3/19, mm. 78, 117 (Walton); SROB HA504/3/15.1 (Walsham); Stone, 'Managerial problems'.

by 20 per cent between the 1420s and 1440s, and between the 1390s and the 1460s the rental value of the Brandon demesne arable fell nearly 40 per cent. Few of these values show signs of recovery before the end of the fifteenth century, although some upward movement is evident at Brandon between the 1470s and 1480s. Furthermore, some lessees often struggled to meet rental payments, even when the rental value remained stable or had been revised downwards. The rent for the Staverton demesne stood at £9 6s. 8d. for the first three decades of the fifteenth century, but by the early 1430s only half this sum was actually paid each year. In the 1450s Henry Winde, the lessee of the arable demesne of Fornham All Saints, accumulated substantial arrears, eventually forcing the lord abbot to reoccupy the land in 1461 in mid-lease and to sell off the crops in order to recoup some of the debts: even then, Winde still owed over £33. The demesne was then leased to Thomas Edward for £20 per annum, who proved to be a reliable and efficient farmer for the next decade.[7]

Most of these examples have been taken from the estates of aristocratic landlords, which remained well documented even though their demesnes were no longer exploited directly by the lords themselves. Indeed, very few arable demesnes on such estates were exploited directly after *c.* 1400, even on those manors located close to the seigneurial household. The demesnes of many of the manors belonging to the abbey of Bury St Edmunds situated close to the abbey itself were leased, as the example of Fornham All Saints indicates, and Sibton abbey leased all of its local granges with the single exception of part of North grange. The retention of a segment of North grange in direct cultivation provided the abbey with a home farm to keep its household supplied with some of its basic provisions. Similarly, the cellarer of Bury St Edmunds abbey maintained the Grange, located outside the south gate of the town, as a home farm throughout the fifteenth century, and the prior and convent of Ely directly exploited Lakenheath for the same purpose.[8]

The management policies of the great landlords – directly exploiting their demesnes in the thirteenth century, and leasing them in the fifteenth century – have dominated the agrarian history of medieval England, for the simple reason that their estates are the best documented. Few manorial accounts have survived from the estates of the lesser landlords, yet historians have

7 CUL Vanneck Ms, box 6 (Huntingfield); Richmond, *John Hopton*, pp. 35–6 (Blythburgh); SROI HD1538/416 (Wetheringsett); Bailey, *Marginal Economy*, table 5.6; Bacon Mss 664–689 (Brandon); SROI HD1538/356/1–10 (Staverton); SROB E3/15.7/2.10 – 2.13 (Fornham).

8 Denney, *Sibton Abbey*, p. 35; SROB A6/1/13 (Grange); CUL EDC 7/15/11/35–45 (Lakenheath).

often argued that these lords adopted a very different approach to estate management in the fifteenth century. It is usually assumed that the gentry continued to exploit their arable demesnes directly for both household consumption and production for the market, because they had both the motivation and the means to do so: they had a static and local household to feed, and they usually maintained a direct personal interest in demesne husbandry. Indeed, these were precisely the people who sought to expand their farming enterprises through either the purchase of other small manors or perhaps as lessees of the demesnes of larger manors. The supposition that minor landlords continued to exploit their demesnes directly in the fifteenth century is potentially significant for a county, such as Suffolk, where the smaller manor and lesser landlord dominated.[9]

Some gentry manors were certainly exploited directly, although in almost every case the main purpose was to supply the seigneurial household with food: in the 1420s Alice de Bryene deployed Acton in this way and Loudham manor directly supplied the lord's household at nearby Campsey. Tattingstone was partially leased in the late 1380s, but taken back into direct cultivation in the 1390s to provide decent quantities of livestock and grain for the lord. However, all these examples date from the first quarter of the fifteenth century, and the overwhelming majority of later examples indicate that most manors in Suffolk held by lesser landlords were leased. For example, direct exploitation was maintained until at least the 1420s on Littlehaugh manor in Norton, again for domestic purposes, but by the 1450s its demesne arable and pastures had been entirely leased. The majority of manors on John Hopton's estate were leased in the mid-fifteenth century, and in the 1490s his widow, Thomasin, was paid in kind rather than in cash by some lessees to provision her household; in the same decade all nine of Sir Simon Wiseman's Suffolk manors, and all those of Sir William Tyndale, were leased. High Hall manor in Walsham was leased from the late fourteenth century and the small manor of Easthouse, held by Ixworth priory, was leased to the lord of Walsham who then re-let it in five parcels to local people. Walsham manor itself was exploited directly in the 1400s to provide food for the lord's residence at nearby Westhorpe, but by the mid-1420s the demesne arable and pastures were split into a number of leases. Manors held by lesser landlords at Boulge (1430), Cavenham Shardelowes (undated), Cretingham (1441), Drinkstone Timperleys (1475), Gipping (1438), Gislingham Rushes and Geneys (1439), Harkstead (1419), Icklingham Berners (1405), Thorney (1450s) and Woolverstone (1425) were all leased. A similar trend is discernible on the smaller ecclesiastical estates. Rumburgh priory leased the overwhelming majority of its lands by the late fifteenth century, while retaining the manor of Rumburgh as its home farm, Sibton abbey

9 *AHEW*, iii, pp. 575–6.

leased Ufford Hall in Fressingfield and split Rendham grange into a number of leases, and by the early sixteenth century Leiston abbey was leasing most of the arable demesne of Leiston in three large blocks.[10]

Many of the manors cited above were held by lords in the middling to upper ranks of gentry, who clearly pursued the same policy as the greater landlords in leasing their demesnes. It is not difficult to reconstruct their logic: these farms were heavily dependent upon hired labour at a time when labourers were scarce and expensive, when income from a lease posed fewer risks than direct cultivation, and when low food prices enabled a household to purchase its needs cheaply. Furthermore, unless a landlord was able to run a manor personally, he probably struggled to find a reliable local agent to undertake the task on his behalf. This widespread policy handed real opportunities to the lowest ranks of gentry lords and yeomen to lease the smaller manors and run them as commercial farms. Such people were the active, dirty-boot farmers of this period, but unfortunately no accounts have survived to document their activities.

On the few demesnes remaining in direct cultivation during the fifteenth century (for which documentation has survived), the extent of the fall in arable output was striking. Only one-quarter of the arable demesne at Lakenheath was sown each year in the 1450s, compared with almost 40 per cent at the end of the fourteenth century. The Chevington demesne alternated between direct cultivation and leasing in the first half of the fifteenth century, during the course of which the area under cultivation fell dramatically from around 250 acres in the late 1390s to a mere 140 acres in the late 1430s. The only direct measures of the output of peasant holdings are the record of grain tithes collected by the parochial rector, but such data are exceptionally rare. Annual receipts of tithes at Lakenheath reveal that peasant grain production in the parish fell by only 20 per cent between the 1330s and 1370s, which mirrors the resilience recorded on many arable demesnes in the quarter century after the Black Death. However, they then fell by

---

[10] Britnell, *Britain and Ireland*, p. 402; *AHEW*, iii, p. 576; SROI HD1538/295/10 (Loudham); SROI HB8/1/817–840 (Tattingstone); SROB 553/27, 35 (Norton); Richmond, *John Hopton*, pp. 66, 73; SROI HD1538/384/1 for Wiseman's manors of Cranely, Thornham Magna and Parva, Swatthaugh in Gislingham, Collishall in Yaxley, Old Newton, Badwell, Stanton and Assington; BL Add. Roll 63553 (Tyndale's estate); SROB HA504/3/5 – 16.9 (Walsham); SROI HD1538/139/3 (Boulge); PRO sc6/1117/12 (Cavenham); SROI HA10/50/18/4.4 (8) (Cretingham); SROB E7/10/1.4 (Drinkstone); SROI HD1538/236/24 (Gipping); SROI HD1538/237/10 (Gislingham); SROI SI/10/6.6 (Harkstead); Amor, 'Late Medieval Enclosure', pp. 186, 192; SROI HA246/A13/1 (Woolverstone); M. R. V. Heale, 'Rumburgh Priory in the Later Middle Ages: Some New Evidence', *PSIA* 40 (2001), p. 12; Denney, *Sibton Abbey*, pp. 35, 37; R. H. Mortimer, ed., *Leiston Abbey Cartulary and Butley Priory Charters*, SCS 1 (Woodbridge, 1979), p. 24.

one-half between the mid-1380s and mid-1390s, which reflects a genuine fall in output rather than some administrative change. Tithes fluctuated around this lower level for much of the fifteenth century, indicating that by mid-century peasant grain output was 75 per cent lower than it had been in the mid-1330s.[11]

The severe contraction in grain production resulted in the permanent and widespread abandonment of arable land. Measuring the extent to which arable land was abandoned over time is not a straightforward task, because the flexible system of land use across Suffolk meant that it often continued to be classified as 'arable' even though it had not been cultivated for years: after all, the distinction between ley (*frisce*) land and scrub pasture was simply a matter of terminology. For example, in 1387 264 acres, out of a total of 564 acres, of the arable demesne of Brandon were described as '*frisce* land, depastured by the lord's sheep and rabbits', but in reality some of this 'arable' had already been permanently absorbed within the manor's rapidly expanding and hugely successful rabbit warren. Only in a few cases is the permanent conversion of arable to pasture explicitly recorded: in 1372 the Cavenham demesne contained 400 acres of arable land, rated at a lowly 3d. per acre, whereas an extent dating from the mid-fifteenth century records 200 acres of arable at 3d. per acre and a new category of 186 acres of pasture worth only 1d. per acre. The 60-acre arable demesne of Livermere Grange in Brandon, carved out as an assart in the late twelfth century, had reverted to heathland by the late 1380s, and by 1438 the whole grange had become a sheep run exploited by the rector of neighbouring Elveden.[12]

Some tenants simply abandoned parcels of arable land when it suited them. Fifteenth-century accounts are littered with such examples. For example, in the 1410s arable lay untenanted in Littlehey and Holmsey fields in Mildenhall; in 1441 14½ acres of a 19½-acre *tenementum* in Wantisden lay abandoned in the lord's hands; in 1434 John and Margaret Crouch abandoned various parcels of land in Ufford; and in 1471 3 roods of arable in Brandon 'have lain *frisce* in the lord's hands for a long time'. John Hopton made little attempt to seek new tenants for land abandoned at Blythburgh in the 1450s, simply absorbing it as additional pasture for his sheep. Occasionally, uncultivated arable was physically segregated from other grazing grounds in order to allow the regeneration of woodland. Once the wood had sufficiently matured, it could then be managed and cropped for undergrowth. Such practices are discernible at Sotherton in the mid-fifteenth century, and they are also implied by one

[11] Bailey, *Marginal Economy*, p. 214; SROB E3/15.3/2.15 – 2.35 (Chevington); CUL EDC 7/15/11/11–45 (Lakenheath).

[12] PRO SC6/1304/36 (Brandon); PRO C135/230/26, C136/47/27 (Cavenham); Bacon Mss 653, 295/29, and p. 74 above (Livermere Grange).

tenant's desire to acquire 'one rood of land with undergrowth and thorn' in Laxfield.[13]

By the mid-fifteenth century over half of the land that had been in cultivation in *c.* 1300 was now redundant in places such as the Breckland. If just over 50 per cent of the land surface of Suffolk was ploughed for arable in *c.* 1300, then the area probably did not exceed one-third by the end of the fifteenth century. There is no evidence to suggest that the severe decline in the output of arable farming was accompanied by a broad shift from commercial to subsistence production: indeed, Bruce Campbell has shown that the proportion of crops sold on English demesnes was broadly the same in 1400 as it had been in 1300.[14] If anything, the orientation towards the market increased after the Black Death, because the general conditions of oversupply eased the ability of consumers to obtain foodstuffs on the open market at precisely the time when the regularity of employment in non-agrarian occupations, such as leather working and textile manufacturing, was rising: a combination of factors which might encourage a greater proportion of the population to depend upon others to produce more of their subsistence needs. The high proportion of smallholders on many Suffolk manors at the end of the Middle Ages would suggest that this was indeed the case.

The choice of crops on manorial demesnes also underlines the continuing importance of commercial production, because the area sown with the principal cash crops of wheat and barley was often proportionately (and sometimes absolutely) greater after 1349 than it had been before. The improved purchasing power of the lower orders of society meant that the demand for wheat – as the best bread grain – and for barley – as the best malting grain – proved more resilient than demand for other grains, especially rye and oats. The proportion of wheat sown on the Mildenhall demesne rose from around 5 per cent in the 1320s to over 20 per cent in the 1380s and 1390s, and it was hardly grown on Ixworth priory's home farm in the 1300s but had become far more important by the 1470s. The increasing prominence of barley is especially striking on the loams and lighter soils. Before the Black Death barley occupied around one-third of the sown area on many demesnes in north-west Suffolk, yet by the mid-fifteenth century it comfortably exceeded half of the sown area, and, in a few places nearly two-thirds. For example, barley occupied 18 per cent of the sown area at Melton in the 1330s and 31 per cent in the 1370s; 19 per cent

---

13 BL Add. Rolls 53132–53133 (Mildenhall); SROI HD1538/357/5, m. 68 (Wantisden); SROI HD1538/295/1, court held August 1434 (Ufford); Bacon 296/17 (Brandon); Richmond, *John Hopton*, pp. 45–6, 85–6; PRO SC12/27/32 (Kentford). Warner, *Greens, Commons*, pp. 23, 31; CUL Vanneck Ms, box 7, court held October 1436 (Laxfield); Bailey, *Marginal Economy*, pp. 277–8.

14 Campbell, *English Seigneurial Agriculture*, tables 5.01, 5.02.

in 1370 at Tattingstone but 42 per cent in 1412; and 41 per cent in the 1340s at Easton Bavents compared with 55 per cent in the last quarter of the fourteenth century, when, unusually for this manor, a growing proportion of output found its way to market. The area sown with peas also increased on some demesnes in east Suffolk, from 11 per cent of the sown area at Horham in 1330 to 25 per cent in the 1370s, and to 24 per cent at Cretingham in 1372, for use as fodder rather than to prepare the land for the following crop. The only example of diversification into new crops comes from Thornham in the 1490s, when the demesne planted small areas with crocus for use as a medicine (or possibly a dye). Although wastage was high and yields were variable, it generated a stunning £22 for a mere 4 acres of crocuses in 1490, but only £4 in 1494.[15]

Tenant holdings also increased their concentration upon the production of wheat and barley. In the 1330s barley constituted 65 per cent of all grain tithes at Lakenheath compared with a remarkable 90 per cent in 1378–9, and between the 1360s and 1380s the absolute quantities of barley rendered as tithe by the parishioners were as high as they had been in the 1330s. In the 1380s barley comprised nearly 80 per cent of all grain tithes at Mildenhall, 53 per cent at Wickham Market in 1411 (wheat 27 per cent), and 73 per cent at Loudham (1422–32). However, these extraordinarily high proportions and quantities of barley were not maintained during the agrarian slump of the mid-fifteenth century, when barley fell back to 60 per cent of all grain output by the 1450s and 1460s at Lakenheath, and to 70 per cent in the 1450s at Mildenhall. The sharpening of the preference for barley on the lighter soils, and for wheat on the heavier soils, reflects the changing preferences of the lower orders of society, who became dismissive of bread which was not made of wheat and of ale not made with malted barley. The relatively low nitrogen content of Suffolk's sandy soils produced modest grain yields, but very fine malting barley, and merchants were prepared to search farther afield to secure supplies of high-quality malt.[16]

PASTORAL FARMING

Pastoral farming was already a significant component of the Suffolk economy before 1350, and its relative importance grew after the Black Death, as rising

[15] Bailey, *Marginal Economy*, pp. 240, 243–5; N. Amor, 'Ixworth *c.* 1500: Landscape, Economy and Society' (MA thesis, University of East Anglia, 2000), p. 15; CUL EDC 7/16/11/8–10, 19, 22 (Melton); SROI HB8/1/817, 837 (Tattingstone); SROI v5/11/1.1 – 1.6 (Easton); SROI HA10/50/18/4.4 (8) (Cretingham); SROI HA68/484/318 (Horham); SROI HD1538/384/1–2 (Thornham).

[16] CUL EDC 7/15/11/11–45 (Lakenheath); BL Add. Rolls 53133, 43061, 53134 (Mildenhall); SROI HD1538/424/1 (Wickham); SROI HD1538/295/11–12 (Loudham); Britnell, 'Urban Demand', p. 16.

living standards fuelled wider consumption of meat and dairy produce, and generated greater demand for wool (for low-grade clothing) and hides (for various leather goods). It possessed the additional advantage of being less labour intensive than arable, which increased its relative profitability in an era of rising wage rates, although rising costs meant that some forms of pastoral farming became less land and labour intensive after the Black Death. The swing from arable to pastoral activities is especially discernible between 1360 and 1400. Production continued to be orientated towards the market, and some producers developed and exploited new commercial opportunities, such as rabbit rearing. Yet, overall, any absolute growth in pastoral farming was unlikely to compensate fully for the dramatic fall in arable output.[17]

Sheep

After the Black Death the importance of sheep rearing increased relative to grain production, and sheep appeared on some Suffolk demesnes on loamy soils where arable and cattle farming had previously dominated. This trend is particularly evident on the margins of the Breckland, where the cellarer of Bury St Edmunds abbey, whose interest in sheep rearing during the thirteenth century had not extended much beyond supplying the monks' needs, expanded his flock at Risby by 84 per cent between the 1340s and 1380s, and by 60 per cent between the 1330s and 1360s at Fornham St Martin. A similar development occurred on demesnes on the Sandlings. No sheep were kept at Easton Bavents until the mid-1370s, when the lord decided to construct a sizeable flock of 532 hoggs through a combination of purchase and transfers from his other manors. The flock at Loudham rose from about 100 sheep in the mid-fourteenth century to about 300 in the 1420s, and from about 150 at Tattingstone in the 1370s to about 350 in the 1410s. Landlords were enticed by buoyant wool prices, which peaked in the 1370s, and by the low labour inputs associated with sheep rearing during an era of sharply rising wages.[18]

A growing interest in sheep rearing in the second half of the fourteenth century is strongly evident on some tenant holdings located on the lighter soils. In the Breckland the overstocking of existing foldcourses, and the erection of illegal ones, became a problem in the 1370s and 1380s, forcing some lords to respond to the pressing demand by granting temporary fold rights. John Flempton was described as a mere labourer in the 1381 Poll Tax, but by the end of the next decade he was frequently amerced for overstocking pastures in

---

[17] Britnell, *Commercialisation*, p. 58.

[18] D. Stone 'The Productivity and Management of Sheep in Late Medieval England', *AgHR* 51 (2003), pp. 1–2; Campbell, *English Seigneurial Agriculture*, pp. 111–13; Bailey, *Marginal Economy*, pp. 247–8; SROI v5/19/1.6 (Easton); SROI HD1538/295/1–8 (Loudham); SROI HB8/1/817–840 (Tattingstone); *AHEW*, iii. pp. 461–3.

the eponymous village, and had obtained the licence to erect a temporary fold in Lackford for over 200 sheep. In the last quarter of the fourteenth century sheep dominate the damage, overstocking and animal trespass presentments in the court rolls of Lackford, Lidgate, Stanningfield and Walton. The over-stocking of commons with, and damage to crops by, peasant sheep was also a problem in some places on heavier soils, such as Aldham and Huntingfield. For example, by 1363 John Over of Aldham owned a breeding flock of sixteen ewes and thirty-one lambs, and in 1393 John Hankerhacches possessed a flock of eighty-nine sheep.[19]

Yet the swing to sheep rearing in the late fourteenth century was not a universal phenomenon. Increases in flock sizes after 1350 were rare on those demesnes where sheep farming was already well established, and on many – such as Lakenheath, Fornham, Mildenhall and Worlingworth – the number of sheep declined. In part, this was due to a succession of sheep murrains in the 1360s, which reduced the demesne flock at Worlingworth by one-fifth and halved that at Fornham All Saints. The exact causes of these epidemics are seldom explicit, although foot rot, scab and liverfluke were regular killers. Although these flocks recovered from these setbacks over the next two decades, none subsequently exceeded the size it had attained before the Black Death. Similarly, the number of peasant-owned sheep in Lakenheath peaked in the 1340s, and was 20 per cent smaller in the 1390s.[20]

By the very end of the fourteenth century economic conditions for sheep farmers began to change dramatically. Wool prices fell markedly between the 1370s and 1390s, and then halved again between the 1400s and 1450s, due to a weakening in the demand for low-grade woollen textiles and a deterioration in the quality of the wool. Consequently the profitability of sheep rearing dipped, but the problem was exacerbated in East Anglia, where fleece and sheep prices were already among the lowest in the country. Hence after *c.* 1400 the size of many demesne flocks in Suffolk was reduced and some landlords sold off their sheep entirely.[21] The number of sheep at Mildenhall fell by over

---

[19] Bailey, *Marginal Economy*, p. 249; SROB E7/10/10 (Stanningfield); SROB E3/11/1.1 – 1.2 (Lidgate); SROI HA119: 50/3/17, mm. 26, 29, 33; HA119/50/3/19, mm. 88, 91, 94 (Walton); SROI HA68/484/135, including court held October 1363, and CUL Vanneck Ms, box 1, including court held October 1391 (Aldham) and box 5 (Huntingfield).

[20] Britnell, *Britain and Ireland*, pp. 413–14; Ridgard, 'Worlingworth', p. 209; Bailey, *Marginal Economy*, pp. 246–8, 250.

[21] J. Hatcher, 'The Great Slump of the Mid Fifteenth Century', in Britnell and Hatcher, *Progress and Problems* (1996), pp. 249–50; Stone, 'Productivity and Management', pp. 2–7; *AHEW*, iii, pp. 463–4; Bailey, *Marginal Economy*, pp. 289–90; Campbell, *English Seigneurial Agriculture*, p. 161; Amor, 'Riding out Recession', p. 14.

50 per cent between the 1380s and 1420s, and from a recorded peak of 532 sheep in 1377 to around 400 in 1432 at Easton Bavents. The decline continued throughout the century at Lakenheath, where the demesne flock fell by 60 per cent between the 1420s and 1480s. After the 1390s no demesne sheep were kept on manors such as Dunningworth, Huntingfield, Lackford and Laxfield. The flock at Melton, which had been over 200 strong in the late 1370s, was promptly sold after being weakened by murrain in 1400, and a flock of about 400 at Chevington was sold in the 1420s. After *c.* 1450 only a few of the aristocratic landlords retained a direct interest in sheep farming.[22]

Similarly, by 1400 widespread peasant involvement in sheep rearing had begun to diminish. The number of peasant-owned sheep in Lakenheath fell by two-thirds between the 1390s and the 1460s, by which time hardly any tenants owned sheep in places like Aldham and Ixworth. Sheep appear less frequently in presentments involving animals in manorial court rolls. For example, they constituted 34 per cent of animal presentments in the courts of Walsham in the period 1320–35, 23 per cent in 1375–99 and a mere 10 per cent in 1400–14; at Fornham St Martin they fell from 31 per cent of these offences (1377–99) to 16 per cent (1482–1510); and from around one-quarter of such cases in the court rolls of fourteenth-century Brandon to 17 per cent between 1421 and 1460. Furthermore, the number of peasant foldcourses in the Breckland fell, as lords ceased to grant temporary folds and began to absorb permanent peasant folds into their own operations, and after 1432 there are no recorded grants of sheep folds in Walsham. Peasants were gradually subject to tighter controls upon the number of sheep they could place in the seigneurial foldcourse. By the end of the fifteenth century sheep rearing had dwindled to the point of extinction on many peasant holdings.[23]

This evidence for sheep rearing seems contradictory: if fewer aristocratic landlords were maintaining sheep flocks, and peasants were being squeezed

[22] *AHEW*, iii, p. 574; SROI v5/19/1.6 (Easton); Bailey, *Marginal Economy*, pp. 246–8; SROI HD1538/206/6 (Dunningworth), CUL Vanneck Mss, boxes 6 and 8 (Huntingfield and Laxfield); SROB E3/15.12/2.3 (Lackford); CUL EDC 7/16/11/22, 26 (Melton); SROB E3/15.3/2.30 – 2.33 (Chevington).

[23] Manor court rolls routinely record the damage to crops caused by wandering animals (a common problem in irregular open field systems), the overstocking of communal pastures by tenants, and the illegal pasturing of commons by non-residents. Many of these presentments also describe the animals involved, which form the basis of the calculations in this paragraph: the figures are based upon the number of cases in which a particular animal appears, not the total number of animals involved in each case. Lock, *Walsham*, i, pp. 88–281, and ii, pp. 119–208; SROB HA504/1/10.1 – 11.2 and 12.11 (Walsham); SROB E3/15.9/1.5 and 1.8 (Fornham); Bailey, *Marginal Economy*, pp. 249–51, 295; SROI HA68/484/135, HA85/484/315, and CUL Vanneck Ms, box 1 (Aldham); Amor, 'Riding out Recession', p. 132.

from this sector, who then was rearing sheep? Indeed, it also contradicts Richard Britnell's forceful argument that English landlords were withdrawing from sheep operations in this period while peasant flocks expanded. Yet Suffolk was different from much of England in this regard, because the institution of the foldcourse presented landlords with a powerful mechanism for controlling sheep rearing at the expense of the peasantry. As a result, the proportion of tenants rearing sheep was significantly lower in 1500 than it had been in 1200, although it is not possible to quantify this assertion. However, a *few* peasants were able to build up substantial flocks, usually as the lessees of local foldcourses. These included John Man of Lakenheath, who held two sizeable foldcourses in Lakenheath in the 1480s, and Henry Hardegrey of Icklingham: in 1427 Henry illegally overstocked the commons of Mildenhall with his sheep, and after his death in 1459 he was able to bequeath 700 sheep to his two sons. Similarly, a few aristocratic landlords retained control of some of their sheep flocks and pastures, even when they had leased their arable demesnes, although they tended to run these separate flocks as an integrated operation: both the abbot and cellarer of Bury St Edmunds abbey remained significant flockmasters in the fifteenth century, and the cellarer even became the lessee of the small lay manor of Charmans in order to increase the size of his sheep operation at Risby. Yet the main sheep rearers were gentry landlords, who exploited their own foldcourses directly and also leased those of others. Men such as John Hopton, who retained direct control of his demesne foldcourses at Blythburgh and Easton Bavents (even converting the latter's arable demesne to pasture in the 1470s), and Peter Poye, who leased the manorial foldcourse of Walsham in the 1420s. The activities of small numbers of people running enlarged flocks are discernible from the nature of court roll entries. In the 1410s the court of Lidgate tried to regulate a few individuals with sizeable flocks, such as John Hardgrey who had a flock of 480 sheep when he only had common rights for 180, while the court of Santon Downham regularly sanctioned John Barton, a local priest, for overstocking the heath with around 500 sheep, and by the 1420s just five flocks containing a total of nearly 1,500 sheep were grazing on the pastures of the vill.[24]

The economics of fifteenth-century sheep rearing did not favour the smaller operators. As the prices for wool and mutton tumbled after *c.* 1400, worthwhile profits were only possible by driving down unit costs still further through maximizing flock sizes and minimizing costs. Small-scale farmers were unable to achieve such economies of scale, and by the end of the fifteenth

---

[24] Britnell, *Britain and Ireland*, pp. 414–15; CUL EDC 7/15/11/48 (Lakenheath); SROB E18/451/3; Northeast, *Wills*, p. 417 (Mildenhall); SROB E3/15.3/2.22 – 2.27 (Risby); Richmond, *John Hopton*, pp. 45–6, 83–6, 98; SROB HA504/3/15.1 (Walsham); SROB E3/11/1.3 (Lidgate); SROB 651/31/1–4 (Downham).

century most peasant-owned sheep were held for the purpose of either domestic consumption or simply turning a few pennies. Commercial sheep farming became even more concentrated into the hands of a few dominant flockmasters, who sought to achieve economies of scale by concentrating their operations into fewer flocks and by reducing unit costs. By the early sixteenth century Thetford priory ran over 7,000 sheep on the extensive heaths in and around Thetford and by the 1480s the cellarer of Bury St Edmunds abbey had concentrated his sheep on just four manors close to Bury itself (namely the abbey's home farm on the east side of the town, Hardwick, Ingham and Elveden). The cellarer ran these four sheep flocks as an integrated whole, with sheep routinely transferred from one to another: Elveden served as a breeding flock of ewes; Ingham and Hardwick ran wool-producing flocks of wethers, while the home farm was deployed to fatten older sheep for the monks' table. By 1537 Ingham was home to over 2,000 of the cellarer's sheep. Similarly, the abbot of Bury St Edmunds rationalized operations on his estate, abandoning sheep rearing on many outlying demesnes in the early fifteenth century and creating two huge sheep runs across the extensive heathland pastures at Fornham All Saints, Fornham St Genevieve and Culford. By 1397 over 2,000 sheep were organized in three flocks at Culford, and the number of demesne sheep recorded at Fornham All Saints jumped fivefold between the 1420s and 1440s. By the 1440s this physical reorganization was accompanied by a move to centralized management and accounting of the flocks, whose details no longer appeared in the local manorial records. Streamlined and centralized operations are also evident on John Hopton's estate and at Ixworth priory, which maintained a large flock of around 1,000 sheep around its home manor throughout the fifteenth century.[25]

Costs were also saved by reducing the amount of care and attention paid to the sheep. The number of shepherds did not increase proportionately with the size of flocks, partly because of difficulties securing good and reliable shepherds, and consequently standards of supervision declined. Expenditure on extra winter fodder for sheep and lambs was systematically reduced; the practice of introducing new stock to flocks diminished; and the active management and treatment of disease was curtailed. The result of these cost-cutting initiatives was a decline in the health and productivity of fifteenth-century sheep flocks, but this simply represented a rational response to the decline in profitability.[26]

[25] Dymond, *Thetford Priory*, i, p. 33; Bailey, *Marginal Economy*, pp. 247; 291–2; SROB A6/1/13; SROI HD1538/92, f. 29; A. Simpson, *The Wealth of the Gentry: East Anglian Studies, 1540–1660* (Cambridge, 1961), p. 184; Richmond, *John Hopton*, pp. 45–6, 83–6, 98; SROI v5/19/1.13 – 1.14 (Easton); Amor, 'Riding out Recession', p. 13.

[26] Stone, 'Productivity and Management', pp. 7–22.

Attempts to reduce costs in sheep rearing were ultimately mere pallia-
tives for the malaise afflicting the sector, which by the mid-fifteenth century
was in recession. Wool prices had fallen by a half since the beginning of the
century, exports of raw wool had collapsed and profitability slumped. Not
surprisingly, the value of the lease of three sheep folds in Walsham fell by a
third between the mid-1420s and late 1430s. Lords who had retained a strong
interest in sheep farming were unable to sell some of their wool clip in every
year, which was stored until a buyer could be found, and in 1451 the audi-
tors at Lakenheath noted that none of the demesne wool could be sold 'for
want of merchants'. This practice was not desirable, because wool shrinks
in storage and loses some of its quality. Some demesnes were also exposed
to delayed or incomplete payments from merchants who had agreed to buy
their wool, but who then experienced difficulty in finding buyers themselves
in a sluggish market. Textile manufacturers were able to be more selective
about price and quality, and to seek out those sellers who offered the best
local wool at the most competitive prices, and those in Hadleigh and Lavenham sometimes acquired wool from Norwich merchants, representing producers in north-east Norfolk, in preference to local suppliers.[27]

Cattle

As cattle rearing was already well established in Suffolk in *c.* 1300, local
producers were able to respond rapidly to the surge in demand for cheese,
meat and leather products during the second half of the fourteenth century.
Bullish demand is reflected in the price of cheese, which remained stable
until the early fifteenth century, and of cows, which rose from about 9s. 6d.
in the 1340s to about 11s. in the 1360s, and then held at 11s. until the 1410s.
These consistent prices help to explain how lactage rates – the annual lease of
a cow – held their pre-1350 levels at most places, and even rose at others. The
lactage rate at Loudham rose from 5s. per cow in 1353 to 6s. 8d. in 1418, that
at Mildenhall rose from 3s. 5d. (1320s) to 4s. 6d. (1380s), and from 5s. (1370s)
to 5s. 3d. (1380s) at Thelnetham. The highly intensive pastoral regime which
characterized many demesnes in Suffolk before the Black Death continued
afterwards, and a substantial rise in the proportion of legumes sown at places
such as Horham and Cretingham is indicative of the premium placed upon
good-quality fodder. Such evidence supports Campbell's assertion that the

[27] Britnell, *Britain and Ireland*, pp. 418–19; SROB HA504/3/15.1, 15.4 (Walsham);
CUL EDC 7/15/11/41 (Lakenheath); Britnell 'Urban Demand', p. 16; Bailey, *Marginal Economy*, p. 290. Thomas Spring of Lavenham bought the entire wool clip
from the flocks of Norwich Cathedral Priory, NRO DCN 64/9.

output and intensity of English dairying peaked in the third quarter of the fourteenth century.[28]

Many Suffolk demesnes maintained or increased their income from dairying in the second half of the fourteenth century, as constant or rising lactage rates combined with constant or rising herd size on many manors. The dairy at Melton generated around £4 per annum between 1328 and 1342 but over £6 in the 1370s, due to a combination of a rising lactage rate (from 5s. 6d. to 6s. per cow) and an expanding herd (from sixteen to twenty cows), and income from the dairy at Risby in the 1360s and 1370s was nearly three times greater than it had been in the early part of the century. The manor of Loudham purchased fourteen cows in 1372, each costing around 10s., to expand its herd, and other demesne herds were expanded at Thelnetham, Horham, on the Fenland edge, and around Bury St Edmunds. The dairy run by Sibton abbey was small in the 1360s, but during the 1370s was rapidly expanded by purchase. By the end of the fourteenth century some sizeable and lucrative demesne dairy herds had been constructed: in 1392 Flixton [by Bungay] priory ran a commercial herd of sixty-one cows on its home farm, and in 1400 the Ufford demesne generated over £7 per annum from a twenty-six strong herd, leased at an impressive 6s. per cow.[29]

Evidence from court rolls also indicates a lively interest in dairying on tenant holdings in the second half of the fourteenth century. The number of manorial court cases involving animals often rose in the decades after the Black Death, reflecting both lower levels of supervision due to labour shortages and the growing importance of animal husbandry. Significantly, the proportion of cases involving dairy and beef cattle was increasing. Between 1320 and 1335 cows and 'beasts' comprised 35 per cent of all animal presentments at Walsham, yet rose to 62 per cent between 1375 and 1399, and references to cows in the court rolls of Fornham St Martin increased markedly after the Black Death until they comprised around 40 per cent of all animal presentments in the last quarter of the century. Cows dominated the rising number of animal presentments at Winston in the 1360s and 1370s, and they featured significantly in such presentments in the late 1370s at Huntingfield and in the 1390s at Dunningworth. Some tenants constructed large herds. Thomas Sampson in

[28] Britnell, *Britain and Ireland*, p. 421; *AHEW*, iii, pp. 464–5, 457; SROI HD1538/295/2, 8 (Loudham); Bodleian Rolls 21 and SROB E18/455/1 (Mildenhall); SROI HD1538/380 (Thelnetham); SROI HA10/50/18/4.4 (8) (Cretingham); SROI HA68/484/318 (Horham); Campbell, *English Seigneurial Agriculture*, p. 151.

[29] SROB E3/15.13/2.5 – 2.9, 2.15 – 2.19 (Risby); CUL EDC 7/16/11/6–10, 19, 22 (Melton); SROI HD1538/295/2, 8 (Loudham); SROI HD1538/380 (Thelnetham); SROI HA68/484/318 (Horham); Bailey, *Marginal Economy*, p. 257; Bailey, 'Lakenheath', pp. 13–14; Denney, *Sibton Abbey*, p. 26; SROI HA12/63/29 (Flixton); SROI HD1538/400/1 (Ufford).

1381 maintained a commercial herd of fifteen cows and a bull in Freston, and the fourteen cows bought by the Loudham demesne in 1372 were all acquired from local peasants. Stock fattening was also increasingly important. Cows are hardly mentioned in the Leiston courts of the late 1390s, where instead references to 'cattle' and 'beasts' dominate the presentments, which seem to indicate beef rather than dairy herds. The manor of Gipping leased all its demesne pastures to local tenants, the majority of whom were grazing the odd bullock, although one herd of twelve bullocks, and another of nineteen, are recorded. Demand for hay remained strong, judging by local meadow valuations, which generally held up in the late fourteenth century. For example, in the 1410s Donnemeadow in Huntingfield was still fetching 4s. per acre at leasehold, and the value of Flemmings meadow in Norton rose from 3s. 2d. per acre in 1383 to 5s. 7d. per acre in the 1390s.[30]

By *c.* 1400 a growing number of demesnes had withdrawn from dairying, or reduced its scale. This trend was especially prominent in the Breckland and the Sandlings, where lords concentrated upon sheep and pig rearing instead. Modest dairy herds were sold off at Brandon, Easton Bavents and Dunningworth in the second half of the fourteenth century; a herd of a dozen cows was sold at Risby in the 1390s; a twenty-strong herd at Walsham was sold off between the 1400s and the 1420s; and in 1400 about twenty cows at Chevington were included in the lease of the demesne. By the early fifteenth century even demesnes in the heart of the traditional dairying districts – such as Huntingfield, Laxfield and Melton – had disposed of their herds. Where landlords did retain a direct interest in dairying, herd size invariably fell: the Mildenhall herd was reduced from about thirty-six cows in the 1380s to about twenty-three by the 1400s. The declining interest in dairying on demesnes is somewhat paradoxical, because it occurred at a time when cow and cheese prices remained buoyant and local lactage rates were constant. For example, the lactage rate at Chevington was 5s. per cow in the 1390s and at 5s. 4d. in the late 1430s; that at Lakenheath held constant at 4s. 8d. between the 1380s and 1430s; and in the 1410s the Loudham herd was still realizing 6s. 8d. per cow. This paradox is partly explicable by the changing financial circumstances of landlords rather than in the profitability of dairy farming. The fall in grain prices and land rents in the 1380s and 1390s must have sharply curtailed the income received by seigneurial households, who probably accumulated debts

---

30 SROI HD1538/295/2 (Loudham); Lock, *Walsham*, i, pp. 88–281, and ii, pp. 119–208; SROB E3/15.9/1.1, 1.3 and 1.5 (Fornham); CUL EDC 7/17/2, 5, 6, 21–23 (Winston); CUL Vanneck Ms, boxes 5 and 6 (Huntingfield), and box 9, court held February 1379 (Leiston); SROI HD1538/207/3 (Dunningworth); Powell, *Rising in East Anglia*, p. 145 (Freston); SROI HD1538/236/21–23 (Gipping); Campbell, *English Seigneurial Agriculture*, p. 151; CUL Vanneck Ms, box 6 (Huntingfield); SROB 553/21 and 23 (Norton).

as a consequence. The sale of a manorial dairy herd provided a cash windfall to ease those debts (a herd of twenty cows would have realized £10), and also reduced the administrative burden on estate officials. It is also explicable by the general shift to rentier farming, in which lords found it easier just to lease their meadows rather than to manage them as part of the lactage rental. By the third decade of the fifteenth century few of the major landlords maintained a dairy herd.[31]

The demand for diary produce appears to have levelled around 1400, and therefore the withdrawal of many lords presented opportunities for tenants to increase their operations: after all, these people were previously the lessees, and now the likely purchasers, of demesne herds. Just as the economics of sheep rearing suited larger units, so dairy farming in particular was better suited to smaller enterprises using domestic labour, particularly women. The evidence for sustained peasant involvement in cattle rearing is characteristically patchy, but in the fifteenth century cows and 'beasts' tended to dominate animal presentments in court rolls and larger herds become more frequent. By the late sixteenth century the average size of a commercial dairy herd in north Suffolk was around sixteen cows and herds of comparable size – which had been exceptional on tenant holdings in the fourteenth century – begin to feature more regularly in fifteenth-century court rolls. For example, cows had not featured much in the court rolls of mid-fourteenth-century Aldham, but became more prominent in the fifteenth century: in 1402 Thomas Goodman – who had leased the demesne dairy house two years earlier – allowed his herd of twenty-one cows to wander into Ladyswood and in the September court of 1403 a total of thirty-one cows and three calves were recorded in various presentments. Cattle dominate references to animals in the courts of Preston; in 1446 Thomas Pinder kept twenty-four cows around the marshes of Brandon; John Lynge had fifteen cows in Flempton; and in 1464 the bailiff of Dunningworth attempted to seize the twelve-strong herd of Reginald Totting as a distraint for the 10s. rent arrears he owed. Cattle increased in importance relative to sheep on tenant holdings across the county. The late fifteenth century court rolls of both Harleston and Ixworth contain frequent references to cows and cattle, but hardly any to peasant sheep, and cattle account for nearly two-thirds of all animal presentments in the court rolls

---

[31] Campbell, *English Seigneurial Agriculture*, pp. 111–13, 149; SROI v5/19/1.3 – 1.6 (Easton); SROI HD1538/206/6 (Dunningworth); PRO sc6/1304/23–29 and Bacon Mss 647, 649 (Brandon); SROB HA504/3/5b and 15.1 (Walsham); SROB E3/15.13/2.19 – 2.35 (Chevington); CUL Vanneck Ms, boxes 6 and 8 (Huntingfield and Laxfield); CUL EDC 7/16/11/26 (Melton); BL Add. Rolls 53116–53126 (Mildenhall); CUL EDC 7/15/1/25–39 (Lakenheath); SROI HD1538/295/8 (Loudham).

of Walsham between 1400 and 1414, compared to less than 10 per cent for sheep.[32]

After the 1420s the market for dairy produce slumped throughout England, and the price of cows fell. The surge in demand for cheese and butter in the second half of the fourteenth century first stabilized and then dipped as meat became a preferred source of protein. Cheese prices fell from around 9s. to 7s. per wey after the 1440s, reaching their lowest level in the middle decades of the fifteenth century, but producers could not easily offset this fall in prices by reducing their costs, because wages remained high and the price of salt – a significant component in cheese making – did not fall. After the 1410s cows feature less prominently in some manorial court rolls, so that the proportion of animal presentments involving cows at Brandon fell from around 7 per cent in the fourteenth century to 1 per cent in Henry VI's reign. Standards of care for cows probably fell, with reduced stall feeding in winter and lower maintenance of stalls and byres. Hence in 1460 John Parker was amerced 6d. for allowing a cowhouse to dilapidate in Huntingfield; John Jay did likewise in Walsham, and no lessee could be found for two dairy houses there in 1426 and 1436. The reduction in the demand for hay and in intensive stall-feeding is reflected in the fall in meadow values, which everywhere began to slip. Some meadow in Mildenhall lay untenanted in the 1410s; the rental value of meadow on the Cavenham demesne fell from 2s. per acre in the 1340s to 10d. per acre in the mid-fifteenth century; Forbrook meadow in Norton fell from 5s. 1d. per acre in 1394 to 2s. per acre in 1420; the value per acre of Coughfen in Fornham fell by 45 per cent between 1395 and 1426; Broad Dole meadow in Walsham fetched 6s. per acre in 1427 and 4s. 5d. in 1441; in 1435 the value of a sizeable meadow in Huntingfield was noted to have recently fallen by 20 per cent; and Brodemeadow and Smallmeadow in Melton fell from 5s. 10d. per acre in 1449 to 4s. 8d. in 1478.[33]

The decline afflicting dairying over the course of the first half of the fifteenth century is less evident in stock fattening, which remained one of the most resilient sectors of the Suffolk economy. Dairy farming required the

32 CUL Vanneck Ms, box 1 (Aldham); SROB E3/15.17/1.1 (Harleston); Amor, 'Riding out Recession', p. 132; Amor, 'Ixworth', table 6; SROB E3/11/1.3, court held October 1420 (Lidgate); N. Evans, 'Farming and Landholding in Wood Pasture East Anglia, 1550–1650', *PSIA* 35 (1984), p. 308 (Elmham); SROB E7/10/5 (Preston); Bacon Ms 295/40 (Brandon); SROI HD1538/207/8 (Dunningworth); SROB E3/15.12/1.13 (Flempton); SROB HA504/1/10.1 – 11.2 (Walsham).

33 Bacon Ms 292, 295 (Brandon); CUL Vanneck Ms, box 5, court held June 1460 and box 6 (Huntingfield); SROB HA504/1/10.7, HA504/3/15.1 and 15.5 (Walsham); SROB E3/15.6/2.35 and 2.54 (Fornham); SROB 553/23–25 (Norton); SROB HA504/3/12 and 15.1; BL Add. Rolls 53132–53135 (Mildenhall); PRO C135/87/27, C136/47/27 (Cavenham); CUL EDC 7/16/11/36, 38 (Melton).

upkeep of stalls and buildings, as well as daily milking, and was therefore more labour intensive than stock fattening, which merely required supervision of grazing livestock. Beef producers could therefore reduce their costs more easily, a key factor when prices sagged but wage rates remained high. References to 'beasts' – usually signifying beef cattle rather than cows or horses – and 'bullocks' feature more prominently in many fifteenth-century court rolls. For example, they were three times more numerous than references to cows in Walsham, where in 1407 an unknown man leased a demesne pasture to graze twenty-one bullocks and Almoric Pit of Wattisfield herded thirty-one beasts, almost certainly a commercial beef herd. Walter Boon emerged as an active cattle dealer in Chevington in the early fifteenth century, and in the 1450s John Hopton exploited the coastal marshes attached to his Blythburgh demesne to fatten cattle acquired at Harleston fair, which he subsequently sold at a healthy profit: similarly, in 1439 William Tyrell kept seventy-one cattle on his manor at Gipping. The practice of importing cattle from northern and midland England to be fattened for urban markets in the south-east, which was a strong feature of Suffolk farming in the sixteenth and seventeenth centuries, emerges clearly during the fifteenth century. Sibton abbey, Thetford priory and Mettingham college all bought northern cattle, and livestock in Darsham was distinguished between country and northern 'neet'. Woolpit fair acquired a reputation for the sale of northern cattle – and might well have been the destination of seven 'drovers' whose bullocks caused extensive damage in Walsham in 1449. In 1465 the inhabitants of Mildenhall were prohibited from stocking 'northern neet or other beasts' on the commons beyond their stint: two years later Thomas Fenby was duly amerced 20d. for introducing 'northern neet' there.[34]

After the slump of the mid-fifteenth century there are clear signs that both

---

[34] The importance of oxen and horses diminished during this period, Britnell, *Britain and Ireland*, p. 420, making references to them in court rolls less likely. Amor, 'Late Medieval Enclosure', pp. 185–7, is less convinced that fifteenth-century court rolls can be used to identify the animals involved in damage presentments reliably. SROB HA504/1/10.1 – 11.2, Almoric Pit at 10.7, and 13.13, and HA504/3/5b (Walsham); *AHEW*, iii, pp. 385, 391; Richmond, *John Hopton*, pp. 37, 99 (Blythburgh); C. Richmond, 'East Anglian Politics and Society in the Fifteenth Century: Reflections, 1956–2003', in Harper-Bill, *Medieval East Anglia* (2005), p. 199. An interest in the provision of meat rather than milk is evident in the activities of William Miller, who kept nine beasts and eight pigs in Haverhill, and also among residents of Fornham St Martin, where cows, oxen and beasts had comprised 53 per cent of all animal presentments between 1377 and 1399, but 'beasts' alone comprised 76 per cent between 1482 and 1510. SROB E3/15.9/1.5 and 1.8 (Fornham); CUL Ms 4130, box 4, court held October 1422 (Haverhill); Dymond, *Thetford Priory*, p. 403; Denney, *Sibton Abbey*, pp. 37–8; Amor, 'Riding out Recession', p. 135; SROB E18/451/5 (Mildenhall).

stock fattening and dairy farming revived in some places, a consequence of a modest upturn in both livestock and cheese prices. In the 1470s a new dairy was developed at Cockfield Hall in Yoxford; the prior of Ixworth's dairy herd was enlarged between the 1450s and 1470s; in 1467 Rumburgh priory possessed an impressive herd of seventy cows and had constructed a large dairy house measuring 84 × 22 feet; and the herd run by Sibton abbey doubled in size in the early sixteenth century to 140 cows in 1513, by which date the abbey's farm managers appear to have been experimenting with selective breeding among their stock. Rumburgh and Sibton were small religious communities, so their large herds were unquestionably kept for commercial purposes. A similar trend is apparent on tenant holdings: presentments for overstocking the greens of Cratfield with 'beasts' and 'cattle' increased markedly in the 1480s and 1490s, and a similar trend is evident in Huntingfield in the early 1480s. Significantly, Nick Stobbard donated two cows to the gild of St Thomas in Cratfield with the intention that the brethren should establish a dairy herd whose income would sustain a priest's wages, and the lease of donated cows and cattle became a good source of income for St Peter's gild in Bardwell. Many of these examples come from central and east Suffolk, where cattle rearing was most prominent. It is no coincidence that the canons of Thetford priory looked to this area for butter, cheese and fattened beef.[35]

Cattle rearing had increased in significance after *c.* 1350, particularly on tenant holdings, thus strengthening Suffolk's pre-existing specialization in pastoral farming. Dairy farming peaked in both output and intensity towards the end of the fourteenth century, although its fortunes dipped in the middle of the fifteenth. Yet its pre-eminence in the rural economy and its subsequent revival help explain how certain parts of sixteenth-century Suffolk – mainly central and eastern areas, and the Stour and Waveney valleys – acquired considerable national renown for stock fattening in general, and dairying in particular. By *c.* 1600 central Suffolk had a reputation for possessing some of the largest dairy herds in the country, and Woodbridge and Ipswich markets were known nationally for their provision of quality cheese and butter.[36] The shift to stock rearing and dairy farming on the county's heavier soils was facilitated by dramatic changes in both the layout and operation of its irregular open fields, which were gradually replaced in this period by manifold small enclosures and converted to pasture. This development was slow and drawn out,

35 *AHEW*, iii, pp. 465–7; Richmond, *John Hopton*, p. 73; Amor, 'Riding out Recession', p. 132 (Ixworth); *PSIA* 14 (1912), p. 321; Heale, 'Rumburgh Priory', p. 12; Denney, *Sibton Abbey*, pp. 37–8; CUL Vanneck Ms, boxes 3 and 5 (Cratfield, Huntingfield); *PSIA* 1995 (38), p. 261; *PSIA* 11 (1901), pp. 86–9; Dymond, *Thetford Priory*, pp. 33–4, 403, 514, 537, 547, 755, 760; Simpson, *Wealth of the Gentry*, p. 205 (Mettingham).

36 Evans, 'Farming and Landholding', pp. 305–7; F. V. Emery, 'England circa 1600', in Darby, *New Historical Geography* (1973), pp. 261, 265.

and its pace and timing varied from place to place, but its cumulative impact was immense, sufficient to transform vast tracts of the Suffolk countryside from a largely open landscape to one that was largely enclosed. Irregular open fields, which in the fourteenth century had dominated places such as Ickworth, Ixworth, Norton and Walsham, had largely disappeared by *c.* 1600. This enclosure movement was silent in comparison with the contemporary enclosures in the Midlands, and was undertaken mainly by hundreds of small-scale farmers and yeomen.[37]

Pigs

The demand for pork and bacon also rose with the rising living standards of the lower orders of society, and which explains the relative stability of pig prices across the late fourteenth and early fifteenth centuries. A few demesnes, such as Worlingworth, responded to these opportunities by expanding the size of their herds. By the end of the century some demesnes located in small towns such as Framlingham, Bungay and Exning had established large commercial herds of up to 100 pigs. Yet demesne involvement in commercial pig rearing appears to have peaked around this time, and thereafter many sold off their pigs as part of the general shift to rentier farming: hardly any manors retained herds by the middle of the fifteenth century.[38]

After *c.* 1400 the withdrawal of landlords from this sector of agriculture created greater opportunities for tenants, although, as usual, the evidence for their activities is fragmentary and impressionistic. An increasing proportion of households now reared a pig or two for domestic consumption, which is reflected in a growing number of presentments in court rolls for damage caused by the odd pig. The number and proportion of such references in Leiston and Theberton rose markedly between the 1370s and 1390s, from 11 per cent to 49 per cent of all such cases where the animal was identified. Growth on this scale implies that commercial pig rearing was also increasing among the lower orders. Any herd containing more than five pigs was likely to be reared for commercial purposes, and references to larger herds become more commonplace in fifteenth-century court rolls. For example, two Clare residents obstructed the main road with pigsties, and several brewers and bakers in Earl Soham kept larger numbers of pigs. In 1404 Walter Day had twenty pigs in Mildenhall; in 1406 three men ran thirty-two pigs in Aldham; Walter Henman of Huntingfield owned nine pigs in the winter of 1460 (and six that summer); and in 1448

---

37 These changes in Suffolk's field systems are documented and discussed fully in M. Bailey, 'The Evolution of Field Systems in Medieval Suffolk' (forthcoming).

38 Ridgard, 'Worlingworth', p. 209; Ridgard, *Framlingham*, p. 74; SROI HD1538/156/4 (Bungay); Campbell, *English Seigneurial Agriculture*, p. 168.

John Baly had sixteen pigs stolen in Brandon.[39] Pig farmers were subject to tighter regulation by fifteenth-century courts, as reflected in a bye-law in 1459 at Lidgate requiring pigs to be kept in houses (i.e. off the fields) until the bailiff proclaimed otherwise in the church: the penalty against this was a sizeable 6s. 8d., to be split equally between the church and the manor. Growing concern about the damage caused by unringed pigs is also evident at Lackford, Mildenhall, Euston and Fakenham Parva.[40]

The growth of pig rearing was particularly evident on the lighter soils of the Breckland and Sandlings, and by the sixteenth century east Suffolk was well known for its pig herds. Perhaps the gradual exclusion of the peasantry from sheep rearing in these areas during the fifteenth century encouraged peasants to diversify into pigs instead. Pigs had accounted for around 10 per cent of all animal presentments in fourteenth-century Brandon, yet rose to a remarkable 54 per cent during Henry VI's reign, and by the early sixteenth century pigs and horses dominate presentments in the courts of Lackford and Mildenhall. Pig-rearing was closely combined with dairy rearing in sixteenth-century Suffolk, because pigs could be fed on the by-products and waste of the dairy, and this association was slowly becoming established during the fifteenth century. In 1428 a well-established dairy and cattle herd at Mettingham was complemented by a modest pig herd, and in 1467 a seventy-strong dairy herd at Rumburgh was run alongside a herd of thirty pigs.[41]

Rabbits and game

Commercial rabbit rearing proved to be a surprising growth sector of the Suffolk economy in the late fourteenth century. Rabbits remained a rare sight in the medieval countryside, hardly existing in a feral state; most lived in specially created and protected warrens. Although introduced as a source of aristocratic meat and occasional sport, the rabbit's potential for commercial profit after the Black Death was quickly recognized. Demand for its meat and fur rose markedly, particularly among the mercantile elite of London, and warrens in Suffolk were close enough to the capital to respond to this surge in demand. The boom, however, was restricted socially and geographically. The right to rear, hunt and kill small game, including rabbits, was a seigneurial monopoly

39 CUL Vanneck Ms, box 9 (Leiston); Evans, 'Farming and Landholding', pp. 306–7; SROB E18/451/3 (Mildenhall); CUL Vanneck Ms, box 1, court held September 1406 (Aldham) and box 5, court held June 1460 (Huntingfield); Bacon Ms 295/44, court held March 1448 (Brandon); Davis, 'Petty Traders', p. 284.

40 SROB E3/11/1.4, m. 20; E3/11/1.5, court held August 1478; E18/451/6, court held July 1474; E3/15.12/1.8 (Lackford); E7/14/1201 (Euston).

41 Evans, 'Farming and Landholding', pp. 306–7; Bacon Mss 289, 290, 291, 295 (Brandon); SROB E18/451/69 ff. 50–65 (Mildenhall); SROB E3/15.12/1.17 (Lackford); SROB HA507/1/33 (Mettingham); Heale, 'Rumburgh Priory', p. 12.

vested in a single lord in each vill, so that all peasants and many lords were legally excluded from keeping or killing rabbits. Only a few landlords – usually the great aristocrats – were able to exploit the commercial opportunities presented by the rabbit. Furthermore, the medieval rabbit was much more fragile than its modern successor, being particularly averse to moisture and cold, and was largely confined to the porous and sandy soils of the Breckland and Sandlings. The largest warrens were located on the extensive open heathlands of the Breckland.[42]

After the 1370s the output of many of the larger warrens rose dramatically and the focus of production shifted from domestic consumption to the market. For example, in the 1340s around 160 rabbits were culled each year in Brandon warren, of which 11 per cent were sold, compared with 2,300 in the 1390s, when 86 per cent were sold (most of them bound for the London market). Rabbits were expensive, reflecting their rarity, fetching over 2d. each in the 1370s, and so the sale of several thousand generated huge sums of money. Over the course of the fourteenth century income from warrens soared from a few shillings to almost £40 each year at Brandon and Lakenheath, or an extraordinary 40 per cent of gross manorial income.

In the late fourteenth century the output from the commercially orientated warrens was increased by absorbing abandoned arable into the warren area to expand the area of rough pasture available to the rabbits, and by more intensive and careful management of the stock. Fodder crops were fed to the rabbits in winter; fortified stone lodges were constructed to defend the bigger warrens against poachers; and additional labour was hired at key times of the year to tend the stock more carefully. Every year rabbits destroyed between 10 and 20 per cent of the oats crop on the Lakenheath demesne, implying that the oats were being sown close to the warren for precisely this purpose. Elsewhere, the burrows of rabbits were actively protected against damage, so that in 1398 the Leiston court sought the lord's advice after William Gant had blocked 200 rabbit holes in the warren with thorn bundles, and the Walton court took firm action against those who had targeted burrows.

Rabbit rearing was perhaps the only sector of agriculture where output was increased after 1350 by raising the intensity of production and increasing labour inputs, yet the remarkable expansion in demand certainly justified greater expenditure in those warrens geared to commercial enterprise. In contrast, output does not appear to have risen in those warrens geared mainly for domestic consumption, such as Loudham, because their capacity was too low to generate the high levels of income that would justify a large increase in costs and investment. A new warren was established at Tattingstone in the 1380s by introducing rabbits and pheasants from Staverton warren, but little

---

[42] Much of what follows is taken from Bailey, 'Rabbit', pp. 4–19; *HistA*, pp. 68–9.

was subsequently expended on its management, and its output remained modest. Interest in game extended beyond rabbits. The earliest references to wild pheasants in Suffolk occur around this time, perhaps implying that they were being reared more widely in a speculative attempt to supply the market with game, although they did not generate much revenue: in 1402 the Staverton demesne raised a modest 2s. from the farm of pheasants and partridges. Similarly, in the late fourteenth century the Gipping demesne fattened its doves on peas prior to commercial sale, although the exercise never raised more than a few shillings, and a number of tenant dovecotes were constructed in Norton. A few demesnes in the Waveney valley experimented with heron farms.[43]

The bunny boom continued throughout the 1380s and 1390s, after which the output of the largest commercial warrens fell: even this growth industry faltered and then succumbed to the familiar pattern of an oversupplied and then depressed market. Some landlords still looked hopefully to the rabbit as a source of quick profit, because as late as 1431 a royal licence was granted to create a new rabbit warren on an outcrop of sandy soil in Bentley, but such optimism was not jusitifed. From the beginning of the fifteenth century many of the largest and most profitable warrens were leased separately as part of the shift to rentier farming, although they still generated significant revenues: Brandon, Lakenheath and Leiston warrens all attracted rent of £20 per annum, comfortably exceeding the annual income from demesne arable and sheep farming, and smaller warrens, such as Blythburgh and Mildenhall, produced the tidy sums of £8 and £5 per annum respectively. Thereafter, warren values sagged. The rental value of Mildenhall warren halved between the 1400s and 1440s, that of Staverton warren fell from 40s. in 1432–3 to 26s. 8d. in 1471–2, and by mid-century even the largest warrens were suffering from rent reductions and accumulating arrears. The lessee of Lakenheath warren died suddenly in 1418, owing arrears of £13 3s. 4d., forcing the lord to manage the warren directly on a temporary basis. The problem of falling demand was exacerbated by a significant fall in the stocking densities of many warrens after much of their stock was killed off in a succession of dreadful winters in the mid-1430s, reckoned to be some of the coldest of the last millennium. Kingston warren yielded nothing in 1434–5 instead of the predicted 2s. 6d., while the winter of 1436–7 drastically reduced the stock in Dunningworth warren, prompting the estate steward to contract John Oxe

43 Bailey, *Marginal Economy*, pp. 254–5; CUL EDC 7/15/11/31, 34 (Lakenheath); CUL Vanneck Ms, box 9 (Leiston); SROI HA119/50/3/18, m. 51 (Walton); SROI HD1538/295/9–10 (Loudham); SROI HB8/1/817, 821, 822 (Tattingstone); the earliest reference I have found to pheasants dates from 1374 in Winston, CUL EDC 7/17/23, m. 3; SROI HD1538/356/1–2 (Eyke); Rackham, *Countryside*, pp. 50–1; SROI HD1538/236/21 (Gipping); SROI E3/15.3/2.10 and 553/57–59 (Norton).

to act as its custodian for one year, with strict instructions 'to restock it and look after it well day and night'.[44]

THE LAND MARKET

The highly active land market of the late thirteenth century became subdued in the later Middle Ages. It still remained relatively commercialized and fluid, allowing the landless to gain a foothold in the land market and enterprising individuals to accumulate large holdings on a variety of tenures. However, the volume of land transfers declined; the size of the average land transaction rose; and the level of entry fine charged to the incoming tenant fell. In addition, the record of land transactions in court rolls became less exact and rigorous, implying that the seigneurial grip on the land market had relaxed. For example, between the 1340s and 1390s the mean number of annual land transactions in the Walsham courts fell by 60 per cent, and the level of entry fine fell by 70 per cent. The proportion of grants made by the lord to a tenant, rather than tenant-to-tenant, rose significantly in the late fourteenth and early fifteenth centuries, reflecting the tendency for land to stick in the lord's hands until a tenant could be found. Over 20 per cent of all land transactions at Ixworth fell into this category, and the proportion at Brandon rose from 2 per cent in the first half of the fourteenth century to 73 per cent in the second half.[45] In 1451 the lord of Staverton granted to a tenant one pightle 'which had lain in the lord's hands for many years'. Untenanted land soon reverted to scrubland, and untenanted buildings quickly dilapidated, so in the first year or so the new tenant often faced extra work on ground clearance and repair. Consequently, some grants from the lord could carry low initial rents and entry fines as an incentive to prospective tenants. In 1424 the lord of Lidgate granted John Rose a burgage plot, which had once belonged to Katherine Creke, for no entry fine and an annual rent of 12d. instead of the original 2s. 4d., together with four oaks to help repair the house. In 1437 Richard George of Brandon acquired three full-lands abandoned some years before by Thomas Felyps, paying rent at a paltry 2d. an acre for an initial term of three years.[46]

The sluggish land market in the fifteenth century is reflected in the falling

44 *CPR, HVI*, vol. 2, p. 180 (Bentley); Bailey, *Marginal Economy*, pp. 296–302; CUL EDC 7/15/11/34 (Lakenheath); SROI HD1538/207/6, court held October 1437 (Dunningworth); CUL EDC 7/14/c/43 (Kingston).

45 Whittle, 'Individualism', pp. 54–5; Lock, 'Black Death', p. 323; Amor, 'Riding out Recession', p. 10; Bailey, *Marginal Economy*, p. 207.

46 SROI HD1538/357/5, m. 97; HD1538/207/6, court held October 1437; SROB E3/11/1.4 (Lidgate); Bacon Ms 295/31, court held October 1437 (Brandon).

rental values of leaseholds. These often lay between 12d. and 22d. per acre, comfortably exceeding the 4d. per acre demanded by the rebels in 1381, and they proved fairly resilient in the late fourteenth century. However, between the beginning and the middle of the fifteenth century, leasehold values dropped by nearly one-half on many Breckland manors. For example, land in Mildenhall had been worth nearly 22d. per acre in the 1390s, yet values in the mid-fifteenth century were 35 per cent lower than they had been in the second half of the fourteenth century. In 1435 around 90 acres of arable land were granted on new leases at Huntingfield at the low value of 5½d. per acre, and in 1430 18 acres of land in Walsham, previously leased at 4s., were granted to Robert Hawes for 18d.[47]

The falling value of leaseholds was compounded by difficulties in collecting rents. Some tenants were genuinely short of money, or experienced cash-flow problems, while others used the deteriorating economic conditions as an excuse to delay the payment of their rent. Landlords, in consultation with their local agents and officials, had to learn to manage their tenants with guile and flexibility, deploying either concessions or firmness as the occasion demanded, because a tenant in arrears was better than no tenant at all in the worsening agrarian conditions. Rent arrears mounted rapidly at Laxfield in the early 1390s, so that by 1393 over £18 (equivalent to almost half the annual value of the manor) had not been paid. The account for 1393 provides a detailed breakdown of the problem: 25s. was identified as rent that had not been collected over the previous four years, while £11 18s. was still owed by the previous bailiff and £4 19s. 6d. by the previous rent collector. By 1398 the collector of rents on the estate of Bungay priory owed over £35, of which nearly £21 constituted arrears of rent accumulated from numerous tenants over the previous nine years. The prioress carefully noted that these arrears were 'respited', or postponed, rather than 'allowed', or written off, implying that she wanted the collector to continue pursing some of the debtors. Debts owed by previous office holders are also recorded on the account, which bears the mark of detailed and flexible debt management. Landlords accepted that some arrears of rent had to be periodically written off as uncollectable. In the early fifteenth century rental income at Aldham generated just over £20 per annum, almost half of which (£9 4s. 11d.) was written off in 1415 as bad debts.[48]

The management of rent arrears was the single most pressing issue

---

47 SROI HD1538/207/7, court held December 1446 (Tunstall); Britnell, *Britain and Ireland*, pp. 440–1; Bailey, *Marginal Economy*, pp. 228–9; CUL Vanneck Ms, box 5, court held June 1435 (Huntingfield); SROB HA504/3/15.4 (Walsham).

48 SROI HD1538/156/3 (Bungay); CUL Vanneck Ms, box 8 (Laxfield); CUL Vanneck Ms, box 2 (Aldham).

on landed estates in the fifteenth century, and the problem continued in some places, such as Worlington, into the early sixteenth century. A tenant who owed rent might initially be given more time to pay, but, if the problem persisted, the officials had to judge their next response carefully: they could agree a rent reduction; write off the arrears after a suitable period of time; threaten seizure of the land; and, finally but exceptionally, the actual seizure of land, or the distraint of goods and chattels, to pay for the arrears. In general, landlords did not write off arrears lightly, and their management of debt became increasingly sophisticated. The practice of breaking down arrears into component parts, and maintaining a record of the liabilities of individual manorial officers long after they had retired from office, is widespread in fifteenth-century accounts, and by the 1450s those at Norton incorporated separate and detailed schedules of debtors drawn up by the manorial reeve.[49]

The combination of abandoned holdings, falling rental values and rising arrears resulted in a serious fall in income from land rents on most manors during the course of the fifteenth century. The problem was greatest around the middle of the century, and was most acute on the poorest soils. One attempt to calculate the extent to which rental income fell at Lackford during this period indicates a fall of 25 per cent between the 1420s and 1440s, and a further 17 per cent between the 1440s and 1480s. In general, the decline seems to have stabilized by the third quarter of the fifteenth century in most places, and by the end of the century some manors exhibit signs of some recovery in income levels. We might estimate that rental income on many manors fell by one-half between c. 1340 and c. 1460.[50]

OTHER AGRARIAN RESOURCES

In the fifteenth century the income from other agrarian resources – fisheries, turbaries, parks and heathland – also fell dramatically. The value of leases of freshwater fisheries in Lakenheath fen collapsed by 80 per cent between the mid-fourteenth and mid-fifteenth centuries, the value of the manorial pond at Cavenham fell by 33 per cent between the 1370s and the mid-fifteenth century, and fisheries around Bury St Edmunds were similarly affected. Fishing rights in the Little Ouse around Brandon held steady at £4 per annum between the 1360s and 1380s, then at 53s. 4d. from the 1390s to the 1470s, after which the fishery was untenanted and the rent had to be reduced further to attract any interest. Sales of heathland had produced a few shillings each year

49 Bailey, *Marginal Economy*, pp. 269–76; BL Add. Roll 67555 (Worlington); SROB 553/35 (Norton).

50 Bailey, *Marginal Economy*, table 5.4 and p. 180.

in the 1330s at Easton Bavents, but only a few pennies in 1383–4, when the account noted 'and no more for want of hirers'. In 1292 heathland products had been worth over £6 at Dunningworth but barely 9s. in 1392. In 1268–9 sales of turbaries and heath reached over £20 at Staverton, but only 35s. in 1403–4, 7s. in 1422–3 and nothing in 1431–2; similarly, its park had generated over £11 in 1329–30, but closer to £4 in 1403–4 and £3 in 1422.[51]

The contraction in grain production meant less business for the competitive milling industry and the gradual disappearance of millsuit further reduced the activity of demesne mills, many of which consequently suffered a serious reduction in income or were forced to close entirely. Between *c.* 1300 and *c.* 1500 demesne milling revenues fell by one-half in England and more than half of the manorial mills in Suffolk disappeared. The chronology of decline varies from place to place, although the 1380s and 1390s, then the 1440s and 1450s, were especially difficult. In the 1370s Laxfield mill was leased for 53s. 6d. per annum, but in the 1380s its value fell to 33s. 4d., after which it dilapidated. The mill at Fornham St Martin had fallen down in the 1360s; Maiston mill near Felixstowe, Kingston mill near Woodbridge, Westmill in Walsham and Norton mill all disappeared in the 1380s; and even Babwell mill – within striking distance of Bury St Edmunds – was in ruins by the middle of the fifteenth century. The rental value of Brandon mill halved between the 1390s and the 1460s, it stood empty and untenanted for short periods in the 1440s and 1470s, and then it was finally dismantled in the late 1480s; the lease of the main mill in Walsham dropped from 26s. 8d. in 1430 to 20s. in 1440–1 before becoming untenanted and ruinous in 1452.[52]

Those demesne mills which survived the fifteenth century experienced mixed fortunes. The income of Blythburgh mill fell by 29 per cent between the 1420s and 1460s, and failed to recover before the early sixteenth century, and that from Eyke mill almost halved between 1401 and 1471. Yet others which managed to secure a greater proportion of the declining milling market, or

---

[51] Bailey, *Marginal Economy*, pp. 302–3; PRO c135/230/26, c136/47/27 (Cavenham); Gottfried, *Bury St Edmunds*, p. 114; PRO sc6/1304/31–3; Bacon Mss 654, 656–61, 664, 671–2 (Brandon); SROI v5/19/1.8 (Easton); SROI HD1538/206/6 and PRO sc6/999/19 (Dunningworth); sc6/1005/7, SROI HD1538/356/3; Hoppitt, 'Parks', pp. 182–3 (Staverton).

[52] Langdon, *Mills*, pp. 62–4; the Suffolk estimate is based on a sample of twenty-one manors, namely Blythburgh, Bungay, Cavenham, Eyke, Fornham All Saints, Huntingfield, Lavenham, Mildenhall, Melton, Ufford (all survived); and Brandon, Drinkstone, Dunningworth, Icklingham, Kingston, Lakenheath, Laxfield, Mettingham, Norton, Walsham, Wetheringsett (all disappeared). CUL Vanneck Ms, boxes 7 and 8 (Laxfield); SROB E3/15.6/2.30(a) and 2.31 (Fornham); CUL EDC 7/14/c/34, 35 (Kingston); SROB HA504/3/5a, 12, 15.12, 15.13 and 15.4 (Walsham); SROB 553/21 (Norton); Bacon Mss 657–61, 664, 672, 677, 681, and 295/35 (Brandon); SROI HA119/50/3/18, m. 74 (Maiston); *CPR, HVI*, vol. 6, p. 231 (Babwell).

were located close to thriving urban centres, were still able to yield a decent income. The huge mill at Mildenhall increased its revenue from £14 per annum to over £17 between the early 1400s and the 1460s, despite the town's steady economic decline, and that at Melton benefited from booming demand in nearby Woodbridge, as its rental income rose from £4 16s. 8d. per annum in the 1340s to £6 in the 1390s, a level still maintained in the 1470s. Three generations of the Moon family leased the mill at Fornham All Saints, which benefited from its proximity to Bury St Edmunds. In general, the rising costs of maintenance eroded profits, encouraging some landlords and lessees to be less assiduous about repairs, and manor courts contain growing complaints about failures to maintain mills and mill races properly, which could lead to local flooding or damage to the machinery. The miller of Mildenhall was warned in 1468 for allowing weeds to grow 'in the water of the mill and the mill dam', and the lessee of Eyke mill failed to water or grease the spindle in the machinery, causing a fire and extensive damage. The evidence for tenant and domestic mills is very scarce, although handmills are still widely recorded in the fifteenth century, when the independent sector probably fared better than demesne mills.[53]

The fall in income from the various economic resources of the manor, the managerial complexity of leasing them to different tenants, and the difficulties of securing reliable local officials persuaded landlords of the benefits of leasing more of their manors as a single lot. Many of the Suffolk manors of the earls of Clare were leased entirely in the 1370s; by 1435 seventeen of the manors of the cellarer of Bury St Edmunds abbey were leased in their entirety (fourteen of which were in Suffolk); and in the late fifteenth century all four of Thetford priory's manors in east Suffolk were leased. The earls of Oxford had leased their four main manors in Suffolk by the late 1450s, and the earls of Norfolk adopted a similar policy. For example, various components of their manor of Dunningworth, including the demesne arable, had been leased to different tenants in the late 1380s, but in the mid-1420s the whole manor – with the exception of the court, warren and advowson of the church – was granted in a single lease for £21 per annum. This device proved both convenient to the lord and relatively successful, for in 1439 the lease was regranted jointly to three men for seven years at £19 per annum, and then in 1447 jointly to four other men for £19 6s. 8d. A similar approach was adopted at Staverton, where by the 1470s the demesne arable, park, pastures and warren were all granted

53 Richmond, *John Hopton*, p. 40; SROI HD1538/356/2, HD1538/357/5, m. 97, and HD1538/357/6, mm. 16, 33 (Eyke); BL Add. Rolls 53120, 53139 (Mildenhall); CUL EDC 16/11/10, 26, 38 (Melton); Langdon, *Mills*, p. 207; SROB E18/451/5, court held July 1468 (Mildenhall); Bailey, *Marginal Economy*, p. 288; Holt, *Mills of Medieval England*, pp. 163–8.

in one lease to a consortium of ten local tenants. The warren and manor court were the only components omitted from the lease of Dunningworth in 1439, which was taken on by three local men, although in 1447 the new lessees came from further afield: John Doket of Blaxhall, Thomas Fowler of Mendham, and two men from Ilketshall. Perhaps Doket, an established local farmer, undertook the day-to-day supervision of the manor, while his distant partners were probably interested in additional pasture grounds near the coast for cattle rearing.[54]

Leasing manors in their entirety as a single lot eased some of the hassle and burdens of estate management in the difficult circumstances of the fifteenth century, but landlords were still exposed to the problems caused by rogue lessees and difficulties in collecting all the income due to them. In the 1410s and 1420s Richard Mendham, a gentry lessee of Lidgate, systematically stripped the manor's assets in an extraordinary spree of economic vandalism. He removed timber from houses, barns and the mill, cut and sold mature trees in Cropley park, and killed deer there for commercial profit, attracting amercements totalling nearly £19 for his transgressions, which presumably reflected the value of his dealings. The entire manor of Great Saxham was leased for £20 in 1449, but after arrears and the cost of landlord's repairs on houses the lord actually received less than £13. Growing rental arrears were exacerbated by greater difficulties in securing payment for other manorial products, such as wool and grain. Arrears had become a chronic problem on many of John Hopton's east Suffolk manors by the mid-fifteenth century, and in 1456 the accumulated debts of various lessees were equivalent to half the annual value of the lease of Cockfield manor and nearly one-quarter of that of Aldham. A similar pattern is evident at Brandon, where arrears were negligible in the 1390s, but by the 1460s were running at around £30 per annum, and in 1490 around one-half of the rental income due from the farm of Simon Wiseman's small manors around Thornham remained uncollected.[55]

THE CONTRACTION OF SETTLEMENT

The most obvious physical manifestation of severe demographic and sustained agrarian decline was a reduction in the number of houses and agricultural

54 Holmes, *Higher Nobility*, p. 154; Bailey, *Marginal Economy*, p. 235; BL Add. Ms 7096, f. 36; Dymond, *Thetford Priory*, pp. 31, 793; CUL Vanneck Ms, box 2 (Aldham); SROI HD1538/356/3 (Staverton); SROI HD1538/206/5; HD1538/207/6, court held June 1424; HD1538/207/7, courts held November 1439 and June 1447 (Dunningworth).

55 SROB E3/11/1.3, court held April 1421 (Lidgate); SROB E3/15.3/2.37a (Saxham); Richmond, *John Hopton*, pp. 70–2; CUL Vanneck Ms, box 2 (Aldham); Bacon Mss 655–9, 664–72, 684–9 (Brandon); SROI HD1538/384/2 (Thornham).

buildings, particularly the low-grade housing that had accommodated the swollen rural population before the Black Death. The dilapidation and thinning of the housing stock is evident from both abandoned house plots on the ground and through references in manorial court rolls to 'wasting' buildings on villein tenures. A few tenants applied formally to their lord to remove surplus properties from customary holdings before their deteriorating state made them too dangerous, but most just allowed properties to fall down and waited to see if the manorial authorities pursued them. The cumulative scale of these losses could be considerable by the mid-fifteenth century: most settlements shrank (plate 14) and a few were deserted entirely.

The proportion of people possessing their own home probably rose sharply in the immediate aftermath of the Black Death, and consequently the drop in the demand for housing was not as great as the fall in population. Yet many manorial courts of the 1350s and 1360s record a steady trickle of presentments for dilapidation on villein tenements, as the least attractive buildings fell into disuse or were taken down. At this early date the courts usually adopted an aggressive stance towards such wastage. In the early 1370s John Gyn paid the Ufford court 5s. 4d. to remove a house and rebuild it in Melton, while Robert Leman simply allowed two houses to fall down and was amerced 3s. 4d. Thereafter, the flow of wastage presentments in manor courts increased, and had become a torrent in many places by the middle of the fifteenth century. For example, presentments for 'wasted' buildings rose sharply in the 1400s at Aldham and doubled after the 1430s in the manorial court of Lackford. The Dunningworth court struggled to stem the flow of acts of wastage in the 1450s, and in one court six tenants were amerced for allowing five houses, two granges, a hall and a tenement to fall into disrepair. The size of amercements imposed for wastage by manorial courts fell as their number rose. In 1356 Thomas Skinner had incurred the large penalty of 20s., and in 1364 Simon Letewyne was threatened with a 40s. fine, for not repairing their houses in Leiston, but by the late 1390s residents there were only charged a few pennies for similar offences.[56] The growth in wastage was a predictable response to demographic decline and agrarian contraction, but it must be considered alongside the general improvements in the size and quality of the surviving stock of housing. Where in the 1340s perhaps three low-quality houses had been crammed onto a plot, in the 1440s a single house of better quality and larger size now stood. Similarly, industrializing towns and villages continued

---

[56] SROI HD1538/294/2, courts held June 1373, September 1374 and December 1375 (Ufford); CUL Vanneck Ms, box 1, especially courts held September 1405 (six presentments) and September 1406 (14 presentments) (Aldham); Bailey, *Marginal Economy*, p. 309; SROI HD1538/207/7, court held May 1455 (Dunningworth); CUL Vanneck Ms, box 9, courts held April 1356, February 1364, and December 1396 (Leiston).

to experience strong demand for housing, so that, for example, few presentments for wastage appear in the court rolls of Stowmarket where, exceptionally, the population level rose between *c.* 1320 and *c.* 1520.[57]

By the fifteenth century the scale and nature of dilapidations could be difficult to manage, and, in addition to reducing the charges levied for wastage,
landlords had to respond sensitively to individual circumstances. Accidental
damage was often exonerated: in 1466 Richard Dawnald was not required to
rebuild a substantial house in Cratfield, which had burnt down 'as a result of
the negligence of outsiders and not the said Richard', and Margaret Miles
was allowed to leave her ruinous bakehouse after it had caught fire. Lords
also offered support to promising tenants as well as punishing bad ones. This
extended to practical help on occasions, for some lords offered rent remission,
or free timber, to tenants who expressed a willingness to repair buildings. In
1423 Thomas Sherd was granted over 17 acres of arable land and an abandoned
messuage next to his own in Mildenhall, all for a notional entry fine and
long lease on condition that he rebuilt his own messuage, a ruined chamber and maintain other outbuildings on the property. In early 1447 manorial officials of Lidgate distributed thirty-five oaks from Southey wood to
aid the repair of fifteen tenanted buildings of various kinds. However, not all
tenants responded fairly to these incentives, and the bailiff of Higham complained that Roger Potter had not rebuilt a barn after receiving timber for that
purpose.[58]

Fifteenth-century lords understood that some wastage was inevitable, and
empathized with the problems facing their tenants. After all, the declining
output of demesnes and the fall in agrarian profits meant that they faced the
same issue of too many buildings that were costly to upkeep. In 1399 many of
the agricultural outbuildings of Walton manor were in need of urgent repair;
in the same year the grange, granary, dairy, stable and sheepcote of Dunningworth required repairs estimated at nearly £8; and in the 1420s, and again in
the 1440s, different lessees of Lidgate allowed a number of buildings on the
demesne farm to deteriorate. A survey of the manors of Dunningworth and
Staverton in 1462 concluded that all the manorial buildings were 'ruinous and
waste'; those at Sutton had disappeared by 1410; the farm complex servicing the large demesne of Erbury (Clare) had disappeared by mid-century;
and by the 1470s the demesne complexes at Flempton and Lackford had disappeared entirely. Numerous small manor houses, especially those formerly
associated with minor lay landlords, had fallen into disuse, and in 1463 a

---

57 Amor, 'Late Medieval Enclosure', pp. 188–91.

58 CUL Vanneck Ms, box 3, court held May 1466 (Cratfield); SROI HD1538/207/7,
   court held May 1455 (Dunningworth); SROB E18/451/4 (Mildenhall); SROB
   E3/11/1.4, court held January 1447 (Lidgate); PRO SC12/27/32 (Higham).

number of deserted manorial sites are explicitly recorded in Westleton and Yoxford.[59]

Seigneurial empathy with tenants did not, however, extend to indulgence, and in the 1420s the duke of Norfolk's court at Staverton, which included parts of the settlements of Eyke, Chillesford, Butley and Wantisden, made a concerted effort to control widespread dilapidations. After a series of general warnings, and then specific directives, to repair houses had elicited an indifferent response from tenants, a court held in August 1430 amerced nine people a total of 9s. 8d. for disregarding earlier orders, and listed a further twenty who were given days to repair theirs. Eighteen of them responded promptly, for the word 'repaired' is written by a later hand in the margin of the roll next to twelve of their names, and 'allowed' next to six. However, the tenants' resolve soon diminished, because six years later the court listed eleven who had allowed their buildings to become 'wasted'. In 1440 Gilbert Debenham, a steward on the duke of Norfolk's estates, personally inspected properties at Butley and Eyke, and the subsequent court rolls document his findings: twenty tenants had allowed sixteen houses, four granges, five stables, two bakehouses and three other buildings to dilapidate. Again, they were given days to undertake repairs, but within a year seven tenants were amerced for failure to improve the properties, including one who attracted a hefty amercement. Debenham co-ordinated an sustained drive against wastage across the Suffolk properties of the duke of Norfolk, because in the August court of 1430 at Dunningworth four tenants had been amerced for disrepair, and ten others warned under a sizeable penalty of 20s. to repair their houses, and then in August 1440 Debenham attended the court personally to direct action against wastage on the manor.[60]

By the mid-fifteenth century the cumulative impact of a century of piece-meal dilapidations was stark. Surveys and court rolls refer frequently to 'empty places', 'vacant plots' or 'messuages formerly built upon', and a survey of 1435 reveals that thirteen out of forty-three recorded house plots in Culford had disappeared. Landscape historians attribute scores of grassy and indistinct earthworks around the edges of greens and empty moated sites to house losses sustained in this period (plate 4). It is possible that around eighty isolated farmsteads scattered around the parish of Mendlesham disappeared during the later Middle Ages, along with half of the known houses in Worlingworth.

59 SROI HA119/50/3/19, m. 74 (Walton); SROI HD1538/207/3, court held May 1399 (Dunningworth); SROB E3/11/1.3, court held October 1426, E3/11/1.4, m. 5 (Lidgate); SROI HD1538/207/8, court held May 1462; HD1538/357/6, m. 4 (Staverton); SROI HB10/427/4/1, f. 36 (Sutton); Warner, *Greens, Commons*, pp. 40, 50; *PSIA* 39 (1996), p. 109 (Erbury); Bailey, *Marginal Economy*, pp. 310–11.

60 SROI HD1538/357/5, mm. 56, 64, 66–7; SROI HD1538/207/6 (Dunningworth).

Between the early fourteenth and late sixteenth centuries the number of occupied house sites fell by a third around Cranmer Green in Walsham, with other abandoned house sites in Upstreet and East End, and Gershaw green on the edges of South Elmham St James and St Cross was largely deserted by the end of the fifteenth. Most greenside hamlets suffered severe depopulation, although Hunger green in Earl Soham was completely deserted. Peter Warner complains that 'so numerous and repetitive are the deserted greenside sites on the clay lands that time and space do not allow for a complete description': where a dozen houses had stood in the late thirteenth century, often only a couple remained by the late fifteenth. The cycle of expansion and decline over many centuries is a familiar experience on the Suffolk claylands.[61]

Why did a few settlements disappear entirely? The explanation in folklore, that villages were deserted by a plague epidemic, is largely incorrect, although Alston St John (near Trimley) is an exceptional example of a settlement, and parochial centre, whose disappearance is almost wholly attributable to the Black Death. In fact, 'deserted medieval villages' are rare in Suffolk for the simple reason that villages as a settlement form are rare, although the abandonment of isolated farmsteads, hamlets and greenside settlements is a common phenomenon. Where an entire village or parish was deserted, the process of desertion tended to be drawn out over many centuries, with the final act occurring in the seventeenth or eighteenth century.[62]

The most severely depopulated settlements were often small before 1349, relatively late-settled, located in peripheral areas of a large parish or situated on less fertile soils. When these characteristics were combined with the general context of agrarian retrenchment, demographic decline, and the ready availability of work and land in more advantaged settlements nearby, then the incentives for residents to stay in their community weakened: many simply voted with their feet. Alnesbourne, Coclesworth (in Eriswell), Fakenham Parva, Breggestreet and Hethern are good examples of minor settlements on poor soil that had apparently disappeared by the end of the fifteenth century. Dunningworth, a hamlet on the south western approach to Snape bridge, suffered much dilapidation of its housing stock in the 1440s and 1450s, and was severely depopulated by the end of the fifteenth century. Sotherton, a parish of relatively late and dispersed settlement, was entirely deserted by the end of the Middle Ages. Greenside hamlets on the clay interfluves of northeast Suffolk – which had been heavily colonized under extreme population

[61] Bailey, *Marginal Economy*, p. 309; *PSIA* 36 (1986), p. 81; Ridgard, 'Worlingworth', p. 208; Warner, *Greens, Commons*, pp. 39–43; *HistA*, pp. 88–9; West and McLaughlin, *Walsham le Willows*, pp. 108–9 (Walsham); *PSIA* 36 (1986), p. 149.

[62] Dymond and Northeast, *History of Suffolk*, pp. 49–50; Bailey, *Marginal Economy*, pp. 52–4, 309–14.

pressure in the thirteenth century – often exhibited severe contraction, and feature prominently among those places receiving greatest tax relief by the Crown in the mid-fifteenth century.[63]

CONCLUSION

The later Middle Ages is a period of intriguing economic paradoxes. It provides examples of contraction and expansion, of diminishing markets and new opportunities. Marked differences in fortunes are evident from one sector of the agrarian economy to another, and also from one period to another, especially when compared to the more homogenous experience in the period 1200–1350. For example, in the 1360s and 1370s recovery is evident in many sectors of Suffolk agriculture, although over the next two decades dairy farming performed markedly better than grain farming. Finally, all sectors of Suffolk's agriculture – with the possible exception of stock rearing – exhibit signs of real distress in the great slump of the mid-fifteenth century. Clearly, the agrarian economy can only be understood properly by disaggregating it into short periods and individual sectors.

On the eve of the Black Death the agrarian economy of Suffolk had reached its peak in aggregate terms, and was characterized by a mixed farming regime, with some of the most intensive and commercialized dairying and cattle rearing in England. The output of arable farming contracted by at least one-half between this high point and the low point of the 1450s, with the brunt borne by cheaper and coarser crops such as rye and oats, although the production of wheat and barley proved more resilient. Villages were emptier, and the countryside was less cultivated and managed. Pastoral farming became relatively and, in some places, absolutely more important during this period, until by *c.* 1500 cattle rearing and dairying dominated the rural economy. Sheep rearing remained buoyant until the last quarter of the fourteenth century, but then suffered from a sustained decline in profitability. The trend towards larger flocks and fewer owners meant that sheep farming became concentrated increasingly into the hands of mainly gentry landlords with estates on the lighter soils: peasant ownership of sheep declined markedly everywhere. Between *c.* 1360 and *c.* 1410 rabbit rearing and, perhaps, dairying became more intensive than before the Black Death, and the withdrawal of many demesnes from cattle rearing around *c.* 1400 presented greater opportunities for tenants. Dairying, in particular, was better suited to smaller operations drawing upon domestic labour, and herd sizes rose during the fifteenth century on tenant holdings in

---

[63] Bailey, *Marginal Economy*, p. 313; Warner, *Greens, Commons*, pp. 23, 39; D. Dymond and R. Virgoe, 'The Reduced Population of Suffolk in the Early Fifteenth Century', *PSIA* 36 (1986), pp. 76–8.

east and south Suffolk. The acquisition of livestock carried other benefits for peasants, because it provided a viable store of wealth and a source of status. Contracting markets created difficulties even for dairy farmers in the middle of the century, but stock fattening remained relatively resilient.

By 1500 the contours of Suffolk agriculture had become more sharply drawn, both socially and geographically. The lowest ranks of lords (gentlemen) and the upper ranks of peasants (yeomen) were the most active and dynamic agriculturalists, buying land, leasing part or all of demesnes, and constructing sizeable commercial enterprises. Regional specialization was more pronounced than it had been in *c.* 1300. Tenant holdings in the Breckland and the Sandlings grew barley, kept pigs and reared horses, while demesnes dominated sheep and rabbit rearing in a landscape characterized by irregular open fields. The rest of Suffolk concentrated on wheat and fodder crops, but was increasingly characterized by dairying, cattle rearing and pig keeping, especially on tenant holdings. The greater emphasis on cattle was associated with the gradual conversion of some arable to pasture, and with an evolving landscape which came to be wholly dominated by hedged enclosures. Suffolk farming retained a good degree of its commercial orientation, with little sense that economic contraction involved a reversion to subsistence agriculture. The swing to the main cash crops of barley and wheat, the emergence of market-orientated production on rabbit warrens, and the sustained buoyancy of dairy and cattle farming all underline the continuing importance of commercial production. In 1500 the pastoral economy of Suffolk was arguably the strongest in England, and tenant holdings were more specialized than they had been 200 years before.

CHAPTER 10

'The World Turned Upside Down': Rural Society, 1350–1500

THE LOWER ORDERS

The surfeit of land on more attractive terms and tenures, the availability of better-paid employment, and, to a lesser extent, the dissolution of villeinage and serfdom, presented clear opportunities for social and economic advancement among the lower orders of Suffolk society. These opportunities encouraged economic individualism and personal enterprise. Young teenagers now had ample opportunity to leave the family home to work in domestic service, perhaps on a dairy farm or in the house of a textile manufacturer, or to establish their own home while picking up regular work as a labourer. Farmers could expand their holdings or provide their sons with sufficient land to earn a decent livelihood. Many people seized such opportunities readily. The proportion of people who were landless is not knowable, but it must have fallen dramatically after 1349 and remained low. Labourers and petty craft workers acquired modest houses and smallholdings of a few acres, and enjoyed good earnings (over 2d. per day) and enhanced purchasing power. Middling farmers constructed small dairy and pig herds, exploited a dozen or so acres of arable land, and were increasingly described as 'husbandmen', while most villages contained half a dozen wealthier farmers (yeomen), who leased components of demesnes and constructed sizeable holdings (above 50 acres) of their own. If we take England as whole, Gross Domestic Product (GDP) per capita probably doubled between 1300 and 1470.[1]

The problem of escalating costs and rising wage bills on demesnes also reflected the improved earning power of the lower orders of society. The wage rates of skilled craftsmen nearly doubled between *c.* 1340 and *c.* 1440 in England, and unskilled workers enjoyed rises of more than 50 per cent. The day rate paid to harvest reapers on the Mildenhall demesne rose from 1d. in 1324 to 3d. in 1391, the cash stipends received by ploughmen on the demesne of Hinderclay doubled between 1340 and 1400, and those paid at Chevington increased from 13s. to 18s. between 1420 and 1439. Manorial courts sought to punish those labourers who habitually charged high fees to employers or who refused to work locally because they reckoned to earn more elsewhere. Labour

[1] Dyer, *Age of Transition?*, pp. 42–3.

shortages presented greater opportunities for women, who could now find more work in agricultural activities previously dominated by men, although their rates of pay were usually lower. Yet the expansion of textile manufacturing and dairy farming in the second half of the fourteenth century enabled more Suffolk women to increase their earnings, either as sole agents or as part of a household. The proportion of households obtaining regular income from both husband and wife rose after the Black Death.[2]

Evidence for the greater prosperity of the lower orders of society is plentiful from fifteenth-century sources. Their improved standards of living are apparent in better diet and clothing, in the growth of a culture of consumerism, and in a diminution of the widespread poverty which had characterized the pre-Black Death era. Higher levels of material comfort are reflected in the variety of personal possessions recorded in fifteenth-century wills, which often included more sets of shoes and clothes, silver spoons, beads, mazers and comfortable feather beds, all of which represented a significant improvement upon the functional and narrow range of possessions owned by even the wealthier peasants before the Black Death. Clothing also became more extravagant and influenced by fashionable trends, incorporating brighter colours and heavier cloth, and was perhaps lined with fur. In 1450 Simon Clerk, a yeoman of Stanton, bequeathed to his son a large spruce chest bound with iron, chairs, sheets and a feather bed with a red cover embroidered with white roses, while the less wealthy William Campyon of Icklingham left his two daughters all his utensils, 'that is pots, pans, sheets and bedding, except the best green bed cover', and he also gave a friend his blue gown and best hood. Special occasions, such as weddings and major holy days, were likely to be celebrated with modest but agreeable feasts. Maintenance agreements for elderly relatives reveal the plentiful supply of food and fuel, and the comfort of fifteenth-century accommodation. When in 1459 the family home of the widowed Margery Bekisby in Thorpe Morieux was inherited by her son, she continued to dwell in the west wing of the house comprising two ground floor rooms with two solars above, together with the courtyard annexed to them and another chamber. In 1431 Walter and Christine Parker of Eyke entered into a formal arrangement for their retirement with John and Isabella Coket, which, in return for land, gave the Parkers four rooms in the Coket household and access to the well, bakehouse and fuel store.[3]

[2] *AHEW*, iii, pp. 467–83; Bodleian Suffolk Rolls, 21; SROB E18/455/1 (Mildenhall); D. Farmer, 'The Famuli in the Later Middle Ages', in Britnell and Hatcher, *Progress and Problems* (1996), p. 232; Mate, *Women*, pp. 27–56.

[3] Dyer, *Age of Transition?*, pp. 114–22, 128–35; Redstone, 'Social Condition', pp. 180–1; Northeast, *Wills*, pp. 174–5, 225, 426, 438, 442, 444, 449, 451; SROI HD1538/357/5, m. 33 (Eyke).

These maintenance agreements indicate that the rising living standards and disposable incomes of the mass of the populace were also reflected in widespread improvements to their housing. The demand for housing fell after 1350, and many buildings fell into decay or were taken down, but the fall in the number of houses contrasted with an improvement in the quality of the remaining stock. Some houses were upgraded and extended with good materials to higher standards of construction, while others were rebuilt entirely. The hall remained the central feature of late-medieval houses, with its eating table and hearth, but in some new builds it was narrower and taller than in thirteenth-century aisled halls, incorporating windows which provided more light to the interior: consequently they are dubbed 'raised aisle halls'. Raised aisle-hall houses of high quality dating from the late fourteenth century survive in Chediston and Linstead Parva; Broadend farmhouse in Stradbroke is a fine example of the same style dating from *c.* 1380; and Paradise farm in Worlingworth is a later example from the mid-fifteenth century. Another feature of some new builds was a greater emphasis on privacy, such as the addition of separate chambers and rooms at the end of the hall, and on display, such as the inclusion of ornate carvings and structures. Hence houses built or upgraded after *c.* 1350 often contained wings at either end of the hall; a second storey, especially over the end bays, to provide segregated accommodation for storage, sleeping or servants; and separate kitchens and chamber blocks. The thirteenth-century aisled hall at Purton green, Stansfield, was significantly altered in the mid-fifteenth century by raising the aisles and adding wings (plate 3), and in *c.* 1400 a detached kitchen range was added to Sawyers farm in Bures. Surviving fifteenth-century houses from Ixworth are impressive structures, comprising two or four bays with demountable internal partitions: Dover house was first built in the early fifteenth century and then substantially modernized a century later, complete with decorated fireplaces. Suffolk also contains the largest concentration of 'Wealden'-style houses outside the eponymous region of Kent and Sussex, most of which date from the late fourteenth century. Fashion dictated that these houses increasingly featured impressive queenposts (mainly in north Suffolk) and crownposts over the centre of the open hall: such ostentatious roof features and decorations reflected higher wealth and status. Court rolls, too, hint at the emergence of more commodious residences. In 1493 Robert Fuller acquired 'an insethouse with a shop, three chambers, a solar as an annex, plus a well and bakehouse in the garden' in Walsham.[4]

---

4 Dyer, *Age of Transition?*, pp. 52–3; *HistA*, pp. 174–83; Warner, *Greens, Commons*, p. 39; Amor, 'Riding out Recession', p. 128, figs. 28, 29; *PSIA* 29 (1963), pp. 336–41; *PSIA* 38 (1998), pp. 400–1 (Bures); *PSIA* 36 (1986), p. 159; *PSIA* 37 (1991), p. 288;

Many of Suffolk's surviving late medieval houses were built by wealthier yeomen and merchants, but there is no doubt that those built by the poorer members of society were also constructed to a good standard, often conforming to the common format of a small hall, parlour and first-floor accommodation. Even a humble labourer was able to fund the construction of an aisled cottage on the edge of Depden green in *c.* 1500. The ease with which land could be acquired after *c.* 1350 enabled people to create more space around their houses, and therefore to enjoy greater privacy. The Quedwell family amalgamated properties around Sawyer's tye in Bures to construct a new house and farm complex on a grander scale, while the acquisition of a sliver of land by John Cripps and his wife next to their existing messuage in Laxfield, and of an abandoned house plot next to his own in Brandon by John Pepyr, imply similar motives.[5] As any modern estate agent knows, impressive houses in attractive locations continued to be in demand. John de Huntingfield paid a large entry fine of 10s. for a cottage in Leiston in 1364, and in the mid-1370s a cottage and 2 acres in Sutton was granted at leasehold for twenty years to a new tenant who was prepared to pay a decent rent of 6s. 8d. per annum.[6]

Despite the availability of cheap land on easier tenures, smallholdings continued to dominate the landholding structure of fifteenth-century Suffolk. Chris Dyer has estimated that in the 1380s 85 per cent of Suffolk tenants held under 20 acres, and a mere 3 per cent had holdings in excess of 30 acres. In 1409 60 per cent of tenants at Fornham All Saints held under 5 acres, and only 16 per cent held over 30 acres, and in 1424 smallholders dominated the holding structure of Melton. In the 1480s 61 per cent of tenants on Mettingham college's manors of Mettingham, Shipmeadow, Ilketshall, Bramfield and Mellis held under 10 acres, while 72 per cent of holdings at Bawdsey and Hollesley were under 10 acres, and only 5 per cent were over 30 acres. The continued presence of so many smallholders seems incongruous, given the general shortage of tenants, but it is largely explicable by the wide availability and attractiveness of non-agricultural work. These people combined craft work and wage labouring with a smallholding to provide some basic foodstuffs for their household. The fragmentary survivals of the 1381 Poll Tax returns for Suffolk reveal that 80 per cent of taxpayers were described as labourers, servants or non-agricultural workers, and 93 per cent within Thingoe hundred. The proportion of the population who were dependent upon wage earnings and craft manufacture was higher in late medieval

PSIA 38 (1994), p. 230; SROB HA504/1/17.15 (Walsham); for Essex, see Poos, *Rural Society*, chap. 4. I am grateful to John Walker for sharing his ideas with me.

5 *HistA*, p. 174; *PSIA* 38 (1998), pp. 400–1 (Bures); CUL Vanneck Ms, box 7, court held April 1472 (Laxfield); Bacon Ms 295/32 (Brandon).

6 CUL Vanneck Ms, box 9, court held February 1364; SROI HD1538/294 (Sutton).

Suffolk than in many areas of England, although it is broadly comparable with that for Norfolk and Essex.[7]

The prominence of smallholders and the low average farm size does not mean that the landholding structure had remained unchanged, because the size of the largest tenant holdings increased markedly. In *c.* 1300 very few peasants had holdings in excess of 30 acres, but by *c.* 1500 a small number in almost every village held significantly more than this. For example, in 1409 the 16 per cent of landholders in Fornham who held more than 30 acres actually controlled 80 per cent of all tenant land on the manor, as well as featuring prominently among the lessees of the demesne, and in the 1480s 40 per cent of tenants in Bramfield held under 10 acres, while another 40 per cent held over 30 acres. Hence the plentiful supply of land after *c.* 1350 did not result in its more equitable distribution, but simply stretched the differentiation of land-holding at its upper end. In essence, landholding within local communities had become polarized between the smallholders, who were primarily labour-ers, craft workers and even servants, and the husbandmen and yeomen whose primary interest was commercial agriculture.[8]

Yeomen were busily acquisitive of land on a variety of tenures, and the ready availability of land enabled them to construct substantial enterprises. Nicholas Fyket was an energetic accumulator of land in Bramford between 1380 and 1420, and in 1454 Geoffrey Atgor of Brantham owned land in three villages, a cattle herd, a sheep flock and considerable quantities of grain. The purchase of land required reserves of cash or good credit worthiness, because freeholds and copyholds were usually traded at between £1 and £3 per acre: one land transaction cost Thomas Stodde of Stonham Aspall over £26, which he repaid to the vendor at the rate of £1 6s. 8d. per annum. Others supple-mented their free and copyhold lands with land on leasehold for a fixed term, while others also leased arable demesnes from local lords. For example, by the 1470s Robert Parman had bought more than 100 acres of arable in Chevington, in addition to the lease of 200 acres from the local demesne. In 1444 Simon Gardner paid the manor of Mildenhall £17 for the right to collect all the grain tithes in Cottonfield and Mundesfield, and twenty years later he was paying £21 per annum as the sole lessee of the vast Mildenhall demesne. Parman and Gardner ran large businesses, which were highly dependent upon significant amounts of hired labour and domestic servants. The intimate knowledge of

7 *AHEW*, iii, pp. 614–15; BL Add. Ms 34689, ff. 37–45 (Fornham); CUL EDC 7/16/11/30 (Melton); Dyer, 'The Rising of 1381', p. 275; Powell, *Rising in East Anglia*, p. 67; Poos, *Rural Society*, pp. 19–21, 30–1; Whittle, *Agrarian Capitalism*, pp. 222–4, 301–3.

8 *AHEW*, iii, pp. 614–15 (Bramfield); BL Add. Ms 34689, ff. 37–45 (Fornham); Whittle, *Agrarian Capitalism*, p. 224.

commerce, leases and legal titles to land increased levels of literacy among the yeomanry. A few harboured political ambitions, establishing themselves as willing supporters within the retinues of knights and aristocrats, although this might also draw them into their political feuds. In one notorious case in 1430 a handful of yeomen in the affinity of the duke of Norfolk murdered James Andrew, a supporter of the earl of Suffolk.[9]

The growing wealth of yeomen farmers during the course of the fifteenth century meant that their local economic and social influence increased. They became the major employers of seasonal and casual labour within their communities, because their large holdings needed a sizeable workforce at key times of the year. They also came to dominate the presentment juries who effectively determined the business of fifteenth-century manorial courts, which therefore enabled them to pursue particular social agendas in their immediate locality. For example, some courts chose to impose the government's labour legislation selectively upon local residents, probably as an initial warning to offenders, after which further breaches would be passed onto a higher court. The leet of Brandon amerced two men 40d. each for 'procuring diverse labourers out of the domain during the harvest period, when they could be employed' locally, and the jurors of Eyke amerced John Grubbe 20d. for charging too much per day for his work as a thatcher and for his unwillingness to work for other local employers. Such prosecutions were not in the interests of labourers, who comprised a good proportion of local residents, and thus reflected the sensitivities of the agriculturalists, whose large and commercialized holdings depended upon hired labour. Social and economic divisions widened in fifteenth-century villages, and may have been accompanied by growing social tensions between smallholders and the large farmers.[10]

One consequence of the emergence of a small elite of agriculturalists is that their lives become better documented. In 1461 John Mell of Bramfield inherited 48 acres and by 1478 he had built up a holding of 150 acres on various tenures through prudent purchases and leases: few such farms in this period were constructed entirely by inheritance. His estate could raise sufficient cash

---

9   *SR* 38 (2002), pp. 22–3 (Bramford); Dyer, *Age of Transition?*, pp. 121, 200 (Brantham and Stonham); C. Dyer, 'A Suffolk Farmer in the Fifteenth Century' (forthcoming); BL Add. Rolls 53137–53139 (Mildenhall); R. Virgoe, 'The Murder of James Andrew: Suffolk Faction in the 1430s', *PSIA* 34 (1980), pp. 263–4.

10 On the social agendas of manorial jurors see M. K. McIntosh, *Controlling Misbehaviour in England, 1370–1600* (Cambridge, 1998), pp. 56–107; M. Bailey, 'Rural Society', in *Fifteenth-Century Attitudes: Perceptions of Society in Late Medieval England*, ed. R. Horrox (Cambridge, 1994), p. 166; Bacon Mss 292/27, 293/7 (Brandon); SROI HD1538/357/5, m. 68 (Eyke). In July 1462 the court of Mildenhall banned resident labourers from working outside the vill, SROB E18/451/5.

to disburse over £26 in bequests after his death, and he was admirably hard headed: his will was craftily constructed to ensure that his son had to borrow money from his executors to purchase the agricultural equipment necessary to run the farm. Men such as Mell built many of the impressive fifteenth-century farmhouses that still dominate High Suffolk. Robert Gerrard of Ixworth, a yeoman who lived in the impressive Dover house, possessed a wardrobe of fine clothes, and his son had a splendid suit of armour to display at military musters. The emergence of a dominant group of yeomen was especially evident in east Suffolk, some of whom developed business interests to complement their farming activities. John Scothaugh of Yoxford built up a decent farm of closes and meadows, owned numerous cattle, and had developed a tanning business alongside his trade in live and deadstock: he employed six servants in his household to help manage all his interests. When he died in 1512, ironically without an heir, he bequeathed large quantities of cash for religious and commemorative purposes. The Mans of Lakenheath – former villeins who became substantial and influential farmers by the end of the fifteenth century – provide another example of the potential for social and economic advancement in this period. John Man served as the bailiff on the main manor of Lakenheath in the 1470s and 1480s, while also running a decent farm of his own which included two sheep folds. In 1488 his son Thomas already held a substantial house and messuage, a holding of 80 acres, and leased the lord's rabbit warren, part of the demesne lands and a wharf. In 1516 Thomas, now described as a butcher, was one of three co-lessees of the entire manor, and the lease arrangements required him to serve in the retinue of the prior of Ely whenever required, and to wear a yeoman's gown in the prior's livery. In 1524 he was assessed as the third wealthiest resident of Lakenheath.[11]

The Mans, John Scothaugh and John Mell epitomize the social and economic gains made by the prosperous ranks of peasant society, the people who made the most of this golden age of opportunity for ordinary people. Unfortunately, we know very little about the smallholders, artisans and labourers who constituted the majority of Suffolk society, although their incomes and purchasing power undoubtedly rose. Perhaps Robert Goddard of Lackford exemplifies the comfortable sufficiency which the fifteenth-century smallholder had come to enjoy. Robert held a few acres of land when he died in early 1496, yet he still possessed sufficient grain in store to cater for the immediate needs of his family, to care for his soul (through small donations of barley to his parish church and to the friars in Babwell and Thetford) and to pay off

---

[11] Dyer, *Making a Living*, p. 362; N. Evans, 'Farming and Landholding', p. 303; Richmond, *John Hopton*, pp. 166–7; Amor, 'Riding out Recession', p. 139; CUL EDC 7/15/11/48; J. T. Munday, ed., *Lakenheath Records*, SROB (typescript); *1524 Lay Subsidy*, p. 226; Dyer, *Age of Transition?*, pp. 117–19.

his modest debts. In addition, he owned three horses, two bullocks and a cow. To his wife he bequeathed their 'new house, and the little garden with the little yard', and Robert counted among his prized personal possessions various cloths, blankets and clothes, plus two candlesticks and a brass pot.[12]

The widening opportunities for economic advancement also extended to opportunities for social mobility. Robert Parman of Chevington educated one of his sons at Bury St Edmunds and Cambridge; the son later returned to become rector of his father's parish. The step from successful yeoman farmer to newly established gentleman was not large, although it did imply the acquisition of certain social graces and attributes as well as sufficient acres of land. The Kebbyl family of Stowmarket began their careers as yeomen farmers, rearing livestock and leasing the small demesnes of local manors, before later generations became wealthy enough to elevate themselves to the ranks of minor gentry. Levels of pragmatic literacy increased after c. 1350, especially among the yeomanry, merchants and lesser gentry, many of whom could read if not write: in c. 1500 perhaps 20 per cent of Suffolk's residents could read English and some Latin. Instruction in elementary literacy and grammar by parish priests and in grammar schools rose, although it is easier to produce evidence for the latter than the former. After 1350 new grammar schools were created in Botesdale, Clare, Hadleigh, Stoke-by-Clare, Framlingham, Long Melford, Lowestoft and Lavenham, and existing secular schools such as Ipswich benefited from enlarged endowments and therefore greater financial strength. Measuring social mobility through formal education is not straightforward, but it did provide advancement for some members of the lower orders of society. Philip Canon was educated and highly literate when appointed as clerk to the borough of Dunwich in the 1410s, although he was neither wealthy nor from an established Dunwich family, and he eventually became one of the town's most influential burgesses and one of its Members of Parliament.[13]

The individual advancement and material comfort of ordinary Suffolk people does not imply an abandonment of communal activity and values, because contemporaries were shrewdly aware that personal achievements and monuments could also benefit the community. This point is perfectly illustrated by the widespread reconstruction of parish churches in the late Middle Ages – communal acts of pride and piety which drew upon higher levels of personal wealth and individual benefaction among the lower orders of society. Evidence for the refurbishment, remodelling or rebuilding of churches in

---

[12] SROB, Bonner 39, proved 15 February 1496.

[13] Dyer, 'Suffolk Farmer'; Amor, 'Late Medieval Enclosure', p. 194; Blatchly, *Famous Antient Seed Plot*, pp. 3, 15–26; Redstone, *Memorials*, p. 178; Redstone, 'Social Condition', p. 165; J. H. Moran Cruz, 'England: Education and Society', in Rigby, *Companion* (2003), pp. 451–71; Bailey, *Dunwich*, pp. 7–8.

the perpendicular Gothic style of the late fourteenth and fifteenth centuries – larger, lighter, grander – is especially widespread in Suffolk, and drew principally upon fund-raising and bequests from ordinary parishioners. Clothiers rebuilt Edwardistone and Waldingfield churches and left money to improve the state of local roads. Individuals also left money or property to support almshouses for the poor, in a manner which had not been apparent before the Black Death.[14]

The explosion in the number of religious confraternities after 1349 also reflects a communal response to the religious and social imperatives of this period, as well as the growing affluence of ordinary people. These rural and urban gilds offered the spiritual insurance policy of a decent burial and intercession long after one's death during an era of frequent epidemics and exceptionally high mortality, but they also provided confraternity, conviviality and other benefits, such as accident insurance and financial loans. Gildhalls constructed from local funds at Cratfield and Fressingfield were recreational in purpose, and church ales were regularly held in Cratfield to raise cash and to provide agreeable social events. The gild of St Peter in Bardwell employed cooks and minstrels, acquired spits for roasting meat and possessed an extensive collection of plate and cutlery for communal feasting. Its membership was cast broadly across Bardwell society, comprising thirty married couples, thirty single men and twenty-four single women, and the gild was empowered to arbitrate in any disputes between them. Thus gilds fulfilled an important social function in a society nervous about the future, providing a sense of belonging and a constant point of reference during an era of epidemic disease, when family ties had declined and geographical mobility had increased: consequently they remained popular and active right down to the Reformation. The willingness of parishes to loan money to local people, of gilds and village communities to rent land and manage it for collective purposes, of jurors in manorial and leet courts to regulate public order and behaviour through the use of communal bye-laws, and of urban institutions to increase their grip upon town life, all emphasize the continuing effectiveness and importance of community action in an age of growing individualism.[15]

For all the evidence of greater affluence among the lower orders, their gains were not unlimited. First, accidents, indolence and personal tragedy could and did trigger a spiral of poverty and destitution for some families, and

---

[14] For example, McClenaghan, *Springs of Lavenham*, pp. 39–42; Middleton-Stewart, *Inward Piety*, pp. 83–5, 95–108.

[15] Middleton-Stewart, *Inward Piety*, pp. 278–80; Hanawalt, *Ties that Bound*, p. 262; Richmond, *John Hopton*, pp. 175–6; Dyer, *Age of Transition?*, pp. 185–6; *PSIA* 11 (1901), pp. 82–5; *AHEW*, iii, p. 623; K. Farnhill, *Gilds and the Parish Community in Late Medieval East Anglia, c.1440–1550* (Woodbridge, 2001), pp. 21–41, 127–52.

'the Wheel of Fortune' was a popular theme among fifteenth-century moralists. Second, gains in purchasing and earning power had peaked by the early fifteenth century, and stabilized or perhaps diminished thereafter. Third, some – though by no means all – labourers and servants opted for leisure pursuits in preference to maximizing their earnings in arduous physical occupations, once they had obtained a decent level of income. The appearance of 'camping' (a violent mix of wrestling and football) closes, the proliferation of taverns, the growing social activities of religious gilds, and the interest in a widening range of games (such as bowls, football, handball, tennis and dice) are all features of fifteenth-century Suffolk. The emergence of an embryonic leisure culture among some groups was another facet of the consumerism which symbolized the social and economic gains of ordinary people, and it proved irksome to those conservative landlords who believed that leisure should define the status of the upper ranks of society: but it also emphasizes that some of those ordinary people were making choices about their lifestyles and not all relentlessly pursued the maximization of income.[16] Fourth, those who chose to construct large holdings or lease demesnes were also exposed to the difficulties associated with maintaining repayments on loans, recruiting labour, the risks of low product prices and the slack demand for grain – the same problems which had persuaded many landlords to abandon direct exploitation of their farms during this period, and which, if mishandled, could lead to crippling debts. Finally, the geographical mobility of the population and the tragic effects of successive epidemics resulted in a decline in family ties: fewer close or extended family now lived in the locality, yet family had provided the main source of economic and emotional support in the pre-Black Death era. Many families failed to produce male heirs, because the evidence from wills points to very low male replacement rates in fifteenth-century Suffolk, with the result that many families died out in the male line. Successful farming enterprises or businesses were often broken up through lack of heirs.[17]

The relationship between landlords and their tenants retained personal elements, but their nature changed subtly during the later Middle Ages. The personal obligations of land tenure, such as labour services and liability for manorial office, gradually disappeared as tenures became increasingly contractual, but the changed economic conditions meant that landlords were now

---

[16] Hanawalt, *Ties that Bound*, p. 63; Dyer, *Age of Transition?*, pp. 232–4. For the emergence of a leisure culture, and for examples of playing various games, see Bailey, *Marginal Economy*, pp. 169–70, 304; Bailey, 'Rural Society', pp. 163–6; McIntosh, *Controlling Misbehaviour*, pp. 96–7, 99; *HistA*, pp. 154–5; CUL Vanneck Ms, box 7, court held 1468; Bacon, *Annals*, p. 105. A mystery play was performed in Ixworth: see Dymond, *Thetford Priory*, p. 251.

[17] For the failure of heirs, and the break up of farms as a consequence, see Gottfried, *Epidemic Disease*, pp. 194, 204–5; Denney, *Sibton Abbey*, pp. 20–1.

forced to understand the individual circumstances and difficulties of their tenants better, negotiating concessions on tenures and managing rent arrears on a case-by-case basis. In addition, the ability and inclination of landlords to regulate the wider life of their tenants through their manorial courts diminished, as the feudal incidents associated with life cycle (such as merchet and childwite) disappeared.

This changing relationship is reflected in changes to the business of manorial courts. In the third quarter of the fourteenth century court income had increased on some manors, as the disruption to the land market in the aftermath of the Black Death, and the determination of lords to reassert their authority over serfs, enlarged the volume of business. Thereafter the volume of business fell almost everywhere, as reflected in a reduction in the number of court sessions (most met just twice a year in the fifteenth century) and a decline in curial income, especially after 1400: by *c.* 1500 few manor courts yielded more than £5 per annum and most yielded less than £3. For example, annual court revenue at Southwold fell by 25 per cent between the 1340s and 1380s; that at Kingston fell from an average of 59s. in the 1360s, to 41s. 8d. in the 1410s and 28s. 6d. in the 1430s; from 79s. 8d. at Laxfield in the 1380s, to 41s. 6d. in the 1420s and 23s. 5d. in the 1480s and 1490s; and at Wetheringsett from 44s. 9d. in the 1420s to 25s. 1d. in the 1440s. These examples are taken from relatively busy courts on large manors, yet many Suffolk manorial courts sat infrequently and yielded little income. In the 1480s the manorial courts of Cranely and Old Newton were not held each year because of a lack of business, the leet of Cotton had nothing to present in 1480, and in 1442 no court was held at Gislingham Geneys.[18] Declining income was exacerbated by mounting difficulties in collecting fines and amercements, which in the mid-fifteenth century proved a particular problem at places like Brandon and Lakenheath, but as early as 1379 the Melton auditor acknowledged that two huge merchets totaling 33s. 4d. were impossible to collect from two women serfs.[19]

The decline in the revenue from manor courts had a number of causes: the contracting number of tenants, a fall in the volume of personal pleas and cases brought by local residents, dwindling attendance (through both demographic decline and growing indifference), the decay of villeinage and serfdom, and the willingness of tenants to use other courts to pursue their claims. The mechanisms of many manorial courts deteriorated through their waning powers of

[18] Dyer, 'Social and Economic Background', p. 29; Whittle, *Agrarian Capitalism*, pp. 48–50; Holmes, *Higher Nobility*, p. 156; CUL Vanneck Ms, box 8 (Laxfield); CUL EDC 7/14/C/25, 27, 37, 38, 43, 45 (Kingston); SROI HD1538/416 (Wetheringsett); SROI HD1538/384/1 (Cranely, Newton); SROB E7/1/1 (Cotton); SROI HD1538/237/12 (Gislingham).

[19] Bacon Ms 670–89; Bailey, *Marginal Economy*, pp. 269–73; CUL EDC 7/16/11/22 (Melton).

enforcement and the declining co-operation of, and attendance by, tenants. The main coercive levers available to lords – the system of pledging and the seizure of a tenant's land for non-compliance with the court's decisions – had lost their power in the economic conditions of the fifteenth century. Disputes were logged, but their outcome seldom reported, and juries became more lax in reporting misdemeanours. The presentment jury of Cretingham in the 1470s failed to amerce William Skynner of Brandeston for illegally occupying and cultivating 120 acres of the manorial demesne for three years, yet they could scarcely have failed to notice his activities. In 1404 a sizeable 40s. penalty was imposed upon the constable and capital pledges of Thorpe Morieux for their failure to maintain the village stocks.[20]

Ordinary people were also less amenable to requests from estate officials to compile new manorial rentals and extents, not least because the process was time-consuming and offered little direct benefit to them. The lord's steward made repeated calls in the 1380s for the homage of Walton to draw up a new custumal after the original had been triumphantly burnt during the Revolt of 1381, and in 1384 he finally lost patience with the homage of Trimley, and amerced them a hefty 20s. for their inactivity. The suitors of Dunningworth failed to respond to similar requests in the late 1390s, taking ten more years to complete the task, and, after repeated problems in the 1420s, exasperated officials at Staverton threatened tenants in 1449 with a £5 penalty if they did not update the manorial rental. The earl of Suffolk's steward regularly ordered the tenants of Ufford to draw up a new rental in the 1390s, and experienced similar reluctance when the rental needed updating again in the 1430s.[21] Estate administration was an arduous task in the fifteenth century, requiring tact, patience and no little skill.

LANDLORDS

The widespread problems of declining revenues from land and perquisites presented the upper ranks of Suffolk society with a severe financial challenge. In the thirteenth century they had taken the risk of exploiting many of their manors directly and, in very favourable agrarian conditions, had enjoyed handsome financial yields. However, in the much less favourable conditions of the fifteenth century many landlords minimized their exposure to risk, and opted overwhelmingly for the security of leasing their manorial assets, so that any

---

[20] SROI HD1538/357/5, mm. 5, 11, 13, 27, 31, 34, 41 and /6, mm. 1–4 (Eyke); SROI HA10/50/18/5.1 (Cretingham); SROB 1700/1/3 (Thorpe Morieux).

[21] SROI HA119/50/3/17, mm. 11, 13, 15, 17 (Trimley); SROI HD1538/207/3–4 (Dunningworth); SROI HD1538/357/5, mm. 19, 27, 28, 93 (Staverton); SROI HD1538/394/2 (Ufford).

rewards accrued to the lessee. This helped to stabilize their income streams, but reduced the prospect of financial windfalls. The fall in manorial revenues, which constituted the main source of seigneurial income, was dramatic and sustained. Large manors, which in *c.* 1300 had often generated in excess of £100 per annum, seldom produced more than £40–70 per annum by the middle of the fifteenth century. For example, Staverton manor had generated cash income of £90 when directly exploited in 1330, but only £59 when largely at lease in 1400, and by the 1470s perhaps as little as £40, while Melton had yielded between £25 and £30 per annum in the 1330s, but less than £20 in the 1450s. The manor of Wetheringsett produced a cash yield of £26 in 1427, but a combination of arrears and falling rent levels meant that in 1447 only £10 was paid to the lord. In 1435 not one of the Suffolk manors leased by the cellarer of Bury St Edmunds generated more than £50, and most produced between £10 and £20. There is some evidence that manorial yields began to rise again at the very end of the fifteenth century, but any recovery was tentative and small scale.[22]

The declining revenues from land posed a threat to the financial stability of seigneurial households. Unfortunately, accurately charting and measuring their fortunes is impossible due to the dearth of long series of household accounts, but the 1380s and 1390s, and the 1440s to the 1470s – when land and product prices dropped dramatically – were critical periods. When faced with a squeeze on their income, lords had three options. First, they could liquidate some of their fixed assets or mortgage some of their land in order to cover a deficit, but this was clearly a drastic and short-term solution. It is likely that the sale of profitable dairy herds and sheep flocks, and the shift to demesne leasing, on some manors in the 1390s and 1400s was driven by an urgent need for cash as levels of seigneurial income contracted sharply. The thorough evaluation of the capital value of timber stocks on the Suffolk manors of the Hastings family in the 1390s must reflect their preparedness, if necessary, to liquidate some of their most valuable assets. The earls of Oxford resorted to periodic and piecemeal asset-stripping of this kind, raising an extraordinary £34 in 1527–8 through sales of woodland products from Aldham, and in 1421 the abbot of St Edmund sold 10 acres of 'wood' – including young trees, undergrowth and faggots – in Chevington at 26s. 8d. per acre to generate a cash windfall of £14.[23]

---

[22] Hatcher, 'Great Slump', pp. 264–6, provides a general background; Hoppitt, 'Parks', pp. 182–3; CUL EDC 7/16/11/7–9, 36 (Melton); SROI HD1538/416 (Wetheringsett); BL Add. Ms 7096, f. 36; Simpson, *Wealth of the Gentry*, pp. 198–201, 203; Richmond, *John Hopton*, pp. 65, 74, 95; Bailey, *Marginal Economy*, pp. 279; R. I. Jack, ed., *The Grey of Ruthin Valor, 1467–8* (Sydney, 1965), p. 25.

[23] CUL Vanneck Ms, box 2 (Aldham); SROB E3/15.3/2.30 (Chevington).

The second option for landlords was to offset the falling financial yields from their assets by acquiring additional land to bolster their income, perhaps through a carefully planned marriage, and by obtaining income from other sources, such as in the service of the Crown or in the retinue of a greater lord. A few landlords were fortunate that new trading or industrial activities developed on their landed estates, such as Woodbridge priory, which benefited from the growth of the eponymous town during this period. In general, such opportunities were greatest for the lesser landlords, the most enterprising of whom took advantage of the misfortunes of others or the availability of cheap land to accumulate small manors into a larger estate and to rationalize their farming units: indeed, the small size of the average manor in Suffolk made them more readily affordable to the acquisitive and upwardly mobile lord. For example, a number of small manors in Bramford and Gislingham were consolidated into single ownership, and by the end of the fifteenth century Simon Wiseman had acquired a number of small manors in Yaxley, Gislingham, Cranely, Braiseworth, and Thornham Magna and Parva, which comprised the geographical core of a Suffolk estate that extended as far as Assington. Similarly, William Capel, himself the son of a minor lord from Stoke-by-Nayland, bought a number of small manors in south Suffolk after making his fortune in London, and the Hotot family acquired at least two manors around Stowmarket and other land in nearby villages. The gradual engrossment of numerous small manors into larger farming units is evident in the disappearance of many of the houses and farm buildings belonging to lower-status manorial sites during the fifteenth century, as the infrastructure required to support agriculture was rationalized and streamlined, and the number of lesser landlords declined.[24]

The third option available to landlords looking to improve their financial position was to reduce household expenditure, because the problem of falling revenues was exacerbated by the rising costs of labour, which swelled the wage bills necessary to run the household and estate. One obvious option was to reduce the size of the household, which usually comprised a significant number of servants and retainers: although Butley priory contained only twelve canons at the time of its dissolution in 1538, its household included seventy-two other people. The number of monks resident at Bury St Edmunds abbey fell by about 40 per cent between the late thirteenth and mid-fifteenth century, and the number of canons at Blythburgh priory fell from seven to four during the course of the fifteenth century, with an implied reduction in the number of servants. A reduction in household size was only one aspect

[24] *VCH*, ii, p. 111 (Woodbridge); *AHEW*, iii, p. 563; *SR* 42 (2004), p. 32; Copinger, *Manors of Suffolk*, iii, pp. 271–2; SROI HD1538/384/1; Bailey, *Marginal Economy*, pp. 51–3; Poos, *Rural Society*, p. 213; Amor, 'Late Medieval Enclosure', p. 192–3.

of cost control, yet many seigneurial households struggled to maintain a culture of careful cost management over major areas of expenditure: none of this was particularly new in the late Middle Ages, but the financial margins for manœuvre were now much narrower, and lords could face spiralling indebtedness with few opportunities for stabilizing their deteriorating financial position. The difficulties of controlling expenditure were greater in larger households, where the authority for financial decision-making was spread across a number of officials. The household of the cellarer of Bury St Edmunds abbey overspent its income in almost every year during the early fifteenth century, prompting an energetic new abbot – William Curteys – to introduce extensive financial reforms in the mid-1430s. Curteys imposed precise monetary allowances for expenditure on the monks' supplies, including a fixed cost per capita for bread, ale, meat, fish and potage, and thus he calculated that the fifty-two monks should cost precisely £338 per year to feed and clothe. Other legitimate expenses and outgoings produced a budgeted expenditure of £885 per annum, which returned a projected surplus of £117 per annum on the cellarer's income. As the very notion of a fixed budget was alien to the culture of large medieval households, imposing it consistently represented an even greater challenge.[25]

The best examples of prudent household management tend to be drawn from the smaller seigneurial households – the type that dominated lordly society in medieval Suffolk – where the head of the household could maintain a strong interest in the accounts, and control over them, and thus personally establish and enforce a culture of thrift: such values were more difficult to impose over larger and more complex households, such as the abbey of Bury St Edmunds. John Hopton maintained his finances carefully during the mid-fifteenth-century slump by retaining the services of experienced personnel and by his active and personal interest in all aspects of estate management, from purchasing bullocks to waiving court fines. Ixworth priory was also prudently managed, enabling the construction of a substantial new brick gatehouse during the recession of the 1450s. Bungay priory contained a prioress and nine nuns in the late fifteenth century – around half its pre-plague size – by which time it generated an income of around £60 per annum. Margaret Dalenger's rule as prioress (1465–90) had left the house with a number of debts, but her successor – Elizabeth Stevenson – was a remarkably robust and effective financial manager. Stevenson began her rule determinedly in 1490 by paying off Dalenger's debts to various merchants of Norwich and Bungay, and she took personal control of the finances of the household and the estate, writing the accounts of both in an immaculate fashion. Within four years she

[25] *Letters and Papers, Foreign and Domestic, of the Reign of Henry VIII, 1509–1547* (HMSO, 1864–1932), vol. 13, I, p. 149; *VCH*, ii, pp. 68–9; Harper-Bill, *Blythburgh*, i, p. 3; BL Add. Ms 7096, f. 37.

had supervised the creation of new rentals and extents for all of the priory's landed possessions, a clear sign of her prudential intent, and under her direction the community lived sensibly within its means. After heavy losses in the late fourteenth century, Rumburgh priory had managed to stabilize its income at around £40 per annum by the second half of the fifteenth century. Although it managed to reduce its debts gradually during this period, it did so at the cost of a frugal existence for the prior and two monks.[26]

The financial troubles of seigneurial households in the late Middle Ages were potentially greatest for the ecclesiastical landlords. They were legally restricted from increasing their landholdings after the 1290s, and their financial difficulties were exacerbated by a fall in the level of charitable donations from lay people and by the sharp decline in income from spiritualities, such as tithes and oblations from parish churches. Fifteenth-century wills reveal that only the friars continued to receive much financial support from the lower orders of lay society, and hardly any of Suffolk's wealthy clothiers in the late fifteenth century left bequests to the older religious houses: among those in Bury St Edmunds, for example, only John Coket bequeathed any money to the great abbey and he confined himself to a nominal 12d. to the shrine of St Edmund in 1479. The fall in revenues from spiritualities contributed significantly to the declining income of Blythburgh priory, which dropped from around £86 per annum in 1291 to about £50 in the 1530s, while Herringfleet priory experienced bouts of financial difficulty. By the early sixteenth century Butley priory was heavily in debt, and the colleges of Mettingham and Stoke-by-Clare had insufficient revenue to meet their liabilities. Such landlords were asset rich but increasingly cash poor, struggling to maintain the lifestyles enjoyed by their thirteenth-century predecessors. It is no coincidence that after the Black Death few ambitious monastic building projects were undertaken in Suffolk. The fabric of the abbey of Bury St Edmunds, and the quality of its workmanship, reached its greatest extent in the thirteenth century – at the peak of the monastery's income from its landed estates – but thereafter building activity mainly comprised repairs rather than new projects, not least when the collapse of the west tower in 1430 and a serious fire in 1465 required extensive and expensive renovation. A humble monastic house such as Rumburgh priory could scarcely afford to keep its fabric in decent order in the fifteenth century, and could certainly not contemplate any substantial rebuilding or extensions; and the buildings of Butley priory became particularly run

---

[26] Richmond, *John Hopton*, pp. 46, 95–9; SROB 553/112 (Ixworth); *VCH*, ii, pp. 81–2; SROI HD1538/156/14–15; M. Oliver, *The Convent and the Community in Late Medieval England: Female Monasteries in the Diocese of Norwich, 1350–1540* (Woodbridge, 1998), pp. 90–9, although her argument that female houses were better managed than those of males (pp. 100–1) does not stand scrutiny on the evidence provided; Heale, 'Rumburgh Priory', pp. 10–15.

down. The exception was Leiston abbey, which had resolved before the advent of pestilence in 1349 to move from its 'bleak and inconvenient site' to a new location further inland. Yet this exception proved the rule, because, in pressing ahead with its ambitious plans, and rebuilding the conventual buildings in the gothic style on its present site in the 1360s and 1370s, the abbey saddled itself with crippling debts for years. Some of the smallest religious houses with modest endowments failed to survive the demanding economic conditions of the fifteenth century.[27]

The mean condition of ecclesiastical buildings was paralleled by the dilapidation of many lesser manorial residences in the later Middle Ages, as tiny manors were engrossed into larger estates and their residential and agricultural buildings became surplus to requirements. Yet a few surviving manor houses were rebuilt in expensive and impressive style, emphasizing the point that some seigneurial fortunes were maintained or made in this period. The most modest improvements might involve the construction of raised aisle halls, with separate kitchen and chamber blocks, and the addition of more ornate and ostentatious roofs. More ambitious projects involved the construction of entirely new manor houses or the significant rebuilding of old ones. Bedfield Hall, Otley Hall and Wantisden Hall were all extensively rebuilt in the mid-fifteenth century on a grander scale than their predecessors. The Hotot family acquired lesser manors around Stowmarket, and in the late fourteenth century constructed a new manor house at Columbine Hall on the edge of the moat, rather in the centre, to conjure a more dramatic appearance to approaching visitors, a project which required the sinking of extensive flint foundations to support the structure against the moat. Its appearance was almost certainly inspired by the design and appearance of Wingfield castle, built by the earl of Suffolk in the 1380s (plate 1).[28]

The builders of these new manor houses were often those successful minor landlords who had accumulated manors and built up other landholdings during the course of the later Middle Ages. There had been over one thousand minor landlords in Suffolk in 1300, many of them relatively impoverished and historically anonymous. By *c.* 1500 their number had contracted by perhaps

---

[27] Northeast, *Wills*, i, pp. xlviii–xlix, and see also Middleton-Stewart, *Inward Piety*, p. 57 for a similar reluctance to donate to religious houses in east Suffolk; Amor, 'Jack of All Trades', p. 424; Heale, 'Rumburgh Priory', p. 11; Harper-Bill, *Blythburgh*, i, p. 23; A. Jessopp, ed., *Visitations of the Diocese of Norwich, 1492–1532*, Camden Society 43 (London, 1888), pp. 131–2, 152, 154, 178, 186; *PSIA* 39 (1998), pp. 127–50; *PSIA* 40 (2001), pp. 12–13; Mortimer, *Leiston Abbey*, pp. 5, 7–8; *VCH*, ii, pp. 91, 99–101, 107, for the closure of Alnesbourne, Chipley and Kersey priories, and the difficulties of Herringfleet.

[28] *HistA*, pp. 60, 174–81; *PSIA* 38 (1993), pp. 107–8; *PSIA* 38 (1994), pp. 229–30; *PSIA* 31 (1983), p. 242; Amor, 'Late Medieval Enclosure', pp. 192–4.

one-half, yet many of these later lords were conspicuously wealthier than their predecessors. In 1327 fewer than thirty vills in Suffolk had contained one person whose taxable wealth dominated the vill in which he resided, but by 1524 a single dominant individual now existed in over 180. Many of these individuals were resident lords, often described as 'gentleman', a new title which had emerged during the course of the fifteenth century. The 1524 Lay Subsidy records the presence of twenty knights and dozens of gentlemen in Suffolk. The emergence of a specific label for this bottom layer of genteel society was partly a social convention to distinguish them from the upper ranks of the yeomanry, but it also recognized their growing involvement in some form of royal service. So, although the status of gentleman was mainly determined by wealth (annual income between £5 and £40), it could also be determined by birthright or service. This explains how William Heigham of Wickhambrook and Thomas Knighton of Little Bradley could be both described as gentleman in 1524, even though William was assessed on goods rated at £50, compared with Thomas's £3 in land. Similarly, Robert Crane was not very wealthy, earning a mere £10 over a two-year period in the late 1430s from his work as an active Justice of the Peace, but his political service to the Crown, if not his wealth, marked him out as a gentleman: indeed, Maddern notes that the most hardworking and regular Justices of the Peace serving in Suffolk in the 1430s were drawn heavily from these ranks. Roger Virgoe estimates that fewer than fifty of such men effectively ran local government in late-medieval Suffolk. Hence the typical late fifteenth-century Suffolk 'gentleman' may have been a distant social relation of the relatively impoverished resident landlord of the late thirteenth century, in that both represented the lowest ranks of seigneurial society, but the later gentlemen were fewer in number, wealthier and wielded greater political influence.[29]

The balance of political power shifted perceptibly away from the nobility towards the gentry during the course of the fifteenth century, and the emergence of some sectors of the gentry as an ambitious, aggressive, acquisitive, pushy and politically adept group is well established in the historical literature. Some made their fortunes as career soldiers or lawyers, while others were farmers or businessmen who were also active in local politics as government officials. William Phelip of Dennington is a good example of the career soldier, who rose rapidly in Henry V's household and became sufficiently influential before his death at the battle of Agincourt to be courted for political favours by the burgesses of Dunwich. Lawyers such as John Staverton of Rendlesham

---

[29] *AHEW*, iii, pp. 562–3; Poos, *Rural Society*, p. 213; *HistA*, pp. 80–1; *1524 Lay Subsidy*, pp. xviii, 295–6; P. C. Maddern, *Violence and Social Order: East Anglia, 1422–1442* (Oxford, 1992), pp. 61–4; Carpenter, *Locality and Polity*, pp. 44–6; Barron *et al.*, *Selected Papers of Roger Virgoe*, pp. 30–1.

and John Glemham earned enough money from a variety of sources – regular appointments on royal commissions, their work as Justices of the Peace in Suffolk, and annual retainers from local gentry and burgesses – to purchase small manors and establish themselves as resident landlords. John Ulveston of Henham was a more powerful and influential lawyer, closely associated with the circle of the earls of Suffolk, whose political career consequently fluctuated with changes in national politics. Thomas Spring III of Lavenham, the great clothier, invested much of his profits from textiles in the purchase of sixteen manors in Suffolk and another ten elsewhere. Some members of the gentry had an impressive number of strings to their bow: John Timperley, an esquire of Hintlesham, directly exploited three manors, and in the 1450s he was also in the service of both the earl of Oxford and the duke of Norfolk.[30]

The growing local political power of the gentry does not imply their segregation from the nobility or from the national political scene. Fifteenth-century society remained hierarchical and deferential, where bonds of loyalty, honour and obedience still drew some of the gentry into the affinities of greater lords, and, by extension, into aristocratic rivalries. The escalation of national political tension between the 1430s and 1450s had discernible local consequences in east Suffolk, because of the presence through residence of two competing noblemen. In this period the earl of Suffolk influenced society in central and north-east Suffolk to an exceptional degree, mainly as a consequence of the strength of his position in the court of Henry VI. A number of local gentry became embroiled in the feud between the earl (who supported the Lancastrian cause) and the duke of Norfolk (an ardent Yorkist). For example, James Andrew, a supporter of the earl of Suffolk, was ambushed and murdered by a small group led by Gilbert Debenham of Little Wenham, a leading gentry administrator on the estates of the duke of Norfolk; and Sir William Wolf, a leading Justice of the Peace in the 1430s, affiliated to the Suffolk faction, was involved in a well-documented dispute with Sir Robert Wingfield, one of Norfolk's men. The fate of Andrew was exceptional according to Maddern, who argues that the threat of violence through ritual challenges was more commonplace than its actuality in these factional rivalries, and that most disputes – however vehement – were resolved peacefully through legal means in fifteenth-century East Anglia. This argument may understate the extent of low-level thuggery and open intimidation in this period, such as that perpetrated upon John Paston and his allies by Charles Nowell of Shelland. Yet it is true that the worst violence was usually the work of social misfits rather than emanating from feuds between noblemen. For example, between 1422 and 1439 John Belsham,

---

30 Horrox, 'Local and National Politics', pp. 391–402; Scarfe, *Suffolk in the Middle Ages*, p. 161; Bailey, *Dunwich*, pp. 10, 57; Richmond, *John Hopton*, pp. 198–201; McClenaghan, *Springs of Lavenham*, p. 77; Richmond, 'East Anglian Politics', pp. 194–5.

a gentleman of Hadleigh, was accused of fourteen serious crimes, including three murders and six assaults upon lowly officers of the law. None of these appears to have been politically motivated, because Belsham possessed few friends or supporters and was ostracized by local society: he was a hotheaded thug, with a pathological aversion to petty law enforcers.[31]

The careers of soldiers, lawyers (the *nouveau riche* of fifteenth-century Suffolk) and pushy newcomers are easier to reconstruct from extant sources than the careers of other members of the gentry, such as the successful yeomen who rose into the ranks of the gentry, or the enterprising minor landlords who bought up small manors, leased others and successfully extended their farming empires. Their lives are scarcely visible, mainly because they often remained politically inactive: as Chris Dyer ruefully remarks, 'the lesser gentry remain something of a mystery.' For example, John Barough of Bardwell was styled a 'gentleman' in his will of 1446, but we know nothing about him beyond the information contained therein. He bequeathed a small manor in Hessett to his wife and cash gifts amounting to £12, a decent rather than lavish sum. His personal possessions contained some fine and valuable objects, including a basilard harnessed with silver, a gold chain and cross, silver spoons and a fine scarlet cloak lined with fur, and, as befitted his status, he was to be buried in the chancel of Bardwell church. Yet we should not underestimate the significance of such people: indeed, their lives provide an important counterbalance to the stereotype of the fifteenth-century gentry. They were likely to be personally involved in the running of their estate, assiduous in their acquisition and management of their property and active lessees of the manors of wealthier landlords, while remaining politically neutral. John Hopton, a wealthy east Suffolk gentleman, was neither politically active nor politically indifferent, but instead attended to the needs of his estate and his family in an 'enterprising, sensible and responsible' manner. Part of the difficulty in tracing the lives of gentlemen farmers from this period is that local families could rise and fall with the wheel of fortune, and the heralded success of some families was paralleled by the silent failure of others. The striking success of the Hotots in building up an estate around Stowmarket in the later fourteenth century contrasts with their rapid decline within a century, because in the 1490s the family was seriously indebted and then died out. Failure of male heirs is the most common explanation for the disappearance of gentry families.[32]

31   Coss, 'Age of Deference', pp. 54–5; Virgoe, 'Murder of James Andrew', pp. 263–4; Barron *et al.*, *Selected Papers of Roger Virgoe*, pp. 53–62; H. Castor, *Blood and Roses: The Paston Family and the Wars of the Roses* (London, 2004), pp. 84–6; Maddern, *Violence and Social Order*, pp. 154–66, 223–5.

32   Dyer, *Age of Transition?*, pp. 97–108; Northeast, *Wills*, i, pp. 218–19; Richmond, *John Hopton*, p. 252; Amor, 'Late Medieval Enclosure', p. 194; Carpenter, *Locality and Polity*, chap. 4.

CONCLUSION

The Black Death brought terror, despair and a heightened fear of sudden and unpredictable death throughout society, but it also provided new opportunities, and, for many of those who survived, economic liberation. If the later Middle Ages was the golden age of pathogens, then it was also the golden age of opportunity. Ordinary people exercised more choice over where and when they worked, and therefore exercised greater control over their own destinies, than those who had lived before the Black Death. Hence the inhabitants of early Tudor Suffolk were fewer in number than those who had lived during the reign of Edward I, but they enjoyed a higher standard of living. Their houses were more comfortable and sturdy, their diet more balanced and tasty, their clothes better made and stylish, and their personal possessions more numerous and varied.

Although Suffolk society in general had become more affluent, the wealth of some social groups had increased more than others. The social structure of rural Suffolk in the early sixteenth-century was still dominated by smallholders, but their material comfort was unquestionably higher than that of their debt-ridden and impoverished predecessors in the thirteenth century. Smallholders in *c.* 1500 were mainly well-paid labourers and artisans, who chose to restrict their landed holdings to a few acres as a supplement to their primary income from trade or employment. In contrast, most smallholders in 1300 had been employed episodically and had been unable to acquire more land. Similarly, the long tail of landless people in *c.* 1300 had been significantly curtailed. Yet the greatest material gains had been achieved by the wealthy yeomen with substantial holdings who now occupied the upper ranks of local society, and their success had polarized the structure of landholding in many communities. They were tough, single-minded individuals who increasingly dominated the juries of manorial and leet courts, and thus were able to dictate social agendas within their communities to a far greater degree than their predecessors: they possessed growing social influence as well as greater economic strength. The large number of relatively poor and anonymous landlords – who had dominated Suffolk society in *c.* 1300 – diminished, and they were succeeded by fewer lords of greater local significance and personal wealth. Some of these gentlemen fulfilled a more clearly articulated and understood political role, perhaps as lawyers or within the affinities of powerful magnates. In *c.* 1500 aristocratic landlords no longer exploited their manors directly, and therefore were less prominent in the lives of local people. The overwhelming majority of Suffolk communities were dominated by a handful of yeomen and perhaps a single gentleman of modest wealth, all of whom were resident and active agriculturalists.

In *c.* 1500 the lower orders of society were not yet 'proletarian', because many labourers and artisans were also smallholders, and many artisans were self-employed workers in their own homes. The landholdings of yeomen and gentlemen were more recognizably 'capitalist', in the sense that they depended more heavily upon hired labour and were strongly geared towards commercial production. Unfortunately we cannot establish just how commercialized they were, due to the absence of many detailed farm accounts, so we cannot be certain of the extent to which they still orientated some production towards household consumption, or the extent to which their land was directly exploited rather than further sublet to others. Fifteenth-century Suffolk was economically and socially progressive, and already exhibited 'capitalist' traits, but its society did not yet conform to a fully fledged system of agrarian capitalism.

– CHAPTER 11 –

Towns, Trade and Industry, 1350–1500

THE expansion of weekly markets and small towns in the thirteenth century had been founded primarily upon local trade in raw and processed
foodstuffs, and in the provision of basic goods and services for nearby farms
and households. The severe and sustained demographic contraction after the
arrival of the Black Death reduced the volume of this commercial activity, and
by extension reduced the volume of trade passing through fairs, weekly markets and towns. Yet the scale of this reduction was not as great as the fall in
population, because consumption per head increased, and both the nature and
structure of local trade changed. One major consequence of the catastrophe in
1349 was that wages rose relative to land and grain prices, reflecting the scarcity
of labour, which also resulted in a rise in the disposable incomes of the lower
orders of society as wages and earnings increased. These improvements in the
living standards of ordinary people stimulated changes to patterns of demand,
such as the swing from grain to meat (especially beef), from crude domestic utensils to professionally manufactured goods, and from basic clothing to
more fashionable attire. Demand for produce made by occasional retailers and
casual craft workers diminished, while demand increased for quality wares
manufactured and distributed by professionals. Maryanne Kowaleski rightly
argues that these changes constituted the beginnings of a consumer revolution,
as ordinary people bought a larger quantity and wider range of goods and possessions. In order to meet this demand, most producers became increasingly
specialist: they operated in larger units of production and kept a sharp eye on
both the quality of their product and shifts in fashion. Cheap local manufactures produced by the village tailor, tanner or weaver were displaced by better-
quality goods manufactured by artisans living some distance away. These new
manufactures were fed through wide mercantile networks rather than peddled
in rural weekly markets, and merchants concentrated upon fewer centres of
trade instead of supplying a large number of local markets. Consequently,
trade became less diffuse and more focused upon those sites that were well
placed strategically. As Campbell states, 'the contribution of the pre-plague
period was to create an infrastructure of trade and exchange, the contribution
of the post-plague era was to rationalise and reconfigure it'.[1]

---

[1] Britnell, 'Urban Demand', pp. 11–14; Dyer, *Age of Transition?*, pp. 128–49; M.
Kowaleski, 'A Consumer Economy', in Horrox and Ormrod, *Social History* (2006),

TRADE AND MARKETING

The fall in the demand for basic foodstuffs, local crafts and services is reflected in a decline in the business transacted in weekly markets and fairs. The growth of markets and fairs in the thirteenth century had met the particular needs of traders and consumers at a time when the demand for food and raw materials was high, and when scores of casual traders sought outlets for their cheap and low-quality produce. However, this structure was less well suited to the different patterns of trade which emerged after 1350, and consequently many established markets and fairs suffered a widespread fall in revenue. Market tolls at Newmarket fell by 27 per cent between the 1400s and 1430s; and between the 1420s and 1470s the average annual income from its market court fell from 49s. 11d. to 8s. 11d., while that generated by its October fair fell from 50s. 7d. to 16s. 9d. The number of stalls leased in Sudbury market fell from 109 in 1337 to forty-two in 1401; in 1425 nine stalls in Clare market were described as abandoned; and income from stalls at Dunwich market fell from around 30s. per annum in the 1410s to just 11s. in the 1430s. The greatest difficulties were experienced during the slump of the mid-fifteenth century, which appears to have adversely affected all trading places. In the 1460s revenue from Blythburgh fair reached its lowest level, in 1465 a number of stalls in Mildenhall market had been abandoned for want of business, and fierce disputes between trading centres (such as the residents of Brandon and Thetford, and those of Ipswich and both Stowmarket and Bury St Edmunds), are symptomatic of harsh competition in a contracting market.[2]

Many of these examples are taken from established markets and towns, yet the decline in the volume of business in smaller rural markets and fairs was sufficient to cause them to cease trading altogether. Of the 100 or so weekly markets founded before 1350, only thirty-two survived into the sixteenth century. The most vulnerable markets were those located in settlements which were already small before 1350: only 19 per cent of markets survived to the sixteenth century in places whose assessed wealth in 1334 had been under £5. By 1391 the Friday market at Leiston had not been held for a number of years; in 1425 an inquiry noted that Wentford (Clare) fair had folded three years earlier for want of traders; and in the 1430s difficulties were experienced

p. 239; B. M. S. Campbell, 'England: Land and People', in Rigby, *Companion* (2003), p. 22.

2 SROB 1476/12, 13 and 359/3 (Newmarket); Britnell, *Colchester*, pp. 83–5; Grimwood and Kay, *Sudbury*, p. 86; PRO sc2/203/67, m. 3 (Clare); Bailey, *Dunwich*, pp. 20–1; Richmond, *John Hopton*, p. 42; BL Add. Roll 53138 (Mildenhall); Bacon Ms 296/25 (Brandon); Bacon, *Annals*, p. 113.

leasing booths for the June fair at Newmarket, which ceased trading soon afterwards. In the late 1390s the Saturday market of Laxfield was generating a paltry 12d. in tolls each year, and by the 1450s it had folded. In 1391 the tolls from Lidgate market were valued at 3s. 4d., yet by 1418 the tollhouse was being used as a pigsty. In 1422 some stalls were repaired and others reconstructed in an unsuccessful attempt to revive the market, but no evidence of further trade is forthcoming: on the contrary, later that decade at least three burgage plots were reported abandoned or ruinous, and by the 1460s two cottages in the bailey, where the market had been situated, were dilapidated. Most of the markets and fairs which survived the fifteenth-century purge were located in larger, established settlements; occupied key positions in the county's transport network, such as key river crossings or arterial routeways; or were situated on the borders of the county's various sub-regions, such as Mildenhall and Brandon on the Breck-fen edge, and Beccles, Saxmundham, Framlingham, Wickham Market, and Woodbridge on the edge of the claylands and the Sandlings.[3]

In a few places landlords tried to adapt to these challenging new circumstances by improving the facilities offered by their markets and fairs, or by changing the dates on which they were held. In 1472 Sir John Wingfield obtained a charter to hold two new fairs (in May and October) in Laxfield and to start a new market each Friday to replace the defunct Saturday one: in 1473 he spent 76s. realigning the old marketplace, clearing houses, and building new shops and stalls. His enterprise yielded mixed results. In the 1490s the two fairs generated a modest income of between 15d. and 4s. each year, although the new market was struggling to find tenants for its stalls and three of its eight shops. Stallage fees from Mildenhall market had risen from just under 9s. per annum in 1323 to around 13s. 8d. during the last two decades of the fourteenth century, but by 1411 they had fallen to just 4s. 5d. and the market was flagging. Consequently, in 1413 royal assent was acquired to switch the market day from Tuesday to Friday, and to change the fair from 1 August to 29 September. The river Lark was dredged to ensure that boats had good access to the fair site; ten new stalls were built for the market; an existing shop was temporarily converted for use as a tollhouse; and a new shambles was constructed in the market square (plate 7). In the next year, 1414, the combined income

---

3 For the 'rationalization' of markets and fairs, see J. Masschaele, 'The Multiplicity of Medieval Markets Reconsidered', *Journal of Historical Geograhy* 20 (1994), pp.255–71. Davis, 'Petty Traders', pp. 28–31; *HistA*, pp. 76–7; Mortimer, *Leiston Abbey*, p. 25; Thornton, *History of Clare*, p. 178; SROB 1476/1, m. 21 (Newmarket); CUL Vanneck Ms, box 8 (Laxfield). The Lidgate evidence is drawn from PRO DL43/4/3, f. 23; SROB E3/11/1.3, court held November 1418; E3/11/1.4, courts held November 1422, October 1425, October 1426, May 1427 and May 1460; E3/11/1.5, courts held April 1462 and August 1470.

from the new fair and market was a handsome 27s. 3d., and the enterprise still generated over 22s. in 1465.[4]

The changing structure and nature of trade is well illustrated by changes in the brewing industry, which gradually transformed from small-scale production, undertaken by large numbers of casual brewers in domestic settings, to large-scale production in the hands of smaller numbers of commercial brewers. Yet the price for ale and beer remained relatively cheap, costing a mere 2d. per gallon, so that it was readily affordable to the masses, who increasingly enjoyed the sociability and conviviality of drinking together in ale-houses and taverns run by those commercial brewers. The disappearance of casual and occasional ale brewers from small towns was particularly marked. In the 1340s around seventy brewers were operating each year in Sudbury and thirty in Lakenheath, but by the 1420s the number had halved in Sudbury, and by the 1480s only four brewers remained active in Lakenheath. Brewing in fifteenth-century Brandon and Newmarket became concentrated into the hands of a small number of leading residents, many of whom also ran successful taverns and were therefore experienced producers with established markets. The professionalization of brewing and the disappearance of casual producers meant that the quality and consistency of ale improved, and during the course of the fifteenth century drinkers in ports such as Dunwich, Ipswich and Walberswick also began to acquire a taste for beer (which, unlike ale, contained hops) brewed by immigrant Dutchmen. The structure of the baking industry underwent a similar transformation: the number of casual bakers operating in weekly markets declined markedly, but those who remained in the trade were usually professional bakers producing bread of decent quality for regular customers. Their produce could acquire a reputation and a client base beyond their home town, so that Augustus Baxter of Ipswich travelled to Felixstowe each week to sell his bread, and in the 1410s bakers from Theberton and Middleton kept regular stalls in Dunwich market.[5]

The collapse in the numbers of active bakers and brewers contrasts with the rising proportion of butchers operating in many towns, reflecting the growing consumption of meat and the relative buoyancy of the pastoral economy. For example, butchers comprised 24 per cent of all food retailers amerced in Sudbury market in the 1340s compared with 35 per cent in the 1390s, and they dominated trade in the markets of fifteenth-century

---

4 Letters, *Markets and Fairs*, pp. 331, 333; CUL Vanneck Ms, box 8 (Laxfield); Bodleian Suffolk Roll 23 and BL Add. Roll 53116; SROB E18/455/1–2; BL Add. Rolls 53127, 53130, 53131, 53138 (Mildenhall); *PSIA* 23 (1939), p. 22.

5 For a general survey of brewing, see Bennett, *Ale, Beer and Brewsters*. Davis, 'Petty Traders', pp. 238–42; PRO SC2/203/63–72 (Sudbury); Bailey, *Marginal Economy*, pp. 261–2; Kowaleski, 'Consumer Economy', p. 243; BL Add. Rolls 40710, 40722 (Dunwich).

Dunwich and Newmarket. In the 1420s and 1430s the income from the meat and leather trades in Dunwich market was twice that from the sale of grain, and in the 1440s the income from butchers' stalls in Woodbridge was four times greater than that generated by bakers and grocers. A growing number of butchers were also graziers, fattening stock themselves as well as selling the hides and skins. John Wolsey resided in the stock-rearing area of Yoxford, and kept a butcher's shop in Dunwich as an outlet for his produce.[6]

The contraction of income from, and the disappearance of, many markets and fairs reflects a change in the structure and nature of marketing as well as a fall in the volume of trade. Public trading in weekly markets and seasonal fairs was gradually supplanted by 'private' deals struck in taverns or by purchases from shops open daily. The burgesses of Ipswich announced a succession of measures in the fifteenth century to prevent the leakage of trade from the market to other locations within the borough and at other times: for example, throughout the 1460s and 1470s attempts were made to ensure that butchers sold their produce from market stalls at fixed times, rather than from their own homes where their hours of business were more flexible. The local shop – open daily and selling a wider variety of goods – became more important in the fifteenth century. For example, the dramatic fall in income from the weekly market at Newmarket contrasts markedly with the rising income from shops and stalls, which grew from £4 4s. in the 1440s to over £6 in the 1470s. Many regular stallholders had gradually encroached upon the marketplace land by converting them into permanent shops with windows to display their wares daily, so that by 1472 there were twice as many shops as stalls there. By the 1430s a number of stalls in Botesdale market had been replaced by cottages and shops, at which date more than twenty-five shops were recorded in the marketplace at Dunwich, and by the 1490s eight shops are explicitly identified around the old marketplace in Laxfield, while the market itself was struggling. Some shops were large and profitable, judging by the combined rent of 17s. 6d. per annum paid for two in Mildenhall market. Architectural evidence of shop fronts in timber-framed buildings has recently been uncovered in places such as Debenham.[7]

[6] A good general discussion of the meat and leather trades appears in M. Kowaleski, *Local Markets and Regional Trade in Medieval Exeter* (Cambridge, 1991), pp. 293–300; PRO SC2/203/63–72 (Sudbury); May, *Newmarket*, p. 45; Bailey, *Dunwich*, pp. 20–1; BL Add Roll 40722; SROI HD1538/435/3 (Woodbridge).

[7] Bacon, *Annals*, pp. 105, 128, 134, 139, 148–9; May, *Newmarket*, pp. 43–5, SROB 1476/12 and 359/3; *PSIA* 40 (2004), p. 526; PRO SC11/886 (Dunwich); CUL Vanneck Ms, box 8 (Laxfield); BL Add. Roll 53116 (Mildenhall), and a number of other shops emerged along the north end of Mill street SROI E18/400/1.3, f. 38; *Eavesdropper* 29 (2005), pp. 5, 11–12.

The structure and nature of overseas trade also changed subtly in the later Middle Ages. Contacts with the Low Countries remained important, links with the Baltic and south-west France continued to be nourished, yet new commercial opportunities opened up with Icelandic merchants as a consequence of changes in the fishing industry. Grain exports were still relatively unimportant. The wool trade declined markedly, but the export of woollen textiles – and probably cheeses and hides – rose sharply, albeit from a small base. Thus around 2,000 sacks of wool were exported annually from Ipswich in the early fourteenth century, but hardly any cloth, compared with only about 1,000 sacks two centuries later and about 2,000 broadcloths. The rapid growth of textile manufacturing in Suffolk, and its development into an industry geared towards exports, is reflected in the threefold growth of Ipswich's estimated share of England's overseas trade, from 0.7 per cent in 1204 to 2.1 per cent in 1478–82. The volume of cloth exported from Ipswich expanded dramatically between the 1350s and the 1430s, by which time it handled 8 per cent of England's cloth exports. Its success contrasts markedly with the decline of other East Anglian ports, such as Lynn and Yarmouth, which failed to adapt to the changing structure of late medieval trade. However, after the 1430s Ipswich lost ground, as local textiles were increasingly exported through London and as Hanseatic merchants drifted away from both Ipswich and Colchester: Ipswich had handled 4.1 per cent of alien trade in England in 1324–9, but only 1.1 per cent in 1478–82. Furthermore, it lost some of its influence in the wine trade with the Baltic and south-west France.[8]

INDUSTRY

Woollen textiles

After the Black Death the manufacture of woollen textiles grew into a major industrial activity in Suffolk. In *c.* 1300 the extent of textile manufacture had been mainly limited to a few urban centres (Bury St Edmunds, Sudbury and Clare) and a handful of industrializing rural settlements, but thereafter the scale of output increased dramatically and production spread to other centres nearby. Woollen textile manufacture represents the outstanding example of a late medieval boom industry, and its success, and the high levels of wealth it generated, are conspicuous in the quality of surviving domestic buildings, and the splendour of perpendicular churches, dating from this period in south Suffolk: contrary to popular belief and the confident assertions of travel guides, these churches owed their splendour to the wealth created by woollen textiles not wool itself.[9]

[8] *UH*, i, pp. 477–9, 490, and table 19.4; Britnell, *Colchester*, p. 175.

[9] McClenaghan, *Springs of Lavenham*, pp. 29–41.

The surge in English textile manufacture in the 1330s and 1340s scarcely faltered in the wake of the Black Death, and from the mid-1350s English cloth exports to the Baltic and south-west France increased markedly. Expanding foreign markets were supplemented by the rapid growth of the domestic market during the second half of the fourteenth century, as rising standards of living among the lower orders of society stimulated a greater demand for clothes which were both fashionable and made from decent-quality cloth. Measuring the exact extent of this growth is impossible from the fragmentary evidence, but during this period the English market for cloth may have doubled, and foreign markets quadrupled. Suffolk producers were quick to seize these new opportunities. A tax levied by the borough authorities on looms indicates that weaving activity peaked in the 1350s and 1360s in Sudbury, when textile manufacture was also buoyant in Clare. The aulnage accounts – which record the sale of woollen cloths in England – show that Suffolk producers increased their share of national output from 3.5 per cent in the 1350s to 5.7 per cent in the 1390s. Unfortunately, the survival and accuracy of aulnage accounts is patchy, but the next reliable batch from the 1460s reveals that cloth making in Suffolk had grown faster than in any other area of England. Its output had increased fourfold since the 1390s, and the county now accounted for 13.2 per cent of all English production (compared with the 2.1 per cent contributed by Norfolk producers): Suffolk manufacturers had captured a rising share of an expanding market. This impressive performance does not imply that the textile industry enjoyed a long period of sustained and uninterrupted growth, because the 1410s and 1420s, and the 1450s and early 1460s, appear to have been periods of contraction. Yet, overall, Suffolk had risen to become England's pre-eminent textile manufacturing county.[10]

Ascertaining exactly the types of cloth produced in Suffolk during this period is frustratingly difficult, because extant sources tend to describe the size and quantity of cloth rather than its style. The sale of woollen textiles was regulated by statute, which dictated that cloths produced for either export or wholesale in domestic markets had to fit one of three standard sizes. 'Broadcloths' measured roughly 28 × 1¾ yards, and were usually the heaviest and better-quality cloths; 'straits', or narrow cloths, were a quarter the size of broadcloths, measuring about 13 × 1 yards; and 'dozens' were half-length broadcloths, measuring about 13 × 1¾ yards. In contrast, 'kerseys' could be exported or sold wholesale without conforming to these statutory sizes. In the 1390s twice as

[10]   R. H. Britnell, 'The Woollen Textile Industry of Suffolk in the Later Middle Ages', *The Ricardian* 13 (2003), p. 86, 89; H. Heaton, *The Yorkshire Woollen and Worstead Industries* (Oxford, 1920), pp. 86–9; Britnell, *Colchester*, pp. 20–1, 83–5; Thornton, *History of Clare*, pp. 143–79; *HistA*, pp. 140–1; Redstone, 'Social Condition', pp. 195–8.

many straits as broadcloths were produced in Suffolk, although by the 1460s broadcloths had become the main focus of production.[11]

Suffolk cloths did not conform to a single or standard type, but were produced in an eclectic variety of styles and colours. This indicates that many different sorts of cloth were being manufactured within the county for different markets, and local producers were particularly adept at adapting to changes in fashion. The finest cloths produced in Suffolk were heavier broadcloths destined mainly for export, such as the famous Lavenham blues, although even these only rated in the middle band of medieval cloths on quality: they did not compare with the luxury Flemish cloths or the finest English products. Some lighter cloths of various colours were also sold overseas, known as 'settcloth' and 'vesses cloth', many of which were probably cheap imitations of the luxury cloths of Ypres, Bruges and Ghent. Although there is no evidence to suggest that many Flemish weavers settled in Suffolk during this period, the county was widely exposed to Flemish influences and consequently the style of its cloth would have been well known locally.[12]

Much of Suffolk's output between *c.* 1350 and *c.* 1450 was pitched at the lower end of the domestic market, supplying good-value cloth to the masses of ordinary people whose disposable incomes had risen sharply after the Black Death. Lighter and less costly cloths such as straits and kerseys were especially popular, both at home and abroad, and the taste for bright and varied colours reflects a growing awareness of fashion in clothing. The targeting of products at the lower end of the market explains the wide variety of cloth styles produced both across the county and within individual towns, in contrast to Colchester's preoccupation with russet broadcloths and Norwich with worsteds. For example, both russet boadcloths and straits in various colours were produced in Stowmarket; William Odeham, a Bury clothier, handled red kerseys, and straits in russet, blue and green; Hadleigh was renowned for its lightweight straits in a range of bright colours, especially violet; producers around Woodbridge made blankets, linens, and violet woollens; and growing references to hemp in the court rolls of Brandon imply an interest in linen manufacture to complement its production of straits. The rapid growth in the relative importance of the London economy would have strengthened demand there for exactly these sorts of cloths, and the proximity of south Suffolk meant that local manufacturers were well positioned

---

[11] Dymond and Betterton, *Lavenham*, p. 37; Thornton, *History of Clare*, p. 147; Amor, 'Jack of All Trades', pp. 421–2.

[12] The lack of immigrant Flemings is noted by Redstone, 'Social Condition', pp. 175–6, while strong Flemish influences are documented in *VCH*, i, p. 637, Hybel, 'Grain Trade', p. 221, and Martin, 'Little Wenham Hall', p. 160.

to supply this market. In *c.* 1400 trading connections between London south and east Suffolk were strong.[13]

The argument that Suffolk producers made an eclectic range of cloths in various styles across the lower to middling sectors of the textile market is further strengthened by the widely varied origins of the raw materials used in their manufacture, which differed according to the type and quality of cloth. The better-quality cloths – such as the Lavenham blues – tended to be made from higher-grade wool, sourced from the east Midlands, and were dyed using fine foreign dyestuffs such as woad and alum obtained through Colchester and London merchants. Yet the lower-grade cloths were made from local wool, which tended to be coarser and lighter in weight, and may have made more use of locally supplied madder. Wool from the main sheep flocks in the Breckland was sold locally, and occasionally farther afield in places like Bungay, and that from the demesne flock in Tattingstone was regularly purchased in bulk by dealers in East Bergholt, Hadleigh and Ipswich.[14]

The remarkable growth in output after the Black Death was also associated with subtle changes in the geography of textile manufacture in Suffolk. The industry continued to be concentrated in settlements along the Stour valley and its tributaries, but the established urban centres, such as Bury St Edmunds, Sudbury and Clare, were quickly supplemented and then overtaken by small towns, such as Hadleigh, Lavenham and Long Melford, and rapidly industrializing villages, such as Bildeston, Boxford, Kersey and Waldingfield. Cloth makers were also active in outlying centres, particularly Newmarket, Mildenhall, Brandon, Bungay, Beccles, Lowestoft, Blythburgh, Ipswich, Needham Market, Debenham and East Bergholt, and some linen textiles continued to be produced along the Waveney valley. In the 1390s Hadleigh was the most prolific manufacturing centre in Suffolk; its leading entrepreneurs dealt with merchants from Colchester, Ipswich and London, and also influenced output in smaller centres nearby, such as Nayland. Bury St Edmunds remained an

---

[13] Kowaleski, 'Consumer Economy', pp. 248–51; Britnell, *Colchester*, p. 167; Amor, 'Late Medieval Enclosure', p. 189; Britnell, 'Woollen Textile Industry', p. 97; Heaton, *Yorkshire Woollen and Worsted Industries*, p. 87; Thornton, *History of Clare*, p. 147. Blanket is mentioned more than once in debt cases at Eyke, SROI HD1538/357/5, mm. 36–7, and John Trankett of Ufford had violet woollen cloth, SROI HD1538/395/1, court held April 1435; Bacon Ms 294/13 (Brandon). The growing importance of London is documented in P. Nightingale, 'The Growth of London in the Medieval Economy', in Britnell and Hatcher, *Progress and Problems* (1996), pp. 89–106, and *UH*, i, pp. 438–9, 529–30, while the strength of trading connections is clear at pp. 577, 579.

[14] Dymond and Betterton, *Lavenham*, p. 26; Britnell, 'Woollen Textile Industry', p. 87; Thornton, *History of Clare*, pp. 174–5; Bailey, *Marginal Economy*, pp. 172–6, 278; Campbell, *English Seigneurial Agriculture*, p. 165; SROI HB8/1/830–840 (Tattingstone).

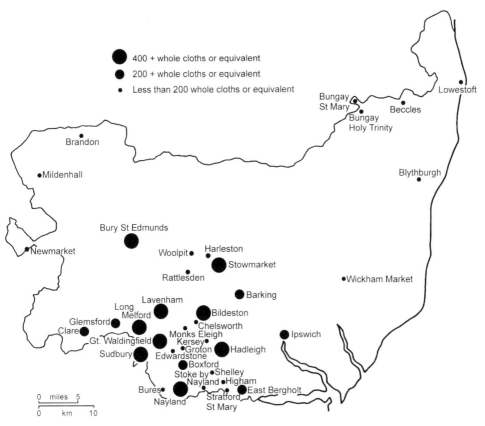

MAP 16 Output of cloth towns, 1465–9 (after Amor)

important centre, controlling rural production in north-west Suffolk, although the upper Stour valley (Sudbury and Clare) had lost its earlier prominence. Map 16 reveals that by the 1460s the scale and geography of production had changed again. The heartland of production remained in south Suffolk, but the balance of power within this area had shifted from Hadleigh to Lavenham, and from Cosford hundred to Babergh: nearly one-half of the clothiers recorded in the aulnage accounts operated in Babergh hundred and over a quarter in Cosford hundred. In the 1460s the leading centres of cloth manufacture were, in rank order: Lavenham, Hadleigh, Bildeston, Bury St Edmunds, Long Melford, Nayland, Sudbury, the Waldingfields, Stowmarket, Ipswich and Boxford, with Lavenham and Hadleigh some distance ahead. Producers in Cosford Hundred, led by Hadleigh and Bildeston, still preferred straits, while those in Babergh, led by Lavenham, Glemsford and Long Melford, concentrated on broadcloths.[15]

[15] Britnell, 'Woollen Textile Industry', pp. 86–9; Amor, 'Jack of All Trades', pp. 418–19.

Between the 1460s and 1520s three significant, and interlinked, changes are discernible in Suffolk's cloth trade: production in some smaller centres lost impetus (such as Kersey and Mildenhall) as fewer towns gained even greater prominence within the industry; control over production fell into the hands of fewer clothiers; and the division of labour within the manufacturing process became more pronounced. Before the 1460s the rural industry was loosely organized, and the involvement of many textile workers was small scale, episodic and usually confined to one or two stages of production: spinning and weaving, for example, were easy to enter and leave, depending upon the availability of other work, and most workers retained a smallholding and perhaps some interest in other forms of employment. Similarly, as late as the 1460s the cloth trade was still run by relatively large numbers of petty entrepreneurs who also maintained other significant economic interests, especially farming. Only sixteen of seventy-two clothiers operating in Lavenham in this decade appeared regularly in the aulnage accounts, indicating that the remainder were 'Jacks of all trades' who were involved intermittently in the cloth trade. The continuing involvement of many clothiers in agriculture is evident from the numerous references in their wills to landholdings, farming implements, grain and dairying interests. Control over production in places such as Lavenham, where the top seven clothiers handled only one-third of the town's total output, and Stowmarket was still shared widely. However, there is some evidence that by the 1460s control over production in a few places had become concentrated into the hands of a smaller number of wealthier clothiers. In Bildeston, for example, John Stansby monopolized textile manufacture, and cloth making in both Hadleigh and Sudbury was now dominated by small elites: just six clothiers handled over two-thirds of Hadleigh's manufacturing. A few of these clothiers possessed the wealth and contacts to lift them above their locality onto a national stage. John Stansby was resident in London and boasted significant Italian connections, while William Forthe had a mansion and shops in London, property interests throughout East Anglia, and his daughter Elizabeth married into London society: yet his main abode remained in Hadleigh where he was buried in 1504.[16]

By the 1520s Lavenham had surged ahead of the other centres of production and the organization of its trade and manufacture – particularly of the higher-quality cloth destined for export – had become more specialized. Lavenham contained many more clothiers than fullers or weavers, in contrast to Long Melford, Bures and Sudbury, which had more fullers but fewer clothiers, and Boxford, which was dominated by shearman and weavers. A clearly identifiable outwork system had begun to emerge, in which textile

[16] Britnell, 'Woollen Textile Industry', pp. 88–9; Amor, 'Jack of All Trades', pp. 422–7; Poos, *Rural Society*, pp. 64–5.

workers were less likely to finish and then sell their cloth personally and more likely to be hired by wealthy clothiers to undertake a particular stage in the production process for a set wage. Clothiers provided the raw materials, laid down strict specifications for quality and style, paid their outworkers by the task, and absorbed the risks – and windfalls – of marketing the cloths themselves. The successful clothiers sought out, nurtured and rewarded the most skilled artisans, which explains why in 1486 a grateful Thomas Spring II left £66 in his will to be distributed 'to my spinners, fullers and weavers', and in 1497 John Golding of Glemsford left 12d. to each of his many spinners. The high proportion of wage earners in the 1520s in Babergh hundred, and the widespread poverty and economic unrest there which followed a temporary disruption to the export of textiles, are strongly symptomatic of the emergence of a broader system of domestic outwork. Indeed, by the 1530s local weavers were complaining that the control now exercised by clothiers had reduced their incomes. In fact, the development of this outwork system was a direct attempt to control costs while imposing some form of quality control on the finished product, as Suffolk increasingly concentrated on middle-grade broadcloths in competitive export markets. The risks of this trade fell on the leading clothiers, but so did the rewards; hence a number of them became fabulously wealthy, forging direct links with London merchants in preference to those of Colchester or Ipswich: the estate of Thomas Spring III contributed over £800 to the extensive rebuilding of Lavenham church in the 1520s (plate 12).[17]

The changing structure of the industry, and the changing fortunes of individual cloth towns, reflects the ability of local textile producers to adapt to changing fashions and markets during the later Middle Ages. In the thirteenth century commercial textile production in Suffolk was mainly focused upon higher-quality cloths for a wealthy clientele, and it was largely confined to the boroughs of Bury St Edmunds, Clare, Sudbury and Ipswich, where craft gilds or urban authorities were sufficiently powerful to impose the necessary quality control over producers, and thus ensure the high grade of the final product. Yet after the mid-fourteenth century the growing demand for clothes and bedding among the lower orders of society opened up a mass market for cheap and colourful textiles, which replicated the style of more expensive cloths and reflected the fashion for bright colours. Suffolk producers were remarkably

[17] Dymond and Betterton, *Lavenham*, pp. 7–8, 12, 14–15, 30, 39–40; McClenaghan, *Springs of Lavenham*, pp. 14–15, 59, 61–88; Britnell, *Colchester*, p. 189; Britnell, 'Woollen Textile Industry', pp. 90–5; Dyer, *Age of Transition?*, pp. 230–2; Nightingale, *Medieval Mercantile Community*, p. 548; *PSIA* 39 (1999), pp. 323–4. Larry Poos identifies an embryonic outwork system in Essex by the end of the fifteenth century, *Rural Society*, pp. 71–2; and Chris Dyer also draws attention to the growing dominance of entrepreneurial clothiers by *c.* 1500, *Making a Living*, pp. 327–8.

quick to respond to these opportunities, judging by the rate at which local output expanded between the 1350s and the 1390s, providing good value-for-money cloth incorporating reliable workmanship at very competitive prices. In *c.* 1400 the manufacture of lightweight straits in a variety of styles and colours dominated output in Suffolk, with Hadleigh and other places in Cosford hundred featuring prominently. The expertise in textile production had originated in boroughs such as Sudbury and Bury St Edmunds, but the new centres of production were based in rural communities or market towns where the workforce was less regulated and therefore less expensive. The liability for taxation – frozen at a fixed rate for each vill in 1334 – was also lower for many of these newer textile towns and villages than for the older boroughs. Controlling costs was crucial to retaining the competitiveness of textiles at the lower end of the market.

During the course of the fifteenth century the most dynamic sector of the textile market shifted away from straits towards broadcloths, which were often heavier and slightly higher-quality cloths. It is likely that the domestic and export markets for lower-quality straits had become saturated by the early fifteenth century, and in the 1440s English cloth exports entered a period of prolonged recession which lasted until the late 1460s. Thereafter, cloth exports picked up sharply, but the dominant style of production in Suffolk was now broadcloths. Straits could be woven on a single rudimentary loom by one weaver, while broadcloths need bigger looms operated by two people, and required much wool to feed them, and consequently broadcloth manufacture was more capital intensive. Both of these developments encouraged the intervention of entrepreneurs better able than smaller producers to minimize costs and to spread the risks of trade by dealing in bulk. Between the 1460s and the 1520s the growing specialization of production in textile towns, and the shift to a rudimentary outwork system controlled by a few wealthy clothiers, indicates that local producers were again adapting the style of their textiles to the needs of changing markets. The outwork system also constituted a mechanism for exercising greater quality control over the work of rural producers, a necessary development in an increasingly competitive market. By *c.* 1500 Suffolk textile manufacture was one of the first sectors of the English economy to develop a high dependence upon overseas markets.[18]

Other industries

An acute paucity of evidence renders the fortunes of the marine fishing industry very difficult to reconstruct. However, there are some indications that the staple trade in herrings and sprats boomed in the second half of the fourteenth century. For example, the number of fishing boats operating

---

[18] Britnell, *Britain and Ireland*, pp. 418–19, on trends in English cloth exports.

from the beaches of Sizewell and Thorpeness nearly doubled in the 1370s and 1380s, when the value of sea weirs in the Deben estuary remained high. This may reflect buoyant demand caused by the growing consumption of fish among ordinary people, as part of a more varied and interesting diet, or simply the success of Suffolk fishermen in breaking Yarmouth's monopoly of the herring trade: Yarmouth's trade suffered declining fortunes in the later Middle Ages. However, the boom in local fortunes did not extend much beyond *c.* 1400, because in the early fifteenth century the number of boats operating from Sizewell and Thorpeness declined, and between 1405–15 and 1415–29 the size of the active herring fleet at Dunwich contracted by a third. Although the size of Dunwich's sprat fleet remained constant over the same period, the volume of sprats and herrings caught fell by one-half. Similarly, the sprat fleet at Aldeburgh had contracted by the middle of the fifteenth century.

The fall in both the number of boats and the volume of fish caught in the herring and sprat seasons may have forced some fishermen to pursue new ventures in more distant waters, because Suffolk mariners were among those pioneers in the early fifteenth century who sought large stocks of meatier deep-sea fish such as haddock, ling and cod in the waters around Iceland and the Faeroes: indeed, they were also accused of piracy and looting off the Scottish coast as a side line. The opening up of new fishing grounds in far northern waters boomed around 1400, although thereafter the involvement of English fishermen was periodically banned by the Crown for political and diplomatic reasons. These royal interventions hampered the trade rather than eradicated it, and by the early sixteenth century it was flourishing again. At this time one-third of all English boats in Icelandic waters originated from Suffolk, and the income from a successful voyage could stretch to hundreds of pounds: in 1535 a boat from Southwold was hired for £120 for the Icelandic voyage, which implies profits which far exceeded those obtained by single boats operating in the herring or sprat seasons.[19]

After 1349 much domestic housing was rebuilt on a wider scale to higher specifications by full-time craftsmen. The decline in large-scale construction projects by monastic communities and aristocrats has to be set alongside the reconstruction of numerous parish churches in the perpendicular style. Brick making developed as a significant new activity in those places where local deposits of clay and brickearth, together with sufficient fuel to fire the kilns, were readily available. Bricks were used increasingly in the construction of high-quality secular buildings in fifteenth-century

---

[19] *VCH*, ii, pp. 208–11, 290–2; Bailey, 'Coastal Fishing', pp. 103, 109–11; H. P. Clodd, *Aldeburgh: The History of an Ancient Borough* (Ipswich, 1959), pp. 17–18; Redstone, *Ipswich*, p. 32.

East Anglia, partly due to the local absence of any good-quality building stone but also because of the rising costs of transporting ashlar from the east Midlands: it is possible that the industry was encouraged by Flemish brickmakers who began to settle in Suffolk around this time. The growing popularity and output of brick is reflected in the rising number of brick kilns recorded in the fifteenth century. In 1459 the Mannock family of Stoke-by-Nayland contracted two men to manufacture 60,000 bricks in Shelley for the redevelopment of Gifford's Hall. Kilns were constructed and leased to tenants on manors such as Chevington (where one fetched a sizeable 50s.), Ixworth, Stanton and Badmondsfield, while private kilns on tenant land would have escaped mention in manorial records. Kilns in Ixworth routinely supplied bricks to Thetford priory; in the 1460s thousands of bricks were made each year at South Elmham; and by the late sixteenth century Woolpit had established a regional reputation for its brick production.[20]

The economic climate of the later Middle Ages was also favourable to the tanning and leather working industry, although its fortunes remain frustratingly difficult to trace. The conspicuous success of the dairy, beef and rabbit trades after 1350 was mainly a response to the improved diet of the lower orders of society, but it also owed something to the buoyant demand for the animal hides and skins used to make shoes, clothing, harnesses and buckets: leather was the most water-resistant material available in medieval England. Ipswich emerged as an important regional market for treated hides and skins, and was exporting leather in the early fifteenth century, while tanners, skinners, curriers and glovers all featured prominently among craft workers in fifteenth-century Bury St Edmunds. Tanners and shoemakers were prominent in Newmarket in the 1470s, and barkers were active in Dunwich. Piecemeal evidence for growing numbers of skinners, barkers and tanners after *c.* 1350 is apparent in the Breckland, as rabbit production boomed and the demand for horse hides and sheep skins remained strong. The claylands of east Suffolk emerged as the most important region in eastern England for leather production, complementing the specialism in dairying, both of which benefited from the relative growth of the London market. Some of the farmers who built up sizeable dairy and cattle herds in the fifteenth century, such as John Scothaugh of Yoxford, also diversified into tanning. In general, tanning and leather working was concentrated in towns, and Beccles, Halesworth, Ixworth, Lavenham, Needham Market

---

[20] *SR* 5 (1983), pp. 173–5; Sandon, *Suffolk Houses*, pp. 69–72, 81–2, 91, 98–9, 202–3; *HistA*, pp. 146–7; SROB E3/15.3/2.42 (Chevington); SROB HA505/3/5b (Stanton); Jack, *Ruthin Valor*, pp. 129–31 (Badmondsfield); Scarfe, *Suffolk Landscape*, p. 182; Dymond, *Thetford Priory*, pp. 27, 768; Amor, 'Riding out Recession', p. 136.

and Woodbridge had all emerged as notable centres by the early sixteenth century.[21]

URBAN FORTUNES

The changes to the patterns of trade and industry after 1350 benefited the economies of Suffolk's towns more than its rural markets and fairs. Dyer estimates that the number of places which could be described as towns in Suffolk increased from over twenty in the early fourteenth century to more than thirty in the early sixteenth century, during which time the proportion of urban dwellers among the population doubled from about 15 per cent to about 30 per cent: the level of urbanization in Babergh hundred was closer to 50 per cent, mainly due to its particularly high concentration of textile towns. In this regard the experience of Suffolk ran contrary to the national trend: Dyer estimates that the proportion of English town dwellers remained constant at around 20 per cent between 1300 and 1500, and Rigby has also concluded that between 1377 and 1524 this proportion held more or less constant. By *c.* 1500 Suffolk had become one of the most urbanized parts of England, and the number of its towns ranked in the country's 100 wealthiest had doubled from five in 1334 to ten in 1524.[22]

The growing strength of the county's urban sector is particularly impressive when considered against the general difficulties facing towns during this period. The contraction in the volume of trade, periodic disruptions to exports, the rising costs of town government, and recurrent outbreaks of epidemic disease all created particular and well-documented problems for late medieval towns. The falling volume of trade through many urban markets was mirrored by a contraction in other staple activities, such as milling. In 1345 Horsewade mill in Ipswich had fetched £6 per annum, but in 1455 its lessees owed £30 in arrears of rent, and so in 1457 it was granted to new tenants at less than £3 per

[21] See M. Kowaleski, 'Town and Country in Late Medieval England: The Hide and Leather Trade', in *Work in Towns, 850–1850*, ed. D. Keene and P. J. Corfield (Leicester, 1990), pp. 57–73, and Kowaleski, 'Consumer Economy', pp. 249–51; *HistA*, pp. 144–5; Redstone, *Ipswich*, p. 27; Gottfried, *Bury St Edmunds*, pp. 111, 117–19; Bailey, *Marginal Economy*, pp. 182–6; Richmond, *John Hopton*, p. 167; Clarkson, 'Leather Crafts', p. 30; Dymond and Betterton, *Lavenham*, p. 62; SROI HD1538/435/3 (Woodbridge); Bailey, *Dunwich*, p. 20; May, *Newmarket*, p. 45.

[22] The increase in the number of places defined as towns is due to the emergence of new textile manufacturing centres with marketing functions, such as Nayland and Long Melford, Dyer, 'How Urbanised?', pp. 174–80; *UH*, i, pp. 755–7, 762–5. For a general background to small towns in this period, see Dyer's authoritative survey in *UH*, i, pp. 505–37. Direct comparisons between the 1334 and 1524 Lay Subsidies are beset with difficulties, but the overall trends are clear enough, see *UH*, i, pp. 325–31; Rigby, 'Urban Population'.

annum. Many towns suffered a sharp contraction in the size of their population. Between the 1320s and the 1520s the number of residents in Ipswich probably fell from about 5,000 to around 3,500, Bury St Edmunds from about 7,000 to around 5,500, and Ixworth from about 550 to around 325. Of course, the precise chronology of decline varied from place to place: Dunwich's population fell from about 1,500 in the 1330s to around 900 in the 1410s, but picked up for a short period in the early sixteenth century to around 1,200, while Gottfried argues that Bury's population increased strongly between *c.* 1470 and *c.* 1520.[23]

Outbreaks of disease tended to become concentrated in towns, adding to the general sense of urban malaise. Mortality rates in Bury St Edmunds remained high throughout the fifteenth century, and between 1430 and 1480 fifteen of the twenty-three places in Suffolk most frequently afflicted by epidemic disease were towns or ports. The fall in the size of urban populations is apparent in the dilapidation of houses and less intensive use of space within towns. Archaeological evidence from Bury St Edmunds reveals a significant decline in the usage of many rubbish sites and gardens between the thirteenth and fifteenth centuries, and in the 1520s considerable areas of Eastgate Street, the eastern end of Risbygate Street, and the north part of Southgate Street were all heavily decayed. In 1447 the chamberlains of Ipswich were instructed to repair the borough's dilapidating houses, and abandoned and decaying properties were also a prominent feature of early sixteenth-century Mildenhall.[24]

Yet these strong symptoms of contraction and decay lay alongside clear evidence of higher levels of personal wealth among urban residents. The dilapidation of houses in Bury St Edmunds in the 1520s was mainly confined to properties held by the abbey, whereas other areas of the town were thriving. In the 1460s a number of houses had been rebuilt in Bury with highly advanced architectural features usually associated with later periods, such as jetties, chimneys and smoke bays. The increased amount and variety of personal possessions belonging to even modestly wealthy town dwellers also testify to strong advances in urban standards of living. John Brook left a sizeable house in Sudbury with an adjacent barn and all its belongings to his wife, but was also able to provide his younger son with another house in the borough as a wedding present and to leave his weaving business – including his loom – to

[23] Bacon, *Annals*, pp. 71, 114–15 (Horsewade mill); Bailey, *Dunwich*, p. 5; *1524 Lay Subsidy*, pp. 114–19; Gottfried, *Bury St Edmunds*, pp. 54, 70; Amor, 'Riding out Recession', p. 129; Middleton-Stewart, *Inward Purity*, p. 53; see *UH*, i, p. 536 for converting lists of taxpayers into population estimates (which recommends a converter of between 1.5 and 1.9 for the 1377 returns, and between 5 and 7 for those of 1524).

[24] Gottfried, *Epidemic Disease*, p. 130; Gottfried, *Bury St Edmunds*, pp. 43–5, 70–1; Middleton-Stewart, *Inward Purity*, p. 53; *PSIA* 39 (1996), p. 89; Bacon, *Annals*, p. 104; SROB E18/451/69 ff. 48, 76, 85, 93, 108, 114 (Mildenhall).

his elder son: his assets were also sufficient to fund the distribution of £60 to charitable activities and in gifts. John Symond of Wickham Market died in 1481 leaving an impressive array of personal belongings, including twelve silver spoons, a feather bed, six pewter plates, a brass pot, fire irons, a chest made of spruce wood and four candlesticks. A wealthy fifteenth-century merchant such as William Wimbill of Ipswich left sufficient money to build a new chancel for St Stephen's church, as well as making donations to every other parish church and religious house in the town.[25]

To some extent, the evidence for the fortunes of urban economies in late medieval Suffolk is paradoxical and conflicting, because indications of higher levels of personal wealth and material well-being exist alongside those of declining populations and contracting levels of trade. Similarly, the economic fortunes of individual towns were much more varied than they had been in the period 1200–1350, when all towns had enjoyed some expansion and prosperity. The experiences of Suffolk towns after 1350 were less homogenous: some suffered unequivocal and extensive decline, others endured mixed fortunes, while a few enjoyed conspicuous growth and success. As a comparison between tables 3 and 6 indicates, Eye, Hoxne, Northales and Orford failed to adapt to changing economic conditions and declined markedly in both size and relative importance, with the last three dropping outside the ranking of the county's ten largest and wealthiest towns by 1525 (plate 9). In the first three decades of the fifteenth century the economy of Dunwich was severely distressed, as the size of its fishing fleet slumped, the income from its market stalls fell by two-thirds, and the borough faced recurrent financial crises. Although Dunwich's port still attracted some foreign visitors and coastal trade, it was losing business to Walberswick and Southwold as its harbour was blighted by shifting shingle banks. It also lacked a decent core of wealthy residents: only one-quarter of its inhabitants contributed more than a modest 12d. to the Lay Subsidies of 1407 and 1422, and in 1524 89 per cent had less than £10 in assessed wealth. Its annual fee-farm payable to the Crown, which had peaked at £108 in the early thirteenth century, stood at just over £14 in 1402, although the town struggled to pay even this sum in the 1410s. In 1449 the borough was relieved one-third of its tax bill due to poverty.[26]

The fortunes of Mildenhall were mixed. It enjoyed a period of prosperity in the later fourteenth century, when local land values were buoyant, cloth

[25] Gottfried, *Bury St Edmunds*, pp. 43–5; D. Dymond, 'Five Building Contracts from Fifteenth-Century Suffolk', *Antiquaries Journal* 78 (1998), p. 281; Northeast, *Wills*, i, pp. 399–400; Dyer, *Making a Living*, p. 312; D. MacCulloch and J. Blatchly, 'Recent Discoveries at St Stephen's Church, Ipswich', *PSIA* 36 (1986), p. 101.

[26] Amor, 'Riding out Recession', pp. 129, 140; Bailey, *Dunwich*, pp. 1–4, 7–8, 14–22, 50–2, 110–13; Bailey, '*Per Impetum Maris*', p. 195; BL Add. Roll 40712; *1524 Lay Subsidy*, pp. 114–19; Dymond and Virgoe, 'Reduced Population', p. 97.

TABLE 6   Rank order of Suffolk Towns in 1524–5

1524		*1525*	
Rank order of towns	*Taxable wealth*	*Rank order of towns*	*No. of taxpayers*
Ipswich	£282	Bury St Edmunds	645
Bury St Edmunds	£180	Ipswich	*c.* 500
Lavenham	£180	Beccles	307
Hadleigh	£109	Hadleigh	303
Beccles	£71	Dunwich	235
Long Melford	£67	Sudbury	231
Sudbury	£61	Lavenham	195
Nayland	£59	Long Melford	186
Woodbridge	£45	Woodbridge	169
Dunwich	£40	Lowestoft	144

Source: 1524 Lay Subsidy (wealth); Sheail, *Regional Distribution*, vol. 2, pp. 321–36 (taxpayers).

manufacture prospered, and its market benefited from the strength of the Breckland economy. By 1377 it was ranked as the seventy-sixth largest town in England, with around 800 inhabitants, and had risen to become the fourth biggest in Suffolk (compared with eighth in 1327). Yet in the early fifteenth century its market began to decline, land values fell rapidly, its cloth production lost momentum, and by the middle of the century its economy was exhibiting clear signs of recession, although there were still enough individuals in Mildenhall with sufficient wealth to fund the construction of a stunning new church tower and nave roof. By the early sixteenth century many houses were abandoned and decaying, especially around Mill Street and East End, and by 1524 its population totalled around 700 people. Mildenhall had now dropped out of the national ranking of towns and no longer featured in the ten largest towns in Suffolk (table 6).[27]

A good number of towns in Suffolk enjoyed a period of sustained relative and absolute prosperity in the later Middle Ages, reflecting the underlying strength of the pastoral economy, the growth in woollen textile manufacture or simply the misfortune of local competitors. Between 1334 and 1524 Aldeburgh, Lowestoft, Southwold, Walberswick and Woodbridge had increased their share of local taxable wealth, with Lowestoft emerging as one of the county's largest towns. Many of these ports benefited from east Suffolk's trade in leather and dairy produce, but they also developed a range of other economic interests. A number featured prominently in the exploitation of new

[27] *UH*, i, pp. 758, 763; Bailey, *Marginal Economy*, pp. 304–5; SROB E18/451/69, ff. 36–8, 48, 69, 76, 85, 93, 108, 114; E18/400/1.3, f. 51; *1524 Lay Subsidy*, pp. 219–20.

Icelandic fishing grounds in the fifteenth century, particularly Lowestoft, Southwold, Walberswick and Woodbridge, whose fishermen also traded other goods with Icelandic merchants. The further expansion of these fisheries for a short period in the early sixteenth century even lifted Dunwich's fortunes. Aldeburgh gradually supplemented its fishing industry with boatbuilding and an involvement in the coastal trade in coal between Newcastle and London. The magnificent fifteenth-century church at Southwold testifies to the town's rising prosperity and self-confidence, crowned in 1489 by the receipt of a charter of incorporation as a borough. During the late fourteenth and early fifteenth centuries settlement at Walberswick expanded towards its port to the south of the present village, and artefacts discovered there dating from this period indicate links with Germany, Holland and south-west France. A new quay and haven were built in the 1460s and 1470s, when the town's church was extensively and expensively rebuilt.[28]

Woodbridge increased its wealth and importance in the later Middle Ages, rising from a small town with fewer than forty taxpayers in 1327 to become one of England's top 100 towns in 1524 (judged by both taxpayers and wealth), when it contained around a thousand residents. Its fine church dates mainly from the late fourteenth and early fifteenth centuries, reflecting rising levels of prosperity, and the tolls from its market rose from about £4 per annum in the 1340s to about £7 in the 1440s. The town's success was founded principally upon rising wealth in its immediate hinterland (map 18), based upon the burgeoning local trade in livestock, leather and dairy produce: its market was dominated by butchers and leather workers. Yet it also developed a reputation for processing hemp and producing rope, it dabbled in some textile manufacture, and in the 1370s its port was attracting Flemish ships and trade in oysters.[29]

None of these examples implies that even the successful late-medieval towns experienced continuous economic growth, because periods of prosperity were interspersed with periods of real difficulty. For example, the 'Great Slump' of the mid-fifteenth century afflicted the economies of most towns, and in the 1480s a temporary disruption to the Icelandic fishing trade caused

[28] *HistA*, pp. 82–3; *VCH*, ii, p. 211; Scarfe, *Suffolk in the Middle Ages*, p. 132 (Dunwich); Middleton-Stewart, *Inward Piety*, p. 27; PSIA 41 (2005), pp. 138–9; F. D. Longe, *Lowestoft in Olden Times* (Lowestoft, 1898), pp. 51–4 (Lowestoft); *PSIA* 39 (1998), p. 255; *PSIA* 40 (2004), p. 519 (Southwold and Walberswick); R. W. M. Lewis, ed., *Walberswick Churchwardens' Accounts, 1450–1499* (Walberswick, 1947), pp. iii–iv. E. Power and M. Postan, eds., *Studies in English Trade in the Fifteenth Century* (London, 1933), p. 173; *PSIA* 9 (1897), p. 348; Arnott, *Alde Estuary*, pp. 31, 37, 40; *PSIA* 12 (1906), p. 204.

[29] Bacon, *Annals*, p. 71; SROI HD1538/435/3; Ridgard, *Framlingham*, p. 88; Arnott, *Suffolk Estuary*, pp. 113–14; *UH*, i, p. 758; *PSIA* 9 (1897), pp. 347–8; SROI HD1538/394/1, December courts of 1365 and 1367.

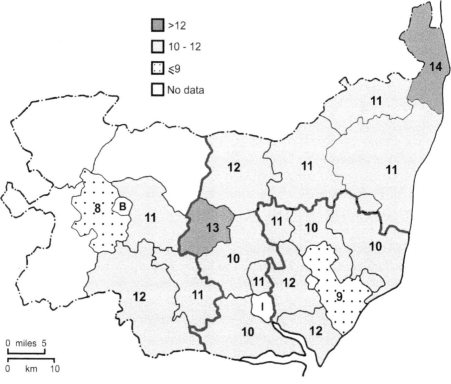

MAP 17 Number of taxpayers per square mile in 1524 (by hundred)

difficulties for most fishing ports. In 1449 around one-half of Suffolk's towns
were granted between 10 and 20 per cent relief from tax payable to the Crown
that year due to their impoverishment: these included Aldeburgh, Bungay, Ipswich, Northales, Southwold and Woodbridge. The common quay of Ipswich
fell into partial decay, and had to be reconstructed in the 1470s through a special financial levy on the burgesses, whilst in the 1430s one of Woodbridge's
three quays was untenanted and then subsequently leased at a reduced rent.
Furthermore, the overall success of ports such as Lowestoft, Southwold, Walberswick and Aldeburgh was achieved at the expense of places such as Orford
and Northales. The borough of Orford was cash strapped in the late fifteenth
century and the economic difficulties of Northales (plate 14) may have been
compounded by coastal erosion.[30]

The dominant textile manufacturing towns performed exceptionally well,

[30] Dymond and Virgoe, 'Reduced Population', pp. 88–97; Power and Postan, *Studies
in English Trade*, pp. 181–2; Bacon, *Annals*, pp. 139, 142; the Woodbridge quay was
leased at 18s. per annum in September 1371, but was let from the lord's own hands
in October 1438 for 13s. 4d. SROI HD1538/394/1 and 395/2; Arnott, *Alde Estuary*,
p. 36.

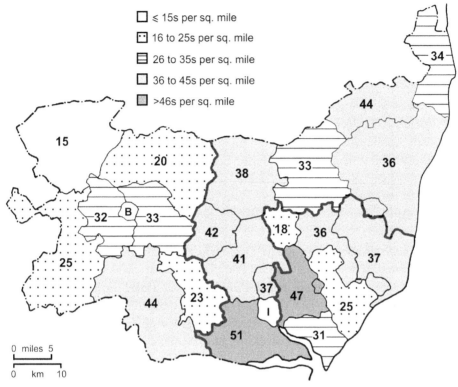

MAP 18 Taxable wealth per square mile in 1524 (by hundred)

and they represent some of the most unequivocal examples of urban growth in late medieval England. Lavenham and Long Melford appear in the ranking of Suffolk's ten largest towns in 1524, with Nayland and Stowmarket just outside, although none had featured in 1327 (tables 3 and 6). Lavenham grew impressively in absolute and relative terms, from about 600 inhabitants in 1327 to perhaps 1,100 in 1524, by which time it was the eighty-third largest, and fifteenth wealthiest, town in England. Between 1470 and 1520 Lavenham emerged as Suffolk's leading textile town, when a growing number of wealthy clothiers with sizeable trading operations became resident there. Rising and high levels of personal wealth in this period are reflected both in an increase in the size of bequests among the will-making population and in the widespread reconstruction on a grander scale of perhaps 70 per cent of Lavenham's housing stock, including the Grammar School house, a merchant's house containing exceptional internal features such as a dais beam carved with angels and a spiral staircase of painted brick. Hadleigh contained a population of around 1,500 in 1327, which had probably increased to around 2,500 in 1377, when it was ranked as the thirty-ninth largest town in England and more than one-fifth of its adult population worked in textiles. The manorial rent roll had grown dramatically between the 1330s and 1370s, swelled by numerous 'new rents', and the income generated by the manor court and fulling mill also rose impressively. Like Lavenham, a booming population and rising levels of personal wealth transformed its housing stock, and by the 1470s a splendid new market hall had been constructed with projecting oriel windows and decorated pilasters (plate 13). Stowmarket had been a typical small agricultural town in *c.* 1300, yet by 1381 20 per cent of its trade people were involved in textile production, and by the 1460s it ranked ninth among Suffolk textile manufacturing centres. It too possesses a number of high-quality buildings dating from *c.* 1400 clustered around the marketplace, and its population rose from about 400 people in 1381 to around 600 in 1524. The relative wealth of south Suffolk rose markedly in the later Middle Ages (map 18).[31]

A concentration upon textile manufacture was not in itself sufficient to boost urban fortunes. The fortunes of individual cloth towns were often volatile and influenced by capricious shifts in markets and fashions, and the overall growth in textile manufacture in Suffolk was not shared equally, especially in the fifteenth century when many smaller centres lost ground to the larger ones. The conspicuous success of Lavenham, Stowmarket and Hadleigh contrasted with the fortunes of other places. Textile manufacture boomed in Kersey in the later fourteenth century, judging from the quality of extant timber framed housing dating from this period, and in the 1390s new houses and stalls, a cloth house and a linen drapers' hall are all recorded for the first time. Yet its fortunes slumped thereafter: there is little evidence of high-quality domestic buildings after the early fifteenth century and its population in 1525 (about 380) was lower than it had been in 1327 (about 450). Sudbury and Clare were early leaders in textile manufacture, but after the 1370s both lost ground to newer centres of production. Growing indebtedness recorded in the borough court of Sudbury between the 1390s and 1420s is a clear symptom of rising economic distress, and between 1262 and 1381 income from the borough of Clare fell from £15 10s. 1½d. to £6: in 1425 the troubled burgesses sought a reduction in the level of their annual fee farm.[32]

---

[31] *UH*, i, pp. 759, 762–3, 765; Dymond and Betterton, *Lavenham*, pp. 4–15; Britnell, *Colchester*, p. 184; R. Shackle and L. Alston, 'The Old Grammar School: The Finest Merchant's House in Lavenham', *Historic Buildings of Suffolk* 1 (1998), pp. 48–9; *PSIA* 39 (1998), p. 398; M. Mate, 'The Agrarian Economy after the Black Death: The Manors of Canterbury Cathedral Priory', *EcHR* 37 (1984), p. 351; Davis, 'Petty Traders', p. 14; *PSIA* 40 (2004), pp. 529–30; Amor, 'Jack of All Trades', pp. 419–21, 434; Amor, 'Late Medieval Enclosure', pp. 189–90.

[32] Leigh Alston, personal communication; PRO SC6/1001/3; *1327 Lay Subsidy*, p. 157; *1524 Lay Subsidy*, pp. 159–60 (Kersey); Britnell, *Colchester*, pp. 83, 190–1; Thornton, *History of Clare*, pp. 21, 40; Davis, 'Petty Traders', p. 290.

CONCLUSION

The difficulties endured by the agricultural sector (chapter 9) are apparent to some degree in the urban and industrial sectors. The aggregate volume of commercial activity contracted; nearly two-thirds of the county's original markets and fairs disappeared, and the profits of many of the survivors slumped; the number of casual traders and producers operating around the fringes of various trades diminished dramatically; many towns had fewer residents and parts of their housing stock became dilapidated; and the great slump of the mid-fifteenth century troubled most places and most sectors of the economy. Yet in other respects manufacturers and traders enjoyed greater opportunities than agriculturalists, because the rising disposable incomes and living standards of the mass of the populace had increased the demand for basic consumer goods – clothes, shoes, leather products, household goods and tableware – manufactured to a decent standard by specialists. In addition, the growth in the relative importance of London as a centre of consumption during the fifteenth century stimulated demand for the produce of Suffolk's manufacturers and farms. The trade in such goods was increasingly handled by merchants with wide geographical contacts operating in fewer trading centres, rather than peddled by the manufacturers themselves in local weekly markets. Places where these wares were manufactured, or where they were traded, could shake off the general commercial and agrarian malaise of the period.

Many producers and places in Suffolk responded to these challenges with conspicuous success. In *c.* 1300 the Suffolk economy had been impressive for its diversification, yet by *c.* 1500 it had become impressive for its degree of specialization. The explosion in the manufacture of woollen and linen textiles – mainly in south Suffolk and the Waveney valley, but also in a number of other individual centres – constitutes a dramatic industrial transformation: textile manufacturing was not widely established in Suffolk in 1300, yet by 1500 no county in England produced more cloth. The exact secret of this success is explored in chapter 12, although the style and quality of Suffolk cloths were aimed at precisely those sectors of the market which expanded most rapidly in the later Middle Ages, both at home and abroad. The market for lower- to middling-quality cloths was also fast changing, yet Suffolk producers possessed a canny ability to adapt their product to changing fashions and different markets, which by the late fifteenth century incorporated a shift to more discernibly capitalist forms of organization. Such eclecticism and adaptability meant that various styles of Suffolk cloth was used by tailors to create fashionable clothes of decent quality for people across England and north-west Europe. The wealth generated by textile manufacture stimulated activity in other local crafts and trades, particularly the domestic construction industry.

When combined with the buoyancy of the leather trade, and the determination of marine fishermen to seek new fishing grounds, then it is clear that many aspects of industrial activity flourished in late medieval Suffolk, and that the relative and absolute wealth of those places concentrating on such trades increased (map 18). The availability of well-paid industrial work explains why the structure of landholding in Suffolk continued to be dominated by smallholders. By *c.* 1500 over one-third of the population of Suffolk was engaged predominately in non-agricultural activities, although many of these craft workers maintained a smallholding and worked in their own homes. This is a high proportion by the standards of the age, but falls well short of the proportion of the population in this category in industrializing regions of England in the eighteenth century (70 per cent). This statistic, together with the continued dominance of agricultural smallholdings, indicates clearly that – for all its advances – the late-medieval Suffolk economy was neither 'modern' nor free of poverty.[33]

While some Suffolk towns suffered unequivocal economic decline in the later Middle Ages, and the ravages of epidemic disease meant that most were physically smaller, the urban sector generally benefited from the changing complexion of trade and industry. Rising levels of consumption, personal wealth and material comfort among urban dwellers are clearly apparent, and the concentration of wealth in some towns increased relatively and absolutely. Between 1334 and 1524 the number of Suffolk towns ranked among the 100 wealthiest towns in England doubled, in contrast with those so ranked in Norfolk which declined from nine to eight. Inevitably, the main gains were made by the new textile manufacturing centres, none of which were boroughs. The efficiency and efficacy of trade in such places must have provided them with a competitive edge over older established urban centres. However, towns such as Nayland, Newmarket, Southwold and Woodbridge were still relatively small by the standards of English, and certainly Flemish, towns, and there were few merchants or wealthy residents in such places. Their leading residents were well-to-do artisans and tavern keepers, not sophisticated or wealthy merchants. The wealthy continued to reside in the largest boroughs or certain textile towns.[34]

The achievements of the Suffolk economy after 1349 are reflected in changes to the distribution of taxable wealth and taxpayers, both within the county and compared with other parts of England. Roger Schofield's analysis of taxable lay wealth reveals that in 1334 Suffolk was ranked eighteenth out of all English counties, and had risen to seventh place in 1515, and that it experienced one of the most rapid increases in relative wealth between those dates. In 1334 the

33 Dyer, 'How Urbanised?', pp. 182–3.

34 *UH*, i, pp. 755–7, 761–7; May, *Newmarket*, p. 38.

assessable wealth per square mile of communities along the Stour, Gipping and Waveney valleys was already among the highest in England, and by 1524 these areas had managed to increase their share of taxable wealth further. The shift in the relative distribution of wealth within Suffolk to the textile districts of south Suffolk, and to the ports and towns of east Suffolk and the Waveney valley, is striking (compare maps 12 and 18), and is illustrative of significant economic realignment and success during a difficult period.[35]

35 R. S. Schofield, 'The Geographical Distribution of Wealth in England, 1334–1669', *EcHR* 18 (1965), pp. 504–6; A. R. H. Baker, 'Changes in the Later Middle Ages', in Darby, *New Historical Geography* (1973), p. 196; Glasscock, 'England in 1334', p. 139.

CHAPTER 12

Conclusion

M EDIEVAL Suffolk possessed a highly distinctive social structure. It was a county of weak manorialism, where the average vill was split between a number of manors; the typical manor was small; and the average manorial lord directly worked his demesne land and was modestly wealthy. In *c.* 1300 at least 80 per cent of all tenants and tenancies were free, one of the highest proportions in England, and conversely the proportion of villeins and unfree tenancies was among the lowest. Head rents on both free and villein holdings were relatively low, and landlords adopted a permissive approach to the sale and transfer of land between peasants, both of which encouraged a thriving land market and the subdivision of landholdings. The reality of villeinage in this predominantly free region was far removed from the onerous burdens of its legal theory, or the experience of villeins in midland England. Consequently, the tight bonds which are traditionally assumed to have shackled feudal society had been significantly loosened in medieval Suffolk, where peasants possessed greater freedom of time and action. Few areas of medieval England had freer or more fragmented social structures, and the example of Suffolk confirms the correlation between such areas and those of advanced economic development.

The average size of peasant holdings had fallen during the course of the thirteenth century, and their output per acre had probably risen, due to demographic pressure and institutional permissiveness. By *c.* 1300 around 75 per cent of all peasant holdings comprised less than 10 acres in Suffolk, and perhaps one-half of the population were landless labourers, servants and townsfolk, which meant that many people were forced to seek alternative employment to make ends meet. The opportunities for such employment – in agricultural wage labouring, petty retailing, craft manufacture, transportation and fuel production – were greater here than in many parts of the country, because of both the degree of commercial activity and the natural diversity of the resource base. These natural resources were expertly harnessed and intensively exploited to yield a range of valuable products from marsh, heath, wood, meadow and pasture. Before the Black Death there was no such thing as wasteland in Suffolk. In addition, the harvest of the sea provided a supplementary income for some people and a nutritious source of cheap food for many, while textile manufacture and leather production had become more specialised in some urban centres and a few rural areas. Yet the inadequacy of the size of many landhold-ings (10 acres of arable land was scarcely sufficient to feed a family of five), and the insufficiency and limited purchasing power of wage labour, meant that standards of living among the mass of the populace were low, and after the 1280s a succession of harvest failures and high taxes pushed many families into a downward spiral of poverty.

The growth of population to a peak of perhaps 225,000 in the 1340s meant that the density of population in Suffolk was comfortably higher than the national average. Rising demographic pressure resulted in an expansion in the area under the plough to around one-half of the county's land surface, a higher proportion than at any time before or since. Local variations in both the main product of agriculture and the intensity of production are apparent across the county, facilitated by complex, labour-intensive but impressively flexible local field systems. These regional and sub-regional differences in agricultural pro-duction were mainly a function of differences in soil type and natural resources, but they were also shaped by commercial opportunity. Agrarian output in Suffolk was relatively commercialized, as evidenced by the high density of weekly markets and perhaps the most intensive regime of pastoral farming in medieval England. Although some produce – notably wool, cheese, processed fish and textiles – was marketed over long distances, most was destined for nearby rural and urban markets. The direct evidence indicates that the com-mercialization of this economy in the thirteenth century was driven primarily by local, predominantly rural, demand, which enabled it to absorb a growing population, albeit at a diminishing standard of living.

In 1086 Suffolk had been one of the most urbanized areas of England, but in *c.* 1300 around 15 per cent of its population lived in towns, compared to a national average of perhaps 20 per cent. From this perspective, the Suffolk economy appears to have lost some momentum relative to other parts of the country between the end of the eleventh and thirteenth centuries. On the eve of the Black Death its towns were neither particularly large nor wealthy, and their core economic hinterlands did not extend beyond 6 miles. Only a minor-ity had acquired the formal status of borough. However, Suffolk possessed one of the highest densities of small towns, weekly markets and seasonal fairs in medieval England. The absence of boroughs, and the proliferation of small towns and rural markets, is a clear indication that the social structure of rural society and the attitude of landlords were broadly encouraging to trade. Indeed, many lords deliberately created a legal framework to facilitate entre-preneurial activity in their manorial market towns, and their townsfolk were canny, aggressive and possessed an eye for profit and commercial opportunity. A sense of independence and individualism, and a keen awareness of wider political issues, permeated Suffolk society at all levels, overlain by a distinctive sense of regional, East Anglian identity. The social constraints imposed by traditional family structures, lordship and local custom had been severely eroded by the multiplicity of lordships (which meant that many tenants held land from more than one lord), high levels of commercial activity, a fluid and active labour market, and geographical mobility.

In the first six months of 1349 the Black Death culled half of Suffolk's population in a brutal and tragic manner: the great pestilence represents the worst human catastrophe in its recorded history. The population level fell from about 225,000 in *c.* 1300 to around 120,000 in 1377, and then fell further to about 100,000 in 1524. The impact of prolonged demographic decline was everywhere apparent, not least because the economy was now smaller in aggregate terms. By *c.* 1500 the proportion of the county's land surface under the plough had fallen from one-half to one-third; arable farming was less profitable; meadows, marsh, heath and woodland were managed less intensively, and some had become genuine wasteland; around one-half of demesne grain mills had disappeared; most rural and urban settlements were physically smaller, with abandoned or empty house plots; and two-thirds of its original markets and fairs were no longer held.

Yet new opportunities had emerged within this context of decline, and subtle but important shifts had occurred within society and the economy. By 1500 regional specialization in agriculture was more pronounced, and a clear distinction was apparent between the 'sheep–corn' district on the lighter soils and open fields of west Suffolk, and the dairying and stock rearing region on the enclosed clays of 'High Suffolk'. A wave of piecemeal enclosure had transformed the landscape of many areas of the county, and its pastoral economy was arguably the strongest in England. East Suffolk now enjoyed a regional if not national reputation for its cheese, butter and leather, while the Breckland was renowned for its horses and rabbits. A growing proportion of these products were being consumed in more distant markets.

In *c.* 1500 farm structure continued to be dominated by smallholdings, with more than one-half of all tenants still holding fewer than 10 acres of land, although most of these smallholders earned the greater share of their livelihood through craft work, retailing, labouring or servanthood. As work was now plentiful and real wage rates were high, they enjoyed a comfortable standard of living, unlike their vulnerable predecessors before the Black Death, and the proportion of landless had fallen. The improved standards of living of the lower orders of society are evident in the good quality of the surviving housing stock, the wider range and higher quality of personal possessions, and a nascent culture of consumerism. The dissolution of customary tenures and the leasing of demesnes, which accelerated between 1380 and 1420, increased the supply of land onto local land markets, which further enabled a handful of enterprising individuals in each village to construct large holdings (in excess of 40 acres) on a variety of tenures, often featuring sizeable cattle and pig herds. These wealthy yeomen and lesser gentlemen wielded increasing social influence within their communities, and ran commercial farms based on hired labour.

Commerce was now conducted through a leaner marketing structure concentrated in fewer centres of trade, and specialists operating in larger units of production manufactured wares of higher quality. Industrial activity was more specialized and widespread, and perhaps more than one-third of Suffolk's population was now engaged predominately in non-agricultural activities. In particular, in *c.* 1500 Suffolk produced more woollen textiles than any other English county, and its manufacturers were heavily dependent upon overseas markets, while its leather trade was the most substantial in eastern England, and its fishermen dominated the English fishing fleet trawling the North Sea and the North Atlantic. This changing complexion of trade and industry brought direct benefits to the urban sector in general. In the Lay Subsidy of 1524–5 ten Suffolk towns ranked in the top 100 in England (compared with five in 1334), and the number of identifiable urban places had increased to more than thirty. In 1525 around 30 per cent of all taxpayers lived in these towns, making Suffolk the most urbanized county in England. It also ranked as the seventh wealthiest county (a rise from eighteenth in 1334), with very high concentrations of wealth along the lower reaches of the Gipping, Stour and Waveney valleys, and in east Suffolk.

The strong emphasis on pastoralism and industrial development – two of the most buoyant sectors of the late medieval economy – help to explain why Suffolk coped better with the paradigm shift caused by the Black Death than many parts of England. While aggregate agricultural output inevitably declined, the economic flexibility and adaptability exhibited by stock rearers, rabbit farmers, textile makers, tanners and fishermen across the county is remarkable, and must reflect a pervasive culture of enterprise. The confidence and willingness to take risks in new circumstances, which underpinned the many successes of the late-medieval Suffolk economy, must also have drawn upon – and fuelled – the political, religious and social radicalism of its society. The tumultuous relationship between the burgesses and abbey of Bury St Edmunds, the chilling ferocity of the Peasants' Revolt, the endemic anti-clericalism, and the willing involvement in Cade's rebellion all point to an edginess and impatience in the character of local society, which helped to precipitate economic and social change at a faster rate than in many parts of England.

By *c.* 1500 many aspects of the Suffolk economy were well developed by the standards of the age. It was more urbanized and industrialized than probably any other area in England: the proportions of rural inhabitants earning a living predominantly from crafts of various kinds (around one-third), and of urban dwellers (around 30 per cent), were high. A textile industry highly dependent upon exports, and increasingly underpinned by an identifiable system of outwork, was well established in south Suffolk. These represent significant economic achievements, and Chris Dyer correctly reminds us that such successes were the result of many ordinary people overcoming challenges and making everyday decisions, which cumulatively effected structural change of real importance. This book has tried to document those changes, while rescuing some of the people responsible for them from the anonymity of economic history: people such as Katherine Dowe, the remarkably successful manager of Sibton abbey's dairy farm; Philip Canon, the poor scholar who rose to become Member of Parliament for Dunwich; the Hotots of Stowmarket, *nouveau riche* gentry farmers who built Columbine hall; John Stansby, the great clothier of Bildeston; and even humble Robert Goddard of Lackford, who had a little garden and little yard around his new cottage. One of the most profound ironies of English history is that the catastrophes of 1349 and 1361 created great opportunities for advancement and prosperity among the ordinary people who survived, irrespective of the emotional and psychological scars they inflicted, and the stable population levels of the late fourteenth and fifteenth centuries helped them to preserve their gains.[1]

Dyer also points out that the facile distinctions which historians once drew between 'medieval' and 'modern' societies, and between 'feudal' and 'capitalist' economies, do not bear close scrutiny, and medieval Suffolk exhibits many commercial, capitalist, non-feudal and therefore 'modern' characteristics. The degree of such enterprise, consumerism and individualism is impressive enough to confound many traditional notions of medieval society. Yet this is not the same as arguing that in 1500 the Suffolk economy was demonstrably capitalist or industrialized, or that its people were self-obsessed materialists and relentless seekers of profit. Around one-third of its rural population were involved in crafts, compared to over two-thirds in industrializing regions in the eighteenth century. Furthermore, individuals still had a clear sense of their own place within a hierarchical, and by extension deferential, society, and a strong awareness of their responsibilities to a wider community, such as the borough, the vill, the gild, the parish or the family. It is possible for commercial activity and entrepreneurial attitudes to exist without full-blown capitalism. The labour force was not a wage-dependent proletariat, but largely comprised artisans working in their own homes, live-in domestic servants, or part-time labourers who also maintained their own smallholding; the major landowners still geared some estate production to their household needs, or leased

[1] Dyer, *Age of Transition?*, pp. 243, 246.

sizeable chunks of their estates to others, rather than adopting a remorselessly profit-driven approach to their landed resources; and, finally, industry in Suffolk was not broadly based, occupying comfortably less than half of its residents and being heavily skewed towards textile production.[2]

A summary of the key economic and social changes between the thirteenth and early sixteenth centuries should not obscure the strong elements of continuity across the same period. Agriculture remained organic and animate, subject to the vicissitudes of the weather, and farming techniques and equipment changed little. A majority of landholders possessed less than 10 acres of land. Commercial activity was dominated by the sale of raw foodstuffs, fuel and processed food, which was largely localized in scope, and the amount of coin per head in circulation was small. The level of urbanization was low by modern standards, and units of production were small and based upon the household. In common with the rest of England, Suffolk's economy and society in *c.* 1500 retained many 'medieval' characteristics.[3]

The key temporal and spatial changes in Suffolk's late-medieval economy can be usefully illustrated, and further analysed, by comparing its progress with that of Norfolk, which in the thirteenth century had possessed the most advanced economy in England. Although at this date the economy of Suffolk was also relatively advanced, its vanguard lagged behind that of Norfolk in a number of ways. In eastern Norfolk, for example, in *c.* 1300 the level of urban demand, the intensity of arable farming, the density of population, the fragmentation of manors and landholding, and valuations of taxable wealth per acre were all higher than even the most progressive parts of Suffolk. The leading towns of Norfolk were much larger and wealthier, which meant that urban demand was more concentrated and thus wielded greater influence upon local rural production, while its arching coastline and the Ouse river system provided a higher proportion of producers with the ability to reach distant markets more cheaply through water-borne transportation. Furthermore, the alluvial soils of the silt fens and the Flegg district are among the most fertile in England, and therefore could better sustain the intensive arable farming and heavy subdivision of holdings necessary to support a dense population.[4]

In many ways the Norfolk economy proved better equipped to cope with the prolonged and sustained rise in population of the twelfth and thirteenth centuries than almost any other area of England. It was certainly better equipped than the Suffolk economy, which appears to have lost ground in relative terms between *c.* 1100 and *c.* 1300. Yet these achievements came at a cost,

---

[2] Dyer, *Age of Transition?*, pp. 41–2, 245–6, which also provides a useful discussion of the main features of a 'capitalist' society.

[3] Britnell, *Britain and Ireland*, pp. 510–16.

[4] Campbell, 'Agrarian Problem', p. 69; Williamson, *Origins of Norfolk*, chap. 7.

because the hyper-sensitivity of Norfolk communities to the succession of external shocks and crises which afflicted late thirteenth- and early fourteenth-century England was a direct consequence of the widening fault lines in its underlying economic substructure. In absorbing such a dense population, and in progressing so far down a particular pathway of commercial development, the Norfolk economy in general, and that of eastern Norfolk in particular, had become choked by a long tail of poor taxpayers, severe underemployment, chronically low labour productivity and congested smallholdings. Small farms, smallholders encumbered by debt and bereft of capital, inequitable rents, and an inefficient marketing system generated negative economic feedback. On the eve of the Black Death the limited disposable incomes of lesser lords and the mass of ordinary people were acting as a brake upon aggregate demand, and the Norfolk economy had reached the limits of its capacity within its existing structures. To a lesser extent, such strains were also apparent within the Suffolk economy.[5]

By 1500 the Norfolk economy was still prosperous and dynamic, but in many respects it had lost ground to Suffolk, which was now more urbanized and industrialized. This bold assertion can be illustrated by comparing changes in the relative distribution of wealth per acre. In 1334 the taxable wealth of many areas of Suffolk lay between £10 and £20 per square mile, just above the national average, compared with between £20 and £30 across much of Norfolk, and over £30 in parts of north-western and eastern Norfolk. Yet in 1524 most areas of Norfolk were now taxed at just above the national average (between 20s. and 39s. per square mile), whereas large areas of south and east Suffolk rated among the wealthiest regions of the country (i.e. above 40s. per square mile, see map 18). Similarly, the rate of growth of taxable lay wealth had increased more than fourfold in Suffolk between 1334 and 1515 (compared with just twofold in Norfolk), one of the fastest rates in England, with particular gains in east Suffolk.[6] When demographic pressure was highest, and when the production of grain was at a premium, Norfolk was better equipped to succeed than any other county in England. However, when the demographic pressure had been released, and grain production was less profitable, Norfolk lost its economic pre-eminence to parts of southern and east Suffolk. Why?

The economic development of east Suffolk after 1350 was founded principally upon pastoral farming, supplemented by leather production, some textile manufacture in the Waveney valley and deep sea fishing from coastal ports, and these developments are evident in the area's relative rise in taxable wealth (compare maps 12 and 16). The strong foundations of pastoral farming in the

5 Campbell, 'Agrarian Problem', pp. 66–9.

6 Glasscock, 'England in 1334', p. 139; Baker, 'Changes in the Later Middle Ages', p. 196; Schofield, 'Geographical Distribution', map 6.

late thirteenth century provided a basis for further development after *c.* 1350, when market conditions were even better suited to dairy, cattle and pig rearing, and when the growing importance of London brought this area within the capital's provisioning zone. Stock fattening and pig farming increased in scale, especially on the farms of yeomen and gentlemen, and subsequently east Suffolk gradually built a national reputation for the quality of its cheese and butter. Its success in building further upon the strong foundations of its pastoral economy contrasts with eastern Norfolk, which, despite a strong pastoral regime in *c.* 1300, subsequently failed to develop pastoralism to the same extent. Farms in east Norfolk remained locked into grain production, despite reduced profits, for exactly those reasons which had contributed to their success before 1350: the region's inherently fertile soils and its location near to the major markets of Norwich and Yarmouth. In contrast, the heavier clays of east Suffolk were better suited to grassland, and its field system contained more hedged enclosures than the heavily subdivided open fields of east Norfolk. Hence the conversion of arable to grassland, and of open fields to enclosures, met with less resistance, and the presence of many hedges and fences reduced the costs of supervising livestock in an era of escalating wage rates, and enhanced the flexibility and competitiveness of Suffolk's pastoral farmers. Its coastal ports benefited from the trade in cheese, butter and hides, and the success of the deep-sea fishing fleets further increased their relative wealth and prosperity.[7]

The booming economy of south Suffolk was based upon a similar swing to pastoralism, but owed more to the spectacular growth of woollen textile manufacture. Why did a successful woollen industry develop here? Joan Thirsk has argued cogently that rural industries thrived in areas with a high population density, pastoralism, secure tenures and a proliferation of smallholdings. These features created a sizeable and stable labour force prone to underemployment and seasonal unemployment, which was therefore readily available for the supplementary work provided by crafts and industries. Thirsk's hypothesis has been tested independently by Poos and Whittle to explain the development of late medieval textile manufacture in rural parts of north Essex and eastern Norfolk respectively, although in both cases pastoralism was considered to be less important than the proliferation of smallholdings and a high population density.[8] All four of Thirsk's prerequisites were strongly evident in south Suffolk: free tenures were dominant (maps 5 and 6), population density was

---

[7] *HistA*, pp. 80–4.

[8] J. Thirsk, 'Industries in the Countryside', in *Essays in the Economic and Social History of Tudor and Stuart England*, ed. F. J. Fisher (Cambridge, 1961), pp. 70–85; Poos, *Rural Society*, pp. 63–5; Whittle, *Agrarian Capitalism*, p. 248.

high (map 7), smallholdings were prevalent, and intensive pastoral farming was widespread (map 11).

While it is clear that rural industries in general, and textiles in particular, were unlikely to develop in regions lacking these four attributes, it is also apparent that industries did not always develop in every area where these favourable conditions prevailed. Indeed, *most* parts of Suffolk – and East Anglia – possessed secure tenures, a high population density, a high propor-tion of smallholdings and a strong pastoral tradition (and, of course, a well-established culture of entrepreneurialism, opportunism and independence); yet only a few areas developed textile manufacturing on any scale. In other words, the principles established by Thirsk are very useful in sketching the conditions most conducive to the growth of rural industry, and are broadly confirmed by Poos and Whittle's more detailed local research, but they do not explain why a particular rural industry developed in one favourable area but not another. Hence the search for a more precise explanation must involve the further consideration of three more questions. Why did a significant textile manufacturing industry develop in south Suffolk but not in many other areas, such as rural east Suffolk, which possessed similar economic characteristics? Why was textile manufacture in south Suffolk more successful than in other areas of textile manufacture, such as east Norfolk? And, finally, why did tex-tile manufacturing take root in some settlements in south Suffolk, but not others?

The most obvious specific explanation for the development of textiles in south Suffolk after 1350 is that a pool of expertise already existed there, mainly within the three urban centres of Bury St Edmunds, Clare and Sudbury. This expertise had been built up during the thirteenth century, and by the early fourteenth century it was already transferring to other locations such as Hadleigh and Lavenham, and a string of fulling mills had been built in vari-ous rural locations. So when the domestic and overseas markets for textiles expanded rapidly after the 1330s, this area possessed the skill base, and the requisite labour force, to react to the new opportunities and to raise produc-tion quickly. This leaking of textile expertise from the established boroughs into the countryside also extended over the county boundary into north Essex, where it was augmented by expertise spreading westwards from Colchester, another successful thirteenth-century textile town. The speed with which new markets in cloth expanded in the middle of the fourteenth century was a significant factor, and it meant that those areas with the established expertise, workforce and infrastructure were best placed to respond rapidly.

Hence the combination of pastoralism, high population density, secure tenures from an early date, the continued proliferation of smallholdings, a pre-existing infrastructure and local expertise in textile manufacture, and, finally, entrepreneurial verve all help to explain the growth of cloth making in south Suffolk. However, these factors do not provide a full explanation for the remarkable scale and success of that growth: the key to this is the nature of the local product. South Suffolk targeted a wide variety of fashionable and colourful, but cheap and imitation, cloths for a new mass market that after the mid-fourteenth century was expanding rapidly across western Europe. Competitiveness at this lower end of the textile market was mainly a factor of minimizing costs; consequently manufacturers depended upon cheap rural labour with a decent skill base, unhampered and unregulated by urban gilds or authorities. Even when the growth of this market first slowed and then stagnated in the first half of the fifteenth century, producers in south Suffolk shifted their focus to the manufacture of better-quality broadcloths for overseas markets. Their inventiveness at finding and exploiting new markets explains the growing dominance of Suffolk producers in English textile production, from 3.5 per cent of national output in the 1350s to 13.2 per cent in the 1460s.

This remarkable success contrasts with the experience of east Norfolk, which also had an established textile industry in the thirteenth century, based on Norwich, North Walsham and Worsted. However, the scale of its production and the extent of its rural manufacture in the late fourteenth and fifteenth centuries were not as widespread or successful as in south Suffolk: for example, Norfolk accounted for only 2 per cent of national output in the 1460s, with Norwich accounting for the overwhelming majority of production. East Norfolk concentrated mainly upon fine worsteds, a light cloth with a niche – rather than mass – market, for which demand did not expand as rapidly as that for lower-grade cloths. The production of fine worsteds was heavily dependent upon Norwich craftsmen to finish the cloth to the requisite standard, which in turn required robust systems of quality control and fine craftsmanship. Urban authorities possessed the power and wherewithal to impose fines upon those who produced inferior cloth and to enforce a strict system of apprenticeship to develop the requisite skills, and the geographical concentration of the workforce greatly facilitated their task. In contrast, a widely dispersed rural workforce was much more difficult to marshal and control for purposes of quality control. Such factors help to explain the continuing importance and prominence of the city of Norwich at the centre of worsted manufacture.

Answering the final question – why did textile manufacturing take root in some settlements in south Suffolk, but not others? – is more difficult and speculative. We have glibly referred to 'south Suffolk' as if it was an identifiable region with cloth manufacturing in most settlements, but in reality the industry was concentrated in the hundreds of Babergh and Cosford, and, even there, many places did not possess any identifiable textile production (map 16). This observation reinforces Britnell's point that industrial development in the Middle Ages was not a genuinely regional phenomenon.[9] Furthermore, the finishing trades in textile manufacture in south Suffolk (weaving, dyeing, cutting) were concentrated in small towns (led by Bildeston, Boxford, Hadleigh, Lavenham, Long Melford, Nayland and Stowmarket), and only spinning was strongly established in many rural settlements. Market towns proved attractive to industrial workers, because they offered many of the benefits of boroughs, such as the convenience of a regular market, easy access to commercial networks, readily available accommodation, plus a robust curial framework to provide an effective means of redress in the event of disputes with other traders. Yet towns like these carried few of the costs associated with boroughs, such as a formal structure of town government, a higher tax burden, and invasive regulation of the quality of their cloth and the habits of their workforce.

The concentration of groups of textile manufacturers in a single location brought additional benefits, such as accrued reductions to transaction, search and production costs, through a process known as agglomeration economics, and thus further encouraged other specialists to settle there. Such advantages were particularly important to producers operating in a sector of the market where cost control and reduction was essential to competitiveness. There must also be some significance in the fact that most of these textile towns were settled on the large manors of major landlords, such as the abbey of St Edmund (Long Melford), the earls of Oxford (Lavenham), the bishop of Ely (Glemsford, Needham Market) and Canterbury cathedral priory (Hadleigh), who may have encouraged their tenants by buying their wares, but who certainly offered patronage and security in uncertain times. Powerful landlords could provide their tenants with protection, more effective manorial courts and a greater degree of stability than could lesser lords. Yet even this cannot explain why settlements such as Boxford, Chelsworth and Waldingfield, which were essentially rural and held by lesser landlords, developed as cloth-making centres. Perhaps, beyond a certain point, the explanation for their development defies rational explanation. Chance may have determined why a few enterprising and energetic individuals or families, who unfortunately are historically anonymous, established manufacturing in one place, but not another, and thus why others followed suit.[10]

The contrasting fortunes of the leading sectors of the Norfolk and Suffolk economies between 1200 and 1500, and the multi-faceted explanation for the emergence of a highly successful textile manufacturing industry in south Suf-

---

9 Britnell, *Colchester*, p. 85.

10 For the modest status of landlords in Boxford and Waldingfield, see Copinger, *Manors of Suffolk*, i, pp. 22–30, 237–49.

folk rather than elsewhere, provide useful insights into the processes which lay behind economic development in medieval England. In doing so, they also indicate that the simple and important questions often posed by historians – such as, 'why did textiles develop here?' – do not have simple answers. This may appear so obvious as to barely merit iteration, but the economic history of medieval England has been characterized by a sustained enthusiasm for relatively simple models of economic and social development. It is no longer satisfactory to seek a simple or single explanation of economic change, either at the macro- or micro-economic level, and most historians now accept that such change was usually a highly complex process involving a range of variables acting together. Many of these variables were themselves moulded and influenced by other economic and social events, and such interactions subtly altered the weight and power of each variable in shaping a particular outcome. Very few variables acted as autonomous agents, although even their influence was mediated through economic and social structures. For example, the Black Death could be regarded as an autonomous agent, in the sense that it was a consequence of the independent mutation of a particular micro-organism, but still its spread was partly determined by existing patterns of trade and population densities.[11]

The adoption of a more active and open dialogue between the general and the particular in historical studies has contributed to the wider acceptance of pluralist explanations of economic change, and, by extension, a willingness to explore the complex interaction of a multiplicity of different causes laying behind particular historical processes. It is also helpful to distinguish between conditions and causes when evaluating the nuanced interplay of numerous variables. Hence we might regard the presence of a dense population, many smallholdings and pastoralism as essential *conditions* for the development of a sizeable rural textile industry, whereas the nature of the product (i.e. the type of cloth being produced), the changing nature of the market for that cloth, and the local availability of a pool of appropriate expertise were the decisive *causes* in determining why, where and when that industry flourished. It follows from this line of reasoning that great weight might be attached to the influence of a given variable in effecting economic and social change at a certain time and place, without any implications for its significance at other times and places. The factors constraining the development of the Suffolk economy in the thirteenth century were largely those contributing to its development after *c.* 1350, when a very different set of economic circumstances and opportunities prevailed.

The emergence of more complex, pluralist explanations of economic and social change reflects the inadequacy of the simple models popular with an ear-

---

[11] Hatcher and Bailey, *Modelling the Middle Ages*, pp. 208–40.

lier generation of historians. General principles and broad models can provide a valuable framework for understanding and explaining historical events when they are deployed as tools to serve and shape the historian's craft, although the selective quarrying of historical events to 'prove' the validity of a particular model is counterproductive. As Steve Rigby remarks, we must 'abandon the quest for historical prime movers and welcome the latest explanatory factors provided by historians as one more piece of the historical jigsaw, even though, by definition, no piece is ever the most important bit of the puzzle: the picture we create is the sum of all the pieces assembled together'.[12]

This book has attempted to refine further one small part of that jigsaw, and to champion the importance of local and regional studies in reassessing our understanding of that bigger picture. The selection of a county – an essentially artificial and political construct – as the unit of study for an economic and social history might appear incongruous and constraining. Certainly our understanding of textile manufacturing in south Suffolk would be improved by studying it alongside that in north Essex, and the particular economic experience of a highly distinctive region like the Breckland transcends the county boundaries that divide it. Yet the county of Suffolk is large enough to encompass whole regions, and diverse enough to offer useful contrasts and comparisons carrying clear implications for our understanding of other areas of medieval England. The motto adopted recently by England's smallest historical county is perhaps on odd way to close a history of another, much larger, county, but the study of medieval Suffolk does offer *multum in parvo*.

---

[12] S. H. Rigby, 'Historical Materialism: Social Structure and Social Change in the Middle Ages', *The Journal of Medieval and Early Modern Studies* 34 (2004), pp. 511–13; S. H. Rigby, 'Introduction: Social Structure and Economic Change in Late Medieval England', in Horrox and Ormrod, *Social History* (2006), pp. 29–30.

Bibliography

EDITED TEXTS

Allen, D., ed., *Ipswich Borough Archives, 1255–1855: A Catalogue*, SRS 43 (Woodbridge, 2000)

Astle, T., S. Ayscough and J. Caley, *Taxatio Ecclesiastica Angliae et Walliae* (London, 1802)

Bailey, M., ed., *The Bailiffs' Minute Book of Dunwich, 1404–1430*, SRS 34 (Woodbridge, 1992)

——, ed., *The English Manor, c. 1200 to c. 1500* (Manchester, 2002)

Chibnall, M. C., ed., *Select Documents of the English Lands of the Abbey of Bec*, Camden Society, 3rd series 73 (London, 1951)

——, ed., *Compotus Rolls of the English Lands of the Abbey of Bec (1272–1289)*, Camden Society, 4th series 34 (London, 1987)

Church, S. D., ed., *The Pakenham Cartulary for the Manor of Ixworth Thorpe, Suffolk, c. 1250 to c. 1320* , SCS 17 (Woodbridge, 2001)

Curia Regis Rolls (HMSO, 1922–)

Denney, A. H., ed., *The Sibton Abbey Estates: Select Documents, 1325–1509*, SRS 2 (Ipswich, 1960)

Dymond, D. P., ed., *The Register of Thetford Priory*, part 1: *1482–1517*, NRS 59 (Oxford, 1994), part 2: *1518–1540*, NRS 60 (Oxford, 1995)

Glasscock, R. E., ed., *The Lay Subsidy of 1334*, Records of Social and Economic History n.s. 2 (London, 1975)

Greenway, D., and J. Sayers, eds.,*Jocelyn of Brakelond's Chronicle of the Abbey of Bury St Edmunds* (Oxford, 1989)

Harper-Bill, C., ed., *The Cartulary of Blythburgh Priory*, vol 1, SCS 11 (Woodbridge, 1980); vol. 2, SCS 12 (Woodbridge, 1981)

Hervey, F., ed., *Pinchbeck Register of the Abbey of Bury St Edmunds and Related Documents*, 2 vols (Brighton, 1925)

Hervey, S. H. A., ed., *Suffolk in 1327: Being a Subsidy Return*, Suffolk Green Books 9 (Woodbridge, 1906)

—— *Suffolk in 1524: Being the Return for a Subsidy Granted in 1523*, Suffolk Green Books 10 (Woodbridge, 1910)

Horrox, R. E., ed., *The Black Death* (Manchester, 1994)

Illingworth, W., and J. Caley, eds., *Rotuli Hundredorum temp. Hen. III et Edw. I*, 2 vols (London, 1812–18)

Jack, R. I., ed., *The Grey of Ruthin Valor, 1467–8* (Sydney, 1965)

Jessopp, A., ed., *Visitations of the Diocese of Norwich, 1492–1532*, Camden Society 43 (London, 1888)

Letters, S., ed., *Gazetteer of Markets and Fairs in England and Wales to 1516*, part 2, List and Index Society, Special Series 33 (2003)

Letters and Papers, Foreign and Domestic, of the Reign of Henry VIII, 1509–1547, 22 vols. (HMSO, 1864–1932)

Lewis, R. W. M., ed., *Walberswick Churchwardens' Accounts, 1450–1499* (Walberswick, 1947)

Lock, R., ed., *The Court Rolls of Walsham-le-Willows*, vol. 1: *1303–1350*, SRS 41 (Woodbridge, 1998); vol. 2: *1350–1396*, SRS 45 (Woodbridge, 2002)

Martin, G. H., ed., *The Ipswich Recognisance Rolls, 1294–1327: A Calendar*, SRS 16 (Woodbridge, 1973)

Mortimer, R. H., ed., *Leiston Abbey Cartulary and Butley Priory Charters*, SCS 1 (Woodbridge, 1979)

——, ed., *Charters of St Bartholomew's Priory, Sudbury*, SCS 15 (Woodbridge, 1996)

Munday, J. T., ed., *Eriswell Notebook*, SROB (acc. 1938)

——, ed., *Lakenheath Records*, SROB (typescript)

Northeast, P., ed., *Wills of the Archdeaconry of Sudbury, 1439–1474*, vol. 1, SRS 44 (Woodbridge, 2001)

Pobst, P. E., ed., *The Register of William Bateman, Bishop of Norwich, 1344–1355*, part 1, Canterbury and York Society 84 (Woodbridge, 1996)

Powell, E., ed., *A Suffolk Hundred in 1283* (Cambridge, 1910)

Richardson, W. H., ed., *The Annals of Ipswich by Nathaniell Bacon, AD 1654* (Ipswich, 1884)

Ridgard, J., ed., *Medieval Framlingham: Select Documents, 1270 to 1524*, SRS 27 (Woodbridge, 1985)

Tanner, N. P., ed., *Heresy Trials in the Diocese of Norwich, 1428–31*, Camden Society, 4th series 20 (London, 1977)

Vanderzee, G., and J. Caley, eds., *Inquisitiones Nonarum* (London, 1807)

Woolgar, C. M., ed. *Household Accounts from Medieval England*, part 1 (Oxford, 1992)

BOOKS AND ARTICLES

Allen, D., 'The Descent of the Manor of Ampners in Thrandeston', *PSIA* 40 (2002)

Amor, N., 'Riding out Recession: Ixworth and Woolpit in the Late Middle Ages', *PSIA* 40 (2002)

—— 'Merchant Adventurer or Jack of all Trades? The Suffolk Clothier in the 1460s', *PSIA* 40 (2004)

—— 'Late Medieval Enclosure: A Study of Thorney near Stowmarket, Suffolk', *PSIA* 41 (2006)

Andrews, S., and T. Springall, *Hadleigh and the Alabaster Family* (Bildeston, 2005)

Armstrong, P., *The Changing Landscape* (Lavenham, 1975)

Arnott, W. G., *Suffolk Estuary: The Story of the River Deben* (Ipswich, 1950)

—— *Alde Estuary: The Story of a Suffolk River* (Ipswich, 1952)

—— *Orwell Estuary: The Story of Ipswich River* (Ipswich, 1973)

Bailey, M., 'The Rabbit and the Medieval East Anglian Economy', *AgHR* 36 (1988)

—— *A Marginal Economy? East Anglian Breckland in the Later Middle Ages* (Cambridge, 1989)

—— 'Blowing up Bubbles: Some New Demographic Evidence for the Fifteenth Century?', *Journal of Medieval History* 15 (1989)

—— 'Sand into Gold: The Evolution of the Foldcourse System in West Suffolk, 1200–1600', *AgHR* 38 (1990)

—— '*Per Impetum Maris*: Natural Disaster and Economic Decline in Eastern England, 1275–1350', in *Before the Black Death: Essays in the Crisis of the Early Fourteenth Century*, ed. B. M. S. Campbell (Manchester, 1991)

—— 'Coastal Fishing off South East Suffolk in the Century after the Black Death', *PSIA* 37 (1992)

—— 'Rural Society', in *Fifteenth-Century Attitudes: Perceptions of Society in Late Medieval England*, ed. R. Horrox (Cambridge, 1994)

—— 'The Prior and Convent of Ely and their Management of the Manor of Lakenheath', in *Ecclesiastical Studies in Honour of Dorothy M. Owen*, ed. M. Franklin and C. Harper-Bill (Woodbridge, 1995)

—— 'Peasant Welfare in England, 1290–1348', *EcHR* 51 (1998)

—— 'Trade and Towns in Medieval England: New Insights from Familiar Sources', *The Local Historian* 29 (1999)

—— 'An Introduction to Suffolk Domesday', in *Little Domesday Book: Suffolk* (London, 2000)

—— 'Villeinage in England: A Regional Case Study, 1200–1349' (forthcoming)

—— 'The Evolution of Field Systems in Medieval Suffolk' (forthcoming)

—— 'The Decline of Villeinage in Suffolk' (forthcoming)

Baker, A. R. H., 'Changes in the Later Middle Ages', in Darby, *New Historical Geography* (1973)

Barron, C., C. Rawcliffe and J. T. Rosenthal, eds., *East Anglian Society and the Political Community of Late Medieval England: Selected Papers of Roger Virgoe* (Norwich, 1997)

Benedictow, O., *The Black Death, 1346–1353: The Complete History* (Woodbridge, 2004)

Bennett, J. M., *Ale, Beer and Brewsters in England: Women's Work in a Changing World, 1300–1600* (Oxford, 1996)

—— 'Writing Fornication: Medieval Leyrwite and its Historians', *TRHS* 13 (2003)

Bishop, P., *The History of Ipswich* (London, 1995)

Blatchly, J., *A Famous Antient Seed Plot of Learning: A History of Ipswich School* (Ipswich, 2003)

Bonfield, L., and L. Poos, 'The Development of Deathbed Transfers in Medieval English Manor Courts', in Razi and Smith, *Medieval Society* (1996)

Britnell, R. H., *Growth and Decline in Colchester, 1300–1525* (Cambridge, 1986)

—— *The Commercialisation of English Society, 1000–1500* (Cambridge, 1993)

—— 'Morals, Laws and Ale in Medieval England', in *Le Droit et sa perception dans la littérature et les mentalités médiévales*, ed. U. Muller, F. Hundsnurscher, and C. Sommers (Goppingen, 1993)

—— 'Urban Demand in the English Economy, 1300–1600', in Galloway, *Trade, Urban Hinterlands* (2000)

—— 'The Woollen Textile Industry of Suffolk in the Later Middle Ages', *The Ricardian* 13 (2003)

—— *Britain and Ireland, 1050–1530: Economy and Society* (Oxford, 2004)

—— and J. Hatcher, eds., *Progress and Problems in Medieval England: Essays in Honour of Edward Miller* (Cambridge, 1996)

Cam, H., *Liberties and Communities in Medieval England* (Cambridge, 1942)

Campbell, B. M. S., 'Commonfield Origins: The Regional Dimension', in *The Origins of Open-Field Agriculture*, ed. T. Rowley (London, 1981)

—— 'Agricultural Progress in Medieval England: Some Evidence from Eastern Norfolk', *EcHR* 36 (1983)

—— 'The Complexity of Manorial Structure in Medieval Norfolk: A Case Study', *Norfolk Archaeology* 39 (1986)

—— 'The Livestock of Chaucer's Reeve: Fact or Fiction? in *The Salt of Common Life*, ed. E. B. DeWindt (Kalamazoo, 1995)

—— *English Seigneurial Agriculture, 1250–1450* (Cambridge, 2000)

—— 'The Agrarian Problem in the Early Fourteenth Century', *Past and Present* 188 (2005)

—— 'England: Land and People', in Rigby, *Companion* (2003)

—— 'The Land', in Horrox and Ormrod, *Social History* (2006)

——, J. A. Galloway, D. Keene and M. Murphy, *A Medieval Capital and its Grain Supply: Agrarian Production and Distribution in the London Region, c. 1300*, Historical Geography Research Series 30 (1993)

Campbell, E., 'Domesday Suffolk', in Darby, *Domesday Geography* (1952)

Campbell, J., 'Hundreds and Leets: A Survey with Suggestions', in Harper-Bill, *Medieval East Anglia* (2005)

Carpenter, C., *Locality and Polity: A Study of Warwickshire Landed Society, 1401–1499* (Cambridge, 1992)

—— 'England: The Nobility and Gentry', in Rigby, *Companion* (2003)

Castor, H., *Blood and Roses: The Paston Family and the Wars of the Roses* (London, 2004)

Childs, W. R., 'Moving Around', in Horrox and Ormrod, *Social History* (2006)

Clarkson, L. A., 'The Leather Crafts in Tudor and Stuart England', *AgHR* 14 (1966)

Clodd, H. P., *Aldeburgh: The History of an Ancient Borough* (Ipswich, 1959)

Copinger, W. A., *The Manors of Suffolk*, 7 vols. (Manchester, 1905–11)

Coss, P. R., *Lordship, Knighthood and Locality: A Study in English Society, 1180–1280* (Cambridge, 1991)

—— 'An Age of Deference', in Horrox and Ormrod, *Social History* (2006)

Darby, H. C., ed., *A Domesday Geography of Eastern England* (Cambridge, 1952)

——, ed., *A New Historical Geography of England before 1600* (Cambridge, 1973)

—— *Domesday England* (Cambridge, 1977)

DeWindt, A. R., 'Defining the Peasant Community in Medieval England', *Journal of British Studies* 26 (1987)

Dodwell, B., 'Holdings and Inheritance in Medieval East Anglia', *EcHR* 20 (1967)

Douglas, D. C., *The Social Structure of Medieval East Anglia* (Oxford, 1927)

Dyer, C. C., 'The Social and Economic Background to the Rural Revolt of 1381', in *The English Rising of 1381*, ed. R. H. Hilton and T. H. Aston (Cambridge, 1984)

—— 'The Rising of 1381 in Suffolk: Its Origins and Participants', *PSIA* 36 (1988)

—— 'Documentary Evidence', in *The Countryside of Medieval England*, ed. G. Astill and A. Grant (Oxford, 1988)

—— *Standards of Living in the later Middle Ages* (Cambridge, 1989)

—— 'How Urbanised was Medieval England?', in *Peasants and Townsmen in Medieval Europe*, ed. J.-M. Duvosquel and E. Thoen (Ghent, 1995)

—— *Making a Living in the Middle Ages: The People of Britain, 850–1520* (London, 2002)

—— 'Small Places with Large Consequences: The Importance of Small Towns in England, 1000–1540', *Bulletin of the Institute of Historical Research* 187 (2002)

—— *An Age of Transition? Economy and Society in England in the Later Middle Ages* (Oxford, 2005)

—— 'Gardens and Garden Produce', in *Food in Medieval England: Diet and Nutrition*, ed. C. M. Woolgar, D. Serjeantson, and T. Waldron (Oxford, 2006)

—— 'A Suffolk Farmer in the Fifteenth Century' (forthcoming)

Dymond, D. P., 'The Suffolk Landscape', in *East Anglian Studies*, ed. L. Munby (Cambridge, 1968)

—— 'Five Building Contracts from Fifteenth-Century Suffolk', *Antiquaries Journal* 78 (1998)

—— and A. Betterton, *Lavenham: An Industrial Town* (Lavenham, 1982)

—— and E. Martin, eds., *An Historical Atlas of Suffolk*, 2nd edn (Ipswich, 1989)

—— and P. Northeast, *A History of Suffolk* (Chichester, 1995)

—— 'The Parson's Glebe: Stable, Expanding or Shrinking?', in Harper-Bill *et al.*, *East Anglia's History* (2002)

—— and R. Virgoe, 'The Reduced Population of Suffolk in the Early Fifteenth Century', *PSIA* 36 (1986)

Eiden, H., 'Joint Action against Bad Lordship. The Peasants' Revolt in Essex and Norfolk', *History* 83 (1998)

Emery, F. V., 'England circa 1600', in Darby, *New Historical Geography* (1973)

Evans, N., *The East Anglian Linen Industry: Rural Industry and Local Economy, 1500–1850* (Aldershot, 1985)

—— 'Farming and Landholding in Wood Pasture East Anglia, 1550–1650', *PSIA* 35 (1984)

—— 'The Holy Ghost Gild and the Beccles Town Lands Feoffees in the Sixteenth and Seventeenth Century', *PSIA* 37 (1989)

Farmer, D., 'The Famuli in the Later Middle Ages', in Britnell and Hatcher, *Progress and Problems* (1996)

Farnhill, K., *Gilds and the Parish Community in Late Medieval East Anglia, c.1440–1550* (Woodbridge, 2001)

Fussell, G. E., *The English Dairy Farmer, 1500–1900* (London, 1966)

Galloway, J. A., ed., *Trade, Urban Hinterlands and Market Integration, c. 1300–1600*, Centre of Metropolitan History Working Papers, no. 3 (2000)

——, D. Keene and M. Murphy, 'Fuelling the City: Production and Distribution of Firewood and Fuel in London's Region, 1290–1400', *EcHR* 49 (1996)

Glasscock, R. E., 'England in 1334', in Darby, *New Historical Geography* (1973)

Goldberg, P. J. P., *Medieval England: A Social History, 1250–1550* (London, 2004)

Gottfried, R. S., *Epidemic Disease in Fifteenth-Century England: The Medical Response and the Demographic Consequences* (Leicester, 1978)

—— *Bury St Edmunds and the Urban Crisis, 1290–1539* (Princeton, 1982)

Gray, H. L., *English Field Systems* (Cambridge, Mass., 1915)

Grimwood, C. G., and S. A. Kay, *A History of Sudbury* (Sudbury, 1952)

Hallam, H. E. , ed., *The Agrarian History of England and Wales*, vol. 2: *1042–1350* (Cambridge, 1988)

Hanawalt, B. A., *The Ties that Bound: Peasant Families in Medieval England* (Oxford, 1986)

Harper-Bill, C., 'English Religion after the Black Death', in *The Black Death in England*, ed. W. M. Ormrod and P. Lindley (Stamford, 1996)

——, ed., *Medieval East Anglia* (Woodbridge, 2005)

——, C. Rawcliffe and R. G. Wilson, eds., *East Anglia's History: Studies in Honour of Norman Scarfe* (Woodbridge, 2002)

Harrison, D. F., 'Bridges and Economic Development, 1300–1800', *EcHR* 45 (1992)

Harvey, I. M. W. *Jack Cade's Rebellion of 1450* (Oxford, 1991)

Hatcher, J., 'English Serfdom and Villeinage: Towards a Reassessment', *Past and Present* 90 (1981)

—— 'The Great Slump of the Mid Fifteenth Century', in Britnell and Hatcher, *Progress and Problems* (1996)

—— and M. Bailey, *Modelling the Middle Ages: The History and Theory of England's Economic Development* (Oxford, 2001)

Heale, M. R. V., 'Rumburgh Priory in the Later Middle Ages: Some New Evidence', *PSIA* 40 (2001)

Heaton, H., *The Yorkshire Woollen and Worsted Industries* (Oxford, 1920)

Hesse, M., 'Domesday Land Values', *Landscape History* 22 (2000)

—— 'The Early Parish and Estate of Ickworth', *PSIA* 39 (2000)

Holmes, G. A., *The Estates of the Higher Nobility* (Cambridge, 1957)

Holt, R., *The Mills of Medieval England* (Oxford, 1988)

Horrox, R. E., 'Local and National Politics in Fifteenth-Century England', *Journal of Medieval History* 18 (1992)

—— and W. M. Ormrod, eds., *A Social History of England, 1200–1500* (Cambridge, 2006)

Hybel, N., 'The Grain Trade in Northern Europe before 1350', *EcHR* 55 (2002)

Jessopp, A., *The Coming of the Friars* (London, 1889)

Kanzaka, J., 'Villein Rents in Thirteenth-Century England: An Analysis of the Hundred Rolls of 1279–80', *EcHR* 55 (2002)

Keene, D., 'Changes in London's Economic Hinterland as Indicated by Debt Cases in the Court of Common Pleas', in Galloway, *Trade, Urban Hinterlands* (2000)

Kerridge, E., *The Common Fields of England* (Manchester, 1992)

Kershaw, I., 'The Great Famine and Agrarian Crisis in England, 1315–22', *Past and Present* 59 (1973)

Kitsikopoulos, H., 'Standards of Living and Capital Formation in Pre-Plague England: A Peasant Budget Model', *EcHR* 53 (2000)

Kosminsky, E. A., *Studies in the Agrarian History of England in the Thirteenth Century* (Oxford, 1956)

Kowaleski, M., 'Town and Country in Late Medieval England: The Hide and Leather Trade', in *Work in Towns, 850–1850*, ed. D. Keene, and P. J. Corfield (Leicester, 1990)

—— *Local Markets and Regional Trade in Medieval Exeter* (Cambridge, 1991)

—— 'A Consumer Economy', in Horrox and Ormrod, *Social History* (2006)

Langdon, J., *Horses, Oxen and Technological Innovation* (Cambridge, 1986)

—— 'Lordship and Peasant Consumerism in the Milling Industry of Thirteenth- and Early Fourteenth-Century England', *Past and Present* 145 (1994)

—— *Mills in the Medieval Economy: England, 1300–1540* (Oxford, 2004)

Lee, J. S., 'Feeding the Colleges: Cambridge's Food and Fuel Supplies, 1450–1560', *EcHR* 56 (2003)

Letters, S., *Gazetteer of Markets and Fairs in England Wales to 1516*, List and Index Society, Special Series 33, 2 vols. (2003)

Lloyd, T. H., *The English Wool Trade in the Middle Ages* (Cambridge, 1977)

Lobel, M. D., 'The 1327 Rising at Bury St Edmunds and the Subsequent Trial', *PSIA* 21 (1933)

—— *The Borough of Bury St Edmunds: A Study in the Government and Administration of a Medieval Town* (Oxford, 1935)

Lock, R., 'The Black Death in Walsham-le-Willows', *PSIA* 37 (1992)

Longe, F. D., *Lowestoft in Olden Times* (Lowestoft, 1898)

McClenaghan, B., *The Springs of Lavenham* (Ipswich, 1924)

MacCulloch, D., and J. Blatchly, 'Recent Discoveries at St Stephen's Church, Ipswich', *PSIA* 36 (1986)

McIntosh, M. K., *Autonomy and Community: The Royal Borough of Havering, 1200–1600* (Cambridge, 1986)

—— *Controlling Misbehaviour in England, 1370–1600* (Cambridge, 1998)

McKinley, R. A., *The Surnames of Norfolk and Suffolk in the Middle Ages* (London, 1975)

Maddern, P. C., *Violence and Social Order: East Anglia, 1422–1442* (Oxford, 1992)

Maitland, F. W., *Domesday and Beyond*, 3rd edn (Cambridge, 1987)

Martin, E., 'Little Wenham Hall', *PSIA* 39 (1998)

—— 'Suffolk', *Medieval Settlement Research Group* 15 (2000)

Masschaele, J., 'Transport Costs in Medieval England', *EcHR* 46 (1993)

—— 'The Multiplicity of Medieval Markets Reconsidered', *Journal of Historical Geography* 20 (1994)

—— *Peasants, Merchants and Markets: Inland Trade in Medieval England, 1150–1350* (Basingstoke, 1997)

Mate, M., 'The Agrarian Economy after the Black Death: The Manors of Canterbury Cathedral Priory', *EcHR* 37 (1984)

—— *Women in Medieval English Society* (Cambridge, 1999)

May, P., *Newmarket: Medieval and Tudor* (published privately)

Middleton-Stewart, J., *Inward Piety and Outward Splendour: Death and Remembrance in the Deanery of Dunwich, 1370–1547* (Woodbridge, 2001)

Miller, E., *The Abbey and Bishopric of Ely* (Cambridge, 1951)

——, ed., *The Agrarian History of England and Wales*, vol. 3: *1348–1500* (Cambridge, 1991)

—— and J. Hatcher, *Medieval England: Rural Society and Economic Change, 1086–1348* (London, 1978)

—— and —— *Medieval England: Towns, Crafts and Commerce, 1086–1348* (London, 1995)

Moran Cruz, J. H., 'England: Education and Society', in Rigby, *Companion* (2003)

Morgan, M. C., *The English Lands of the Abbey of Bec* (Oxford, 1946)

Morris, M., *The Bigod Earls of Norfolk in the Thirteenth Century* (Woodbridge, 2005)

Nightingale, P., *A Medieval Mercantile Community: The Grocers' Company and the Politics and Trade of London, 1000–1485* (London, 1995)

—— 'The Growth of London in the Medieval Economy', in Britnell and Hatcher, *Progress and Problems* (1996)

Oliver, M., *The Convent and the Community in Late Medieval England: Female Monasteries in the Diocese of Norwich, 1350–1540* (Woodbridge, 1998)

Palliser, D. M., ed., *The Cambridge Urban History of Britain*, vol. 1 (Cambridge, 2000)

Palmer, R. C., *English Law in the Age of the Black Death, 1348–1381* (London, 1993)

Parker, R., *Men of Dunwich: The Story of a Vanished Town* (New York, 1979)

Platts, G., *Land and People in Medieval Lincolnshire* (Lincoln, 1985)

Poos, L., *A Rural Society after the Black Death: Essex, 1350–1525* (Cambridge, 1991)

——, Z. Razi and R. M. Smith, 'The Population History of Medieval English Court Rolls: A Debate on the Use of Manor Court Rolls', in Razi and Smith, *Medieval Society* (1996)

Postgate, M. R., 'The Field Systems of East Anglia', in *Studies of Field Systems in the British Isles*, ed. A. R. H. Baker and R. A. Butlin (Cambridge, 1973)

Powell, E., *The Rising in East Anglia in 1381* (Cambridge, 1896)

Power, E., and M. Postan, eds., *Studies in English Trade in the Fifteenth Century* (London, 1933)

Putnam, B. H., *The Enforcement of the Statutes of Labourers, 1349–1359* (London, 1908)

Rackham, O., *The History of the Countryside* (London, 1986)

Raftis, J. A., *Tenure and Mobility: Studies in the Social History of an English Village* (Toronto, 1974)

Rawcliffe, C., 'On the Threshold of Eternity: Care for the Sick in East Anglian Monasteries', in Harper-Bill, *et al.*, *East Anglia's History* (2002)

Razi, Z., 'The Myth of the Immutable English Family', *Past and Present* 140 (1993)

—— and R. M. Smith, eds., *Medieval Society and the Manor Court* (Oxford, 1996)

Redstone, L. J., *Ipswich through the Ages* (Ipswich, 1948)

Redstone, V. B., 'Social Condition of England During the Wars of the Roses', *TRHS* 16 (1902)

—— '*Nomina Villarum*, Suffolk, 1316', *PSIA* 11 (1902)

——, ed., *Memorials of Old Suffolk* (London, 1908)

Richmond, C., *John Hopton: A Fifteenth-Century Suffolk Gentleman* (Cambridge, 1981)

—— 'East Anglian Politics and Society in the Fifteenth Century: Reflections, 1956–2003', in Harper-Bill, *Medieval East Anglia* (2005)

Rigby, S. H., *English Society in the Later Middle Ages: Class, Status and Gender* (London, 1995)

——, ed., *A Companion to Britain in the Later Middle Ages* (Oxford, 2003)

—— 'Historical Materialism: Social Structure and Social Change in the Middle Ages', *The Journal of Medieval and Early Modern Studies* 34 (2004)

—— 'Introduction: Social Structure and Economic Change in Late Medieval England', in Horrox and Ormrod, *Social History* (2006)

—— 'Urban Population in Late Medieval England: The Evidence of the Lay Subsidies' (forthcoming)

Royle, E., 'Need Local History be Parochial History?', *University of Cambridge, Institute of Education, Occasional Paper* 4 (2001)

Rubin, M., *Corpus Christi: The Eucharist in Late Medieval Culture* (Cambidge, 1991)

—— *The Hollow Crown: A History of Britain in the Later Middle Ages* (London, 2005)

Sandon, E., *Suffolk Houses: A Study of Domestic Architecture* (Woodbridge, 1977)

Scarfe, N., 'The Body of St Edmund', *PSIA* 31 (1967)

—— *The Suffolk Landscape* (London, 1972)

—— *Suffolk in the Middle Ages* (Woodbridge, 1986)

Schofield, P. R., 'Tenurial Developments and the Availability of Customary Land in a Later Medieval Community', *EcHR* 49 (1996)

—— 'Dearth, Debt and the Local Land Market in a Late Thirteenth-Century Village Community', *AgHR* 45 (1997)

—— 'Peasants and the Manorial Court: Gossip and Litigation in a Suffolk Village at the Close of the Thirteenth Century', *Past and Present* 159 (1998)

—— *Peasant and Community in Medieval England, 1200–1500* (Basingstoke, 2003)

—— 'Seigneurial Exactions in Eastern England, *c.* 1050 to 1300', in *Pour une anthropologie du prelevement seigneurial dans les campagnes medievales*, ed. M. Bourin and P. Sopena (Paris, 2004)

—— 'The Market in Free Land on the Estates of Bury St Edmunds, *c.* 1086–*c.* 1300', in *Le Marché de la terre au Moyen Âge*, ed. L. Feller and C. Wickham, Collection de L'École Française de Rome 350 (2005)

—— 'The Social Economy of the English Village in the Early Fourteenth Century', *EcHR* 60 (2007)

Schofield, R. S., 'The Geographical Distribution of Wealth in England, 1334–1669', *EcHR* 18 (1965)

Shackle, R., and L. Alston, 'The Old Grammar School: The Finest Merchant's House in Lavenham', *Historic Buildings of Suffolk* 1 (1998)

Sheail, J., *The Regional Distribution f Wealth in England as Indicated in the 1524/5 Lay Subsidy Returns*, List and Index Society, Special Series 29 (1998)

—— and M. Bailey, 'The History of the Rabbit in Breckland', in *Thetford Forest Park: The Ecology of a Pine Forest*, ed. P. Ratcliffe and J. Claridge, Forestry Commission Technical Paper 13 (Edinburgh, 1996)

Simpson, A., *The Wealth of the Gentry: East Anglian Studies, 1540–1660* (Cambridge, 1961)

Smith, R. M., 'Kin and Neighbours in a Thirteenth-Century Suffolk Community', *Journal of Family History* 4 (1979)

——, ed., *Land, Kinship and Life Cycle* (Cambridge, 1984)

—— 'Families and their Land in Redgrave Suffolk, 1260–1320', in Smith, *Land, Kinship and Life Cycle* (1984)

—— 'A Periodic Market and its Impact upon a Manorial Community: Botesdale, Suffolk, and the Manor of Redgrave', in Razi and Smith, *Medieval Society* (1996)

Statham, M., *The Book of Bury St Edmunds* (Buckingham, 1988)

Stone, D., 'Medieval Farm Management and Technological Mentalities: Hinderclay before the Black Death', *EcHR* 54 (2001)

—— 'The Productivity and Management of Sheep in Late Medieval England', *AgHR* 51 (2003)

—— *Decision-Making in Medieval Agriculture* (Oxford, 2005)

Thirsk, J., 'Industries in the Countryside', in *Essays in the Economic and Social History of Tudor and Stuart England*, ed. F. J. Fisher (Cambridge, 1961)

Thornton, G. A., *A History of Clare, Suffolk* (Cambridge, 1928)

Twigg, G., *The Black Death: A Biological Reappraisal* (London, 1984)

Underhill, F. A., *For Her Good Estate: The Life of Elizabeth de Burgh* (London, 1999)

Unwin, G., *Essays in Economic History* (London, 1927)

Victoria County History of Suffolk, ed. W. Page, 2 vols. (London, 1907)

Vinogradoff, P., *Villeinage in England* (Oxford, 1892)

Virgoe, R., 'The Murder of James Andrew: Suffolk Faction in the 1430s', *PSIA* 34 (1980)

Walker, J., 'Purton Green, Stansfield: Some Later Observations on the Early Aisled Hall', *PSIA* 38 (1994)

Ward, J. C., 'The Honour of Clare in Suffolk in the Early Middle Ages', *PSIA* 30 (1964)

Warner, P., *Greens, Commons and Clayland Colonisation: The Origins and Development of Greenside Settlement in East Suffolk*, University of Leicester Department of English Local History, Occasional Papers series 4 no. 2 (1987)

—— *The Origins of Suffolk* (Manchester, 1996)

West, S. E., and A. McLaughlin, *Towards a Landscape History of Walsham le Willows, Suffolk*, East Anglian Archaeology 85 (Ipswich, 1998)

Whittle, J., 'Individualism and the Family–Land Bond: A Reassessment of Land Transfer Patterns among the English Peasantry, *c.* 1270–1580', *Past and Present* 160 (1998)

—— *The Development of Agrarian Capitalism: Land and Labour in Norfolk, 1440–1580* (Oxford, 2000)

Williamson, T., *The Origins of Norfolk* (Manchester, 1993)

—— *Shaping Medieval Landscapes: Settlement, Society, Environment* (Macclesfield, 2003)

Winchester, A., *The Harvest of the Hills: Rural Life in Northern England and the Scottish Borders, 1400–1700* (Edinburgh, 2000)

UNPUBLISHED PAPERS AND DISSERTATIONS

Amor, N., 'Ixworth *c.* 1500: Landscape, Economy and Society' (MA thesis, University of East Anglia, 2000)

Davis, J., 'The Representation, Regulation and Behaviour of Petty Traders in Late Medieval England' (PhD thesis, Cambridge University, 2001)

—— 'Administering a Fifteenth-Century Small Market Town' (unpublished paper)

Hoppitt, R., 'A Study of the Development of Parks in Suffolk from the Eleventh to the Seventeenth Centuries' (PhD thesis, University of East Anglia, 1992)

Phillips, J. L., 'Collaboration and Litigation in two Suffolk Manor Courts, 1289–1364' (PhD thesis, Cambridge University, 2005)

Ridgard, J. M., 'The Local History of Worlingworth to 1400 AD' (PhD thesis, University of Leicester, 1984)

Smith, R. M., 'English Peasant Life-Cycles and Socio-Economic Networks' (PhD thesis, Cambridge University, 1974)

Stone, D., 'Managerial Problems and the Crisis in Demesne Farming after the Black Death' (unpublished paper)

Index

www.ingramcontent.com/pod-product-compliance
Ingram Content Group UK Ltd.
Pitfield, Milton Keynes, MK11 3LW, UK
UKHW021942260225
455626UK00010B/75